A GUIDE
for
EXUBERANT LIVING

Clark L. Corey

Plymouth, Michigan

Published by C. L. Corey TLW
9357 Haggerty Road, Plymouth, MI 48170

Manufactured in the United States of America.

Cover by: P. Powers

Library Of Congress Cataloging-In-Publication Data
Corey, Clark L.
>   A guide: for exuberant living.
>   p.   cm.
>   Includes bibliographical references and index.
>   1.   United States - Social and Cultural
>   Life - 20th Century.
>   2.   Education - History - Language - Family.
>   3.   Indictment of liberals.
>   4.   Word Meanings and Understandings for
>   Humanness.
>   5.   What To Do.

ISBN:
0-9644698-0-4 (Hard)   94-93978
0-9644698-1-2 (Paper)   CIP

ACKNOWLEDGEMENTS

First of all I wish to acknowledge my debt to my parents. They were prairie homesteaders under the brow of the Rocky Mountain front, with the others, all Brett Harte men and Grant Wood "Daughters" -- men and women who "upheld the ways and institutions of their forbearers", and without whom my early life would have been far poorer. So too I owe so much to my brothers and sisters.

Then I wish to acknowledge and thank all of those who have helped over the past dozen years to bring this book to its completion. Especially I thank Michael Warder of Rockford Institute who induced David Bovenizer to give the manuscript a thorough reading.

Finally my sincerest thanks to Ginny Eades, whose Letter Writer organization and unstinting efforts produced the manuscript in its finished form.

Clark L. Corey
Plymouth, Michigan
1994

iii

PREFACE

This *Guide* is intended to move people, all people who value Western civilization, to reassert support of our human society. It encourages all people to become a part of a positive and progressive movement.

It is only in recent decades that scientists and others have succecded in gaining knowledge of the true nature of man, of his natural human society, and the significance of an associated culture, sufficient for the first time to permit the rational combination of reason and tradition in social guidance. A great forward movement toward this end is essential protection against an encroaching Statism.

With understanding, certainly the vast majority of people would wish to support the rebuilding of our society. This *Guide* seeks to foster that understanding and urges the cooperation of all groups, classes and races.

It should be clear to nearly all people -- scholars have warned us -- that an evil party has taken over the "establishment" of our country where perceptions and purposes are promulgated. It has been their announced, yet often obscured, intent to destroy the culture which is so essential for our social guidance and to replace it with socialism, or Statism. A number of authors pretending to be "conservative" have excused those attacks as mere errors, on "a road paved with good intentions". Not so at all; perhaps many of the supporting jackals had no idea of the evil they were doing, or did know but forced their eyes closed. But the core "overhead planners" have admitted their hate and intent to destroy "with necessary violence".

It is the purpose of this *Guide* to identify human society and its culture, to identify the evil party of renegades who struggle to enslave us in Statism, and to prove that there is no "middle way" between them. There is only the abyss of chaos where only the terror of fascism can regain order. Recognition of how near this evil party has come to total control can and must be used to awaken people to the danger and to fire them to drive its incorrigible core to the fringes of society.

It is necessary that children and youths comprehend, not just believe; they must be taught the ways essential for social living even more so than are young robins. What you are taught today in schools and by entertainment and on TV is to be, and to expect to be, dumb clients of the State. Education in "doing your own thing", in your personal conscience, condoms and free needles and more, obviously is for life confined by outer forces, like chickens in a vast Arkansas farm. On the other hand to be free to seek your own limits requires comprehension of responsibility, and support for human institutions of family, culture and law that provide nurturing and guidance. Survival, of the individual and of freedom, alone imposes the responsibility.

Young men and women must recognize that all things decent and human: homes, safety, freedom, promising children, rule of law, even companies for careers, jobs and production, depend critically upon a society of families, stable through marriage. Women must recognize that their primary duty and joy in the world comes from nurturing a family. Men must even more intently come to understand that their primary duty and hope can only come from providing internal support and the external protection for their family and the responsibility and authority for a society of human purpose.

Seniors must see that they are sucking up far more of what society produces than is justified, even as they have failed to demand and enforce a social responsibility for stable families and a society and culture of decency, morality and freedom. Freedom and spiritual guidance come only through a culture; human beings cannot exist long without the psychological and spiritual support of a culture and society. Those of the West and of Christianity are all we have or can ever have; to lose them would be to lose all humanness. We can only improve by rising up on what we have.

But that is but a beginning. The great positive challenge is the rebuilding of human society, based on that which is innately proper to man, and upon reason in the service of that purpose.

Plymouth, Michigan   April, 1994

CONTENTS

1. INTRODUCTION

TO UNDERSTAND IS TO WILL

Thinking back into the past, the writer hesitated with his pen. He recalled long ago standing at the side of a great commander as they watched the destruction of a beautiful city. His own country had fallen when he was a young man; taken as a hostage, he had been befriended and educated by the commander's family. Throughout his life, he had observed the ways of these people. Words finally came.

"Who is so worthless and indolent, as not to wish to know by what means and under what system these people in less than fifty years have succeeded in subjugating the entire world to their purpose -- a thing unique in history? Who can regard anything of greater moment than the acquisition of this knowledge?"

Such was written over two thousand years ago about the Romans. Some twenty-five years ago a scholarly journalist wrote, "As an eyewitness throughout the years (1933-1967), I formed the opinion that the United States merits the dubious distinction of having discarded its past and its meaning in one of the briefest spans of modern history." Since then the genocidal, deliberate and systematic destruction of our culture and society has continued with even less resistance.

Huge sections of our great cities have been Lebanized into Third Worlds -- Beiruts. Our government has been occupied by jackals and jackasses and run by crooks, cons and renegades. Our schools are a world disgrace. Aliens and wastrels demand rights ahead of the essential needs of our society. Crime and obscenities, alien enclaves, and destruction of families make social coherence and limited government impossible. Our accustomed liberties cannot exist without a prudent morality, a guiding purpose, and rule of law. Without these, only Statism (fascism) can keep order.

This corruption of all things decent must be halted and our human society rebuilt. Your life and that of your children and the life of your society, from which you receive all joy and all real protection and meaning, must be revived, and it can be through a renewal of purpose. As nothing is more disastrous than to lose all purpose, so nothing can be more exhilarating than getting it back. Lenin himself assured us that "No situation is so bad it cannot be saved." Motivation can come only through understanding; rational and effective action must be guided by a great purpose. And what could be more admirable than the rebuilding of our human society and Western culture? The purpose of this *Guide*, is to urge all people to comprehend the urgency, and to indicate how to rebuild.

Nobelist Konrad Lorenz has asserted that, "The progressive decay of our civilization is pathological in nature," and any attempt at recovery must be based on a comprehension of the workings of society, and of its nemesis - - Statism.

This is a task for which ordinary people must grasp the nettle and assume responsibility. The bureaucratic network that controls the media, academia, and government, even many churches, will sneer and snarl to divert you, but don't be dismayed. Most great human movements have been carried out against an entrenched elite. If you are going to be ashamed of your ancestors and your heritage of struggle for freedom and dignity, you are already dead. To face ridicule requires not so much bravery as a comprehension of the situation. That is the key to motivation, and it will come as indignation comes, with an awareness of the renegade forces that arrogantly seek to uproot all that human beings cherish and have struggled thousands of years to achieve. Purpose and morality, truth and honor, love and beauty, and all the spiritual chords on which ride hope and bursting joy: these are the great generators of coherence and identification in a human society.

There is a war of subversion that has been going on for many years against human society and, if you don't join the fight to stop it, you are certain to be "used" to help destroy it. Arise, you have the opportunity of the ages to be a part of a truly noble effort. Conviction, like truth and morality, arises from purpose. Purpose grows on understanding. Knowledge of the true nature of man, of human society, and of the threat of its strangulation by Statism will provide the guidance.

Our poet, Lowell, has given us assurance, "Amid all the fruitless turmoil and miscarriage of the world, if there be one thing steadfast and of favorable omen, it is the rooted instinct in men to admire . . . to admire what is better." To rise up is the rule of life. Lowell adds that it is the touchstone of a society to provide that which is worthy of this sentiment. What could be more worthy than the rebuilding of our human society?

The struggle going on between human society and Statism has no middle ground, no third way, as Lenin also insisted. People must be sparked like an engine, motivated to move, to work or struggle. They can be moved by the vision of a great and admirable purpose which can make a joy of all of life, or they will be moved by the knout of terror. There is no middle way.

THESIS - AN OPPORTUNITY

The very mark of this century has been the holocausts, crushing some 100 million souls. And they are not over, for they are a natural product of Statism which still flourishes throughout the world, nowhere more virulently than in Washington, in our media and universities.

People have evolved only two ways to organize their cooperative activities; there is no third way. Human society is voluntary; it has a free market and a constitution of consent, and controls through award of respect. Statism is tutelage to an elite, it coerces through indoctrination backed by fear. People must be motivated to exert themselves; in human society it is by award of respect and so by self-interest. Under Statism, only the forbearance of the powerful stands between the naked individual and terror. The great evil of today that must be defeated is the renegade corrupting of human decency, of human society, so that Statism may take over.

Holocausts take only lives; far worse is the Statist's uprooting and destruction of all humanness, all that is driven by respect and a desire to be better: decency, personal responsibility, and rationality itself. Statists Anthony Lewis and the *New York Times* denounced even <u>criticism</u> of the most brutal of all the holocausts, that in Cambodia, as "cultural arrogance." And the renegade establishment that largely rules media, education, entertainment, much of our government and, even churches, never questioned them.

Statists claim that there is no right or wrong, good or bad, no reason for respect or contempt -- only preferences. John Rawl's *Theory of Justice*, that would have the State outlaw contempt, is answered by Allen Bloom: "This folly means that men (must not) seek the natural human good, (nor) admire it when found . . . instinct and intellect must be suppressed."[1] The flow is downhill, in all things; the normal is rejected for the abnormal, the inhuman. This can be reversed only with a great purpose which demands a right with respect and a wrong with contempt.

Why? Why reject respect? Why dumb-down schools, skimping on language and arithmetic for studies in sex, masturbation and sodomy, and the evils of white men? Why

----

[1]Allen Bloom, *Closing of the American Mind* (1987), p. 31.

has the tax exemption for children dropped to about one-fourth of the 1950-60 value? Why are mothers forced to work while we pay tens of billions to louts and aliens? Why are churches, the traditional teachers of morals and social purposes, pushed from the public square? Why is immigration virtually unchecked as we stagger towards Lebanization, our great cities fast becoming Beiruts, teeming with uncompromisable dissonance? Why?

Bloom gave the answer quite openly. It was the "purpose," the very intent of the intellectuals of this century to destroy our culture, our civilization, all that holds together our human society. Now our great universities proclaim it every day; their Deans find more guidance in the mad terrorist, Fanon, "kill the white man and enslave his women," than in Locke, a founder of modern democracy. When human society has been beaten down, Rule of Law rejected by renegade courts, families destroyed, language corrupted, hatred and violence rampant, only in this chaos can Statism enter, as only terror can then regain order. Fascism of the intellectuals is the goal.

This is the war of subversion, of lies and irrationalities of Marxism's "taught hatred" for all humanness that is waged so ruthlessly in Washington, New York, Hollywood, in our universities and schools. If anything, it has been intensified since the fall of socialism.

Actually the struggle is more massacre than war, with society being raped while people look on like eunuchs, not comprehending what is going on, not knowing how to resist, or too wimpish to try. But understanding can provide the indignation to motivate action. Many people and organizations are already in the field.

Thomas Jefferson has told us how to proceed. He recognized, in later years, that an important link between the people and their government[2] had been left out of our Founder's plan. He proposed that the people coalesce into

---

[2]Remember, it was the people's government, with the State subservient to the people -- not people as "consumers", as "clients".

local "wards"; these would provide media-uncensored news and information, and an opportunity for education and discussions for reaching agreements on actions. Above these would be correlating councils; thus would be provided an organization, a core, necessary to execute purposes. Such groups have been used throughout history; the <u>ekklesia</u> of the early Christians, the Jacobin Clubs of the French Revolution and the "cells" of communists are examples. The number of truly active socialist-communists in these cells was astoundingly small, compared to the gigantic feats that they accomplished with their host of liberal jackals, in destroying America. So America must immediately organize into a network of interconnected wards and rebuild. We must act quickly, it is not too late.

If only say 12,000 real leaders arose, who firmly believed in saving Western human society and were cognizant of its danger, although a dozen times that many ought to be available; each could search out and convince a score or more of other leaders: in industry, in unions, churches, senior groups, youth groups, especially veterans' groups, private clubs, schools, Kiwanis. And each should begin immediately to gather members for a ward, even as searching for new leaders for other wards. A purpose of the wards would be in a sense to make each member also a leader. Everyone rise up! Especially the youth. Tens of millions of people could be mobilized in a short time. The three tasks of the wards are: motivation through understanding the <u>truth</u>, action to gain control of our society and, most important, but longer term, planning for the beginning of a new human community.

Nothing is more important for a free people than active participation in their own governance.

You have truly been chosen by time to participate in a great movement -- as spiritual as the creation of Christianity, as intellectual as bringing the Age of Reason, and as active as the settling of America -- to rebuild our human society. The Age of Reason has degenerated into an Age of Irrationality. Reason is a far more dangerous tool than nuclear power, but it is from our Creator, and we must learn how to use it, or the dregs of mankind will use it against all humanness. People have deep spiritual needs that arise from innate social "forces"; in fact, it was in searching for an understanding of these spiritual feelings that our ancestors developed science and philosophy. Earnestly accept this opportunity and your life will come alive with the hope and joy of struggling in an admirable purpose: to bring decency and humanness back to our society -- to rise up.

Young people, did you ever wonder who might bury you? Does the possibility ever bother you that some Beruitized L.A. street may, in a few years, be decorated with your dog-gnarled body? That weight ought not overload your TVed brains. But instead, think of the possibilities, the honor and joy of doing and having a real and permanent part in turning Western human society away from certain catastrophe, and lifting it up to a new level of humanness. Many young people are ready and needed.

Seniors, what do you think is to become of your grandchildren? You have seen how quickly all things solid and precious have been crumpled, gutted. Who do you think will bury them, or on what shattered street will their broken bodies lie? I know this is on your minds.

Boomers you are old enough to be acutely aware of the degradation, the corruption that has poisoned our society especially since the 1960s. Yours is the most favored generation that ever lived, and what have you done? You know that the world is ruled either by human decency or by the force of terror. Humanness is decency, truth, and loyalty: loyalty to a family and community, with spiritual bonds that can grab your very soul, as in homesickness or conscience. When children grow up with "day care", without fathers and with squats for mothers, schools become clientized centers for State indoctrination; when truth is denied everywhere, and decency and modesty jeered, when Rule of Law is pushed aside by bureaucratic courts, only the terror of fascist Statism can regain order. Young and old people may become enthusiastic about fighting back to a human society, but only you boomers have the numbers, the positions, and the strength to do the job quickly.

Study the facts about what went wrong; if you don't like what I have written read the references -- many before 1960; there have been so many lies since then. Excuse the many quotes; I'm not a scholar. Besides you need comprehend not what I think but what has been thought and believed through the ages. Tradition is truth through repeated testing. You owe this effort to the human society that you uncomprehendingly were accomplices in bashing. Look to your end.

Veterans, never to be forgotten! How shameful are the obscene fruits of our struggle. We would never have gone to WW II or any of the others, had we known. But now you are needed to correct the wrong. We need only the truth; make the truth be known in every school, every church, every veterans post. "Steady now, we have seen worse."

To all Americans, all people of the West: a Nobel scientist has warned, "The progressive decay of our civilization is pathological . . . shows the symptoms of mental sickness . . . concerns man's social and moral behavior . . . understanding the causes requires us to break down the barrier between humanities and science . . . "[3] We can see it, and the time is late. It is a priceless opportunity and a honor to act in so great and admirable a cause. This is not a crusade for left or right, or for democracy. It is a struggle to save human society and for survival of free human beings.

I came late to this understanding. Raised in deepest want of the Depression, but not to the misery of today, I was inclined to an active interest in "liberalism." I saw my party destroyed in 1968, voted for the candidate, but never went back. It took time from a busy professional career to discover what was going wrong; neither media nor universities were about to let it be known. In time I discovered a few of the modern Jeremiahs, philosophers, ethologists, and sociologists:

---

[3]Konrad Lorenz, *Behind The Mirror* (1973) p. 18. An indispensable text for any study of human beings.

Kirk, Babbitt, Durkheim, Chambers, Lorenz, Ropke, Morley, Tocqueville, Hayek, Weaver, Lyons, J. F. Cooper, Paul Johnson, Spencer, Bloom, and many more. The purpose of this *Guide* is to start you on the way.

Motivation for this effort can only come from an increasing understanding of the problem, and in beginning to act, seeing things happen. Action will point to a need for more information, and further understanding. You can usually recognize a truth as something you really knew or unconsciously expected.

Society and culture are the real concerns; scientists believe that people cannot survive without the physical, psychological, and spiritual support they receive from a human society and culture. Human society will cease being human when it ceases to be voluntary. Nothing is promised but the opportunity to follow the Law of Life -- to seek to rise. You must begin even as you read this *Guide*; organize a ward tonight. Create the beginning of a new society.

To get a feel for the alternative, read Tocqueville's next-to-last chapter, in *Democracy In America*, "Despotism in Democracy." The State gradually accumulates all power, while destroying all bulwarks against it: church, family, private associations, Rule of Law, and private property. Then it stands forth as a great "tutelary power . . . alone to secure the gratification of the people . . . like the authority of a parent if the object were to prepare men for manhood . . . on the contrary it seeks to keep them in perpetual childhood . . . man is not shattered but softened . . . it compresses and stupefies, to a flock of timid animals . . . They are led to surrender exercise of their own will . . . spirit is broken . . . gradually losing the faculties of thinking, feeling and acting . . . gradually falling below the level of humanity."

This is not a struggle between liberals and conservatives, or of left and right; these terms have been so corrupted that a hard-line communist has become "right" and protectors of human society are called fascists. Remember that Confucius warned that the easiest way to destroy a society is to corrupt its language. When I was in high school everybody knew that integral to socialism was the Big Lie; we have heard the new Russian leader vow, "No more lies."

Also, this is not a struggle against any minority: Blacks, Hispanics, Jews, Asians, or Indians. Everybody does understand that Western civilization or culture is essentially the White man's creation -- with a number of important additions from Egyptians, Semites, Hindus, Chinese, even American Indians. The essential point I want to make is that Western culture cannot be saved without saving the white man, and the white man cannot be saved without saving his culture -- except as an artifact; he and his culture are an endangered species. When I was in grade school, an old grey geography book put the white race as nearly one-third of the world's population. Today it is approaching one-tenth and is falling rapidly. A speaker at an academic conference a few years back -- there are certainly more today -- announced that within a very few decades "what the white people want will no longer be of concern to the world". Our existence is threatened by a smothering influx of aliens, destruction of our families, and destruction of our essential cultural guidance, through the renegade tactics of "multiculturalism", relativism, education "reform", and hate America.

It is of great concern to the world, whether any race, white, black, or any other color, is eradicated, and it certainly is to us. We have as much right to exist with a culture and a territory as do Blacks, Asians, or Hispanics. If we are eradicated, as many anticipate, it will be our own fault; it will be because you refuse to help prevent it.

You must understand, in the beginning, that a culture is essential guidance for the survival of a society, or a race. The Jews have always known this. And it is entirely obvious, even generally admitted, or vowed in some quarters, that current thrusts are intended to uproot our culture, our society, and our Western civilization.

A document, deposited in a Gotha church steeple in 1784, reads as follows: "Our days are happiest . . . princes descend . . . and become their people's father . . . Religion emerges . . . divine . . . from tattered clerical gown.

Enlightenment makes strides . . . hatreds disappear. The arts and science prosper.   Artisans like artists, approach perfection . . . a faithful picture. Do not look down on us if you (who open this) have attained greater heights . . . acknowledge how much our courage has raised you . . . Do likewise and be happy."[4]

Five years later, the French Revolution broke out and the fruits of the Enlightenment began to fall in ever increasing torrents of hatred and terror. Where can one find today the optimism and sureness of this 18th century writer. Now there is doubt that even truth exists; people fear to look 10 years ahead. I know no grandparent who does not fear for his grandchildren.

Our intellectuals have become renegades, enemies of their own people and society. Their predecessors for generations back have increasingly ignored the spiritual and cultural nature of society's guiding purpose, and its essentiality for people.

You must know the pain and horror of a person who has "lost all purpose in life", but that is insignificant compared to the case of a whole society that has lost purpose, and the people gallop madly like the swine of the Gadarenes. A single person may be cared for; even strangers will seek to prevent his doing harm to himself. But when a whole people lose guidance, they stampede like a frightened and maddened herd.

The common people must rise up and take over the leadership from renegades who have been leading us to destruction.

---

[4]Wm. Ropke, in his *Human Economy*, recited this story in the forward. The text asserted: "In a sound society, leadership, responsibility and exemplary defense of the society's guiding norms and values <u>must be (an) exalted duty and unchallenged right</u> . . ."

2. PURPOSE AND CORE

PURPOSE

Chinese Tao, "the way": asserts absolute values in the universe, moral rights and wrongs, no less than in mathematics.

"If there is no God, then everything is allowed"; for the secularist this becomes, "If there is no Purpose, then everything is allowed."

Without purpose, there can be only confusion and chaos. Irrationality means without purpose. Life cannot exist long without purpose; the implacable urge of all life is not just to survive, but to rise up. Hence all Nature is rational. "Without purpose," declared Scotus, "there is nothing. God is primarily Will (purpose)."

Purpose is will and will is purpose; without the other neither is potent. No wind is favorable, the poet said, to him who knoweth not where he is bound. Rationality itself demands, for what purpose. Purpose tends to lead to actions. Science looks for connections, and is about connections and being. Science permits us to see purpose in all the universe, in life, in evolution, in everything of Nature -- a will to unfold, to rise up. Life cannot exist long without purpose; the implacable urge of all life for some billion years has visibly been not just to survival but to be better, to rise up. This is the Law of Life. Thus with purpose, all Nature is rational.

A will to rise up urged our pre-human forbearers to condense into an interdependent society, to struggle to communicate, and with the coming of reason, it urged an additional purpose: a purpose that could captivate and guide reason upwards.

Purpose marks the living from the dead. Your purpose, that big purpose that guides all your smaller purposes, is your religion, however confused and unkept it may be: that which guides your essential thoughts and acts. To "struggle for a greater dignity for man", or similarly to "do the will of God", guided Western civilization, first of the Greeks and then of Christianity.

What is your purpose, your religion? Surely no sadder words are ever spoken than, "He has lost all purpose in life." With purpose, life is exuberant, all things have meaning and flavor. Truth and beauty, justice and respect no less than hope and joy can rise only on the wings of purpose.

If you do not have a well-defined and active, conscious purpose in your life, there is little doubt but that you are being used for the purposes of others. All who do not support the purposes of Western human society, particularly as to supporting families, morality, truth, culture, and especially Rule of Law and limited government, to that degree, they help Statism. In his *Idea of Progress*, J.B. Bury claimed that the fundamental assumptions of socialism prohibited the idea of progress; it denies a "rising-up". Bury saw that socialism was taking over all thought, (in 1920) albeit subversively, and the idea of progress was being replaced by a "directing idea of humanity." Bury asked whether the idea of "progress itself suggests that its value is only relative . . . ?" Not at all! Progress is the result of the whole guiding purpose of humanity -- to rise up.

It is an intention that this *Guide* bring a renewal to your life. The beginning requires your acceptance of Nature's purpose to rise up. With that act, you feel an immediate freshness, a hope, and a desire to understand. When you can comprehend who you are, and what is proper in your life for rising up, you become part of an admirable movement. Learn to reflect and to depend upon your own common sense; ask whether statements sound reasonable. When you find the meaning for yourself, yours to grasp, as a drowning man gasps for air, you will want to tell others. Begin with the recognition that there is truth: You want to rise up.[5] If you didn't, you wouldn't be reading this.

CORE

"No action is possible without leaders." (Gibbon)

If you do not actively plan and work for your human society to survive, it most likely will not. Any purpose of more than temporary importance needs coordination and a core of responsibility -- an administrative hierarchy. The central administration of any business, school, or even club, acts as such a core. The Catholic Church, in addition to its central Vatican core, with its cardinals, had a very powerful extra core in the Jesuits aiding the Pope. It performed well the three essential core functions: teaching, exemplification and advancement of the purpose.

The Communists had a very special core which every person who is against them needs to comprehend; it provided an excellent example of the minimum that a human society must have. It is important to be aware that as the core of the Communist movement grew, its first aim, beyond its own success, was to attack the core of human society as it faltered from inner corruption.

Communism was, to its "true believers", a religion in a very real sense, and this should reinforce your understanding that the essence of any religion is purpose. In the beginning of modern socialism and sociology, the founders, St-Simon and Auguste Comte referred intentionally to their "faith as a

---

[5]R. M. Weaver, *Ideas Have Consequences*, (1948), p. 19, asserts that "We begin . . . (with) the categorical statement that life and the world are to be cherished". James Russell Lowell, the poet, declared that above all else, is "man's rooted instinct to admire . . . that which is better."

church."[6] For the Soviet Communist Party, the Communist elite and their "theoreticians" constituted the core. They declared the accepted "world view", and "the way things really are." Whittaker Chambers has given us a powerful image of their hierarchal core for guidance in a total purpose. Communists were the only part of mankind, he wrote, that had retained the "power to hold and to act on a conviction" -- a purpose. The purpose was as simple as that of the Greeks or Christians: "It is necessary to change the world," so that the elite could "be as Gods." That was the purpose, the "tie that binds them across frontiers of nations, across barriers of language, class, education, in defiance of religion, morality, truth, love, honor, and the weakness of mind and body, even unto death."[7] The driving purpose and fanatical will was what made Communism the most powerful idea and purpose for some seven decades. Their tactics, strategies, and general methods are worthy of careful study,[8] but keep in mind their evil ends.

That is what I mean by a core. Statism has a powerful advantage over human society in this matter; its core is always an intellectual elite, easily organized and motivated by visible rewards. All they have to do, as Machiavelli advised them, is to make fancy promises. The core of a human society must do much more than convince and organize. It must present an admirable purpose, within which the common people can find meaning and identification and will voluntarily want to adhere to, with morality, charity, truth and justice.

Tribal aspects in society existed in much of Europe even after the time of Christ. They are still controlling in

---

[6]G.G. Iggers, *The Doctrine of St-Simon*, (Preface by C.D.H. Cole, Fabian) 1958 p. XLIV.

[7]Whittaker Chambers, *Witness*.

[8]If you doubt their terrible, fanatical intensity, read Koestler's *Darkness At Noon*. "It is no accident" that Mr. Clinton drives for "change".

much of Africa and are strong in Asia and Latin America. That's why families in all of these areas are so much stronger than Aryan families.[9] Evidence indicates that the core of all tribal societies was a Council of Elders. Some thirty thousand years ago or more when the big cats or cave bears still snuffled about just beyond the clan firelight, loyalty and responsibility required no harsh discipline. Then the job of the core was quite simple. The problem became acute only after affluence through agriculture had removed any very visible or felt urgency; only then did motivation for social cohesion, or more to the point, restraint of reason's imagination, become a pressing problem for a core of Elders -- to be covered in more detail later.

Roughly since that time, the core for Western civilization has been a fluctuating combination or even competition, of church, king, and aristocracy. Now the central fact of modernity is that beginning about at the time of Machiavelli, all of these elements began a decline. The horrors of the 20th Century in the West are directly attributable to the fact that few nations any longer possess a core of intellectuals who are willing to stand up and protect, or even to warn the people of the need of protecting, the legitimate prerogatives of their society, its culture and place in the world. That is why the West has often staggered blindly during the past two centuries. However, there was the decreasing remains of a church, and some loyal intellectuals up to the 1960s that carried some weight. Some still exist to remind us, but carry little weight, even in their own communities.

Note that an even more damaging factor, beyond our society running nearly blind, has been the increasing presence of renegades with subversion and lies to distract and confuse,

---

[9]I use the name Aryan after V. Gordon Childe, the British historian. It suffers no drawbacks not possessed by the designation Semitic. If there are stains on the name, there are equally bad stains on all other names. Most Westerners would prefer not to be hyphenated Indo-Europeans. We must have some name. To be without a name, particularly in an age of rabid ethnicity, is to be a nobody, a nothing.

who have led us into one disaster after another. It is not only arguable, I believe that the historical record clearly shows, that in not a single war which we have been dragged into in this century was there any intention of its benefitting America or simple humanness in any significant way. We, perhaps, merely blundered into Korea and Vietnam, but WW I and II were engaged in principally for the benefit of socialism, here and abroad. They could have been fought to save, or to strengthen Western civilization, but they surely were not.

Before WW II, America had a minimal core that could, at times, exert pressure: churches, prominent figures, etc. There were many more newspapers and perhaps much more useful news. It is surprising how many senators and congressmen, regardless of party, were then generally well thought of. Walter Lippmann, was a brilliant and educated observer with entrance for first-hand witnessing nearly all important events. Hence he had a wide background. As an astute witness, he described in 1936, what had largely taken over as a prime controller of America. In essence, he identified a core that could act on almost anything. It generally had to do it subversively, and this remained largely true until 1965; it is still marginally true today. The new core was made up of liberals and socialists, "overhead planners". "No other approach to . . . human affairs is seriously considered . . . only a handful here and there, groups without influence, isolated and disregarded . . . challenge it . . . collectivism has become the working belief of nearly every effort which lays claims to being human and progressive . . . no one is taken seriously who does (not seek) to magnify the power of public officials . . . unless he is . . . collectivist, he is a mossback, a reactionary . . . swimming hopelessly against the tide."[10]

"Within every society . . . there is a small group of intellectuals who give to society its tone . . . What one thousand professors, writers, and bishops think, write, or

---

[10]Walter Lippmann, *The Good Society* (1936), p.4.

preach is handed on by 300,000 teachers, journalists and ministers to the 130,000,000 Americans. The process is as inconspicuous as it is overpowering . . . (A) book which has made an impression on 3,000 teachers and 2,000 journalists alters our . . . (perception more) than a novel read by 2,000,000 housewives. Ninety-nine and nine-tenths percent of Americans have never held a book by John Dewey in their hands, but all Americans have been educated by him . . . (by) the transmission belt of our educational apparatus . . ."[11]

And what did socialist, John Dewey say? "The first step . . . (is to inform) students about the present state of affairs of society in a way that enables them . . . to be ready to take part in aggressive participation in bringing about a new social order" (socialism).[12]

Human society and socialism (fascism) are totally incompatible. Human society requires constant building up, like love in a family, honesty in a bank, courage on a battlefront.   This is not easy, and people are slothful. Socialists seek first to corrupt, disorganize and disable the society, before they have any chance of taking over. This tearing down is much easier than building up; furthermore, the socialists demand that certain things "need fixing". Our health system, we are told from Washington, needs something -- we are not told what, but to fix it requires socializing some one-seventh of our economy. Over the years, socialist "fixing" is what has in fact destroyed our cities, our schools, disabled our families, corrupted the youth, and generated inequalities and hatred and violence. The socialists have succeeded, and not a hand and hardly a voice is raised against them.

Re-read Walter Lippmann's description of America's core since 1936 (on p. 17); and reread what socialist John Dewey was urging young people, in " . . . bringing about a

---

[11]W.S. Schlamm, quoted by Van Wyck Brooks in *Opinions*, (1941) p. 209.

[12]John Dewey, *Education for the New Social Order*, League for Industrial Democracy (1934).

new social order" (socialism). A famous educator, Nicholas Murray Butler, President of Columbia University for decades, wrote, in 1921, to his Board of Governors: "It is now proposed to bureaucratize (socialize) the educational system of the whole United States, while making the most solemn assurance that nothing of the kind is intended."

That is the universal pattern. Since the 1930s, socialists, enemies of human society, have increasingly controlled the core in America.[13] By stealth, deception, dissembling, and lying, they have destroyed our institutions.[14]

Nowhere is the deceit and dissembling more blatant than in the destruction of our communications, our language. Thus the word "liberalism" received a noble reputation as a supporter of freedom through limited government; yet today, and for the past 30 years, the so-called "liberals" of the West have carried the major load for communism: in Western disarmament; in spreading Soviet disinformation; in supporting Vietnam "peace demonstrators" chanting for a Communist victory over our own sons, for support of communists in Central America, Communists and various Marxists seeking to destroy Western culture in our schools and universities.

---

[13]Read Eugene Lyons's, *Red Decade.*

[14]The story is that terrorist Rudi Deutsch was asked how he could possibly expect to crush communism down upon free peoples; his answer was a confident, "By going through the institutions."

3. SOCIETY AND CULTURE

INTRODUCTION

All Americans -- young people, boomers, seniors -- are becoming aware that no one is in control of our nation any more. It was largely criminal gangs that took over L.A. and looted and burned for three days, and it was the cops' fault. Some $300 billion were looted from Savings and Loans; we know that Senators were coercing bank examiners to keep crippled institutions open while the bank looting went on. Increasingly there is no law but judge mandates; no education except indoctrination. Millions of illegals flood across our borders, creating problems whose magnitude will not even be assessed.

There is, however, a more dangerous problem. It has become far larger since it was described some 25 years ago by the eminent child psychiatrist, Selma Fraiberg, due to immigration, to welfare and to degraded families. She warned of the increasing numbers of young people who remain outside the bounds of any society; " . . . they are unable to fulfill the most ordinary human obligations in work, friendship or marriage. 'Alienation' leaves a void where conscience should be." There is a growing horde of these people who, of course, are commonly illiterate and unfit for work, waiting for a Stalin or Hitler to provide them a home in a Soviet Cheka or Nazi SS. And there is no force, no social institutions to stop them when society fails.

SOCIETY

The central issue of all human society and culture is the recognition, not a belief, of the reality of a fixedness, a normality in our natural society. It is not an anthill nor a herd; rather it is something "proper to man." The Rule of Life, as revealed on all sides and throughout a billion years, is that all life seeks not only to survive but to rise up. That is, implicit in the 5,000 year old Egyptian recognition, "Righteousness is what is loved," to Hegel's "impulse of perfectibility." It is being ended by Marx's vision of a stateless, classless anthill. Rising up requires a platform of normality. All life is guided to its innate or natural character in each species by encoded DNA, which is extremely resistant to change. It specifies exactly how a species shall look and act. Minor changes in DNA can occur and thus there is an evolution, but these changes are biased so that only those which aid survivability and rising up generally become permanent adaptations.

The poet Lowell wrote in his essay "Democracy": "Amid all turmoil and miscarriage of the world, one thing is steadfast . . . it is the rooted instinct in man to admire, to admire the better. (It is) the very taproot of civilization . . ."

You should understand why a comprehension of the nature of society is so very important today in this age of modernity. Very simply, the truth is that since the modern age began, some hundreds of years ago, Western intellectuals have increasingly sought to destroy their human society, principally by subversion of its culture, from which it must obtain guidance. Especially during the past century, the denigration and destruction have been savagely successful and we have been told that that was the very "purpose" of a whole party of intellectuals. They teach and force the perception that man's mind comes as a blank slate, a *tabula rasa*, that people have a right to an individuality, a lifestyle, with no responsibility to society.

It is very wrong to picture human society as the "thinnest of veneer." It is culture, something quite different that is the veneer. Society is not at all like an eggshell, rather it is the nurturing medium within which all humanness has evolved and solely where it can survive. It is strong and resistant to its external enemies but is susceptible to internal rot as by the past century of intellectuals. Poisoning it with such things as multiculturalism, relativism and hate, kills the human essence leaving only hollow scheming brutes, like the Chekas, Gestapo, and renegades everywhere.

People have been made aware of the considerable disaster that could result from upsetting a delicate ecological balance. Yet more critical for mankind is a social balance between a socially invigorating freedom and the stabilizing restraints of morality, loyalty, and belonging which keep a society from tearing itself apart. Western civilization has been tearing itself apart for a century or more.

The essential and fundamental question concerning human society is: Is there a normality and natural fixedness to human society, is there some condition "proper to man," as the Greeks put it? Further, does Nature or Nature's society provide some form of guidance toward that "proper to man"?

The answers to these questions are quite well known and are generally agreed upon by scientists and by ages of common sense and tradition. It is a measure of the power of the renegades who control our education and media that the answers are not generally known. It has been the dissembling, deception and lying about religion, culture, society and purpose that has been responsible for creating the catastrophic horrors of today. Thus, it is essential to straighten things out from the beginning.

First, there was a creation. Though we have no idea what that might mean, we know at least that the universe in all of its rational complexity came about, even if it was "always here," by processes not a part of the natural physical world known to man. Thus, to summarize, the existence of the universe is superhuman and supernatural.

Actually whether the universe was created is not even a significant question. The only question that might be asked is: is the Creator still around adjusting things? One look at the world today must strongly bias any person's belief, but as will be shown, even that question is hardly significant. A brief introduction to what is known today about society and about culture and their origin in the history of our forbearers -- totally unknown to Rousseau and even to Darwin -- can provide some fair answers. As scholars have always believed, there is a natural human society and, if it is destroyed, the chaos, corruption and barbarity of today is to be expected.

Our natural society is innate; man no less than the bee or baboon has adapted to an existence in an interdependent society as a strategy for survival. It is innate for a bee to live in a beehive; likewise, it is innate for people to live in a human society, and scientists tell us that one "cannot live without the supporting structure that society and a culture provide".

But "innateness" can be looked at more specifically. A ciliated protozoan on running into an obstacle will stop the oaring motion of the cilia, pause as if thinking, and then will oar off in an opposite direction. If a ship did that, one would never doubt the act of thinking by the captain. This kind of thinking, without sense organ for information, or nerves to carry the message, or brain to store information and to rationalize, is not unique. A Portuguese man-of-war can sense even a stealthy approach of a person, and follow his circling around him, yet he too has no organs of any kind. Clearly, he is conscious of his surroundings and responds to them. Where resides his rationality and will to survive? It can only be within or very closely connected to a molecule of DNA. We may even add, if necessary, that a dog or a chimpanzee may stroll down a street, noting and reacting to artifacts of the environment, not unlike a person. Perhaps they even live as consciously as some people.

The point I want to make from all of this is that if a single-celled creature, even an amoeba, can act as though consciously and rationally reacting to environmental artifacts, then there is no reason that there could not have been also within its DNA an order to survive and to rise up. In fact, we do see the conscious response to such a genomic injunction -- to rise up -- not only in all life, but in all life for a billion years. Finally, this rule of all life, to rise up, is actually the essential core of the Greek injunction, to struggle toward that "proper to man".

So to bring the whole argument to an end, we know also that various ultimate particles "know" what kind of statistics and physical laws they are to obey. Thus, it is essential, not to believe, but to <u>comprehend</u> that whatever form the creation of the universe did have, a part of that creation was the encoding of instructions somehow within ultimate particles. Hence there is nothing supernatural or "religious" about the possibility that whatever Creator there was, He also provided for the encoding of "struggle upwards" in all DNA.[15] It is not necessary to believe that a "creator" provided this encoding; if you can find a better answer, take it.[16] It is necessary to recognize that encoding <u>does exist</u>, and

------

[15]Look at a tiny mustard seed; within it is a tiny bit of DNA. If the amount of DNA within the seed of a Great Sequoia were ten times as much, it would still be minute beyond normal comprehension. Yet within that bit is all the information not only for the construction of needles, branches, trunk and every single bit of the subsequent plant, whether mustard or Sequoia, but there is a whole other information bank of how to adjust for improper (abnormal) light or temperature, how to heal wounds, and we know not what else. Certainly people who claim that man is born with a "blank slate" mind, are as idiotic as those who claim the absence of truth.

[16]We know the encoded behavior for say hadrons is an important determinant in the cosmos; things would be much different out there if their encoding (inherent behavior) were different. We are quite sure that an encoding on DNA must be the source of the urge for all life for a billion years to rise up. We know that out on the desert of Mesopotamia stands a slab of stone upon which marks taken to be a readable message are inscribed. All of these may be the result of pure chance, the eddies

it is that injunction, the imperative of the encoding, that provides purpose, and hence rationality to all life and to the whole universe.

Some hundred million years ago four new life-forms came into existence. Insect-like invertebrates had existed for some time, but now flowering plants appeared among the dinosaurs, bringing the insects we know; and the birds came. A little later as the dinosaurs died out, small rodent-like mammals appeared. Note that in these three animal forms, we find the beginning of societies, a strategy for survival and rising up. There were the bee hives, flocks of geese in whose "triumph ceremony" was heard the first *Hallelujah Chorus*, declaring a belonging to a communion, and finally the rat and then baboon packs.

About ten million years ago (the time is not critically important) most scientists believe that baboon or chimpanzee-like primates descended from a somewhat individualistic, sheltered existence in the trees to an embattled existence on the ground. Now their very survival depended upon cooperation in the close interdependence of a society. Responsibility to self had to be broadened to a first responsibility for a pack, a clan, or society. Modernists refuse even to consider this; equally loathsome to them is the fact that in return for the yielding of sovereignty came not only more assured survival but all that man his ever considered most precious.[17] Not just brotherhood and a great protectedness in a belonging; in the future was to come language and culture, inconceivable and unneeded among lone individuals. At the time, it was principally a strategy for cooperative survival that these individuals gradually adapted themselves to: an interdependent existence with non-aggression and altruism as principal standards -- not choosable "values" but <u>standards</u> for stable operation. This

---

of cosmic winds; the only alternative is that a purposeful agent, or agents, arranged things this way.

[17]At least up to modernity.

non-aggression and altruism applied only to those within the clan. Later that was to undergo a fundamental shift.

It is interesting that chimpanzees are said on rare occasion to condense into a hierarchal hunting pack and make a foray out into the open grasslands. It cannot remain permanent because it lacks a source of cohesion. For stability there must be an identification and a deep sense of belonging, a sacredness, commonly celebrated by shared rituals, such as the "triumph" ceremony of geese and in humans shared symbols and purposes. The adoption of standards of non-aggression and altruism were later to become the deep roots of morality and charity, without which the cultural additions would have been meaningless.

All evolved adaptations for survival, such as non-aggression in a society, and later a verbal communicability, presumably occur much as did the movement of our thumb to an opposed position. Slow step-by-step movements occurred by mutations each from the beginning being advantageous and thus promoting the chance of a subsequent move, until a position of approximate stability was reached.[18]

While living in the trees, our forbearers had a very great need to look forward and actually to focus their eyes sharply in order to catch the next branch. Forward focusing eyes brought an emphasis on the close environment. After attaining an even partially erect position and with hands out in front as manipulators for carefully viewing of objects in the close environment, the surroundings became far more intently and centrally experienced for these primates than for other animals.

This became an important factor in a far more significant change that accompanied the transition to social being. Our forbearers had neither the defensive nor offensive weapons of bees, wolves, rats, and baboons. It is rather clear that the principal advantage of a human group was to be its collective, cooperative strength, and hence the society or clan had to be very close and thus communicability would be of

---

[18]Reverse changes, of course, preferentially die out.

prime importance. It has recently been reported that even rodents, the progenitors of primates, have far more complex verbal signals than previously recognized. We know too that the higher primates possess a wealth of gestures, expressions, purrs and grunts of various kinds, and rituals.[19] Certainly it was the possession of this extensive pre-syntactic-language communicability that permitted sufficient communication for these forbearers to cooperate for survival on the ground, and, in fact, to communicate extensively about the physical world and social affairs.

It is very important to recognize that these non-syntactic forms of communication required considerable development of the essential cognitive structures for conscious recognition of aspects of the environment: enemies of a certain kind, food of a certain kind, strategies useful for hunting, and much more, demanding or soliciting communication. Thus a cognitive awareness, an expanded and alert consciousness of surroundings, required brain space for itself and particularly for long-term memory to store patterns of situations to be recognized. Reasoning for the formation of exact and recognizable messages had to be developed, along with an expanded code for transmission. On the receiving end, these all had to be reversed.

These demands forced a degree of brain development not commonly recognized before syntactic language had evolved to any significant degree. In fact, it seems probable that the cognitive powers of our forbearers had increased to the point that an objective awareness, a consciousness of surroundings and a reasoning power well beyond any other modern primate, had combined with long term memory so as to have produced considerable conceptual thought. A significant conscious awareness, combined with this growing power of conceptual thought could have brought to our forbearers not just an awareness of "feelings", but also an interest and concern for these new "forces", as Durkheim called them. Conscious innate "feelings" arise from innate

---

[19]See Note on Ritualization.

emanations, produced when the unconscious mind processes genomic information. Without sufficient consciousness this processing of DNA information would have produced only emanations commanding instinctive action. Even today, we react at times instinctively and "do things quicker than we can think."

The importance of our forbearers becoming consciously aware of these emanations stands above all else in our universe: it marks the beginning of humanness. These feelings and the emanations that produce them are in essence innate commands that result from "genetically specified and phylogenetically programmed" behavior patterns.[20] Durkheim called them forces: "commanding, helpful and kindred, and coming as from the outside."[21] When genomic knowledge (from DNA) produced a feeling that commanded restraint in the conscious mind, our forbearers came to recognize this as "conscience." Genomic knowledge processed through the unconscious might produce feelings in the conscious mind during recognition of brotherhood, or of belonging, or recognition of a great and unexplainable power of a protectedness in the collective which came to be recognized as "us". This was the origin and sound basis of man's

---

[20]It is necessary to have the word "emanations", for commands from the unconscious that are unfelt and go directly to actions, reserving "feelings" for messages that arise from them and go also to the conscious mind. It is important to recognize that these emanations were exactly what produced instinctive guidance before our forebearers became consciously aware of them. They have always produced animal guidance, even for the smallest "germ".

[21]Emile Durkheim, *Elementary Forms of Religious Life* (1915). Durkheim was perhaps the only socialist to believe strongly in human society. See later "Note On Feelings".

E. H. Lenneberg, in *Biological Foundations of Language*, 1966, p. 71, declared it "repugnant" to science to attribute man's vocal tract peculiarities "to any primeval need for communication or for making speech sounds." He ignores such specific peculiarities in other animals such as birds and even frogs.

spiritual life, of religion. Our forbearers were profoundly affected by this new insight; it had to be discussed, ritualized and speculated about. This required far more abstract thinking then any previous concern about the physical world; it also produced an urgent need for more precise, detailed and complex messages than were possible using gestures and expressions. A syntactical language was the answer.[22] Consciousness, reason, and memory continued to increase as accessories to all communicability.

Our deepest feelings concern our society, home, and family; we feel forces of brotherhood, belonging and protectedness. Many feelings came to be conceived of as due to spirits; the spirit Pan caused flocks to "panic" and to stampede, due to a felt force. The most profound feelings became related to the greatest spirits; the Great Spirit, or Spirit of the people, came to be associated with a feeling of belonging to a great collective protectedness.

There is another quite different set of feelings, related to "parental affection," which are prior even to society.[23] There is an often-reproduced photo of a chimpanzee mother with an infant in her lap, holding a mildly protective hand

---

[22]This suggestion that syntactic language followed not only consciousness and reason, but even man's first awareness of innate "feelings" as the substance of his spiritual world, is supported by, among other things, a claim by the poet W. H. Auden. In his Forward to Owen Barfield's *History In English Words* he declared the primary function (of syntactic language) was "personal speech, to which its use as a (mere) code is subordinate." By personal speech, he referred to speech about feelings, emotions. "Speech in the true sense is the medium in which, as unique persons who think in the first and second person singular, gratuitously disclose ourselves to each other." Note and remember how far removed this is from communication about the concrete physical world. This is about as close as we can come, briefly at least, in probing the distinction: spiritual versus physical. For reflection: Hooton tells us that chimp phonetics are entirely subjective; they express only emotions, never objects. Perhaps it has been shown that training can modify that.

[23]E. Westermarck, *Origin and Development of Moral Ideas*. Note that all the following "parental feelings" are primarily personal, prior to society; the previous "forces" were innately social, collective.

between it and an inquisitive, somewhat older sibling. "From this emotion (parental tenderness) and its impulse to cherish and to protect springs generosity, love, pity, benevolence, and altruistic conduct of every kind". Harm toward a child evokes resentment and anger. "This intimate alliance between tender emotion and anger . . . is the germ of all moral indignation . . and the greater part of public law."[24] Darwin, long ago, surmised that most feelings and the behavior patterns pertaining to them were innate.

"Parental affection is not a late product of civilization, but a normal feature of the savage mind".[25] Is it not monstrous that today "liberals", intellectuals, would destroy this in State day-care centers? And for what possible purpose, in peace time and with millions on a dole? This is as arrogant as Stalin wiping out millions of people with the snap of a finger, for "a new vision of society"!

Our ancestors moved into the conscious world of feelings and reason gradually, as slowly coming out of a fog. But they found a world waiting; they did not have to create a committee to promulgate natural law, morality, truth, or even social customs; they were to become aware that these had long existed; they needed but to become conscious of them. And we have continued to become conscious of new truths, as the history of words will show. (See Barfield.)

---

[24]W. McDougal, *Intro To Social Psych.* This is the root of natural law.

[25]J. H. Breasted, *Dawn of Conscience,* p. 18. "Savage" was Breasted's word not mine, but people do ask why we should be concerned with innate instinctive feelings. Are they not in fact from brutes, savages and are all morals relative? This must be answered, and clearly. The so-called savage mind we know feels parental tenderness and all the aforesaid feelings of generosity, pity, benevolence, plus all the later social feelings, and they are the predominate determinors of his behavior. A Christian may be usually all of these, but very unnaturally refuse to eat meat at a certain season; the savage may likewise unnaturally eat people during a certain season. These cultural artifacts, good and bad, have universally been imposed by intellectuals.

The world was then new, the world of Adam and Eve, and men had become as gods. They had eaten of the tree of wisdom and had obtained reason, but soon discovered that reason could be very dangerous. It was through reason that wrong and evil come into the world. Reason was but a tool, as useful for evil as for good. Before there had been no wrong, no evil, only Nature's way. It was reason's imagination, which by then seemed always to have been with them, like natural law, that became in the Adam and Eve lesson "original sin", as Miamonides suggested.

But an even greater catastrophe was to come. Reason brought progress and agriculture. Agriculture's plenty brought population in the great river valleys and so security. With plenty and security, purpose, as the driving need to struggle to survive, became radically attenuated. And without purpose irrationality brought chaos and terror.

You see when the shining eyes of the great cats were right there, just beyond the firelight, loyalty and responsibility required no harsh discipline; they were the overflowing offerings of beseeching followers. Over a million years of adaptation to a specific hunter-gatherer's struggle for existence had shaped every human sinew and cognitive program. Reason upset all of that. Reason could destroy human society! It invented inhuman Statism to replace the fallen society.

In the great river valleys where agriculture flourished, the old tribal society was unable to keep order for its disciplining force was gone. Chaos followed its uprooting, and it was, of course, the intellectuals who properly sought to do something about it. You understand that the disaster was unprecedented --quite unlike ours today -- for there was no history, no experience to refer to for guidance. The intellectuals were not evil men, evil being quite limited in those days, but what happened should be taken as a warning. They used reason, <u>but without a clear purpose</u>, to re-establish order; in the process they lost the very idea of purpose as they stamped out the remnants of the old society -- repeated following the Age of Reason.

They grabbed a monopoly on knowledge of seeds, soils, and storage. Gradually people were put back to work, some baited with food, until the elite reached a critical strength. Coercion then increased, the masses were pushed into slavery. Angry gods and a horrible hereafter were invented to coerce through terror, and a bureaucracy came to power, holding up a god-king symbol. Statism was in control.

Men will act through desire or through coercion but will not long follow two masters. Voluntary adherence to an admirable purpose does not mix with terror enforced indoctrination. There is no Third Way, as Lenin agreed.

Statism is very powerful internally but very weak externally; it is an anthill but man is not an ant. He will not fight to preserve his enslavement. Statism, modern or ancient, is not a civilization; the so-called ancient civilizations, the god-king empires, were not proper civilizations. They utilized very extensively what was known; they did make some very slow progress, did absorb innovations -- as the alphabet and we don't know what else -- from peripheral traders. Their stultification was the result of priestly fear of not being able to control the new; the Soviets came into the same problems with Lysenkoism. Everything remained rigid, as Plato described Egyptian art forms.

Intellectuals blame such rigidity on religion; but intellectuals' deceit and lies of a bureaucratic priesthood are not religion. Real religion is based on man's spiritual feelings and incentives, supreme of which is the will to rise up. There is no natural quarrel between science and proper religion, both are activities in the struggle to know. Intellectuals may have been pushing some magic and superstition into their "religion" before agriculture, but afterwards especially in the god-king empires, where human society had been pushed back into slaves' huts, it became widespread, as planned deception, innate as Orwell noted for Statism.

But out on the barren hills, where struggle kept humanness alive, tribal societies still maintained a fierce hold on freedom. The Greeks were fascinated by the collected learning of the Egyptians and never seemed to war with them; they admired especially their mathematics, something priestly censors ignored.

The Greeks developed a culture that has never been surpassed, if even equalled, but their greatest gift is hardly known, probably barely realized by themselves. They feared no social bonds; it was the enslaving bonds of a bureaucracy of the mind that frightened them:

> What good have prophets brought to men? Craft of many words, evil your message speaks. Seers bring terror to keep men afraid.

This was written before Plato was born; certainly the thought must have predated Aeschylus. It seems probable that it was this fear that urged an intuitive adoption of a guiding purpose, or more likely forced a much greater awareness of and emphasis on such a purpose, to keep them from this seen abyss.

The Greeks clearly did not fear their own priests, for they were never asked for advice; loose talk about the gods was referred to the Council of Elders. It was the intellectual priesthood that they had met in Egypt or in the East that raised the terror. It is innate for tribal (human) societies to seek to rise up; it is not clear that the Greeks fully comprehended the influence of their consciously conceived purpose to seek that "proper to man". What we can understand in retrospect is that a great purpose, consciously taught and held up for a society, is essential for the monopolizing of reason and its imagination for the service of that purpose. Only purpose can maintain rationality, morality, truth and all human guidance; without purpose, irrationality and madness will bring chaos.

The Christian world, which according to many including Simone Weil is basically Hellenic, was guided similarly in rising up -- as following the will of God -- perhaps embedded in Nature at the creation. Under it, Europe was created from a barbarous wilderness in one of the great creative ages (500 - 1000 A.D.). The next eight or nine hundred years brought a more worldly expansion. Beginning about 1000 A.D., reason was returning in force to the intellectuals of the West; the early Scholastic philosophers sought to use reason to build an alliance between social and spiritual guidance. But it was turned back; confusion increased for a couple of centuries and, finally, Machiavelli threw up his hands and suggested to his intellectual colleagues that they take to loading the commons with promises and take over.

Thus it was that around 1000 A.D., reason began to reclaim Western culture, but by 1500, the seeds for the destruction of reason, and the uprooting of all humanness had been sown. It is fascinating and tragic, heart-rendering in its obscenity to watch a giant reptile capture and "incorporate" a small animal. So too, it is to examine the struggle of intellectuals to destroy human society and reason so that our great universities deny the very existence of truth and reason; decency and virtue have become dirty words and even motherhood avoided. Christianity, once widely praised, even by non-Christians, is scourged from the schools and from the public square. And renegades seek to submerge all of the West in a Third World tidal wave.

NOTE ON FEELING

We are now at the point of making the transition in the discussion from society to culture. Neither term is well understood; the definitions used here for them are those common to most science.

Animal societies are guided nearly totally by instinct. Human beings living in reasonably healthy human societies are guided in their behavior to a large degree by their emotions -- feelings -- which are innate. Innate behavior patterns require a large number of generations to change, but cultural patterns, it is widely claimed, can be changed in a generation. The fact is that a culture can largely be destroyed in a generation, but it takes much, much longer to build a new one. It may not even be possible to rebuild before the society to which it belonged dies out for lack of cultural guidance. The aim of the current savage assault in Western culture is to destroy our human society. It is society that nurtures humanness, provides bonding to a purpose, and protects. It is this society that must be destroyed before Statism can take over, and this can be done most readily by subversively undermining culture.

Culture is knowledge acquired for the purpose of aiding society to survive and to rise up. Culture evolved innately and is necessarily conformable with the innate customs and purposes of natural human society. As civilization has advanced, people have lost touch with or even an understanding of society. When an intellectual denies any fixedness to man's society, he actually denies its existence. Many things that are called culture -- all of "adversary culture", all of Statism, and the like -- are actually poisons to society; they decrease its ability to survive. And when society is poisoned and dies, all that we call humanness and decency, which arises largely from innate roots in society, will die with it. All that we think of as human and we hold as most precious will die as society dies.

Culture is activated and communicated principally by language, but society is moved by innate, sometimes nearly unconscious, feelings. Some so-called feelings are little more than temper, imagination and intuition. Some innate feelings are rather short-range in time and space; fear, hunger, anger and happiness are psychological responses to situations over which we may have little control except for a reasoned response to them.

Brotherhood, belonging, a protectedness in the collective and conscience: these great social imperatives are the deepest and most lasting feelings; they usually come mixed with some short-range feelings. Conscience, the great social policeman of all the world has nothing to do with "my personal conscience", claimed in "values clarification." These four form the principal bonds of social cohesion, the purpose of which is to achieve a common social will.

It must be understood that even long before our forbearers coalesced into a society, they were subject to powerful imperatives, a natural guidance for survival. These were "genetically specified and phylogenetically programmed" behavior patterns, or we can say that emanations from the unconscious, produced from processed genomic information, commanded certain actions. There was little conscious awareness of the emanations because of the near absence of objective consciousness or adequate long-time memory, but there were consequences. If these imperatives were not obeyed anxiety, guilt, even fear -- as we know from animals today that are coerced into unnatural behavior -- could become debilitating.

The oldest of these imperatives is to survive and to rise up. Imperatives for non-aggression and altruism came with society. Prior to consciousness, our forbearers were nearly totally guided by emotions from the unconscious processing of genomic information. With consciousness, these emanations become immediately accessible to the reasoning mind which could act upon them. Reason could reject an innate command and thus culture joined DNA in guiding behavior. The difference in rates of change in cultural and to phylogenetic processes is very great. DNA is very resistant to change but, on the other hand, culture being a matter of merely acquired characteristics can be altered readily. Many things are innate or phylogenetic that are commonly taken to be cultural. "One of the most important (and often quite difficult) tasks facing ethologists is to differentiate between the affects of the two processes . . . completely different therapeutic measures were indicated in pathological disorders according to . . . " the process.

Lorenz discusses various strategies for distinguishing phylogentic from cultural processes and he gives two examples which we will outline briefly. Lorenz declared that if we discover that a certain pattern of social conduct is found in <u>all</u> human cultures, we can be quite certain that it is genetically specified, for it is manifestly impossible that such norms could remain unchanged, and to the same degree, if they were mere products of culture. In discussing these examples, note the detailed pervasiveness of innate behavior patterns.

In the first example, the anthropologist Eibl-Eibesfeldt[26] added a prism to the front end of a movie camera. His assistant could then take pictures while casually fiddling with the camera with it pointed off to the side; thus natural behaviors could be recorded. Pictures were taken of essentially all types of human societies, from Australoid aborigines and Papuans, Kalahari Bushman, Orinoco Indians, and Western representatives from Americans to cultured Europeans. Films were taken of many standard situations: greetings, farewells, quarrels, fear, and so on. Contrary to what anyone would assume, Lorenz states, "From closest analysis, even in slow motion the behavior patterns . . . of all proved to be identical." By behavior patterns, he meant

---

[26]See Lorenz.

gestures, expressions and body language, which are at the heart of ritual.[27] Remember that these were all the primitive forms of communication. Much of social conduct is motivated by feelings and they contain a large number of phylogentic factors. Even Darwin was quite certain that the ways in which we often express our emotions involve a large number of innate behavior patterns.

The other example is the story of a unique life, that of Helen Keller.[28] Helen, deaf, dumb and totally blind from near birth communicated with only two grunts until age seven. Then she obtained a teacher who turned out to be as exceptional as Helen. A normal child, when he starts to school, does not know the noun, verb, pronoun, up to subjunctive mood, but he knows what they "say" when he hears them. Also, he appreciates beauty, light, and many other things. Helen had no conception of these at least in her conscious mind. Yet in four months, she could read in Braille and write coherent letters quickly and legibly with a pencil. A year later, she used the subjunctive correctly and with pleasure in the conditional. Helen's complete experience, including a comprehension of what was beautiful and good, came first only through the pressure of fingers on her palm, and later by Braille. The idea that any person could come to form "abstract concepts of the most complex kind" solely from pressures in the hand "must strike . . . behaviorists . . . as utterly incredible". Her teacher, Anne Sullivan, explained properly that "It would indeed be a Herculean task . . . if the ideas did not already exist in the child's mind". Lorenz asserted that "there is not a single account to be found (in the scientific literature) with the clarity of this underestimated book (Sullivan's account). Yet it has been almost completely shunned."

---

[27]Remember that gestures and expressions (facial), body language generally, are a large part of all ritual, ritual being in a sense a sort of story or scenario told by largely body language. Hence body language, including specific signs, not mere gestures, plus a complex but primitive verbal language, constitute a major portion of primitive communicability. Even today much of our most deeply felt communication is in gestures, facial expressions, and ritual. Syntactic language is for reason. Hannah Arendt tells us that the "language of passion and compassion consists in gestures and expressions of countenance."

[28]Anyone who seeks or claims to have a knowledge of either social behavior or learning should be very familiar with it. Read her *Story of My Life* or Lorenz's account of it in his *Mirror*.

"The learning of language is based on a phylogenetic program which insures that a child's innate power of abstract thought is integrated and reintegrated with the vocabulary of its cultural tradition." "(S)yntactical language . . . is <u>the</u> vehicle of tradition *par excellence* and one of the most vital factors in cultural stability." And our schools very largely shun, even refuse to teach it.

In an important sense, it doesn't make much difference whether the Creator is still keeping an eye on us or not, because we receive emanations from our unconscious processing of DNA as commands into our conscious minds exactly as though He were. It is the encroachment of evil imaginings here that gave rise to the concept of original sin and makes it imperative that a society, having reason, cling zealously to a purpose to rise up. These feelings are real and the most sacred aspect of human life; celebrating them in song, rituals, and communion as in a church is far more reasonable and human than the denying of all that is the very essence of humanness.

RITUALIZATION

The situations and enacted behavior norms studied by Eibl-Eibesfeldt demonstrate a number of significant features. The necessary conformity between an innate behavior pattern -- which we now may recognize as a phylogentic ritual -- and, as it were, an adsorbed film of culture is characteristic of nearly every innate custom, ritual or behavior. In the case of language, there is a "phylogenetic program which insures that the child's innate power of abstract thought is integrated on every occasions with the vocabulary (of) the cultural tradition."

The situations studied by Eibl-Eibesfeldt were phylogenetic ritualizations, or acting-outs, for the purpose of communication; you "can tell by the way they act." Perhaps better than anything else these may demonstrate the pervasiveness of innate rituals -- these are <u>innate</u>, although they also possess a cultural veneer -- in social conduct. Rituals communicate and channel other feelings. There is no one ritual for greeting or one for quarreling, there are nearly as many for you as the number of people that you know. Exactly what you say or give to each is cultural but underneath them all is a certain ritualized structure immersed in a flood of feeling. The totality of these in a society provides a framework within which we express ourselves.

Groups larger than those held together by personal relationships "owe their cohesion entirely to symbols . . . evolved by cultural ritualization". (So much for cohesion, and the accompanying restraint on violence, when our highest Court actually "urges by permission" the burning of our national flag). "The development of verbal language (a symbolization for communication) presupposes . . . conceptual thought (and) ritualization, which codify the symbol and make it a part of tradition."[29]

Julian Huxley announced in 1914 his discovery that coordination of behavior within an animal society is effected by a system of communication in which the signals symbolize a particular behavior pattern. Thus, courting in certain birds involves nest building movements. Dominance is often expressed by an ostentatious display of aggressive weapons. He called this ritualization. Lorenz tells us that the idea that these behavior patterns -- expressive displays as ritualized means of communication, together with their variability in various species -- could be as reliable indications of generic relatedness as are physical characteristics, marked the proper beginning of ethology, the study of behavior.

After communication, the second major function of phylogenetic ritualization has been to redirect or channel aggressive behavior. Displays of antagonistic behavior commonly replace or preclude active combat.

The motivation of behavior is the major purpose behind all ritualization. Commonly with social animals, the entire structure of the community is largely determined by ritual. Geese and other birds of the same family commonly

---

[29]These quotes are from Lorenz. I hope I can suggest the fascination of his *Behind The Mirror* to motivate you to read it. There are other books -- wordy, pale substitutes; in Lorenz, you recognize a scholar.

possess a "triumph ceremony" in which mates, parents and siblings participate. The entire flock forms groups of mates or families, within which the members face together while stretching their heads and necks high in the air while honking for all they are worth. This triumph ritual dominates the entire life of the family, the flock and of the entire species. The ceremony is said not to create a bond, but rather it _is_ the bond; it expresses the bond and reaffirms it. Such rituals give rise to a new and "autonomous" _motivation_ in social behavior.

Cultural ritualization follows the innate rituals in most all details. Practically all phylogenetic behavior patterns, motivating an associated behavior, are colored over by cultural ritualization, except those socially tabooed, such as nose picking and similar "comfort" activities, including elimination. Normal social behavior is thus perceived to be dominated by cultural ritualization and it has been designated as both a straight-jacket and as a framework, a skeleton, for our social, cultural and intellectual life.

It is this structure that provides a known and practical order and meaning to life. It is within this structure that each individual finds his place, finds an identification and a belonging which supports his outward personality and his inward spiritual wholeness. Without this identity, Lorenz tells us a man loses contact with his society and becomes a nobody, a nothing, a disinherited alienate. The "despairing emptiness of so many young faces" presages a "dogged autism" or a violent social terrorist.

To be civilized is to be ritualized. All normal people have always sought to wear the customs and mores, the rituals, of their age, of their society. It was a matter of respect, of decency and dignity; all people desire to conform.[30]

---

[30]Perhaps never were people required to conform more precisely than under modern collectivist socialism. Our current P.C. is but the beginning. You should conform to basic human principles so that you then can have freedom to find that which seems to you "proper for man".

To conform is a great desire and a powerful urge. "To have his path made clear for him is the aspiration of every human being."[31] Whatever we acquire from our parents and older relatives and even neighbors and community -- certainly if it is a reasonably normal, human community -- we are bound to perceive as precious. Identifying with and obeying the canon of a father-figure is of exactly the same order as obeying the Great Spirit of the people. It provides an inner security and a bonding that makes belonging and conforming with loyalty and responsibility a sacred duty and a wish.

Oh, but people say, that is not true; not only do modern people refuse to abide by a "worn-out" tradition, we can also see that all progress comes from non-conformists. Ok, look at them: Isaiah, Buddha, Christ: the non-conforming conformists. It is not whether you are a conformist or not; it is what you are conforming about. Nonconformists who settled in the American colonies, or even St-Simon and Comte, whom Marx followed, every one of them, and many more, wanted to revive a lost order, a corrupted purpose. It was a matter of the purpose for which the conformity served that is at issue.

Examine the conformity of Puritan America, that (1) produced the Mayflower Compact and other such documents which formed the model for our Founder's vision of free men under written law, (2) produced Harvard University and a system of public education, unfettered by a State bureaucracy, and (3) provided a paradigm for personal growth and accomplishment through a concentration on reforming self, rather than others. Compare this with the modernists: St-Simon, Comte, Marx and followers, who (1) created modern anti-Semitism and its strategy of taught hatred, and the focusing of hatred by Marx's tactic of "one enemy", (2) murdered some 100 million brutalized and often tortured souls, for the convenience of a priestly bureaucracy and (3) manufactured the Big Lie of socialism and a mass of deceptions, lies and subversions beyond any previously

---

[31]Joseph Conrad.

imagined. Orwell and many others (we will examine a number of cases later) declared that lying became not an expedient but was endemic to their modern totalitarianism, revived from the bureaucratic enslavements of ancient god-king empires.

4. CULTURE

INTRODUCTION

To what combination of circumstance should we attribute the fact that in Western civilization alone, "cultural phenomena have appeared which lie in a line of development having universal significance and value?" That is the problem that the great scholar, Max Weber, set for himself in his famous work on *The Protestant Ethic*. He presents it at the beginning of his introduction and then answers. "Only in the West" was there a rational science, a structure like the canon law, a rational music. Over and over he repeats, "only in the West," a rational and written Constitution, and much more; printing came from China, but a printed literature, a culture, a press, and periodicals appeared only in the West.

So too with the "most fateful force in our modern life, capitalism". Capitalism, he explains is not at all the greed that Marxian sycophants in universities have pretended. It may, in fact, even be identical with restraints to irrational impulses. "Unlimited greed is not in the least identical with capitalism." The impulse to acquisition, gain of money of the greatest possible amounts, has nothing to do with capitalism; that impulse is universal, common in all sorts, in all conditions, all times, all countries. Scholars from von Mises to Simone Weil have agreed that the imposed perception of "capitalism" as a grab-bag of all the evils of man and of society is subversive nonsense.

The point that Weber made was that Western culture evolved as the only rational culture. We know that that means that it was guided by a central purpose; to be without purpose is to be irrational. But exactly what is culture?

NOTE ON CAPITALISM

There has been great pressure for over a century to force the perception onto the public that capitalism is a value system like Communism. This is corrupt bunkum from idiots or renegades. Communism is a "value system" only through its ability to control the minds of many Western sycophants. And anything claimed by anybody to be capitalism, beyond a free market which any free society must have to be free is, in reality, a human society; it may or may not be corrupted in a variety of ways by the use of wealth for anti-social destruction. Renegades who hate human society quite generally force the perception that capitalism is a grab-bag of all the known evils of men or society, and socialism (or communism) is a similar bag of all the known virtues. Such fatuous claims are not worthy of consideration. This is an example of a straw-man that is made the focus of Marx's "one-enemy" hatred. Only a human society, with an admirable purpose, can possibly judge human values in its culture. Human values can only exist by virtue of a great purpose for a human society, which capitalism is not; most certainly communism is not, it being in no manner human.

You must recognize that the claim: to be destroying "evil capitalism", is a deception. There is no such thing as "capitalism": what is called that is but a human society that renegades have corrupted. Our human society, trashed as it is, is what they are destroying.

CULTURE

Blackbirds and crows have been found to pass on knowledge of certain dangers, as of man, to their young. Rats have long been known to pass on knowledge of specific poisons. When Lorenz raised a generation of jackdaws from eggs, they had no fear at all of men, and when rats are totally deprived of a specific poison for a generation, knowledge of that poison as a danger becomes lost. Primates have been found to teach their young a number of life enhancing practices, such as washing their food; again if a reasonable facility for the washing is removed, this knowledge disappears.

Animals generally must and do depend near totally upon knowledge stored in their genome -- in DNA. Plants too have such stored knowledge for guidance -- how to adjust for lighting, temperature and other variables. Our forbearers once were guided totally by such innate knowledge, but even today we know from science that our emotions, "feelings" which arise from phylogenetic factors -- instinct -- still direct much of our most basic social behavior.

Superimposed on these deep-rooted, innate behavior patterns, our forbearers began to evolve a veneer of acquired practices based on experienced knowledge (tradition) which made the phylogenetic programs more effective or more complete. Obviously, the veneer had to be made conformable with the solid pre-existing phylogenetic patterns.

This "acquired knowledge for survival", as distinct from genomic knowledge has been designated as culture by scientists. It must be taught, for people no less than for rats. Animal species within their society -- pack or flock -- are absolutely truthful; a rat could not conceive of teaching its young that some poison was a nutrient or that some valuable food was a poison. Culture thus evolved as <u>truthful</u> information for <u>survival</u>, or to rise up, for every animal wants more than mere survival. We have such robust laws and enforcement concerning the distinguishing of toxins, or poisons, from nutrients in foods that no one would dare to label a poison as a nutrient. But in our culture, upon which the decency and the very survival of our society -- as a people -- depends, truth is often denied, and irrationalities spread confusion, distrust and chaos. Today vulgar, inhuman, heinous practices are acclaimed as our "culture", while knowledge long proven to be most essential for the survival of a human society is openly denied, jeered, even proscribed by law. A rat couldn't imagine being so stupid.

If someone sought to poison you, they might pretend to confuse nutrients and poisons; an elite seeking to destroy a culture could similarly "pretend" to confuse culture as knowledge for betterment, with social poisons: such as "rap", "modern art", much of entertainment and music, as well as "multiculturalism", an inordinate "equality" above responsibility, and "rights" above duties. An "adversary culture" is a contradiction, an oxymoron, an euphemism for renegadism.

Sociologists commonly show an ingrained confusion on the subject of culture; Carleton Coon, a writer of special perception, is rather typical. He defined culture as the total of all that people do, "as a result of being taught." But being taught is no restriction; in a generally accepted sense, everything is "taught," both the innate and the cultural. However, Coon soon demonstrated that he really believed that "culture" must aid a seeking of that proper to man; he declared for his very early "biological phase of history", that "culture gave *Homo sapiens* a decisive advantage, an opportunity for the future". Clearly the detrimental, taught as it may be by ignorance or intent, cannot give advantage.

It is important to recognize, as is particularly well substantiated by the Eibl-Eibesfeldt results, that the foundation or root of <u>all</u> human cultures resides in human nature. There is only one "proper to man", and hence only one basic culture. Or take the matter of language; Helen Keller went from zero in language to an ability to write a coherent letter "legibly and quickly with a pencil" in four months. She was able to do so only because the innate cognitive structures pre-existed in her mind, and on this innate structure any cultural language could have been superimposed. Hence as Noam Chomsky suggested, all of these human cultural languages must have a structure in common. This plus the commonness of the cultural veneer over the Eible-Eibesfeldt innate ritualizations, and the commonness among all peoples of so many basic concepts:

the Golden Rule, something like the Commandments, and concepts of justice, morality, charity and truth essentially guarantee a common basis for all human cultures. They vary only in the non-essential surface designs, as in language.

A human society is voluntary; a taught and understood purpose is essential to keep it rational. Though much of basic social behavior stems from innate roots, it nevertheless must be taught, just as young robins must be taught. And what is taught is not arbitrary; it must conform with the phylogenetic structures of innate human society. Rationality requires conformability --no clashing of gears; that requires truth in intent and fidelity in communication. Fixed truth in culture is imperative in order to assure conformability with the innate foundation.

Rationality, truth and fidelity of messages demands fixed meanings to words and expressions. "Uncontested terms" must provide a stable structure to any communication so that its meaning can at least be approximated. When meanings of the most fundamental words, such as "mother" or "family",[32] and when even the most approximate understanding of the natural character of man and human society, are forced to remain totally open, and all questions resolve themselves into "the condition of Negroes in Mississippi", then all communication, all reasoned progress, and even humanness are terminated.

Culture, as this acquired knowledge for survival, evolved in three phases. In the beginning, it was predominantly about the physical world: dangers in the environment, just as for rats and crows, and of food, clothing and shelter. Obviously, much of the acquired knowledge related to an understanding of, and was an addition to, innate or genomic knowledge. They both require being taught, as we saw for the rat. Lorenz has emphasized the difficulty of

---

[32]The editor of a large and influential newspaper recently condemned "the use of the word 'motherhood', as a ploy of the pro-lifers". The media would have "family" include a pair of pederasts (who, not long back, would have been hanged) as recipients of social protection and tax support.

determining the boundary between the innate and the cultured.

The second phase in the development of culture is marked by the beginning of its involvement in social guidance. It began when people became consciously aware of innate "feelings" -- Durkheim's "forces" as discussed previously. These were felt as commands, but friendly and as coming from the outside: conscience, a powerful force for brotherhood and belonging, a collective protectedness, and always most elusive, an urge always for something higher, better. Rituals in dance and song constituted man's first attempts to communicate, to commune about and to celebrate these forces. Durkheim declared that man was never so near his god; intellectuals had not yet sought to corrupt this elementary religion.

Mankind's evolution has been marked by two or three great turnings, the mere existence of which, to say nothing of their importance, is scarcely recognized in our education. The first occurred when our forbearers condensed into a society; the second we have just come to, the beginning of a world of reason and consciousness, and feelings. Scholars go on at great lengths about claims that man has not yet adjusted to the industrial world, or about the evils of capitalism, or racism. Why not add bad beer, "German bands and all other discomforts that have vexed the souls of them that go in chariots"? The fact is that people have not yet learned to live with reason.

The third phase of the evolution of culture concerns man's attempts to control reason. Reason has been extolled as the true mark of humanness, or God's greatest gift, and other fancies, unaccompanied by any significant whiff of comprehension. Reason is the one source of all evil, assuming God's Nature to be only good.[33] Reason is more dangerous than nuclear power, for the latter can be controlled by reason, but only purpose can control reason; reason cannot, but it can help us to take and to follow a purpose.

---

[33]In that in all of Nature's world, there was no evil only Nature.

And that man <u>must</u> do, if he is to seek to continue to rise as a human being.

When our forbearers were guided by Nature's instincts, or a Creator's embedded law, there was no problem because there was no reason. Even after reason came, when people and their cultures were predominantly concerned with things of the physical world, there was no problem. When the glowing eyes of the great cats could be seen by everybody, culture as knowledge for survival was snatched up like bread by the starving. "Adversary culturalists" would have provided but a few moments of entertainment. The problem came when reason brought agriculture, which brought leisure and security. Security ended unquestioned guidance, and man first met the abyss of irrationality. The question is, is it possible for him to escape? Of course, the answer is yes, if he will use reason. One looks around today and finds sheer madness most everywhere.[34]

When agriculture's security terminated the authority for guidance by the eon-old, tribal Council of Elders, the intellectuals properly sought to end the chaos. They did it by gaining a monopoly on knowledge, teaching terror to the ignorant commons who were pushed into sub-human enslaved masses.

We know that these ancient god-king empires that arose in the great river valleys of the world were not really civilizations. As in modern Statism, the elites were aware that free minds might discover something that would cause them to lose control -- Lysenkoism is but a modern version. They capitalized on known knowledge, creating a Stalinesque culture, not only their external works such as architecture and sculpture, but also in their culture of the mind as in frozen Egyptian art forms commented on by Plato. They

---

[34]We teach boys and girls the joys of masturbation and sodomy during ages of normal sexual quiescence, when people have long known from primitive times that this is when they need to comprehend their culture. We perniciously discourage families, while using tax dollars to promote a flood of aliens, who have already vowed to overwhelm us and enslave or kill us; a Dean at Stanford urges the teachings of Fanon.

borrowed from peripheral traders; the alphabet is probably a late example. But there apparently were periods of relapse when some people, even the elite priesthood, reasoned. Considering the amount of time, people and facilities available to the Egyptians, their contributions were not great. Perhaps they, in some way, however, provided a necessary step to a free culture. It was over 3,000 years before Christ, 1,000 years longer than from Christ to us, when men first were becoming aware, as the Egyptian priest wrote, that "Righteousness is what is loved". That was the beginning of conscious philosophy, of religion and science of the mind when they were still one: the total product of man's "desire to know".

You should recognize that these god-king empires might still exist, nearly unchanged today, had it not been for the outside -- the neighbors. In fact that very plaintive whine came out of Moscow a couple of years back. But, out on the barren hills of Greece, tribal bands still lived in freedom, guided by reason in a purpose to survive.

Their greatest contribution to mankind was not produced by reason; it was probably an intuition, hardly recognized by them any more than it is today. They had a powerful feeling for freedom, and rather certainly had never been under the thumb of an elite. They declared a hatred for deceitful "seers who would keep man afraid". It was likely an intuitive response to this fear that urged them to guide their society towards that "proper to man". It was through this purpose that they gained guidance and rationality, and from these they forged a culture never surpassed, perhaps never equalled. It was in their literature, philosophy, history and in art, that they wrestled with the problems of virtue, and truth, justice and guidance towards a higher dignity for man. These works are the very foundation of our canon, our knowledge for survival. Only a renegade or idiot would discard them.

The Greeks, of course, fell away from their purpose, likely without realizing its real significance; few people today seem to. Reason's imagination is the source of all of our conscious problems. For if it weren't for reason, there would be no conscious problems; all things would be guided by Nature's rationality. Reason's imagination is the essence of that which early men sought to identify as original sin. There has been much argument as to whether man was naturally good or naturally evil. This is absurd; these men recognized thousands of years ago that man was both; he had a dual nature. What the Greeks demonstrated to be possible was that a great social purpose can monopolize reason's attention; then like a working boy, it won't have time for destructive imaginings.

The result was a tremendous expansion in the extent and especially in the importance of culture. Previously culture as acquired knowledge for survival was largely concerned with the physical world. When the Greeks set out to seek that "proper to man", in government, in ethics and philosophy, in all things, culture had its real beginning in its modern structure and purpose. Culture became something profoundly new; intellectuals today seek to obscure or even to deny its significance.

Previously society had been kept rational by a clear and visible purpose: to survive largely through defensive or sustaining efforts, largely in the physical world. With reason and agriculture's affluence rationality became undermined because its purpose had become irrelevant. But mankind could not abandon society; people had psychic and social needs demanding cooperation -- the essence for which society was entered into initially. Clearly the major need was no longer defense; it was for coherence. And the Greeks, by somehow involving their entire society with the great purpose of seeking a higher dignity for man, were able to make a non-tribal, affluent society to cohere in a freedom which encouraged the most spectacular achievements.

I must remind you again of that picture, of "the glowing eyes of the great cats, right there;" how that could "concentrate man's mind so wonderfully". No room for deceits or lies or imagination; no need to call for order. For a million years, our forbearers adapted every innate cognitive pattern in their minds, every social habit or more, every cultural integument supporting an innateness with that picture focused on their consciousness. Suddenly it was gone.

The Greeks greatest victory was in achieving a combination of an intuition with reason which carried them by the abyss of purposelessness. They achieved a voluntary commitment to a purpose which gave them cohesion. And the Christian world which rose in their wake was soundly based on their genius.[35]

But the problem will never go away; mankind is like Sisyphus with his huge rock on the mountain-side. We have all seen families, groups, nations that one month are all in accord while facing danger, and the next month are at each other with lies and deceits. Commonly these are held within bounds. But people forget not only their purpose but even their need of one, and for what use; or they find outside, renegade, reasons for subversion.

We must consider a specific irrationality, which is nearly always a confusion of purposes before going on. Most people are familiar with the value, the supreme importance that big league club managers, or financial analysts, place on records and experience, on history, as does anyone under a stress to produce results. But the above jobs are simple; if they demand records and history, how vastly more important is history for the task of guiding a human society. A club manager would throw up his hands in horror at the way intellectuals ignore, deny, dissemble the history, the record that is needed so vitally. Culture is a veneer, an integument, which must conform with a fixed, phylogenetic structure underneath. Truth is imperative in culture to assure the rational fitting, and certainly without responsibility, truth is but artifact. Intellectuals often jeer both Henry Ford and history, for his declaration that "history is bunk". What he clearly meant was that the history of historians was so often bunk. A few years back, the editor of an important journal declared something to the effect that to him, the Civil War

---

[35]*Simone Weil Reader*, p. 180.

was as irrelevant as the War of the Roses. My God, is he not aware that the roots of our most pernicious problems today lie in the debris left by the Civil War?

So too are most of our worst problems in Western culture and its survival, rooted in the irrationalities and subversions resulting from the Middle Ages and its consequences. The Dark Ages, contrary to popular opinion, were a time of vigorous growth in Europe. Consider the 500 years from the fall of Rome to the announcement by Roscelin of contradictions in Christian dogma (nothing central but merely an artifact inserted in a lay creed by some clerk). A continent of dense, often impassable forests, was, to a considerable extent, turned to fields, navigable rivers and canals, villages, cities, cathedrals, universities and wealth. Scholastic philosophers had entered into the most vigorous use of that dangerous weapon -- reason.

Consider what a marvelous future the 12th and 13th Centuries seemed to promise for Europe. The Scholastic philosophers renewed the use of reason, and "Logic, ethics, and metaphysics gave to (them)", wrote Condorcet, "a precision unknown to the ancients". But there were bugs in the establishment; one called <u>filioque</u> had already split the Church and was nearly to down Roscelin. Another bug called "universals", caused no end to troubles. There is much, much more very exhilarating, very tragic. The only real problem was that they were not able to handle reason; perhaps the lack was a real, vigorous core. Instead some sought to use reason where it was invalid, and others refused to allow it to be used to loosen obvious contradictions.

This kept on, with much growth in Western culture, until the 16th Century, but with considerable chaos in intellectual circles and denigration of religion. Finally Machiavelli threw up his hands and urged intellectuals to cease restraining the commons, begin promising them their wildest fancies, and they will follow and you can again become Shamen.

In 1987, Allen Bloom, who certainly should have known, declared that it had been the "purpose", the very intention of 20th Century intellectuals to destroy the culture that supported them -- "even while making the most solemn assurances that nothing of the kind was intended", declared the President of Columbia University.

The challenge by Machiavelli to promise and take over was answered by the Reasoners' promise of material wealth from science, by the Enlighteners' promise to release people from the bonds of society, by the liberals' promise to free them from all restraints. Modern socialism arose early in the 19th Century in the movement by Henri de St-Simon and his secretary, August Comte. They conceived of inventing a total social science; their central intent was to return society to an ordered state by establishing "an industrial feudalism based on the rule of a self-appointed elite". But this "Utopian" socialism did not sell. Already the Enlighteners had come to realize the errors, even deceit, in their movement -- Diderot in particular. And there was much backtracking during the 19th Century -- read Mill on "Coleridge". And various liberals came to recognize, as did Disraeli and Marx (we are told) that Liberalism was but an exotic parasite growing on the decaying trunk of a fallen order. It was unable to support an order of its own for it had no guiding purpose only a "palpitating humanitarianism". "I would like to share with you . . . " How nauseating!

Marx found the answers in the 1840s and published a number of papers (see under Socialism); Lenin remarked that these papers signaled his turn from Utopian socialism (which did include totalitarianism) to communism. Idealism and promises were not enough, something hard was needed. Marx invented mass taught-hate; he outlined the tactic of focusing the hate on one enemy; subversion and lies could intensify the hate.[36]

But in America, even that didn't work. It is detailed briefly in the section on "Education" what did work. Socialist

---

[36]It is bizarre that the one enemy for Marx should be the "Judaistic manifestation", and Hitler followed, also utilizing Marx's "one enemy tactic".

cells were created and joined in a network that spread through our major universities. What came to be known as Gramsci's strategy, to go through the institutions, was well under way by 1900: Dewey in education, Morris Cohen in law, and a little later, Franz Boas -- and his women, Mead and Benedict -- in "cultural anthropology", whose purpose was to uproot physical anthropology and to denigrate Western culture.

This was what Allen Bloom referred to as the "purpose" of the intellectuals. Actually, the rot had started much earlier, beginning perhaps with Flaubert, or with Freud, Joyce, Proust, and especially Lytton Strachey. It has been noted by scholars that the books most praised by Western intellectuals began to be those that violently or subversively opposed the civilization's supporting beliefs.

Books most admired should celebrate the achievements of individuals attained by personal excellence. The minds and conscience of people, nurtured by a culture guided by a purpose "to seek that proper to man", should respect and insist upon an ability and a motivation to distinguish renegadism from constructive criticism. It is irrational, or renegadism -- which means in the service of a foreign purpose -- to bestow the dearest honors on those most intent on social destruction.

Read Paul Johnson's account of the assault of modernism on Western culture.[37] In 1905, impresario Sergei Draghelev of the *Ballets Russes* announced "a new and unknown culture . . . created by us . . . will sweep us away." Johnson notes the confusion, promoted or otherwise, between scientific relativity, a mathematical concept, and relativism, a cultural poison. Havelock Ellis declared Freud a great artist not a scientist. Sir Peter Medeavar called psychoanalysis akin to Mesmerism and phrenology -- isolated nuggets of truth, but the theory is false. Freud was first of the Century's messianic idealogues to regard those who disagreed with him as unstable. Freud mixed dreams, myth and sex; he invented

---

[37]Paul Johnson, *Modern Times* 1983).

almost as many words and phrases as Rudyard Kipling. He was intent on atomizing religion, encapsulating emerging trends, and presenting an explanation for everything.

Marcel Proust, according to T.S. Eliot, "destroyed the nineteenth century". James Joyce's *Ulysses* demonstrated the extent to which Freud's concepts had entered culture. *Ulysses*, and *A la Recherche* by Proust, marked "the destruction of individual heroism as the central element" in literature. "The exercise of individual free will ceased to be the supremely interesting feature of human behavior". These views of Johnson's seem obvious today. Yeats claimed that "mere anarchy had been loosed upon the world". Personal conscience, which stood at the center of Judeo-Christian ethics, was dismissed by Freud as a mere safety-valve. Guilt was unjustified; maybe all were guilty.

J. B. Bury, in 1920, *(The Ideal of Progress)* declared an end to progress; was it not merely "relative to a certain advanced stage of civilization"? No, writes author Johnson, it was killed by the sheer enormity of the horrors of WW I, perpetrated by civilized Europe. Exactly what do you suppose Mr. Bury means by "civilized Europe", and where, Mr. Johnson, has there been a proportional fallout from the often tortured killing of some 100 million souls since that time, largely in peace times, and initiated principally by intellectuals related socially to the victims, for the sake of "a new vision of society"?

The example of Weimar, Germany, from 1920 until the advent of Hitler, well covered in *Modern Times*, is significant. Read it there but we need the gist and culmination of it. Weimar was comparable perhaps, as a minority government, to Clinton's Washington. The liberal, intellectual avant-garde socialists took over. Few Americans have any concept of the cultural density in Europe, particularly before WW I in Germany. Berlin was the center but there were world famous opera houses in Dresden and Munich, art centers in Hamburg and Weimar, theaters in Frankfurt, Nuremburg, Leipzig, and on and on. Very briefly, the point is that the leftist intelligentsia deliberately sought to incite conservative Germans to fury. Sexual freedom, homosexuality, negro dancers and jazz, the cosmopolitan, erotic and immoral, and pacificism were exalted. That which had been sacred to Germany: the army, the State, the university, the Church and the volk, were savaged and ridiculed.

In this intelligentsia complex, the Jews were far from a majority, but they held conspicuous positions everywhere. They were very important if not dominant in publishing, department stores, and especially in popular entertainment. Kurt Tucholsky is but an example; he was a Jew and wonderfully gifted in satire. He intended to give pain, to arouse to fury and hatred. He succeeded. He wrote, "These is no secret of the German Army, I would not hand over readily to a foreign power". Johnson presents a summation by Friedrich Hussong: "They claimed they were the German *Geist*, German culture . . They represented Germany to the world, spoke in its name . . . Everything else was mistaken, inferior, kitsch, philisitinism.

"They always sat in the front row . . . awarded (themselves) knighthoods. What they did not permit did not exist . . . whoever served them was sure to succeed. He appeared on stages, wrote in journals, was advertised, his commodity recommended, whether cheese or relativity . . . patent medicines or human rights, democracy or bolshevism, propaganda for abortion, rotten negro music or dancing in the nude . . . there was never a more impudent dictatorship".[38]

Johnson asserted that "nothing is more galling than a cultural tyranny", real or imaginery. And Marx had provided the most comprehensive of hate theories and had, in fact, done so for the very purpose of attacking the "Judaistic" emanation of capitalism. He wrote of "The practical

---

[38]Paul Johnson's *Modern Times*, p. 115. Compare this with Walter Lippmann's description of America's renegade establishment in 1936, or Clinton's Washington.

domination of Judaism over the Christian world . . ."[39] Hitler borrowed Marx's tactic of "one enemy".

Only a lack of imagination can prevent a comparison being made between the intellectuals' attack on the society and culture in Wiemar, Germany and in America since 1965. Read Myron Magnet's *Dream and Nightmare, The Sixties Legacy;* Magnet adds . . . *Legacy To The Underclass,* which states his intentions of relating this attack on our culture to the horrors of our "underclass", no likes of which we suffered even in the Great Depression, which FDR dragged out to nearly a decade.   Recall that Bloom has admitted the intellectuals of this Century had deliberately intended to destroy our society and culture. Of course, really since 1965 that has been admitted: "Ho! Ho! Ho!". Also recall Walter Lippmann's designation of just who "We" had come to be: those "who sat in the front rows" were the "overhead planners", the Statist elite, all who "belonged", who "were allowed to be called humanitarian".

Magnet described the horrible savagery with which our human society was assaulted. But, he declares, it was all so unintentional and was done for a good cause. "We", Magnet writes, "made a Herculean effort to" do a whole lot of things. "We turned our entire culture inside out, only to make things worse . . . "

Then he turns around and submits that "we" were not the American people at all. It was the academics at great universities from coast to coast -- Duke to Stanford -- who declared Western literature to be the product of "high Anglican ass holes". The "turning upside down" created Bret Ellis' *American Psyche,* a "spiritual wasteland" where everything human had "died along with individual responsibility".

Magnet denounces Norman Mailer and Felix Rohatyn. It was a whole decade before "the summer of love" when Mailer produced "The White Negro". Learn from the Negro, he urged, "divorce oneself from society", "forget the single

---

[39]K. Marx, *Selected Essays,* p. 90.

mate, the solid family, the respectable love life". Choose a life of kicks, orgasms and marijuana.

Felix Rohatyn sneered at "people who live dead-end lives", and Magnet himself answers: if parents bring up children to respect hard work, to be curious about the world, stay in school, take pleasure in family and community life, to value themselves and have grandchildren -- surely that is worthy of social respect. And I would add that anyone like Rohatyn or Mailer, or all of the evil party who sneer at respect, ought themselves to be sneered out of decent society.

Decency, civil society, civilization, are not givens; they are goals to be attained by cultivation and by vigorously cutting out the weeds.

In summary, note that it has been determined that much of what is commonly perceived as cultural is but a veneer covering over innate behavior patterns that guide so much of basic social life and behavior. And these must be taught, just as young robins; and if they are not then young people will fail to become social humans, just as untaught robins will fail to fly with the flock. Tocqueville has warned of the sub-human consequences, which in a mild initial form appear as failure to become adults.

This must not be perceived as denigrating culture. What could be more important to reasoning beings then knowledge acquired through sensed experience, and utilized by reason and imagination for this purpose of survival? That we properly call culture, but it is certainly of equal importance to distinguish those urgings of reason's imagination that do not serve survival. These poisons can no more rationally be called culture than can toxins in food be called nutrients, or lies presented as truth.

Certainly when scholars declared, very short-sightedly, that all knowledge came as experience through the senses they would never have included in this knowledge -- culture -- such poisonous indecencies and renegadisms so destructive of human society as are today paraded as "culture". Nothing can be of greater importance to a human being than a true comprehension of <u>society</u>, <u>culture</u>, and their <u>poisons</u>.

"Society is the most complex of all living systems on earth, and our knowledge of it has barely scratched the surface. Yet I believe that man stands at a turning point, and has at this moment the potential to scale new and unknown heights". So wrote Lorenz, who goes on to describe Gestalt perception (as something like intuition, instinct and conscience); it perceives, stores, and unconsciously monitors vast quantities of observation for the significant from the noise -- in babies and in animals. Discussed more fully under Language, we need note here a most valuable example of its product: it informs animals and humans, most surely of that which is normal, "proper to man" and that which is abnormal, sick, poisoned.

MODERNITY

Modernity is the philosophy of liberalism. It demands a "coming out from under society", a release, an unbuttoning. Let it all hang out. The modernist insists that creativity requires spontaneity, not tradition, and similarly originality is seen to consist in uniqueness. "Modern man has ceased to believe without ceasing to be credulous." Modernity sees no future; it is so fascinated with "now." Hence its childish ways.

Conformity, conventionality and normality are straitjackets; the modernists seek nonconformity, a breaking away from tradition, from the moss-backs. Change is the touchstone. It was claimed, erroneously, that Hegel's dialectic demanded change. "Where to?" asked Councillor Mikulin softly.

A palpitating humanitarianism goes back to Rousseau; the conventional was loathsome. Man could be perfected by reason, as was assured by Condorcet. Love replaced charity in Corinthians; yet we know that charity is much different; it brings impartiality and peace, while love often brings the opposites. Modernity's freedom is hostile to order and responsibility; it forgets that its heroes, the "nonconformists", such as Isaiah, Buddha, Christ and Marx were actually great conformists, seeking to regain what had been lost.

The most profound characteristic of modernists, however, is their irrationality. Woody Allen explained, "I believe in sex and death". Mr. Rover found Freud and Dewey to be "seminal thinkers". An acknowledged educator of standing, returned from China, some years back at its opening, gushing about "all they had to teach us". Modernists believe in private judgments, private conscience -- except where their "beliefs" are concerned. Cultural modernism is to be retained, while rejecting the social implications. Marquis de Sade gloated, "If there is no God, then everything is permitted", and his children of the 1960s surged into the abyss. A century earlier it was asserted that people confused creature comforts for civilization; now it is irrationality confused as originality.

Surely most people will recognize the mad irrationality of this modernity. Let us look to its origins. In the early 19th century socialists began to realize and to complain that the "nexus between man and man", or human community, had disappeared. Some hundred years earlier, a growing population's desire for more "goods", promised from sciences by the Reasoners, had urged utilization of a "division of labor", thus making man a mere cog, a proletarian in a mass production industry.[40] It is well known that the early socialists, St-Simon to Marx (of 1840), sought to regain a lost order in society; they looked back to the ordered structure of the Middle Ages -- eulogized by followers even up to the beginning of the 20th Century.[41] When "utopian socialism . . . first appeared . . . as a consistent theory, it was largely a

---

[40]Before that people had been largely independent producers, bartering somewhat for what was produced locally at the weavers or blacksmith.

[41]See Max Beer, *The General History of Socialism* (1957).

reactionary protest against a new, progressive . . . economic movement, an appeal to turn the clock backwards."[42]

We know the origin of the problem of "nexus" and community order that vexed St-Simon and Marx. Back around the year of 580, some clerk in Toledo added a *filioque* to a recitory Creed, and it split Christianity. In another 500 years *filioque* returned to inflame again. Church intellectuals knew that reason was a powerful gift from the Creator and that it could not abide with a contradiction, but instead of recognizing the profound nature of man's long struggle to reason toward a great comprehension of that Creator's purpose, they clutched. The upshot was that Machiavelli urged his intellectual colleagues to go for the old shamanship and, through promising anything, gain the worship of the masses.

The ultimate and irrefutable result of this intellectual arrogance and stupidity was the near end to Christianity. But that in no way has ended man's spiritual needs. People were cut off from the greatest and most beautiful purpose and vision man had ever known. He did not, however, cease to worship visions. Man will always worship, either some great visioned purpose that he finds deeply admirable and sacred, and will struggle and fight for, or he will be given one and made to work and fight for some terrible, inhuman vision, such as socialism. There is no middle course.

That is how the Aryan, the Christian, how Western culture came to lose purpose, lose rationality, and thus began the decline into modernity's irrationality, and alienation and loss of nexus.

For want of meaning and beauty men sought the spontaneous, the expedient; always beginning, always leaving. Don't bother to right the ship, burn it. Having no idea where to go, it is yet necessary to leave, seek change.

Human society is uprooted. Language, grammar, morality, decency, family, literature, and standards of any

---

[42]*Socialism and American Life*, ed. Egbert and Persons (1952), article by E. H. Harbison "Socialism in European History".

kind, are all unnecessary and impossible when everything is permitted. But there is always the abnormal, the perverted, all "palpitating deliciously". "I want to share with you -- ." "Goodness of heart," delights the modernist; it is substituted for common sense, but is only something to say.

NOTE ON H.G. WELLS

Somewhere in H.G. Wells, he has been belaboring the Church, left and right, for all the evils known to man and for all the disasters of a thousand years. But, at the end, he seems to pause and reflect; he writes, but think of the millions of simple men and women who over that period dedicated their entire lives to sharing if but briefly the burdens of the common people, consoling them in their grief, sharing some small joys, and always trying to bring some beauty and hope into their dark lives. Never before nor since have there been such people. That was the true Church of Christ. It had nothing to do with the corrupt intellectuals who found their way from time to time into the hierarchy, generating wars of greed and other corruptions.

But why, people ask, must their lives have been so "dark". Maybe, they were in fact not so dark, for darkness is largely a matter of expectations, and lightness but a hope of receiving. Compare Brueghel's peasants with modern masses under Marxism, or compare the exuberance of the writer of Gotha with the disinherited alienation of so many of our own youth. The only solid joy and hope in this world is to be found in a purposeful struggle to rise up. Darkness, in hall or hut, comes with the death of hope.

SNOW'S TWO CULTURES

C.P. Snow presented his concept of *Two Cultures*, science and humanities and their separateness even hostility, in his Rede Lecture for 1959.[43] It is valuable but not for the

---

[43]Lionel Trilling's account in *Beyond Culture* has been followed briefly.

concept itself as for the bright light that it throws on the thinking of the intellectual class in America as well as in England even before the uprising of 1965 -- before Vietnam and Watergate.

Snow's 1959 lecture was a continuation of the argument of 1882 between Matthew Arnold and T. H. Huxley. Arnold had contested the assertion by Huxley that science, not "culture", must supply the knowledge essential for a rational, technological society; in his Rede Lecture, he had claimed that science does not "serve" the instinct for conduct and the instinct for beauty so necessary for human social guidance. Snow took a completely opposite position, "a position of extreme antagonism toward literature".

Snow began by noting the near total lack of any community between humanities and science, and presented a quite even-handed description of the "split". Thus in the beginning of his lecture both sides were to blame for the "gulf of mutual incomprehension", but soon Snow had it that the scientists were generally "in the right of things" and literary men in the wrong. Scientists were inclined "to see if something can be done" about problems; they were "tough and good men". It was this spirit that made them "regard the (literary) culture's social attitudes as contemptible". Snow then quotes "a scientist of distinction": "Yeats, Pound, Lewis, nine out of ten . . . of literary sensibility, weren't they not politically silly, wicked? Didn't . . . all they represent bring Auschwitz nearer?" Yeats might be "magnanimous and a great poet", but Snow would not "defend the indefensible."

With that the virtues of the scientists "boiled over": a natural decency, free from racial feeling, lovers of equality, cooperative and, above all, have "the future in their bones". That future was nothing but good, like the history of Marxism, always triumphing in the right.

On the other hand, Orwell's *1984*, Snow claimed, showed "the strongest possible wish that the future shall not exist". This proved that the culture of literature, the "traditional culture," was "hostile to the future," and it is this "which manages the Western world"; <u>and</u> <u>thus</u> <u>mismanaged,</u>

the "existing pattern" must be "broken" completely (emphasis added). Snow details the blame for all the ills of the 19th and 20th Centuries: intellectuals of the humanities "did not comprehend what was happening . . . they contracted out . . . Ruskin, Morris, Thoreau . . . (little) more than screams of horror . . ."

Did Snow expect the literary men, unorganized and few in number, to manage parliaments and congresses, ministries and armed forces, massive commercial and scientific enterprises, promises to citizens, and so on? Certainly men of memorable names: Coleridge, Carlyle, Mill, Dickens, Ruskin and Arnold, did decisively change perceptions and practices; it was not management but guidance as intended by culture. But in Snow's opinion, it rated no praise. Arnold and many others understood Hegel's announcement that the French Revolution had marked an absolute change; Idea or Ideology or Imagination had become decisive in human affairs, theory replaced purpose.

But Snow had unwittingly come very close to the real problem; he assumed that the intellectual culturalists should have provided or contributed a core, capable of using the culture for social guidance, as it theoretically is supposed to. But the then liberal establishment, going back to the Enlighteners, had rejected the concept of a core, by rejecting social responsibility for individualism. And Snow was well aware that the literary culturalists had never conceived of the responsibility of taking the real place of the church; they lacked the organization and a network of communication to the people. Snow's most arrant nonsense was to urge that scientists now form a new core, not to bring focus and organization to the culture, but to "supplant" culture, undoubtedly under the State. Let them guide society with no questions asked. These scientists could soon settle all problems with the Soviets -- where have we heard that before; thus politics is rejected by Snow. Intellectuals thus dream of taking over management of the world, and soon. These irrational ideas received high approval, but not unanimous, on both sides of the Atlantic. It is not clear that even Trilling understood what was wrong with them.

Allen Bloom, in *Closings*, tells this following account. The president of a well known research university, inspired by Snow, proposed to help heal the breach between "Snow's silly two-cultures," science and literary culture, by exposing scientists to cultural experiences and culturalists to science. Accordingly he invited a professor of music to give a lecture on musicology to which the scientists came "with their brown lunch bags."

The *New York Times* picked up the story, and quoted the university president, who had recently dumped the school's philosophy department, as declaring that Snow was on the right track but had counted wrong. There were not two but many cultures and he pointed to that of the Beetles. To Bloom this was "the ultimate trivialization of a trivial idea . . . just a rest station on the downward slope." To the president, the humanities were just another "peep show;" in a sea of relativism, only natural science "stands like Gibraltar." You see, science with nearly only Marxism alone, holds strongly to a purpose.

WHO ARE YOU?

Man is by nature a social being, and cannot live without the supporting structure of a society and culture to which he belongs. The Greeks at Marathon, Christians facing the lions, Schoolmen grappling with reason, our Founding Fathers, the Pioneers, the Unknown Soldier, and the cowboy or fireman provide a continuity and an identity, without the real experience of which young people can have no concept of who they are or of belonging to something real and solid. The desperate struggle for an identity -- marked by alienation, irrational behavior, and suicide among youth -- is a symptom of a hiatus in the continuum of our culture. If a person loses contact with his culture, he becomes a nobody, a nothing, as one can see in the emptiness of the faces of some many young people. Losing one's cultural inheritance is to cease "to belong"; indeed to be disinherited. No man can preserve his spiritual well being without identifying with other men.[44]

It seems likely that most all white Americans belong to a family of people who lived for thousands, perhaps tens of thousands, of years along the edge of the glacial icecap. The struggle to survive may well have been the eugenic imperative which stripped out many weak constitutions and, most significantly, engendered a powerful and nurturing social order which, on retreat of the ice, led to a massive population growth.

Perhaps sometime after five thousand years ago a tremendous outflow of people began to occur from the plains north of the Black and Caspian Seas. They moved slowly southward into northern India as a warrior and ruling class. It is from these people that the name Aryan, the Sanskrit language, and the *Upanishads*, and the *Bhagavad Gita*, arose.

Let us skip ahead momentarily to the 18th Century. In 1767, a certain similarity was noted between Sanskrit and European languages by the French Jesuit Coeurdoux and, in 1786, the Britisher Sir Wm. Jones noted that Greek and Latin bore a "strange affinity (to Sanskrit), both in root of verbs and form of grammar, than possible by accident -- no philologist could have failed to believe them to have sprung from a common source." What was soon recognized was a familial relationship among all European languages and Sanskrit. Philology became the central study for many scholars because it was assumed that the very ancient commonness of this root of language and thereby of culture, marked a common people, that came to be called the Aryans.

What came out of this study is certainly one of the most fascinating accounts in all of history. The history of these Aryan people is not found in books, on monuments, or in archeological digs so common for other peoples. Helen Keller learned to read and to write, and learned of all things good and beautiful, beginning solely with the pressure of a

---

[44]Paraphrased from Lorenz's *Behind the Mirror*, p. 206.

teacher's fingers on her palm. All that we know of our ancestors before the time of the Greeks, or original Aryans in India, has been gleaned from just words, in the Aryan languages. The story is too fascinating to attempt a simple, surely to be butchered condensation.[45]

We may note briefly some ways in which information and some inter-Aryan relationships were obtained. Dr. Johnson's culture saw *electric* or something related to a property that some bodies exhibited when rubbed. It came from the Greek word "electron," designating "amber," actually a derivative of a verb meaning "gleaming." From this we deduce that the Greeks did not have a word for, nor know of electricity, and that modern electricity was recognized somehow through the properties of amber. This is a rather simple example of the way relations were derived.

Barfield discusses the deduction of information from the presence or absence of certain words. Some words appear in all Aryan languages; thus there is *brother* and *frater* in English and Latin; and Sanskrit, which is assumed to be close to the original common root language, gives the half way in between, *bhratar*. There is a common word for 'waggon'; *wheel* and *axle* are common, but not "spoke", suggesting solid wheels. "*Wand* in English means 'slender rod', but in German it is 'wall'; combining these suggests wattle huts, with a 'wind's eye' or *window*. On and on it goes.

We will continue now with the outflowing of the Aryan peoples, particularly after 2000 B.C., at which time they were perhaps beginning to descend from the Danube Basin into what is now Greece and Italy. By the time of Julius Caesar much of Europe had been taken over by the Aryan Celts, but Teutons and other Aryans were making their way westward.

These people were all Aryans, but that in no way inhibited them from invading and decimating each other. For instance in the British Isles, the Celts, who presumably had ousted some previous inhabitants, were in turn invaded and

---

[45]For a brief account see Owen Barfield's *History in English Words.*

set to flight by Jutes, Angles and Saxons, who were in turn slaughtered by Danish invaders, who in turn were subjugated by the Teutonic Franks, in 1066.[46]

The Aryan waves moving south produced the *Upanishads* in India, the Parthenon in Greece, the beginning of Western Civilization in Greece and Rome, and the great cathedrals of Europe. On arriving at the western verge, they halted momentarily, then leaped the ocean to a New World, then on to the Antipodes and both poles. Finally to the moon.

There was also Dante and Da Vinci, the Schoolmen and Shakespeare, Kant and modern sciences. The scholar Max Weber declared that the culture of the West alone, had universal significance -- because only it was rational, due to a great guiding purpose. This is the Aryan heritage, your inheritance, something of which to be proud.

This is the society and the culture that is responsible for order and progress in America. There is no other. It is for this reason that it is far more important for Aryans to recognize and to comprehend these roots than it is for Negro or Jew[47] in America to comprehend theirs. You must recognize that at its center is a great purpose and it is this

---

[46] It is important to note that the so-called American Indians did precisely the same thing in the Americas, and so too did Negro tribes in Africa -- some of whose current tribes decimated the previous occupants in historical times. C.S. Coon tells us that imports of taro and banana plants, and the art of ironmaking had been introduced into East Africa after 500 AD, presumably by Arab traders. With these food plants and iron tools, the population of eastern and central Africa grew rapidly. By 1500 Bantus were pushing southward, and it has been claimed that the Hottentots and Bushmen might well have been extinguished had not the entrance of white Dutch saved them. Coon concludes that had it not been for the Arab imports, there might have been few blacks in South Africa today. *C.S. Coon, The Story of Man.*

[47]Only if and when they control society and culture and thus become responsible for order, will theirs exceed in importance that of Western culture.

that makes it rational; it is the Christian purpose to rise up towards a higher life.

The central purpose of this *Guide* is to urge people to go beyond the mere perception that Western culture is under attack, and perhaps near its end. You must comprehend, grasp, the enormity of this catastrophic event. Sartre was astonished that Western intellectuals could toss out God, and then pretend to go on "as though nothing had happened." It is much the same thing, perhaps even more real seeming and thus more horrible to even consider giving up one's culture. It is suicidal to allow it even to be attacked, and genocidal to do so. Perhaps the fears of an L.A. talk show host, Dennis Prager, may be more real to you. "As a Jew in America," he said, "I greatly fear a post-Christian America. It is symbolized in American youths' lives by the difference between the Boy Scouts and Guns 'N' Roses . . . The L.A. riots . . . (are) a preview of what such an America will look like." Well a post-Christian and a post-Western-culture America are the same thing. So too is a post-purpose-to-rise-up America. It is in fact the very reason-for-existence of Christianity, of any religion, of any human culture of a human society to seek to understand and to attain that higher level "proper to men."

I would draw your attention to the rather total misunderstanding of "the idea of progress." "Progress," as used in the literature, is commonly only some new "thing," resulting from purpose, just as "values" are fancies dependent upon purpose. Thus the real purpose of all human societies -- to rise up -- might properly and did at one time mean more food, better shelter, an easier life, more leisure, more rights, more freedom. But today a gluttonous populace is overfed, over-sheltered; life is so easy and leisuresome that most people suffer from boredom, and the more "rights" and "freedom" they have, the more they lack any civil restraint, so essential to true humanness. Never before were the words more apt, "What profiteth a man that he gain the whole world but lose his soul?" Or, "(Man ought) to live according to the highest thing that is in him, for small though it may be, in power and worth it is far above the rest."

"To find the soul," to paraphrase the old Greek, "is hard, and having found it is impossible to utter." If we understood the soul, we would understand what was "proper to man," and what it meant to "rise up." We can see that all life, for a billion years, struggled to rise up. Our forbearers struggled endlessly for a million years, and monatonically they did rise up. That struggle to do more than merely survive is what all life and existence, what all culture is about.

Durkheim has warned us that "a people cannot exist without a name." To have the hyphenated name, Indo-European, given to you, is to assent to a subjugation. The liberal's much quoted *Golden Bough*, by Fraser, tells of "Aryan races from India to Ireland." The British historian V. Gordon Childe supports the use of "Aryan" for the "brevity and familiarity," and because of the clumsiness of alternates.

Ancient claims of being "Chosen People" or a "Middle Kingdom" have not totally been given up, but the claim of "Aryan supremacy" was not Aryan in origin; it came from the socialists, even Marx and Engels, as also did modern anti-Semitism, and taught hatred. Liberals have supported socialists in pushing the odium for these inventions on to Aryans, and in attacking any who would deny these calumnies.

Without a name, and a name that you can be proud of, you are a nobody undeserving a name, and this is increasingly true due to the liberal-socialist Balkanization of culture. Are you proud to be named "non-Hispanic white" by your Census Bureau, or gringo, anglo, WASP, or heathen (the meaning of gentile)? These are commonly used, vituperatively, for all Aryans -- while the use of nigger or kike, actually self-given names, are made hate-crimes; but let not the hun or the dago feel exempt from the cut of WASP or anglo. What is being slashed is not the lone limey, but Aryans, all of Western people, and their society and culture.

WHAT IS WRONG

City "A," as we will call it, was some thirty years ago terrorized by crime; secret criminal gangs ruled drugs and prostitution. City A and its surroundings were miserably poor, with no industry, but notorious with slums. It barely subsisted. A peoples' movement came to power; a social not a Marxist movement. Laws were passed and enforced; criminals were shot and the gangs scattered. Traffic in drugs brought the immediate death penalty. Prostitution and pornography were halted; even littering could cost $300. Business picked up; industry moved in; families were rebuilt. Today it is one of the most prosperous and safest cities on earth.

In city B, a paroled felon, high on drugs, led police on a high speed chase through traffic lights, endangering untold lives and property. Finally, ramming a chain blocking the entrance to a dangerous area, he halted, and scared a female on patrol into pulling her gun on him. The police came and may have saved his life by ordering guns away. The felon continued to mock police when arrest was attempted. A prison-developed physique enabled him to throw off police "swarms" like a "professional linebacker." Hit twice with a Taser that should have knocked out a bull merely took the drug empowered felon to his knees. He arose in a quick and savage attack, and police were forced to use sticks. Though ordered to quit resisting and to lie down, he continued to attack. This kept on for some 81 seconds until he was forcibly cuffed.

The graduated force used by the police was according to departmental instructions. The felon was taken to medics who declared "no serious injuries" and was treated for "superficial lacerations."

All was brought out in the trial, a much more detailed description of the controlled use of sticks, only when the felon sought to rise up. Nothing was withheld. There was not one single criticism in the trial, except the venue.

A number of concerned lawyers watched nearly the entire trial; all seem to have agreed, if not that the jury's verdict was totally correct, at least that it would be difficult to fault them.

Roger Orloff wrote his findings in the June issue of *American Lawyer*: prosecution and defense witnesses agreed on speeds close to 100 mph; two black passengers arrested with no problem; Rodney King refused to obey police orders, "danced around wiggling his hips;" police tried to cuff him, "King threw or shook them off;" Koon warned King to get down or get Taser, King refused, second Taser, King fell to pavement; King recovered and lunged for officer as video starts and baton blows start, first eleven blows not faulted by either side. From 11 through 56, the (officers) defense used slow motion replays, with officers pausing (Orloff writes) "to observe King's behavior . . . Like it or not, that is what the video shows," Orloff wrote. King refused to be flat, remaining in a spring-position, but was eventually forcibly cuffed. Orloff supported an oft-ridiculed statement by one juror, that King was in control all the time; he argues that King refused to obey.

Orloff wrote more, in "lowered voice." "I might have done the same as the jury . . . I have never felt so hesitant to say what I believe . . . I'm concerned about reactions . . . people see headlines and never read the rest . . . I'm terrified at prospects of quotations out of context. . ."

The above blow by blow analysis was supported by National Audio Forensic Lab analysis of the tape; it also denied King's charge of racial slurs. The video shows the constant leg-cocking, rising to knees, Folsom Rolls, etc.

"I think a jury of 12 having heard all the evidence might conclude that the officers used reasonable force," wrote Harvard Law professor, Arthur Miller. Note that Mr. Miller's connections with Harvard and with ABC as a legal commentator, must be seen as biasing in favor of the media, not the police.

The felon had violated parole; he had run from the police at speeds up to 100 mph, at high speed through a reported six or seven stop lights or signs; had resisted arrest; assaulted officers. He was never charged with anything. Instead he has been given some $3.8 million in "damages".

A video and audio was taken from the point when the felon leaps up from the second Taser was used intensively during the trial as noted above. The incident was winding down during the last ten or twenty seconds; that last part was <u>all</u> that the great majority of Americans were aware of. Most all that wasn't shown was not contested; that is, it was accepted as legitimate police coercion. Only the last dozen seconds, according to one reliable source, was all that was declared excessive.

We come now to one of the fraudulent aspects of the media presentation. The felon wasn't charged with anything; the police were charged with "assault with intent to do great bodily harm". Now, if a person is eventually handcuffed by the police, and he receives according to a doctor, only "superficial lacerations", even as he is attacking the police, how can the police have "<u>intent</u> to do great bodily harm"? But there is a far more important story.

From the time when the deceitful, cut video began to be played over and over, with a near total censorship of all other facts -- a "motorist" had been beaten by racist cops -- the media began planning a pernicious deception, a criminal libel of America. Where has there been a single important trial at which every scrap of information was not publicized immediately. Here not a single inkling, even as Orloff and Miller could see clearly that a not-guilty verdict was almost inevitable, on the charges. The American public was held, <u>held</u>, in near total ignorance -- like FDR's setting up Pearl Harbor. When the verdict came, the media played it as a bomb bursting, like Pearl Harbor all over. Black L.A. Mayor Tom Bradley and the media incited to riot; "express our outrage," ordered the Mayor. "A miscarriage of justice!" "Racist America!"

Then began the most evil, treasonous attack on the very society which alone can bond our order; an attack was made upon the right of trial by jury for which Western people have given much blood. The sneering renegades who laced their promoted-riot with a hate-twisted "beaten into insensitivity", deserve nothing less than a public hanging. Otherwise America cannot escape Lebanization.

Can it really be true that the felon is given millions of dollars from the taxpayers while the arresting officers, who may have been risking their lives to bring him in with only "minor laceration" (largely self-inflicted), have prison terms? Or that the police officers bringing into custody a known felon, in the act of bringing great danger to lives and property, were widely equated to <u>animals</u>, while brutes who took an innocent passer-by's head into their hands and mashed it into pulp with a piece of cement are "victims of society"?

That Western people's culture as knowledge for survival had reached such desperate depths has been known for some time. Some 51 years before, a Senator arose to demand, are we to war against one set of thugs in order to save a larger more evil band of brutes? He received no answer.

For a dozen years after the "blockbusting" into existence of our Third World cities, there was a very occasional news story of the death of some old woman, of which there were certainly tens of thousands left behind. When blockbusting swept an area, or an entire city as Detroit, there were many old couples soon to be just widows, too old to run, and couldn't afford it. First their flowers were pulled up, then the screen door torn, a window broken, a TV stolen, finally the desecrated, broken body of an old woman, whose calls for help had been laughed at, was sacked for the morgue and a bull-dozed funeral. A dozen millennia ago if a tribe abandoned an aging parent along the trail who couldn't keep up, it was essential for survival of the tribe. Here there was no necessity; some hundred thousand souls were merely inconvenient, and it was considered "insensitive" even to mention such cases, after all, they were but Aryans.

The question out of all of this is, can a people whose purpose, whose core, whose culture, have become so rotted, can they ever even hope to recover? The answer is of course;

most all new life is generated in rot or chaos. The only question is whether it will be a new truly human society or the slavery of a new Statism.

5. SOCIALISM

INTRODUCTION

Our society is innate, the result of millions of years of adaptations. The human society which we have had in America over the last century and a half has become increasingly corrupted and unsupported. A society is voluntary, therefore it must have an admirable purpose to attract the support of people. This guiding purpose makes it rational, which requires truth and a culture.

Human society has broken down twice, the first time perhaps some eight or ten thousand years ago when extensive agriculture developed in a river valley, thus destroying the entire basis of the old hunter-gatherer tribal society. How it occurred can only be guessed; presumably intellectuals recognized that by grabbing a monopoly on knowledge they could gradually gain hegemonic control. These intellectuals were not necessarily evil men; to a degree they had no choice. But once in control they had no way to go but ahead, and they recognized that that meant a close retention of all knowledge, and coercion of the masses through terror.

It is not clear why this anti-society that we have called bureaucratic Statism[48] has returned; or it may be

---

[48]It is understood that fascism and communism are merely variants, different theories or ideologies, of socialism. The great majority of socialists were communists in idealogy and loyalty. Today the nationalist or fascist form seems the only possibility.

said that there are many possible reasons for its return in modern times. The most common theory is that it arose out of the misery of the industrial revolution. That is simply not even reasonable.

Quite likely its origin has to do with the same factors which produced it the first time: a breakdown in social guidance caused by loss of social purpose. Machiavilli's proposal, at the beginning of the 16th Century, that intellectuals regain control of society presumes exactly an intellectual bureaucracy which is the essence of Statism. The intellectuals' efforts, continued over four or more centuries, to destroy social purpose, to destroy first religion, then the cohesion and the bonds of society, then education, and law, and responsibility of any kind. They "went through the institutions," and destroyed society's immune system, all the bulwarks that had been fashioned to support it.

Society is unique. It evolved over millions of years of trial-and-error; evolution is a learning experience in Nature as to what works. Statism is an ideology, a theory for some artificial construct designed to be forced into replacing society. Song, dance, human hope and joy, art, literature, truth and morality, all things human and decent evolved at or even before the dawn of humanity, as adaptations to support and to celebrate society. Under Statism, all these are crushed from the masses and are replaced with hated indoctrinal substitutes. The stultification which Plato found in Egypt has been demonstrated again and again in this century, in every place in which socialism achieved total control.

It is to be noted that Bismarckian socialism is not total Statism. Tribal societies were ruled, not in details, but mostly in long-term social guidance by a Council of Elders as a core. These old men were the heads of large families and had served their tribe long and faithfully. They had as a purpose only the welfare of the tribe as a protective home for their grandchildren. In a sense European aristocracies, with some noted rotten exceptions, partially filled this need, as did some kings, and Bismarck. They served as a core. Bismarck's bureaucracy, was like a corporation's bureaucracy, yoked to a people's purpose -- as reason and power must always be yoked for rationality. The bureaucracy of Statism is the arm of the intellectual elite, whose only purpose -- of both elite and bureaucracy -- is staying in power or achieving more power. This corrupt purpose has no essential need for truth and morality, or for culture beyond indoctrination.

Deceit, lies and viciousness are the everyday tools of socialism. There is a description somewhere of how Communists were to operate when infiltrating some target: get into the policy making positions if possible and take over, if not get on important committees and write the reports, if not possible at least change some of the words in the reports. Leave no stone unturned.

The eminent Jewish scholar, Lucy Dawidowicz revealed the evil renegadism of the whole continuum of intellectuals, from liberals to communists, in *The New Leader* (12, 22, 1952); she charged it with "attempting to use Jews as it had long used blacks in its 'war against America'."[49]

As for deceit, go back and compare the description of the German Weimar establishment with Lippmann's statement on America's "overhead planning" establishment in 1936. Thus in Germany, ". . . Everything else was mistaken, inferior . . . What they did not permit did not exist . . . They 'made' themselves and others. Whoever served them was sure to succeed . . ."; and in America, "No other approach seriously considered . . . only a handful here and there . . . without influence . . . isolated, disregarded, continue to challenge it . . . From (them comes) every effort which lays claim to being enlightened . . . no one else taken seriously . . . mossbacks, reactionaries."

Trying to tell anyone in 1936 that the establishment that secretly was at the controls in America as Lippmann described, would have been equivalent to trying to show someone today that FDR consciously sacrificed some 2,500 young men at Pearl Harbor and twice that on Bataan. Like a chess player, he sacrificed a couple of pawns and a rook

---

[49]R. Radosh and J. Milton, *The Rosenberg File*, p. 353.

for board position, to get into the war. He could get away with it because the whole establishment was already controlled by "overhead planners" (a.k.a. collectivists). FDR was able to "trick" America into the war, as A.M. Schlesinger, Jr. put it, and then, far worse, he was able to conceal that the <u>reason</u> he was so desperate to get into the war that he knowingly sacrificed Pearl Harbor was that he wanted to save Stalin and Communism. Schlesinger roundaboutly admitted in 1990 that FDR had a "vision" of America becoming 40 percent Communist. Ask a Chinaman or a Russian or a Czech what that means.

Diana Trilling, whose husband was long within the very eye of the renegade establishment -- the cell at Columbia University -- has recently reinforced Lippmann's account of the collectivist's control of the establishment in America, operating largely in secret, while as Nicholas Murray Butler, President of Columbia insisted, "making the most solemn assurances that nothing of the kind was intended." Nobody would have believed Mrs. Trilling had she written in the 1930s that: "In art, journalism, editing and publishing, in the theatre and entertainment, in the legal profession, in the schools and universities, among church and civic leaders, everywhere in our cultural life the Soviet Union exercised control which was all but absolute." Perhaps a bit overstated as *The New Republic* charged but read Eugene Lyons' *Red Decade*.

You start to read and you discover as I did -- a former rather left-wing democrat up to 1968 -- that you find lies, lies, lies, lies, lies and deceit on everything that exists in the "mainstream" today. Recently a professor at California, claimed that B. F. Skinner (the "behaviorist") and Keynes, who led the West to economic stagnation, were not renegades; they were "credulous." Margaret Mead too, with her Samoan story, and Alfred Kinsey with his homo convicts, they all were merely "credulous," and Ruth Benedict, still quoted as an elite source, and Franz Boas, all merely credulous.

And of FDR at Yalta, "Well you know, he was sick." Numbskull Stettinius spiked that, "No, these agreements had all been made long before." "Well, you know, FDR trusted Stalin." Of all the sins and weaknesses that FDR, Harry Hopkins and Eleanor had, credulity was not one of them.

Kennedy wanted to "withdraw" from Vietnam but evil America killed him. Actually JFK had spent much time in the previous months before his death with a group to "Get Diem!," so that the war could be <u>moved</u> <u>along</u>. Two days before the killing off of the Vietnam government, JFK was told that the entire system of rule by village chiefs would be overthrown, with obvious chaos -- in the midst of war! -- and besides no one had any idea who was to take over. (See Ellen Hammer's *A Death In November*, p. 274-277.) Any rational person would have cried out, "Stop the coup. We're trying to ease out. We can't leave, and leave such a disaster behind. Stop immediately!" He might have added that Ho Chi Minh was dickering with Diem for a settlement, and hence it would be an ideal time to leave, but not with the government destroyed. There has been much fatuity about, "Oh, if only Bobby had lived." The real shame is that John didn't live to take the load of doo-doo that was then dumped on America.

Lies on end. Why doesn't Oliver Stone make a movie of the facts which point (allegedly) to John Dean, and a brothel date-book for high Democrats, as being central to Watergate; and Nixon didn't know what hit him.

Near the end of Johnson's administration, Cambodia's Sihanouk told LBJ's Minister to India that he "was not opposed to hot pursuit" into the Communist sanctuaries along the border where ran the Ho Chi Minh Trail, that it "would be liberating us." This has been little publicized, along with the fact the Sihanouk insisted that bombing the sanctuaries be kept secret; it must not appear that he was in on it because Big Brother Mao was just across the border. The attacks were necessary to protect American soldiers in Vietnam, had been requested by Cambodia, and were "secret," only for Sihanouk's sake. Renegades have claimed this not to be the case because of Sihanouk's later denial -- when he was actually a hostage in China. The whole Kent State affair was founded on a lie.

Paul Samuelson, MIT Nobelist declared (1976), "It is a vulgar mistake to think that people of Eastern Europe are miserable"; Bruce Morton, CBS, (1986), The Soviets Are "satisfied people"; Dan Rather, " . . . do not yearn for Western style democracy." M. Scammel, Cornell (1991), " . . . communism miraculously retained a moral edge . . ." S. P. Dunn, Director of Social Science, U.C. Berkley: "Marxism will retain its intellectual force and attraction for those who think in terms of broad hypotheses . . ." Arnold Beichman, former editor of pinkish *PM*: "You never forget how otherwise intelligent people will lie with a straight face in order to safeguard the image of the Bolshevik Revolution."

"Americans have not been told how much courage and hope Iron Curtain democrats took from Reagan's 'evil empire' charge."

Few socialist proselyters have ever urged socialism because they believed it would bring abundance, equality and cooperation. Nor did they envision themselves as one of a large brood of happy piglets nursing from a great fat sow-state. Rather, as C. S. Lewis explained, they see themselves as wise poultrymen caring for a weak and dim-witted flock. They hold a dark and vengeful faith that they should be as gods. All of human society and humanness itself must be corrupted and obliterated that they might achieve this apotheosis.[50]

---

[50]The most noted economist of this century, John Maynard Keynes, never altered as a vigorous anti-Marxist. Marx's *Das Capital* he declared to be "an obsolete economics text, not only scientifically erroneous but without interest or application to the modern world . . . nothing but out of date controversializing".

On Socialism, "how a doctrine so illogical and so dull can have exercised so powerful and enduring influence on the minds of men . . . perhaps the most useless . . . the most boring form of verbal creation."

On Soviets, "having been brought up in a free air undarkened by the horrors of an (overseeing bureaucracy) with nothing to be afraid of . . . (the Soviet) holds to so much that is detestable. Comforts

The Big Lies of socialism begin with the idea that you don't have to pay; the State will provide it "free." Next comes the claim that the opposite to socialism is "capitalism." Socialism means "overhead planning" if it means anything at all. To get people to accept this planning and to do irrational things requires indoctrination, control of people's thoughts. That is why "idealistic" socialism, or utopianism, is a fantasy. Socialism requires total control, thus comes totalitarianism.

Capitalism is an economic system at best; any control it may gain over society's other arm, politics, or over society itself can only come by corruption of society. At its worst that would be but limited and temporary. The fact is "capitalism" has been a straw-man created by socialists by stacking all the evils of man and society in a big heap and labeling it "capitalism." There is greed and cruelty, narrow-mindedness and corruption in the world. One tends to find them wherever unrestrained power is allowed to grow. The very purpose of socialism is unrestrained power, total power. Capitalism is but the market. In a free society, the market must be free, except that it must be restrained to serve a free people.

In 1884, Herbert Spencer warned that every state interference strengthens the belief that it is the duty of the state to interfere and to provide all benefits. As state interference creates gross mistakes and evils, new compulsions will be necessary to correct for these unforeseen corruptions. By *1984* people could discern far greater evils. The disaster has been predicted by Tocqueville, Schweitzer, Nietzsche, C. S. Lewis (Abolition of Man), Orwell, Lorenz, and by Allen Bloom.

---

foregone, but . . . a creed which knows not how much it destroys liberty and security . . . uses the weapons of persecution, destruction and international strife".

These thoughts Keynes wrote around 1925. By 1936 being favorable to Communism was almost a social necessity and Keynes changed; he became "impressed".

ORIGIN AND DEVELOPMENT

The father of modern socialism was the French aristocrat and speculator, Claude Henrie de Rouvroy' Comte de Saint-Simon. He was afflicted with severe mental disorders through much of his life; it was while temporarily imprisoned during the French Revolution that he had a hallucination one night, during which his ancestor Charlemagne supposedly appeared. From this delusion St-Simon was motivated to envision a "scientific" solution to social ills.

Charlemagne was one of the founders of feudalism and he established state control over most economic activities. After the French Revolution, much of the old order was gone and powerful new forces were creating a fluidity and disorder; St-Simon sought to use science to bring a new order with stability. Thus the roots of socialism lay deep in the medieval concept of a closed socialistic society. "The modern era seemed . . . built on quicksand, to be chaos . . . utterly immoral . . . which must lead to . . . extremes of wealth, and poverty, and to a universal upheaval. . . The Middle Ages with its firm order of church . . . feudal tenures, autonomous associations and its guilds appeared . . . like a well-compacted building."[51]

August Comte was St-Simon's secretary during much of the formative stages of socialism; he too suffered from severe mental disorders. He invented sociology after he had been declared insane. The St-Simon-Comte system included much of the tyranny of modern Socialism, either Communist or Fascists -- Totalitarianism: "in both its conception of the scope of state power and the inner organization of the state . . . The goal is universal association . . . all men on the entire surface of the globe in all spheres of their

---

[51]Max Beer, *A General History of Socialism* (1957)

relationships".[52]   Substitution of arbitrary decisions by "administrators" in place of law, punitive labor camps, "everything in the State," were features of their system.

The Middle Ages were held in high favor by socialists until the beginning of the 20th century. "The truly 'radical' movement of the . . . early modern period was the growth of economic individualism, not the appearance of . . . (socialism) . . . when it first appeared . . . as a fairly consistent theory, it was largely a reactionary protest against a new progressive . . . economic movement, an appeal to turn the clock backwards." "Early modern socialism was a conservative critique of a new and strange individualism (promoted by the Enlightenment)," "Pre-Marxism socialism . . . (expressed) optimistic faith in human nature, the everweening emphasis on environment and proper (controlled) education . . . exaggerated uniformitarianism which is the measure of every utopian (system)."[53]

It is interesting to note that Karl Marx, in his *Manifesto,* did not claim that capitalism had degraded man from the higher level of the Middle Ages. Marx blamed, "The bourgeois" for "ending all feudal, patriarchal, idyllic relations . . . who had pitilessly torn asunder the motley feudal ties that bound man to his 'natural superiors', and left no other nexus between man and man than naked self-interest . . . changed personal dignity into market value, and substituted . . . (free trade) for the numerous chartered liberties of the middle ages."[54] Compare this with a typical "Marxist", P. M. Sweezy, "Capitalism and the doctrine of human equality can be described without exaggeration as the (claimed) true

---

[52]*The Doctrine of St-Simon,* compiled in 1829 by followers, translated to English by G. Iggers. (1958)

[53]E. H. Harbison, "Socialism in European History," article in *Socialism and American Life,* editors, Egbert and Persons, 1952.

[54]*Communist Manifesto* (first English translation) Woodhull & Claflin's Weekly, Dec. 30, 1871.

parents of socialism."[55] Recent socialists are thus extremely intent on dissembling any connection with the medieval reaction -- the true parent of socialism. Note too the reversal of the meaning of the words, "progressive," "liberal," and "reactionary." It is the mission of sociology and "social sciences" (applied socialism) to make fast these deceptions.

Karl Marx's father was a prominent German lawyer and a friend of the autocratic Ludwig von Westphalen, privy councillor in the government, and a descendent of one of Germany's most aristocratic families. Karl learned St-Simon's socialism from von Westphalen whose daughter, Jenny, was to become his wife.

In the mid-1840s, Marx published a group of papers which constitute the core of his idealogy. In these papers he developed "historical materialism" or the "economic interpretation of history." Marx, there in one stroke, deprived man of "Morality, religion, metaphysics, all the rest and their corresponding forms of consciousness . . . (and their) semblance of independence. They have no history, no development; but men developing their material production . . . alter, along with their real existence, their thinking and the products of their thinking."[56] Thus he says the human mind depends on production in the same way that a hog is determined by the slop he eats.[57]

Those ideas, if not entirely fraudulent are at least arguably so, and have served principally to fuel the chatter of intellectuals. The real essence of Marx lies in his identification and treatment of capitalism. If one examines Marx's eulogistic description of capitalism in his *Manifesto*, it seems impossible that he was against it, as an abstract

---

[55]*Science & Society* (Marxian) Winter 1948, Vol. XII, No. 2, p. 65, P.M. Sweezy, "Origins of Present Day Socialism."

[56]Marx and Engels, *The German Ideology*. 1845. International Pub. 1939, p.14.

[57]*The Great Deceit*, A Veritas Foundation Staff Study, Z. Dobbs, Director, (1965), P. 83.

concept, or even as a system -- which it hardly is, for it lacks any systemization. What he denounced was a class, the "bourgeois" (don't use the word, it has no meaning, is but a curse). The "bourgeois" that Marx hated was a "Judaistic manifestation," "The practical domination of Judaism over the Christian world . . ." Marx urged the elimination of individualism and the Jews: " . . . abolishing the empirical essence of Judaism, the huckster and the conditions which produce him . . ." ". . . money has become a world power and the practical Jewish spirit has become the spirit of Christian nations."[58]

Uprooting this hated class came to include the uprooting not just of "huckstering" entrepreneurs, not just the means of production; it meant the complete elimination of human society and Western culture. Men would be made equal and all government would fade away -- a veritable anthill. Clearly nothing human could be such.

Lenin claimed that Marx's papers, "On the Jewish Question" (undoubtedly the most bigoted trash ever published) and *The Holy Family*, marked Marx's transition from idealistic socialism to radical communism and the class struggle.

Marx's class struggle was against the bourgeois, a Judaistic manifestation. More simply, this was the modern invention of taught-hatred. It included the tactic of "one enemy," which Hitler used and credited to Marx; after all, Nazi was an abbreviation for national socialist. Marx noted the strategic advantage in "concentrating all the defects of society on one class . . . the embodiment of social obstacles and improvements." Hitler recognized this Marxist doctrine as "the genius of a great leader to make adversaries . . . appear always belonging to one category, because to weak . . . (followers) various enemies will too easily lead to doubts

---

[58]Karl Marx, *Selected Essays* (1844): "On the Jewish Question" p. 89-92 (International Publishers, Soviet, 1926). Also "Hegelian Philosophy of the Right." See also G. Sprio, *Marxism and the Bolshevik State*, Red Star Press (1951) for *The Holy Family*, by Marx and Engels.

. . . war waged against one enemy only . . . strengthens the belief in one's own cause and increases one's bitterness. . ."[59]

Marx learned his anti-Semitism from his father-in-law and the St-Simonians generally. But almost all Socialists were harshly anti-Semitic. Fourier, another insanity candidate, was the source of the "transcendentalism" of Emerson, Brisbane and Horace Greeley -- the left wing of the Unitarian Church, which in 1805 had grabbed control over Harvard University. Edmund Silberner has written a number of papers on socialism, including "Fourier and the Jewish Question." He wrote, "Convinced that the Jews were the incarnation of commerce, the basis of Fourier's anti-Semitism is potent." "Has there ever been a nation more despicable than the Hebrews . . . at every page their bothersome annals make you sick," Auguste Blanqui, originator of "dictatorship of the proletariat" and "armed seizure", and with whom Marx had come in contact, asserted that "Semitism must be eliminated from Aryan society".[60] Moss Hess and Ferdinand Lassalle -- the latter a leading organizer of socialism in Germany -- were both Jews and both supported harsh anti-Semitism. Lassalle declared that, "The workers movement has to be freed from capitalists and Jews." The roots of Hitler's Nazism run directly to Lassalle - Marx socialism. Marx and Lassalle were rivals for the control of the German Socialist movement. This led Marx to characterize Lassalle as "the Jewish Nigger Lassalle . . . the obtrusiveness of this fellow is nigger-like."[61] Marx and Engels also taught Aryan (and to a lesser degree Jewish) racial superiority. Marx simultaneously denounced Lincoln for his compromise and easing of hatreds and, at the same time, shed crocodile tears for the fate of U.S. Negroes.

The German philosopher Johann Gottlieb Fichte

---

[59]Adolph Hitler, *Mein Kampf*, 1940, p. 82.

[60]E. Silberner, *"French Socialism and the Jewish Question"*, Historia Judaica, April 1954, P. 5.

[61]Marx-Engels, *Briefwechsel* Vol. III, p. 424, Aug. 7, 1866 Marx to Engels.

influenced Marx's development of socialism; his political theory of supremacy of the state, which Hegel later took over, was used by both Marx and Lassalle. This supposedly provided a theoretical foundation for socialism, however the theoretical foundation is as spurious as the scientific claim.

The Christian Socialist Workers parties of Europe came from Marxian-Lassallian Socialism. The Catholic parties were organized initially by Bishop Baron von Ketteler in 1863, the Protestant party in Germany by Adolf Stocker in 1877. The Pan-German movement of G. R. von Schoenerer was an offshoot of Stocker's Christian Socialists, and from these Nazism was developed.

A further important aspect of Socialist anti-Semitism needs to be explained. During the Middle Ages, the Jews were excluded from nearly all social activity, meaning economic and political life: the army, land, trade corporations, and the artisan guilds. The pastoral Semitic was transformed into a practiced dealer in money and a commercial middleman. Oppressed by the church and the state, his conservative traditions lost their hold on his ways, and he became devoted to democratic politics and to radical change. So when the medieval world began to break-up, the Jew was a ready-made agent for unrestricted free enterprise. Isolated by guild restrictions, his free-lance industry was forced to utilize unskilled labor, to seek new methods such as the division of labor and use of machinery. More efficient production and cheaper products in more volume led to growth of vast wealth and to the overthrow of the mercantile-guild social order.

But it was especially the intellectuals that were pinched; their old patrons among the aristocracy and the landowners no longer held the big money. The industrial bourgeois became the ruling power in Europe and the "semblance of a Jewish domination presented itself." It was this apparent domination that was exaggerated by the socialist intellectuals: St-Simon, Comte, Fourier, Fichte and Hegel, Blanqui, Marx, and Proudhon. Thus was created modern anti-

Semitism.[62]

More needs to be explained about racism in an appropriate section, but it is essential here to point out that "racism" is not a simple thing. Distrust, fear and even "dislike", whatever that is, is innate to all animals and people. Attempts to crush it leads invariably to the worst tyranny. The church and Europeans generally did not express a fondness for Jews; all people have always resented, distrusted and disliked strangers. But the socialists brought a new dimension to racism; it was to be taught, as a weapon of ideology. The Dreyfus Affair is a good example of socialist deception.

Karl Marx lauded the Paris Commune (1871) as a shining example of the use of violent means to institute socialism. The Communards established a reputation for murder, shooting of hostages, and destruction of priceless art treasures. Benoit Malon had been a leader and was, of course, violently anti-Semitic. He promoted Edward Drumont, a leading anti-Semite and editor of a periodical, *Liberal Parole*. Drumont's paper was the main source of the invective which was responsible for the railroading of Captain Dreyfus. Dreyfus was accused of spying for Germany, was convicted and sentenced to Devil's Island. Both Dreyfus and Drumont were Jews. The falsehoods were revealed and Dreyfus exonerated.

The fallout from this famous case was in line with socialist tactics. On January 20, 1898 a manifesto was published by the entire French Socialist press, as signed by most of the socialist notables, including a number of Deputies. Jean Jauris is mentioned in E. A. Shils's introduction to G. Sorel's *Reflections* for his "mighty effort on the side of Dreyfus," along with other prominent Dreyfusards.

---

[62]Intellectuals tend to denounce everything but their own ideas. Voltaire, a savage enemy of the church or more realistically of the priesthood, was also anti-Semitic: Jews "have ever been vagrants, robbers . . . seditious . . . vagabonds in the earth, abhorred by men, yet affirming that heaven and earth were created for them alone." *Philosophical Dictionary*.

The manifesto urged "non-participation in the Dreyfus affair on the grounds that while the reaction wishes to exploit the conviction of one Jew to disqualify all Jews, Jewish capitalists would use the rehabilitation of a single Jew to wash out all the stains of Israel." Sort of, "on both your houses." But Jean Jaures was the leading orator of the French Socialists, and look what he has to say:

". . . these Jews, closely knit together. . . separated from other men as enemies. . . isolated by blood, religion, lucrative profession, and a common hate of the rest of humanity . . . control all business, all wealth, bend free men under the yoke of money. What is Jewry if not a dangerous state within a state?"[63]

Who was it that got blamed for the Dreyfus affair? Never is a socialist ever mentioned[64]. It was the "philistines" -- the Christians, Catholics, Aryans. Note the recent National Endowment for the Arts stink; the liberal establishment that controls media, academia, etc., raised the claim of the same "philistines's" attack on the French impressionist artists. The truth is that it again was the communists-socialists-fascists that detected anti-revolutionary tendencies in the New Art. It was the same socialists who were anti-Dreyfus; Degas in particular broke with Zola over *J' Accuse.* The art establishment, the modernists, were socialist and anti-Dreyfus. More lies.

As we noted, Lenin declared that Marx had abandoned "idealistic" socialism in the 1840s; it was never going to sell. Marx turned to deception, the teaching of hate as class struggle, and a "science" and history that were obviously fraudulent. By 1870, many young, wealthy and educated Jews were pushing into socialism, and by the end of the century anti-Semitism was going underground in the socialism

---

[63]G. Spiro, *Marxism and the Bolshevik State* p. 790, also Edmund Silberner, *Historia Judaica* April, 1954, p. 16.

[64]Martin Peretz (TNR 2,10,92 p. 41) accused "the old Catholic right" of having "the Jewish problem," and mentioned "the Dreyfus Case."

that was to become the Communist Party. The Christian socialist parties, being closed to Jews, remained openly anti-Semitic.

In the U.S., Fourier socialists fed the Abolitionists' hate-the-South campaign; they were not particularly interested in the welfare of the Negro, as was openly expressed by the mainstream poet, Lowell, in his *Bigelow Papers*. They were primarily interested in secession, ending the dirtying of their skirts in association with the South. Dislike of the Negro was far more intense in the North than the South. The Abolitionists' hate-radicals formed the core of the reconstruction radicals who nearly destroyed our republic.

Fourier and Owenite socialists were greatly augmented around 1850 by German immigrants who brought a susceptibility for socialism with them. The socialist populism of the Midwest, and the associated anti-Semitism in Ohio, Missouri, and Wisconsin, came largely from these people.

A great change came over socialism between 1880 and 1920 in the U.S. It was taken over by university intellectuals, and became a distinctly subversive movement. Anti-Semitism and Aryan superiority were both hidden, and rejection of the Negro changed to patronage. There was a gradual move to blame all this on the "philistines" - on conservatives and Christians. Lester Ward and E. A. Ross were important pegs in the socialist network of the U.S. major universities near the end of the 19th century. Ward asserted in 1883 that the Negro's "nasal bones are completely ossified . . . not found in man . . . (a) normal condition for monkeys."[65] Ross claimed that, "The Negro is not simply a black Anglo-Saxon deficient in schooling, but a being who in strength of appetites, and in power to control them differs considerably from the white man." "The higher culture should be kept pure."[66] But by 1929 all had changed; Ross declared that, "but cultural background and special experience" makes Negroes different.

---

[65]L. Ward, *Dynamic Sociology*, Vol. 1, p. 418 (1883).

[66]E.A. Ross, *Foundations of Sociology*, (1905) p. 356.

"Given our training, their minds would work as ours."[67] Booker T. Washington had made great progress in teaching black independence and the virtues of work, thrift, and responsibility. In order to counter this, white socialists organized the NAACP to back blacks in "demanding their rights." The following year, they induced the Harvard educated W. E. B. DuBois to front-office for them.[68] Ross and Ward had a long list of communist-front association, as did G. W. Allport. Allport, along with many others, sought to force the perception that the "tolerant person is liberal. Prejudiced individuals are more often conservative".[69]

By 1965, socialism changed again. Largely through the efforts of "fanatics" such as Harry Truman, Joe McCarthy, Nixon, Whittaker Chambers, and others not accused of fanaticism, such as J. Burnham, W. F. Buckley, Sidney Hook and the FBI, socialism-communism had been forced to hide after 1948. The ADA, ACLU the AAUP, NAACP and others publicly denounced communism, but it lasted only briefly. By 1965, socialists and many mainstream liberals came out as avowed enemies of everything America and Western culture had ever stood for, and as supporters of Communism in China, Cuba, Vietnam, and in America.

---

[67]E.A. Ross, *Principles of Sociology*, 1929.

[68]This was the beginning of their "war against America," as Jewish scholar Dawidowicz charged. See p. 79.

[69]G. W. Allport, *Nature of Prejudice*, 1958.

6. EDUCATION

INTRODUCTION

"Within every society, be it ever so democratic, there is a relatively small number of intellectuals who give that society its tone and character. What 1,000 professors, writers, and bishops think, write and preach, is handed on by 300,000 teachers, journalists, and ministers to the 130,000,000 Americans, and forms the consciousness of the entire nation . . . Ninety-nine and nine-tenths per cent of Americans have never held a work of John Dewey in their hands, but all Americans have been educated by him . . ."[70] "Overhead planning's" advocate, Stuart Chase, bragged that "a society could be completely made over in 15 years -- the time it takes to inculcate a new culture into a new crop of youngsters."

Gerald Grant has written of such schools that have "imposed a new moral order on the country," in *The World We Created* (1988). An upstate New York town opened a new high school in a middle-class neighborhood in 1953. A dozen years of high performance and conformity was followed by the "new order of the mid-60s". By the 1970s, the principal had a full time bodyguard, his predecessor's skull had been fractured, achievement plummeted, three-quarters of the teachers quit, and cheating flourished as did violence. Professional therapists, employed not by the principal, protected student's rights. From institutions dedicated to improving the opportunities for the next generation, schools have become -- everywhere to a greater or lesser degree -- instruments for the destruction of our culture, of all that can

---

[70]Van Wyck Brooks, *Opinions of Oliver Allston* 1941, p. 209, quoting W.S. Schlamm; Brooks, a socialist, was himself boasting "how far intellectuals influence the mind of a country."

make improvement possible and for sowing shame and hatred for all that has held America together.

Simpleton slobs in the late 1960s, exulting in "freak 'em out", had been set to tearing at social vestments whose purpose and value were beyond their untutored minds. The fault was that America had, way back early in the century, lost its core and its leaders whose function it was to assure that group movements be consistent with a social progress, a rising up. A network of socialist cells in our major universities had taken over and, like thieves driving off the flock, they were organized and knew exactly what they wanted -- the destruction of culture for the empowerment of Statism. Check Lippmann's description of them in 1936 (p. 17). By the end of the 50s, anti-Communism had been made evil, and by the end of the 60s, America also was perceived as evil.

The opinions of important scholars on major aspects of education should provide a reasonable basis for considering our present difficulties. J. S. Mill, a much quoted liberal, has warned that, "If a society lets any considerable number of its members grow up mere children, incapable of being acted upon by rational considerations . . . (it) has itself to blame . . ."

Mill warned against "State education, as a nice contrivance for molding people . . . education controlled by the state should only exist as one among many competing systems." Government interference in social affairs (excluded by our Constitution and Bill of Rights, but perceived to be overridden) is pernicious he declared, not only when individuals or society can do a thing better, but even when they may not do it as well. People and society ought to do everything reasonably possible for themselves: for (1) their mental education, (2) for strengthening their active faculties and judgment, and (3) for giving them knowledge of public affairs.

Up until the beginning of this century, in the big cities, and even until WW II in many rural areas, schools were run by local "school boards" who hired and fired, approved curriculum, and monitored discipline. That authority was purloined -- filched away. It must be gotten back. It was subverted, grabbed away for the purpose, as John Dewey put it, of "organized social planning (socialism) . . . now the sole method of social action" (1935). Note that this preceded Lippmann's statement. Dewey chose his battle terrain with foresight; education is the portal to culture, and the lifeline to that portal, the line of communication, is reading. By squeezing it, Dewey could cut culture down to what he wanted to pass, mere indoctrination.

In 1955, Rudolf Flesch wrote *Why Johnny Can't Read;* he explained how Dewey had intentionally dumbed-down education. In 1970, a veteran of more than 20 years at the University of California, Karl Shapiro, wrote " . . . this generation cannot and does not read . . . university students . . . (at) our best universities." J. Atlas, editor of *New York Times Magazine,* in his *Book Wars* (1990), "We are producing a generation that has no stake in our society . . ." The National Education Association encourages children "to despise the rules and customs that make their society a democracy," was offered by C. A. Finn, Jr.

In 1983, a national Commission on Excellence in Education declared that "if an unfriendly power had imposed on America the mediocrity . . . that exists, we might have viewed it as an act of war . . . for the first time . . . the educational skills of a generation . . . will not equal, not even approach those of their parents."

Most people are aware that SAT scores, which largely measure advancement in the 3Rs, have been dropping. Fewer know that the greatest reduction has been at the top, among those from whom excellence must be expected. Even fewer have heard the excuse, "They (SAT) don't measure what is being taught . . .," from NEA's president; obviously not the 3Rs.

The Assistant Secretary for Education in the 1980s wrote that half of the high school juniors could not determine that 87 percent of ten was less than ten. Only six in a hundred could find the least sum of money in ten coins, if it is known that at least one was a quarter, one a dime, one a nickel and one a penny, as determined by the National Assessment of Educational Progress testing.

This is not really a lack of arithmetic, it is more a lack of an elementary ability to think, perhaps lack of awareness of thinking. A more subtle or sophisticated kind of thinking is that of judgment of truth. It generally requires the weighing of one or more 'pictures in the mind', that have been thoroughly analyzed by thinking of the kind involved in the above two problems.

This destruction of education and culture did not just happen; it did not occur overnight. Allen Bloom, you remember, declared that it had been the purpose of intellectuals for most of this Century to destroy our culture. Actually, it started at least as early as Horace Mann in the 1840s, when he began the bureaucratization of education with the establishment of the first teachers college, or Normal School.

Mann was a socialist and he hated most everything around him; so too did G. Stanley Hall, from a Puritan farm family, who studied socialism in Berlin. He returned in 1871 declaring, "I fairly loathed and hated so much that I saw about . . ." Hall went back to Germany to study psychology at Wundt's Leipzig laboratory, and later attended Harvard, receiving their first Ph.D. in psychology. He established a laboratory at Johns Hopkins, where John Dewey and James Cattell were two of his early students. Dewey, Cattell, and Thorndike from Harvard, in the early 1900s, formed a socialist cell at Columbia University and planned their assault on American education.

By that time, there existed a whole network of socialist cells throughout the major U.S. universities. At Harvard, Morris Cohen, with some help from Dewey, announced in 1913 "judicial legislation," and by 1935, his son Felix was to declare that no part of law or Constitution could not be set aside by the Court, and he pointed admiringly to Hitler's accomplishing just that in Germany.[71] A little later, Franz Boas, also at Columbia, created "cultural anthropology" as a socialist's tool for poisoning human society. The dissembling's of Margaret Mead and Ruth Benedict resulted directly from his efforts; they and other Boas followers were very influential in Myrdal's dissembling *Dilemma*, so convenient for Warren's subversion in the Court. Benedict's *Patterns of Culture* "inculcates socialistic doctrines (and anti-Americanism) under the guise of science." Derek Freeman in 1983 presented a refutation of Margaret Mead's long accepted story of Samoan sexual practices, and was figuratively "lynched" in a "feeding frenzy" by the American Anthropology Association.[72] Even Freeman sought to credit their stand to "cultural relativism", or the "taught to be hallowed" . . . assumption that "all human behavior is the result of social conditioning." It is probably unjust to mark this as dissembling, but it is clearly a misunderstanding. Freeman's attackers are the same liberals as those who similarly attacked David Lehman for a rather balanced presentation of deMan and deconstruction and, since 1965 have attacked any questioner of Marxism or its anti-social lies.

John Dewey was a man dedicated to the replacement of human society by socialism. Our society was far stronger in 1896 than it is today, and he was well aware that subversion, "boring from within" the institutions, was the only feasible method of attack. His President, Nicholas Murray Butler, at Columbia (1921) warned, "It is proposed to bureaucratize the educational system of the whole United States, while making the most solemn assurances that nothing of the kind is intended."

---

[71]Am. Socialist Quarterly, No. 1935, Vol. 4, "*Socialism and the Myth of Legality*", Felix Cohen, p. 21.

[72]See Derek Freeman's article in *Academic Questions*, Sum. 92, p. 23. Much of the "theoretical support" and "public perceptions", which gave acceptance to the anti-social distortions of Alfred Kinsey, Freud and followers, Dr. Spock, and others, came from the writings of Mead and Benedict.

Figures from the U.S. Bureau of Education for 1900 show illiteracy for children 10 to 14 years of age at 42 per 1,000; in 1910 after a decade of heavy immigration of peasants from eastern Europe, the number dropped to 22 per 1,000, who could neither read nor write. A publication by Dewey's colleagues declared that illiteracy soon would be gone.

But, at the end of the 19th Century, Dewey had an experimental school at the University of Chicago where reading was taught by the look-say, or whole word method which had been invented in 1830 by T. H. Gallaudet for teaching the deaf and dumb to read. With this method as a weapon, in a most unobservable way, Dewey would raise illiteracy to a national disgrace, creating millions of illiterates, incompetent for self-government, or anything but socialism's tutelage, and create a multibillion dollar social drain for "remedial reading." John Dewey formulated the notion that high literacy was an obstacle to socialism. In 1896 he wrote, on the basis of his Chicago school, "It is a mistake to make reading . . . the bulk of the school work the first two years . . . language is not primarily the expression of thought, but the means of social communication . . . It is not claimed that by the method (look-say), the child will learn to read as much, nor perhaps as readily . . ."[73]

When Dewey also wrote that "language is not primarily the expression of thought, but a means of communication", what he was in essence doing was rejecting culture, making man but a robot, with whom a tutelary power would need to communicate only orders. Here Dewey reveals his true intent: the rejection of education as a preparation for a thinking, self-governing people, who would have need of reason and culture. Recall Auden's denigration of language as mere "code" (p. 29).

---

[73]Quoted from M. M. Mathews, *Teaching to Read* (1966), p. 128, as noted in S. L. Blumenfeld, *NEA: Trojan Horse* (1984). The latter is an inexpensive book that all parents should read. It has been used extensively here as a source.

Dewey loathed competitive individualism; "Each child sits in his place in a fixed row of desks and faces not his companions . . . but his teacher . . . he studies largely by himself, for himself . . . in direct competition with his mates." Dewey made the chairs movable, the period a social occasion. The teacher was more a leader, bringing "cooperative plans" for discussion and activity. Reform of society had to start in the classroom, preceding reform (socialism) in society at large. The battle was between collectivism and competition for excellence. Collectivism had become his religion, given in his *Common Faith*. Humanity would replace God in a new materialist religion. But humanity was but a word lacking any binding power. He did not say it, but the leaders would do the binding like the poultrymen or herdsman leading their flocks.

HISTORY OF A TREASON

The look-say or whole-word method for teaching reading was developed for the deaf and dumb, people unable to hear and thus unable to sound-out words and to recognize cognates by this sense. Thus words are like Chinese ideographs, memorizable pictures. It has been found that children can commonly make a rather rapid start in this way but, by the end of a year, the number of pictures to be memorized soon slows progress, and children perhaps rebel in frustration. The method was forced into the Boston area schools by socialist Horace Mann, but by 1844, the school masters, then no pussy-cats, threw it out with a scornful attack on Mann and his "reforms". This perhaps should be recognized as the first of a very long list of socialist "reforms". It was, however, kept alive in Mann's Normal Schools, awaiting Dewey while McGuffey's Readers reigned.

James McKeen Cattell, a classmate of Dewey's under Hall at Johns Hopkins, had also gone to Germany, and had made reaction-time experiments in Wundt's laboratory at Leipzig for psychology studies. He had Dewey join him at

Columbia in 1904.

Edmund Burke Huey, another Hall student, in 1908 wrote, with help from Dewey and Cattell, his *Psychology and Pedagogy*, although he had never taught a child to read. It was the power of the growing socialist network that forced the perception that this was <u>the</u> authority on learning to read -- of course, by look-say. When the 1911 *Cyclopedia on Education* came out, Huey's book was praised as the sole authority. Huey even admitted that children often guessed at word meanings, and he praised it as thinking on their own -- hardly reading. Of course, Dewey had admitted a dozen years earlier the method's inferiority.

This powerful gambit, with other schemes and the cooperation of a growing network, resulted by the mid-1920s in a number of school superintendents in large cities adopting primers utilizing look-say. As a result, by the end of the decade Dewey, through the socialist network, had been able to coerce textbook publishers into printing only look-say primers.

For the first time in America, socialism which openly vowed the destruction of human society, would step forward and change the flow of culture, usurping the leadership of a core; their usurpation constituted a fascist monopoly. It was certainly destructive of human society and done in the interests of socialism. Today, an even more coerced fascism has gripped the entire writing, printing and selection of all school textbooks, as the entire public school curriculum has been "incorporated" into the bureaucracy. Texts are screened by radicals, and will not be supported, nor published, if they do not fit the agenda of some radical group assaulting our society. When common people object to the results, the obscenities, the anti-Americanism, the anti-Christianity, they are denounced widely in the media as censors.

But how can one distinguish a proper social core from an anti-social core, such as a socialist clique? Generally, very easily, from the direction of their policies or actions. It didn't take the school masters of Boston long to get the number on Horace Mann and his ideology. Nor did it take long to catch up with Mr. Dewey. By all common sense, all rationality, all concern for probity, look-say should have been dead by 1930. Here's why.

Dr. Samuel T. Orton was a professor of psychiatry at Iowa State in 1929. He was, in fact, becoming a part of the intellectual elite that Lippmann described as the "overhead planners". But Dr. Orton had not totally succumbed. He was a neuropathologist, specializing in speech disorders, and had become alarmed at what he was beginning to observe. He began his report for the *Journal of Educational Psychology* (2, 1929) very apologetically: "I feel some trepidation . . . (in something) somewhat outside my own endeavor . . . ". Look-say readers had been used for a number of years in a number of large systems and their effects were beginning to show, "for the past four years . . . (he had studied) reading disability . . . (in a) large number of cases from many different schools . . . (using) the sight method (look-say) of teaching reading . . . I think we can show . . . (that look-say) often proves an actual obstacle to reading progress and . . . may not only prevent the acquisition of academic education by children of average capacity (implied I.Q., not PC today) but may also give rise to far reaching damage to their emotional life."

But the stock market crashed; the Depression began; districts quit buying books, and Dewey slipped by. But not quite. By 1936 "nearly a half million children in the first four grades . . . with serious disabilities in reading" (Oct., 1936, N.E.A. Journal). Up to 1930 reading disability was akin to walking disability; anyone who had gone to school three years could read, did read. I'm not sure my father finished the fourth grade, but he was an avid reader, mainly of the political, social. He could guess the weight of a load of livestock and, from the price per pound, could figure the check in his head. More than once, he had to tell the man with the scales-weight and pencil and paper to try it again.

The NEA's answer to the problem: fewer words, more repetition. Then Life Magazine (Ap. 1947), "Millions of children suffer from dyslexia." In 1955 Rudolf Flesch published *Why Johnny Can't Read;* it was the look-say method.[74] The NEA accused him of "deliberately attempting to mislead and deceive the people" -- exactly what the NEA was doing.[75]

But the network, the evil party, knew that look-say was not only an inferior method; they knew that Thorndike's conditioning method of applying look-say was causing "educational blockage" and "serious disabilities." George S. Counts of Columbia toured the Soviet Union in 1927 and again in 1929; Dewey and others had been there in 1928. Counts, Thorndike, Dewey, and Judd had all carefully followed Soviet research on "methods for artificially inducing behavioral disorganization in humans". Soviet psychologist L. R. Luria's, *Nature of Human Conflicts*, translated in 1932, noted that Pavlov had obtained disorganizational behavior each time conditioned reflexes collided. Dyslexic behavior is thus artificially produced by the look-say reading method.

Already "remedial reading" had became a growth industry for the NEA: more teachers, money, books, bureaucracy. School-teacher-President Johnson's War on Poverty included federal aid-to-education. The Elementary and Secondary Education Act (ESEA) of 1965 provided $1 billion for "compensatory education" under Chapter I. By 1985, accumulated appropriations would reach $42 billion. Headstart had been initiated in 1964 and Follow Through in 1967. Ten years later, the Disabilities Education Act was passed creating Special Education classes. Chapter I enrollment had climbed (1993) from 2 to 6 million at a cost increase from $2 billion up to $7 billion. Special Education enrollment went from 3.7 to 5 million and from $3 to $23 billion dollars. Of the 5 million Special Education students, 2.5 million are of above average intelligence but for some reason cannot read. Another million have pronunciation

---

[74]Recently he has published "Why Johnny Still Can't Read."

[75]Similarly communists, socialists, liberals have for years, consistently accused "conservatives" of anti-Semitism, yet Marx was the real developer of modern anti-Semitism. Check in his "On the Jewish Question".

difficulties -- stutter, lisp and yet have no known physical or structural defects. Another million are tested as emotionally disturbed, mostly older students of short attention spans, possibly because they have never learned to read. Since 1965, $300 billion has been spent on these programs; no one has even attempted to show that they have accomplished anything.[76] Nearly half of the students in these remedial programs are in grades 6 through 12; most of the 60 million children since 1940, who have reached the 4th grade as illiterate, never learned to read. Virtually all of the 4 million students who are in these programs, yet have no real physical or mental handicap, would have learned to read in 1930.

By 1951, the assault on literacy reached a new stage, noted in the arrogant assault published in the *Bulletin* of the National Association of Secondary School Principals: "We've built a sort of halo around reading, writing and arithmetic. We've said they were for everybody . . . rich poor, brilliant and not so . . . something everybody should learn . . . We've made some progress in getting rid of that slogan."

Dr. Jeanne Chall, a professor at Harvard Graduate School of Education, was a respected member of the International Reading Association. Several years of intensive research on instruction of beginning reading, with mountains of studies, had convinced her that most of the reading problems were caused by the look-say method. These studies were summarized in her 1967 book, *Learning to Read*, and she concluded that look-say was inferior to phonics instruction. Chall was from within the "belly of the beast" and her book was aimed at her colleagues, not at the popular market where it might more readily have been taken as an affront to them. In IRA's *Journal of Reading* (1, 1969), a reviewer explained that Chall's studies "were ill-conceived, incomplete and lacking in . . . methodological criteria. (Furthermore) personal bias . . . (had) moored (her) on a reef of inconclusiveness and insubstantiality. (Thus she had

---

[76]Albert Shanker, Pres. Am. Fed. of Teachers: "No student who has not learned to read by the sixth grade, has ever learned."

failed) to achieve respectability." *Pravda* couldn't have said it better. Contempt for Drs. Flesch and Chall were expressed in the 1983-84 NEA's Annual Edition of *Today's Education:* "(O)veremphasis on phonics with beginners (is now) ready for the scrap heap."

Today the great majority of Americans almost never read for enjoyment; they are not able to. In years past, perhaps since the 18th century, many people did read, as today people watch the boob-tube. The great authors, from Fielding and Johnson on, came into being because a great popular audience was opening up. American writers were enjoyed by million; Irving and Cooper, the poets, Twain, historians, on and on, could exist on popular support. The writing of literature today is almost non-existent.

And most people hardly know what is going on in the world, except as they watch TV, which is based so much on lies and dissembling as to be a poison. Conversation except at the most idiotic level is gone. To ask a serious question today, among educated people, is considered rude or worse. Dewey succeeded. Today America is told even by its TV heads that the "public" is incapable of self government (see p. 212). The difference between welfarism and fascism lies only in a fickle forbearance of intellectuals.

In 1985, R. G. Damerell published an excellent study, *Education's Smoking Gun,* whose central theme was the incompetence and renegadism of the education establishment. He describes the "watering down" of junior and senior high school curricula in big cities and in regional systems: "weeds and flowers for botany, general science not chemistry or physics, general math instead of algebra and trigonometry, "social issues" instead of history, film study and group dynamics in place of English. Some schools even undermine, not just the parents or the students' own lives but all society, with units like, "What can I do with my old fashioned parents?"

Disparagement of the 3Rs, which are so essential to any serious attempt at physics, history, English and literature, and for maintenance of a human culture, has become the constant in educationalist's literature.   Damerell tells an interesting account of his career in the "learning" trade at the University of Massachusetts, and of his encounter with "Illiterates with Doctorates."

Peter H. Wagschel was an associate professor of education at the University of Massachusetts, with a B.A. from Harvard College.   The August, 1978 issue of *The Futurist* (World Futures Soc., Wash, D.C.) contained an essay of his entitled, "Illiterates with Doctorates".   In the not too distant future (he suggested 1995, back in 1978), "America can be a society in which knowledge, ability, and wisdom are widespread in a population that is illiterate . . . We are witnessing the demise of the written word as our primary means of storing and communicating information. By (1995) . . . there will be hardly any compelling reason to be able to read, write and do arithmetic . . . The three Rs are, by their very nature . . . (for the) elite . . . time consuming modes of communication and inherently difficult . . . Only a minority . . . can afford the time and resources required to learn and use the three Rs." Sophisticated audio, video, and computers would replace the 3Rs, and the citizens would be largely illiterate.

Now the fall-out. It was reviewed by John Simon, in *Esquire*, with a "scathing denunciation" as a "horror story". In spite of this it was displayed (proudly) in the Education Dean's showcase, then reprinted in the (Feb., 1980) school's *Alumni Newsletter*. (That's my Pop!) Such reprinting, giving the school's imprimatur, would be "reinforcing," in the behaviorists lingo, to the miseducation or confusion of all.

Damerell sent copies of the *Alumni Newsletter*[77], with notes calling attention to Wagschel's article, to six professors in each of the departments of English, literature, and math. There were half a dozen of them whom he said he liked and

---

[77]The February *Alumni Newsletter* was sent out "in a black context." -- announcing establishment of a center for Equal Ed., emphasis on the "black child," Julian Bond portrait on the cover. This was taken as similar to medievalists putting a cross on the pagan hot-buns.

respected.   Obviously, it was to their own self-interest to oppose the article, even if their self-respect felt no pain. But "fundamental talk about education was taboo . . . unbelievable, eerie silence in the face of nonsense?" Did they not act like German professors, or Russian professors, under far, far more threatening surroundings?

Get this: no guarantee of anonymity except for those who might have agreed with Wagschel would loosen one tongue. One answer would only encourage more questions. "Why not speak out?" "Are you not tenured?" "What about academic freedom?" "Why are you afraid?" Questions would become too threatening; facing one piece of nonsense would invite facing up to who knows what evil nonsense. It could mean an end to a well paying job, lifetime security, a handsome pension. Were they not stupid, or accommodating or cynical?   Three doctorates from Berkley, Illinois, and Michigan State; two from each Columbia, Cornell, Florida, New York University, Ohio State, Wayne State, Wisconsin, and Toronto.   Some dozen or so had degrees, not in education, but Ph.D.s in history, English, law, physics, statistical analyses, economics. Total "Orwellian silence," <u>not</u> imposed by Big Brother, but from <u>within</u> each - conspiracy even though arrived at individually.

John Simon left no escape: (1) The computer science department considered English majors with GRE verbals of +650 as excellent candidates. English is encoding no less than computer language. Would illiterates be able to score on oral GREs? (2) Wagschel claimed that the new computers "call up information instantly from the spoken word." But "how could an illiterate understand the computer speaking in written language's attributes of precision and completeness which, of necessity, it would have to speak to convey information of any complexity?"

What must be comprehended is that many educationalists have not the slightest concept of what "written language's attributes of precision and completeness" mean. There are few educationalists who have any knowledge of the Schoolmen; according to Sir Wm. Hamilton, it is to them, "that the vulgar languages are indebted for what precision and analytical subtlety they possess." "Logic, ethics," said Condorcet, "owe to Scholasticism, a precision unknown to the ancients," and we can add to the moderns.[78]

Recently I had reason to reread an article by Derek Freeman on the Margaret Mead Hoax, and was rather shocked to be reminded that in 1983 anthropologists were "taught to hallow" the assumption that "all human behavior is the result of social conditioning." This old Marxian tale has long been discarded; a century ago Darwin had apprehended that much of social behavior was innate. Read Lorenz's *Behind The Mirror* for a good account of the fatuity of behaviorist theories. Animal breeders back into pre-history have assumed important hereditary aspects of behavior. What you must come to see is that renegades have us on Marxian autopilot aimed right for the depth of the abyss.

"Languages are abstract, rule-governed and the information they carry can be made available across the major senses," that means that a particular word message can be spoken and heard, felt through the touch of Braille, or seen in printed form. Most fantastic is the case of Helen Keller. Totally deaf and blind from shortly after birth to age seven, she communicated with the outer world by a total of two grunts; in the words of a capable and dedicated teacher she was made to want to learn, and in less than a year could write a better paragraph, making proper use of such refinements as the subjunctive, than most current high school seniors. The simple touch of fingers in her palm (later Braille) opened up to her a world of light and beauty, and gave her a delicate understanding of that spiritual world of the mind, almost beyond comprehension.

In some obscure sense languages are super-sensory, "only incidentally sensory." Damerell tells us that all purely

---

[78]I had a very excellent Chinese graduate student; when I asked, "Do you think in English or Chinese?" without batting an eye, she replied, "Oh ordinarily I can think in English, but when it is very difficult, I must think in Chinese." People think in words, and the more their comprehension of words, the more powerful can be their thinking.

sense information can be detected by only one sense. If one should lose his sense of taste, sight, smell or sound, whatever we absorb by that sense becomes lost, gone. But words and the message that they carry can reach us through all of the major senses. Thus all manner of codes have been perfected: Morse Code, hand signals, light flashes, shorthand, computer printer cards, even music notation to carry deaf Beethoven's tremendous spiritual scores.

But a vast subversive movement in education is aimed at ending the teaching of reading, the principal technique by which we gather knowledge for thinking. Grammar, or the structure of logical thinking, has already largely been removed from education, and reading is rapidly disappearing as the primary vehicle for communicating ideas.

This is most debilitating culturally and socially; it is the result of renegadism, and is not based on any real problems or barriers. Donna Connell reported (NEA _Journal_ 9, 69) that all her kindergarten children, regardless of IQ or economic background, learned to read, some up to mid-second grade on Stanford Achievement Tests. We know that Helen Keller readily learned to read and write, without sight or hearing. Marva Collins, without training or experience in teaching, apparently had no great trouble teaching children to read in presumably one of Chicago's most backward schools.

Some minimum desire and disciplined effort will produce prompt literacy, as certainly as it produces golfers or tennis players. It is not difficult to learn, kids five to seven naturally love to learn, and will read in a week or two. Having an active joy in learning and a basic discipline inculcated by parents are necessary, but what is missing more often than these is a decent book. Anything like "See Spot run, run, run, run . . ." will disgust any child. We are told that Marva Collins threw the "run, run, run . . ." readers out and used fables - Aesop's, Fontaine's and other such stories. Children understand and relish meaning, in real feelings of greed, joy, malice, and failure of evil. There is a very similar story told by Lenin's widow, of a school teacher sent to the 1919 front to teach the Soviet troops to read and write.

In 1986, Andre Ryerson examined three popular "peace studies", guides for elementary and junior high published by the NEA and Educators for Social Responsibility. He reported "indifferences to American values" seemingly "designed to arouse in students (feelings of) fear, horror, shame, and finally righteous indignation" towards the U.S. "(R)eferences to the Vietnam War were used . . . to illustrate American deception, brutality and violence." Where oh where was Higgins's *Our Vietnam Nightmare?*

Talk about censorship! The Duke of P.C., Chairman Fish of Duke University urged in a letter to the Provost that members of the National Association of Scholars (an organization supporting that which long has been acclaimed as excellent in American and Western culture) be disqualified from key university committees, such as those involving tenure or curriculum decisions. The University of Texas English Department sought to replace its standard freshmen course in English composition with "readings in feminism and racism."

"NEA will become a political power second to none . . . will organize this profession from top to bottom . . . with power unmatched by any organized group in the nation," NEA's ex-secretary Sam Lambert, bragged in 1967. "Our public school teachers are no longer the benign, neutral servants of our communities . . . their ability to control the minds of our youth," to make them enemies of human society is beginning to be recognized.

Any hope for reform, recovery of some degree of excellence in education depends on getting children out of NEA schools. They have bragged that they have supported every education reform in the last half century or more. Rather they have supported a list of "NEA reforms," which are in fact the cause of our once excellent public education becoming the "shoddy, fraudulent piece" of astronomically priced corruption that it is today.

In 1840, "Americans were probably the most literate and libertarian people in the world." There were no accrediting agencies, no government regulations, no state textbooks, no teaching certification, and very little in the way of taxes.   Home tutoring was common, as were private schools of many kinds; there were charity schools for the poor with tutors, and the common, or church schools. Papal authority had been replaced for the Calvinists by Biblical authority, and comprehension of the Bible, along with Latin and Greek as the original languages, created the literary standards upon which the pre-Civil War culture of both North and South depended. The Calvinists didn't believe that power corrupts man so much as man corrupts power.

These excellent schools constituted no theocracy as renegades have charged; there was competition of all sorts, and the theocratic control of today's NEA is far more rigid and complete than anything previously even attempted.

Education is the very linch pin of society, holding families and culture to society itself. Education is necessary to arouse even innate knowledge; we know that that is true for young robins, and it is essential for activating the phylogenetic programs in man that are the foundation upon which morality and culture must rest. The time allocated by Nature for such training increases with the advance in social complexity of the species. Also fixed by Nature is the timing of physiological and psychological changes.   Both are commonly involved in known changes in sexuality, readiness for learning processes, and changes in social bonding.

Although there is a variance in opinion, it seems true that by the age of six months many of a child's attitudes toward life in general have become relatively fixed. If, by the age of four years, he/she has not learned the proper attitude toward discipline, personal integrity, and responsibility and especially the apprehension that struggle is the only avenue to success, he/she most likely he never will or only quite imperfectly. From age five to around twelve or the beginning of puberty, is claimed to be a period of relative sexual dormancy, during which a child learns, memorizes, and absorbs concepts most readily. Hence this is the time for learning reading, writing and arithmetic. It is said that the critical ages for learning to read are from five to seven, and that if a child has not learned to read by age nine or ten, he may never learn unless driven by a strong inner urge. This is the time for foreign languages and memorizing poems.

Puberty in animals marks the transition to adulthood; not so with humans. Approximately the next eight years are, it seems, set off by innate factors as a time for learning not how to fly, but how to fly with the flock -- in humans the learning of culture. It is commonly understood that education is the transmission of culture. At the end is adulthood in which responsibility, not only for self but for society and the acceptance of its uncontested terms, is to be acknowledged.

Culture is <u>imposed</u> by education, a good example being learning to speak the language. How happy a small child is to rear up on his hind feet, to be toilet trained, to express some thoughts in speech, to show some responsibility for things such as his boots. Yet all of these are in reality imposed, at times, with many tears. The so-called initiation, or trial-to-manhood for young males was imposed, much like the rules of a ball game are imposed. More truly these are gladly accepted. When people jeer about imposing beliefs, it must be recognized that society must impose rules for the game and demand recognition of the umpire. The impositions under Statist ideologies are like prison rules, far more rigorous and inhuman.

Barbarity has been called an impoverishment of the mind to feelings, and therefore an insensibility to a higher life. It is an innate perception of the urge to rise up that produces in the child a desire to learn. In times past we know that the aims of education -- morality, citizenship, and livelihood -- were advanced throughout society. Families were shamed by children's misbehavior; churches joined schools in teaching morality -- what was good and what evil. Policemen, neighbors, doctors, merchants all influenced behavior. Prominent citizens and statesmen expressed the nation's ideals -- necessary for rising up. Journalists were as concerned as English teachers when corruption of language was observed, and many spoke and wrote an exemplary tongue. Families and schools linked the young to the past through history, tradition, ancestors, and stories. A positive attitude toward discipline and rising up must be inculcated in the young before they even reach school. If they are not, they probably never will be learned. Continued examples from every aspect of society, viewed with high respect and reverence, are necessary to solidify these attitudes into habits.[79]

FADS

Fads are principally schemes to avoid teaching. Few are more foolish and expensive than computers, and add TV to that. I refer to computers for instruction not for record keeping. Even hand-held computers, claimed to be used to speed up routine calculations, were and are mere crutches for school students, avoiding their need to think and to memorize. There are in reality no "routine" calculations in K-12 (beyond necessary drill); finding some percentage, or ratio, in a word problem is a matter of thinking, and the numbers used are commonly such as to permit mental calculations, along with the thinking. Mental exercises for the mind are even more essential than exercise for the body.

People think largely in words; what we have no word for is difficult to think about. The history of words is filled with cases of new words marking a distinct change in culture. So too we think with numbers, but inability to manipulate numbers mentally clearly denotes an inability to properly comprehend concepts related by arithmetic.

Button-pushing is a drug in our present education; few teachers can read well, as necessary for enjoyment; few have more than the most shoddy concepts of math and science. So they teach button-pushing. There used to be a number of drivers, and there are still many, who drive cars by pushing

---

[79]A most valuable and fascinating book about education, also used in the preparation of these brief notes, is, *The Dilemma of Education in a Democracy*, by R. H. Powers.

buttons. If the proper thing didn't happen that was supposed to happen, they had not the faintest idea generally what the reason might be. K-12 should concern predominately the reasons, not the routine, hence there should be no need generally for computers.

Computer literacy, the "fourth basic skill" is as much a fraud and fantasy as FDR's "fourth freedom."[80] People like Harry Lewis, Gordon McKay Professor of Computer Science at Harvard is unconcerned with such lack in entering students. The field changes too rapidly, quickly outmoding the button pushing. He says what students need is solid comprehension in grammar which is logic, in spelling and in simple basic math. Most of the educational advantage of computers in K-12 comes from the extra attention to the learning process; and has nothing really to do with the expensive machine. And computers are expensive; like cars, the purchase price is but the down payment; it's the upkeep that kills.

Joseph Wizenbaum, Professor of Computer Science at MIT, inventor of Eliza for computer-person conversations, calls K-12 computers a fad invented by charlatans, like "tired blood." He compared computers to TV, "the child inhabits an abstract world in which actions have no consequences, violence is mindless . . . video games . . . actively teach dissociation" between actions and consequences. Computers, he says, inhibit creativity; "computers program kids", it tells them what to do and when to do it. If computers could reinforce a child's problem-solving ability, then computer professionals ought to lead better lives -- they don't.

People may attribute, he goes on, the success of children of the rich to their computer experience. In reality they have more important other advantages. If you want to reduce inequality, Wiezenbaum advises, give them money. That of course was facetious. If you really want to help them, throw Prof. Wagschal and his computers and TV and unions out and get teachers who can teach children how to

---

[80]Read "The Myth of Computers in the Classroom," *The New Republic*, 9, 19, 1994, p.14.

speak and to write and to think correctly about man's spiritual world; the physical world he can pick-up from anybody.

When "computer literacy" or any other such crutch is used, "the principal effect is to push problems even further into obscurity -- to avoid confrontation with the need to think."

"Outcome based education," OBE, is the latest of a century of "reforms" in public education. OBE, a lucrative business for Colorado activist Wm. Spady, at its most "transformational", strips away grades, semesters, discipline, individual study. He says "We don't want bell curves, standards, expectations and results." Classes would be merged into group studies; subjects listed include: "the homeless" and what to do about them; environment and stewardship; demonstrate understanding of prejudice. Descriptions include "paradigms," contexts, thematic learning, culminating outcomes. Indoctrination for Statism, not education.

"Outcome based" does not mean graded reading or arithmetic. It claims to strive for higher order thinking in the "affective domain", "relating to prejudice and interpersonal problems," being a "supportive person." In Richmond, Virginia, a mostly white fifth grade class was to study the 20th Century by focusing on Cesar Chavez, Eleanor Roosevelt, and Colin Powell. Maya Angelou's Hispanic, feminist and black group indoctrination was to be used to correct attitudes.

"OBE is not only one thing. It's a system, a broad group of strategies."

schooling as psychotherapy
self esteem
multiculturalism
homogenous grouping
no-fail rule
global citizenship

When critics get at them they change and say, "Oh we have never stated that we are OBE," from a Birmingham "director of community relations." "We're not talking about OBE any longer, we're just doing it." OBE is <u>not</u> education; it is Statist indoctrination.

In the last 30 years, the educationalists have moved public schools almost completely away from the 3Rs, from a subject oriented curriculum to "strands", molding attitudes, and openness, to "remediate inappropriate attitudes and behavior." "Restructuring," OBE, Charter schools, magnet schools, integration with TV and computers: these "reforms" mark a total assumption of control by the bureaucratic state.

Children are intellectually uneducated, morally confused, alienated and maladjusted. In Oregon, 3rd graders were surveyed, "Did you ever want to beat up your parents?" In a Tucson talented fourth grade were questioned, "How many hate your parents?" "Desensitizing" programs require children to touch corpses in a morgue, movies show adult male genitals, naked sex in color, masturbation. A Washington state health class requires all boys to say "vagina" and all girls to say "penis." One small girl who could barely say it, was forced to go in front of the class and say it loudly ten times. Children are jeered and required to defend their religion under extreme ridicule from group leaders and class.

SEX EDUCATION

Sex-ed courses are almost perfect recipes for producing personality problems and even perversions. Monogamous, intimate love (which sexologists degrade to a mere option) is an integral part of the sexual instinct. Sex-ed courses disregard, in fact violate, this need for intimacy. Sexual instinct has a physical part and a feeling (affectionate or spiritual) part, which need to be conformable. Sex-ed downgrades or ignores the affectionate and monogamous nature of human sexuality, it desensitizes youth, breaks down instinctive mental barriers of shame, disgust and morality -- the natural mental claims that control base sex urges.

The sexual development of children is far more

complicated than in animals, going through a number of stages. Both Freuds warned of indulging children in any of these; getting hung-up in any of these may prevent further development. Sex growth may cease and "seeing and showing" become the central aim.

Psychologists quite generally have warned of the danger of exposing young children to the viewing of sexual intercourse and mature genitals. Freud warned that to them it is an act of subjugation and may lead to a predisposition to sadism. "Vast amounts of experiences suggest that the majority of adult perverts are products of premature sex experience". Seduction may occur through overexposure to psychoanalytic terms, to "sex activities, including sex courses".

MONEY AND HOMES

We spend somewhere between $200 and $300 billions of dollars[81] each year on education of 42 million public school students. Regina Lee Wood tells us that, for example, in Oklahoma 40 percent of their money for education goes to students in various remedial education programs - 23 percent are in Chapter I and Special Education.[82] Probably more than half of that 23 percent will never learn to read and never be self-supporting, to say nothing of supporting society. Nationally one-fourth of our students are in these special programs, which in themselves, consume $30 billion dollars; only one-fifth ever finish high school of a standard curriculum, and we know that even of those some fraction, perhaps as high as 25 percent, barely have a fourth grade education. The National Adult Literacy Survey, covering 14 million students, recently revealed that 67 percent lack

---

[81]*Human Events* (11,20, 93, p. 18), quoted *Education Week* that $493.3 billion spent total on education 1993, a decade's increase of 50 percent.

[82]R. H. Wood, *National Rev.* (IV, 18, 1993).

"literacy proficiency" to go to high school, and one-fifth can't read.

Before WW II, 80 percent of the blacks over 14 years of age could read, today just over 50 percent. There are 1,000 times more mothers trying to keep their children out of remedial education than there are politicians and NEA agents trying to cram them in. It's the money, you know.

I started to school in a one-roomer, "boys" and "girls" out back, on either end of a shed for horses. For view there was nothing but rolling prairie grass with the blue heights of the Rocky Mountain front, behind which the sun dipped too quickly when walking home. The teacher with two years at Normal, at $80 per month, say five ton of coal at $5 per, and five gallons of coal oil at 10 cents, and maybe at the most five or ten dollars for new books and supplies; that was the total cost of teaching about 30 kids in eight grades. About one-fifth of them finished college.

The 1964 Civil Rights Act mandated a study, which led to the Coleman Report[83]; it was supposed to document the "lack of equality" in education by race, in order to justify spending, and busing to change the black children's peer group (?). Coleman reported (1) he found funding "differed very little," when region and urban versus rural settings were considered. (2) Resource difference did not matter much for anybody. Schools, he explained[84], had even then long been a tight monopoly, and like the industries in socialist countries, operating under bureaucratic management, outputs and input are totally disconnected; the forces that would make a difference were gone.

Only one school resource stood out: teachers' scores on a special vocabulary test conducted by the Survey itself. Teachers' degrees, experience and salary provided no correlation, but vocabulary did. This fact was hushed up for "racial reasons." (3) Undoubtedly the most significant result

---

[83]Ibid.

[84]See for example *Academic Questions*, W. 90-91, J. S. Coleman.

(most people would have known that money would be a minor factor) was the finding that family background was a major determinant. Coleman put it that black children did better in classes which were primarily middle-class. Perhaps he used that as a "code-word" for white, which was the initial urging for busing.   It shouldn't have been; in some communities, as for example in pre-war Harlem where discipline and excellence were more than mere words, there were "middle class" black schools. "Middle class" is not an amount of money anymore than it is a race; it is an attitude. And it must be recognized as that thing in the world that liberals and socialists most hate: "the god damned middle-class." It is the attitude that demands truth, decency, and responsibility; it is human society.[85]

Another report that needs a brief review is that of J.E. Chubb and T.M. Moe, *Politics, Markets,* a report from the liberal Brookings Institution. N. Lehman summarized their book in the *Atlantic Monthly* (1, 91). It dismissed the waves of NEA education "reforms"; that was nothing new. What is relatively new in Chubb and Moe, and largely kept out of the public's perception, is that "the single most important prediction of student achievement, more important than quality of schools", is family background. The authors give "page after page" of evidence, just as Coleman's report noted the importance of "family education", in determining <u>attitudes</u> towards discipline and responsibility, and towards a desire to learn.

The other somewhat original recommendation in Chubb

---

[85]The whole purpose of the "sixties": the hippies, drugs, Woodstock, patched and stained jeans, beards and general unkeptness, "freakin' out," jeering at modesty, even decency, "Vietnam," "Watergate," post -1965 "civil rights," the media and entertainment no less than the universities, and many churches, was to destroy. Allen Bloom said it was to destroy the culture; it was in reality to destroy that which is even more basic then culture: human society, the god damn middle class. And it is <u>true</u>, what they say, without it all things are relative: truth, morality, culture. For without society and society's innate purpose -- to rise up -- there is none of these, nor even rationality.

and Moe is to get rid of "public schools." Along with bits of "Reagan-era jargon," as reviewer Lehman reveals his biases, the authors agree with Reagan, and J. S. Mill, that "government is the problem." Also largely get rid of unions and credentialing of teachers.

But I have found nothing to compare, in "mainstream (Statist) media" with the following: In general, the ghetto schools that are producing good results always seem to have a "visionary" involved ("a small group of visionaries . . . and their hold on power") -- like James Comer in New Haven, Marva Collins and George Clements in Chicago, Joe Clark in New Jersey -- committed to helping <u>students</u> <u>and</u> <u>their</u> <u>parents</u> assimilate into the middle class.

Assimilate into the middle-class, whether the authors were aware of it or not, means assimilation into a human society. Statism doesn't have a middle-class; in fact it demonizes them as bourgeois. Statists have no concern for, even a loathing for, morality, truth, decency, and real culture.

Hundreds of thousands of nuns in parochial schools and teachers in other church-related schools for centuries have performed the task of Comer and Collins, as writers such as Sidney Hook, Tom Sowell and Abraham Lass have testified. Today such people are effectively strained out of the teacher flow, by the nauseous schools of education, and the credentialing that makes them compulsory, and which bars highly competent people from areas in which "ed. teachers" are generally, notoriously deficient: English, science, math. The entire educationalists' establishment is ruled by Statists who blacklist the unaccredited.

Clearly liberals Chubb and Moe have recognized the great "visionary" difference between assimilation into the middle class on one hand, or not on the other, noting the immense value of the former. The middle class is what Dewey sought to destroy, through destruction of reading, and thereby of culture and society, leaving the field open for Statism.

We read or hear "heads" talking about all kinds of "cultures": prison culture, ghetto culture, youth culture, adversary culture. If the word culture is used for those predominately anti-social poisons, then the word for one of the most essential aspects of a human society becomes lost, and the very concept thus trampled with consequent destruction of society. Here we see the great evil of corrupting language. When you have become aware of how long and hard intellectuals have struggled to destroy education, uproot society, override Constitutional freedoms, push the use of such irrationalities as "prison culture" or adversary culture, only to destroy the only culture that Western civilization has or is going to have, when you begin to comprehend the enormity of the catastrophe we face, then you will be moved to act, to remove this corruption.

EPILOGUE

Nothing can possibly be more convincing, that it was the intent of intellectuals to destroy Western culture, than the account of the step-by-step destruction of reading and then of all education.

Their phenomenal success was due to the near total loss of a core of leaders who would watch "with eternal vigilance" for any corruption, not just of freedom, but more especially of truth, morality, and culture.

I feel a need to qualify my harsh criticism of "intellectuals." It should be noted that all of the advances made by man have been the work of intellectuals, some of the people responsible for the disaster documented here were only pseudo-intellectuals.

The solution to our education problems is quite simple. All human experience has shown the destructiveness of unchecked monopoly; remove the government-union monopoly. Remove totally all government imposed regulations. Have states pay directly to any school, say something like seventy percent of the average spent on schooling within the state (total of national, state and local contributions), for each student who passes a comprehensive standard achievement test at the end of each semester or year. After a somewhat lenient working-in period, schools with more than five or ten percent no-passes would be warned and then rejected. More than one no-pass, for one grade, for a student, or more than say five or six for K-12 would have to be accommodated by a special separate program.

It may well be necessary to have two classes of schools, A and B, and associate different levels of achievement tests. In less populated areas it may be necessary to have students given either A or B tests in the same school. It is absolutely essential that the economic progress of our nation and its cultural level of excellence, be cut loose from an anchor to the lowest denominator. Society through their government, has a reason and, therefore, a right to insist that children receive a level of education necessary for them to be supporting of themselves but also of society. But it has no good reason to insist on determining <u>how</u> people attain that goal.

7. HISTORY

PART I

INTRODUCTION

> Upon the presence of the past in the present depends all conduct directed by <u>knowledge</u>.
> R.M. Weaver

Vast and continuing efforts over the years to read and thereby to control the future have embraced astrology, the flight of birds, the reading of entrails, and priestly incantations; Marx used phrenology. On the other hand, a few years ago the editor of *Commentary* was quoted as declaring that the history of the Civil War was as irrelevant to him as the War of the Roses. In 1938 Neville Chamberlain described the problems in Czechoslovakia, discussed at Munich, as a "quarrel in a far away country between people of whom we know nothing." The catastrophe that festered in that ignorance nearly destroyed Western civilization. The results of ignorance in high places are much the same as for treason.

If history were really bunk, unimportant or "irrelevant", why would so many powerful groups take so much trouble to obscure, distort, and to lie about it? Orwell wrote that because of "the poisonous effects of the Russian <u>mythos</u> . . . facts are distorted and suppressed to such an extent as to make it doubtful whether a true history of our times can ever be written." "The continuous alterations of the past, and . . . a disbelief in the very existence of objective truth" are not the demands of just totalitarianism, as Orwell claimed: they are the "adjustments" necessary of any ideology.[86] Idealogy is theory, and facts must be adjusted to its procrustean claims. We can be sure that when Henry Ford declared history to be bunk, he really meant the historian's history; he exhibited a great concern for true history.

Statism you see needs no truth; ideologies make their own truth; that is why liberal Statists have abandoned the claims of truth. Controlling the past was a critical imperative not only for theoreticians in the Soviet Union but also for their extensive vassalage in the West. Designation of non-persons and non-events remains a matter of high policy in Statism everywhere. Winston in *1984* worked in the Records Department, whose business was "the mutability of the past."

Any small boy already is aware of the gear-clashing that arises so readily from lies. The gear-clashing, or unconformability, becomes irrepressible when the true history is revealed. That is the bare reason why real history has been largely expelled from our schools,[87] and without history there is no way for a human society to judge the conformability of today and tomorrow with yesterday. Statist history is intentionally adjusted to conform not with truth and human purpose but with the policies of the Statists. Thus for those who know history, perhaps lived it, the resulting and obvious lack of conformity, the gear-clashing irrationality, becomes the constant character of today, a pathology turning human society to madness. Controlling irrationality and imagination requires implementation of a purpose and the growing out and up of the strengths and knowledge proven of worth in the past. Who today is held more accountable than the sports manager, and what does he rely upon?

---

[86]Ideology is theory, as in Marxian theory, which forms the framework for all socialism or Statism. Human society is based on experience, which in concentrated and proven form is tradition, not theory.

[87]The new history is not of hope but of hate, despair, betrayals. American exceptionalism is turned on its head. Our children are taught to despise their ancestors, their culture, their country.

Traditions and history, "Never change pitchers when . . ." and "How's his hitting?" To be rational is to conform to the best approximation of reality, of truth.

We all learn early of hot stoves and bad consciences. History is experience; there are few things in life more important.   Today most young people have been taught almost no history; thus they approach being social idiots. This ultimately is our fault not theirs, or the teachers. Try starting a conversation with most people about ideas more involved than ball-scores or weather and see how quickly they turn away.   Conversation and reading were long considered to be important joys of living, but no more. If you know but little about tennis then the subject to you is boring, but if you are a fair player, it is very interesting. However, knowing enough about your (1) society, (2) your culture, (3) your community, and (4) your government to be able and desirous of discussing various problems and ideas is vastly more important; it is essential to humanness, to society, to self-government, and even to fulfillment of your own life. Failure to learn enough to make it interesting and important, due to ignorance or indifference, makes a person at least a 50 percent enemy of his society.

Lorenz has explained that the health and soundness of a society, its ability to control violence and to provide an admirable vision, depends critically upon its ability to provide an identification with that society -- one that is honorable and sacred. The need for identification -- to feel that you belong to a brotherhood --is innate, and it must arise from a worthy purpose. It also must be informed with the nature of that brotherhood, with "what has been." It is no accident that the world's great books of purpose, from the Bible to the books of Communism, rest on a foundation of history. German Professor Michael Sturmer wrote, "Whoever supplies memory, shapes concepts, and interprets the past will win the future." All people who have a purpose necessarily put a high value on history; it is the sole source of knowledge for the directing of purpose and for assuring a comformability with the past which is the essence of social rationality.

History is more important today than perhaps ever before because society is under attack by ideologies which rest on indoctrination and force. Human society is the very opposite from an ideology, in the same way that experience is opposite to theory. Facts are rocks upon which theories are shattered, but upon which human societies are built. There is an erroneous idea that science is based on facts and reason alone, and that our spiritual world, so essential to guidance of society and thereby to history, rests on mere beliefs. This is very far from the truth. Our spiritual world of innate feelings guides social affairs as much by reason as is true in the world of science. We see a rock fall, or that the allowed energy levels for small particles act as though they were discrete; we <u>see</u> and believe, hardly needing reason. On the other hand, truth, so fundamental to humanness, also must be reasoned. There was in fact no truth before reason; reason necessitated the concept of truth.

Hence, we see that reason and truth must coexist, work together supporting our society, just as we have seen for the case of purpose and will -- one is impotent without the other. And it was the great flaw in the Enlightenment, which spawned our irrational modernity, that reason was above all else; the truth of man's spiritual world was rejected because it was claimed to rest only on beliefs. Our spiritual world concerning feelings is clearly of necessity experienced; it consists of the efforts of great men of the past to relate inner feelings to the real world and to what is proper for man. Such a heritage in history, from the struggle on the Marathon plain to that of the Pilgrims on a rocky New England shore, provides the experiences of history upon which must rest the belonging, and the identification with an admirable purpose. Lorenz has warned us that unless an individual is led to find such a feeling of belonging he becomes a nobody, an incipient terrorist, a candidate for the Chekas or Gestapo. And the principal means, the experience by which people learn to identify with their society, is through history.

It was Woodrow Wilson who tore American democracy away from self-government and thrust it into an irreversible bureaucracy with a global mission. He was driven by a vision, no less than John Dewey, for restructuring human life under an administrative state. Without Wilson, Franklin Roosevelt, who served under him, could never have had his New Deal nor his WW II. (See his biography by Arthur S. Link.)

The history of WW II is an example from history that confirms the fact that an ideology, being a theory, makes its own truth. It needs commonly to impose "adjustments" on history in order to make the facts fit the needs of the theory, the ideology.

Franklin Roosevelt deliberately sacrificed Pearl Harbor, the Pacific Fleet, some 2,500 young lives at Pearl Harbor and twice that number on Bataan, of the Philippines -- knowingly sacrificed them -- in order to get into the war. The facts are overwhelming; Arthur Schlesinger in 1948 admitted trickery for the American people's "own good," he declared testily. That was the origin of "the good war." The real question, as Schlesinger now realizes, is not whether, but why? We know that FDR received the next-to-last Magic intercept at 9:30 p.m., December 6, and declared, "This means war." Navy Chief Admiral Stark received the final intercept at 9:00 a.m., December 7, and cried out, "My God, I must warn Kimmel." General Marshall returned from a long morning canter, on the most important day of his life, shortly after 11 a.m; he could have reached Pearl Harbor by special phone in a few minutes. But FDR, Stark and Marshall knew that if Pearl Harbor put up as much as a token squadron of planes, signalling to the Japs that surprise had been lost, they had orders to turn away. Marshall finally got off a message almost an hour later; sent by "commercial wire" on a circuitous route; a boy on a bicycle was pedalling it through the streets of Honolulu when the bombs started falling.

Robert Sherwood, responsible for FDR's "again and again"[88] and who thereby "burned" inside, found 1948 to be "inexplicable." Lucky for him to die so soon. John Lehman, a recent Secretary of the Navy no less, a few years ago jeered at Admiral Kimmel, as "dressed for a golf game" the morning of December 7, 1941.[89] Kimmel and Short he judges "deserved the ax and got it." Let Mr. Lehman be judged as he has judged. Kimmel <u>did</u> <u>not</u> <u>know</u>; was allowed no inkling. FDR sat in the White House playing with his stamp collection, knowing that Pearl Harbor would be bombed at 1:00 p.m., as did Marshall who had gone for a long canter.

What evil, what abominable evil! What is it, that even today still crouches so powerfully behind this renegadism?

Schlesinger gave the answer in the *Wall Street Journal* (6,21,90): "FDR Vindicated!" FDR wanted to "narrow the differences . . . between democratic and communist societies." He "had an assured vision of the world he wanted after the war." "The American system might reach 60" as it moved toward Communism, and "the Soviet systems as it moved toward democracy might eventually reach 40." A little slapdash Arthur admits, but "less naive in 1990 than . . . 1950," and with the collectivism that has wormed its way into our nation, a good deal less treasonous. How could the evil intent be made more transparent? Ask half a dozen nations around the globe what happens when you start sharing your bed with communism. Being partly communist is like being a little pregnant.

Dorothy Rabinowitz charged on the pre-ed page of WSJ (12, 2, 91): "This weekend on December 7, Arts and Entertainment presents 'Sacrifice At Pearl Harbor' -- an epic whose title tells the story. In the view of the filmmakers,

---

[88]Robert Sherwood, *Roosevelt and Hopkins* (1948), alone admitted the evil, "I burn inwardly," when he recalled contributing to FDR's re-election in 1940 by providing what he knew to be a deception. " . . . I shall say it again, and again, and agaain: your boys are not going to be sent into a foreign war."

[89]*WSJ*, 10, 2, 1991.

those killed at Pearl Harbor were sacrificed to the aims of an American president determined to bring his nation into the war . . . the filmmakers magnify bits and pieces of accusatory testimony, suspicions, insinuations . . . of revisionists and conspiracy theorists . . ." The reason or cause for all the conspiracy theories is "clear enough. One has only to examine the political prejudice coloring these theories to grasp their origins both among journalists of the fashionable Left and the terminal Right . . . Pearl Harbor was a particularly bitter day for America Firsters. Today's American Firsters and fellow isolationists are among the leading conspiracy theorists accusing Roosevelt and Churchill . . . "

Then H.V. Jaffa wrote (*Mod. Age,* Sp. 92, p. 277) ". . . it is simply grotesque . . . to write, 'the American declaration of war against the Axis powers was a triumph for Churchill and the culmination of many months of careful efforts'. . ."

Starting with Jaffa first, can you believe that he is not aware of the widely publicized cable of Japanese Ambassador Admiral Nomura to Tokyo? "I understand the British believe that if . . . a Japanese-American war (is) started at the back door, there would be a good prospect of getting the U.S. . . . in the European War."[90] Mr. Churchill himself, in *Grand Alliance* p. 606, wrote that he received news of Pearl Harbor with "the greatest joy." Two months later he told his Parliament, "This is what I have dreamed of, aimed at, and worked for, and now has come to pass." Churchill's war production minister Lyttelton, in a speech (6,20,1944) to the American Chamber of Commerce declared, "America provoked Japan to such an extent the Japanese were forced to attack . . . (it) is a travesty of history ever to say that America was forced into war."

Now for Rabinowitz. Can some word other than ignorance or renegadism soften the name for her totally inept charges of "revisionists and conspiracy theorists," aimed at the A & E filmmakers? But immediately she shifts her aim to the

---

[90]Stanford Prof. T.A. Bailey, *The Man On the Street,* (1948).

"fashionable Left and the terminal Right." This she pinpoints as the "American Firsters" and "isolationists," and can it be denied that by "terminal Right", she aims at them the charge of Nazis, fascists? And did the ADL, ACLU, AJC or NAACP find this to be lying renegadism, hateful racism, or even "unconscious racism"?

In 1938-1939, I was in the last two years of high school, reading the *American Observer*, was strongly pro-FDR, and when war came volunteered. I would like to inform Mrs. Rabinowitz that better than 80 percent of America was solidly all "American Firsters" in spirit against any war, were as strongly anti-Nazi as anti-Communist -- as revealed by old Senator Hiram Johnson of California, who demanded to know whether America had sunk so low as to choose to support "one cutthroat out of the two?" My observation has been that, as with socialism v. human society where there is no middle way, here too one is either an "American Firster" or an "American Laster."[91] What could America be second to other than socialism, the very opposite of a human society.

Then Rabinowitz refers to the "fashionable Left"! Just who made Communism "fashionable"? Why has it been that something so "fashionable" has had to hide behind lies and deceits to this day? Even after the mid-60s only a few "leftists" came out of the closet and openly expressed their hatred for America and everything it has stood for, and vowed to uproot that which the American Firsters went to war to protect.[92]

This "fashionable Left" was identified by Lippmann as the "overhead planners" -- socialists . . . (to) liberals . . . all who claimed to be enlightened . . . collectivists". '"There sat Harry Hopkins,' Churchill writes in *The Grand Alliance*, 'absolutely glowing with refined comprehension of the Cause!' This 'Cause', as Hopkins told Churchill on behalf of Roosevelt,

---

[91]As for the sneer, "my country, right or wrong," see p. 229.

[92]Read the introduction to *The Rosenberg File*, by Ronald Radosh and Joyce Milton.

was to be 'the defeat, ruin, and slaughter of Hitler, <u>to the exclusion of all other purposes, loyalties or aims</u>' (e.a.). Thus did the President of the United States, through the mouth of Harry Hopkins, renounce adherence to the Constitution and dishonor his pledged word to the American people to keep them out of foreign wars, for the sake of an aim he conceived to be higher . . . "[93]   Note the date of Hopkins's Cause, January 10, 1941.   Why not slaughter Hitler <u>and Stalin</u>? Certainly at that time (Jan., 1941), the American people recognized Stalin as the more evil and more dangerous to Western civilization of the two gangsters who were then allies, carving up Europe from Finland to France. We see the deft hand of Roosevelt, even earlier, in a secret protocol added to Britain's guaranty (early 1939) to come to Poland's aid if attacked by "<u>any</u> European power."   The protocol effectively provided an exemption for the Soviet Union,[94] and we know that FDR had been secretly and illegally communicating with both Eden and Churchill concerning Poland[95] and promising support.

How could FDR get away with it? Apart from the dozen who had fairly direct knowledge of the Magic intercepts and FBI spy surveillance, there must have been thousands who had clear hints, tens of thousands who suspected; in fact the majority of Americans came to have some degree of suspicion. But only two or three muffled

---

[93]So wrote the most scholarly American general of WW II, Gen. A.C. Wedemeyer in his *Reports* (1958), p.9.

[94]So convenient in 1945 for legitimizing Stalin's fruits of aggression.

[95]See H.E. Barnes, *Modern Age.*   Spring, 1958, 139-151.   Also Morgenstern's *Pearl Harbor,* p. 5-6.

cries are recorded.   Robert Sherwood in 1948 found "the present . . . appalling . . . inexplicable." In 1958, General Wedemeyer pointed to the treason in his *Reports*, and some twenty years later it was revealed that the genius of Magic, the principal cryptanalyst, W.F. Friedman, exclaimed when he heard of the Pearl Harbor attack, "They knew!   They knew!"

It has been claimed over and over that FDR and Marshall saw their main task as defeating Hitler. That is corrupt dissembling and marks the purveyor as ignorant or renegade. Their clear and primary Constitutional task was to protect America's interests, and at that time the preservation of Western civilization was unquestioned as in our interest. Communism on the other hand was recognized as posing its greatest danger. In fact, without the Soviet threat, Germany would never have accepted Hitler.

Roosevelt's declaration, through Hopkins, that the "Cause" was the "slaughter of Hitler, to the exclusion of all other purposes, loyalties or aims," is an evil on a much higher level than mere treason. The "slaughter of Hitler" was but a euphemism in misdirection. What was sought was the very termination of the West as a human society, for the apotheosis of Communism.

FDR made saving Stalin his principal task, never once considering any other objective. After the Soviet counter attack at Moscow, 6 December 1941, Hitler could not win; after December, 1942 when the Soviets started west from Stalingrad, not even a stalemate was possible. To supply Stalin after that, and what was generally recognized as the evil empire, was as a prominent historian noted, idiocy or treason. Both the Kennan group in the U.S. and a group in Britain sought to convinced Churchill and FDR to demand concessions for supplies. But Harry Hopkins and Lord Beaverbrook laid down the policy of Soviet needs first, unconditionally.

NOTE ON JOHN CHARMLEY

John Charmley, British historian, was supported in the *London Times* by former M.P. Alan Clark, (author of a history of the Soviet-German War) in an attempt to reassess the performance of Churchill and FDR in WW II, particularly in the early, or Soviet-German War stage. Charmley's professed intent was to show that FDR should "not have been allowed to change the postwar world . . . (nor should he and Churchill have) been as naively pro-Stalin . . . which resulted in a victory which enthroned Communism . . ." His (1993) biography of *Churchill* was rather savagely attacked, from both so-called Left and Right, which may suggest that significant portions of the Right, as well as the Left, are now "continuous with Marxism".[96]

Anyone seeking to cover up this treason as naivete, even at this late date, is as much an accomplice in it as was Adm. Stark: "I must warn Kimmel!": but didn't, or Col. Walter Bedell Smith whose duty it was to get Magic intercepts to Marshall, but sat on his ass instead because he knew that Marshall and FDR didn't want him to.

THE ROOSEVELT CLIMATE

"(W)e knew that all we held dear was under attack and we should not let it perish." So proclaimed the *NY Times* (11, 6, 1941). It turned out that there was a great split in American perceptions of just what "all we hold dear" was. A southern boy hassled unmercifully by an eastern intellectual, finally muttered, "Maybe I don't know much, but I sure 'spects a lot." Another old Alabama boy American-Firster grinned at anti-America-Firster old Honest Ave Harriman when he tried to snow him, "Aw, you're pissin' on ma' laig, govna." Liberal historian of vast human perspective, C. A. Beard, saw in Roosevelt, "only conceits, dreams of grandeur, vain imaginings, lust for power, or a desire to escape (from

---

[96]A. Schlesinger, *The New Rep.* (9,13,1993, p.29) and *National Review* (11,15,1993, p. 54, and 3,1,1993, p. 21).

Eleanor presumably)". Alcide De Gasperi, the Adenauer-De Gaulle of post-war Italy, believed that his "we" of Italy was not entirely to blame for its troubles with post-war Communism because "that evil plant . . . was born and prospered in the Roosevelt Climate". A special American ship had been provided to rush Statinist Togliatti back from Moscow, and U.S. emergency relief supplies began to be used to funnel political status through the Italian Communist Party.

Throughout 1942, FDR insisted over Churchill's violent protests that convoys carrying arms to Stalin keep sailing to Archangel and Murmansk, even though losses were unbearable. Churchill wrote FDR, "On July 14 only four ships have reached Archangel . . . out of thirty three . . ." Yet Stalin refused to allow U.S. or British planes and ships to use Soviet nearby bases, and British sailors who had endangered their lives to bring supplies were subjected to "often ugly treatment." Stalin never deigned to "take notice" of complaints; more revolting was FDR's unwillingness to pursue Stalin on that point. In March 1945, FDR refused when Sovietphile Harriman, "outraged by Soviet brutality and callousness toward American prisoners-of-war rescued from German prison camps, begged the President to communicate directly with Stalin" to get it stopped. "It doesn't appear appropriate . . .," Roosevelt answered.

While FDR and the evil party sought to force the perception that our relations with Soviet Communism were excellent, the memoirs of Generals Deane, Mark Clark, and Wedemeyer, and Admiral Zacharias and Admiral Leahy, FDR's Chief of Staff and thereby superior to Marshall and Stark, tell quite a different story. When Admiral E. M. Zacharias returned from the Pacific to become Deputy Director of Intelligence in the fall of 1944, he was amazed to find that the correct "party line" in Washington was that Japan would fight on for years, thereby necessitating an invasion and especially the need of buying Stalin in on the invasion of

Japan.[97]   Admiral Turner was Chief of Navy War Plans on December 4, 1941 when the "winds" message was received. A Captain A. H. McCollum prepared a warning message for Admiral Kimmel and other Pacific Commanders. The warning was killed by two Admirals, Turner and Wilkinson. When Turner returned from a Pacific duty in 1945, he found to <u>his</u> amazement that the "party line" was that there had been no "winds" message. This was reinforced by the revision that what was claimed as the "winds" was false. But everybody <u>at the</u> <u>time</u> believed it and should have acted upon it. There is no reason to believe that it was not received. Briefly it was a special signal to be sent so that many Japanese abroad not on Magic would know that war was imminent.

In the fall of 1943, our military attaché in Moscow was forced out by Stalin and Hopkins. They had objected to his reporting open military information, which was his purpose. Marshall sent his protege, General Deane, as the replacement but strongly ordered him to seek no information that might "irritate" the Soviets. General Deane became Chief of the Military Mission in Moscow and, when he denied a Soviet request for a second order of 25 very large Diesel marine engines which McArthur needed desperately in the Pacific, and the first 25 received by Soviets were rusting in an open field where they were stored for post-war use, Harry Hopkins overruled him. Hopkins and his aides, like Major General J. H. Burns, Deane wrote in his book <u>Strange Alliance</u>, went at supplying Stalin and "carried it out with a zeal that approached fanaticism . . . (that) could not be tempered."

---

[97]Harry Truman may not have been terribly smart, and was perhaps somewhat narrow minded where his party was concerned, but Harry was not a traitor, nor was he a brutal man. Only some implacable necessity forced him to order the Bomb dropped; that could <u>only</u> have been to hurry the end of the war, before Stalin could claim a seat at the peace table. He claimed it anyway but MacArthur froze him out -- quite different from Eisenhower. Liberal renegades whine over Hiroshima, but never have mentioned the far more horrible fate of millions of people in Europe. The Japs got off easy.

General Wedemeyer, also a protege of General Marshall, was scholarly and able. Later in the war he became the theater commander in China, and often had to deal with Marshall's blunders. He wrote that Marshall "had little knowledge of the complexities of the world conflict and no conception of (communist trickery). He became an easy prey to crypto-communists . . ." Returning to Washington from China in March, 1945, he told FDR that he " . . . felt certain they (communists) would cause trouble as soon as the war was ended. (FDR) did not seem to understand . . . and abruptly ended the meeting."

President Edward Benes visited Stalin in December, 1943, after Teheran. He came to believe that General Patton was kept out of Prague by Eisenhower on orders from FDR through Marshall, as a result of Teheran.

There are facts that point to Harry Hopkins being instrumental in providing Stalin with equipment for his atom bomb, and perhaps more. Major G. R. Jordan was on a kind of detached service as Liaison Officer with Harry Hopkins's Lend-Lease at Newark Airport early in 1942 and later at the big Air Base in Great Falls, Montana, through which most all of the highest priority items to Stalin flowed. In his *Diaries* (Western Islands, 1965, first published in 1952 by Harcourt, Brace), Major Jordan reported 11,912 pounds of thorium nitrate sent to the Soviets on January 30, 1943. "(D)ue undoubtedly to General Groves' vigilance" (head of Manhattan Project) there were no further shipments officially through Lend-Lease. In April, 1943, Major Jordan recorded 1,465 pounds of (mostly apparently) uranium nitrate and 2.2 pounds of uranium metal, when total U.S. stock were reported at 4.5 pounds, shipped to the Soviets, by direct orders to him from Harry Hopkins.

Ambassador William Bullitt heard the Hiss brothers named as Soviet agents by French counter-intelligence officials in 1939. In September, 1945 Igor Gouzenko, a Soviet code clerk in Ottawa, defected taking with him hundreds of documents that proved the existence of a large Soviet spy network in Canada and in the U.S., and gave information on a link to Hiss. At about the same time Elizabeth Bentley reported detailed information on some eighty government employees, a number of whom were at high levels. A number of spies identified in Gouzenko's documents had been named to FDR by A. Berle of State Department Intelligence (from Chambers' report of 1939), and were again named by Bentley. Eleanor's, "My Day," (8, 4, 1948), denigrated Bentley's testimony as "the fantastic story of this evidently neurotic lady." It appears almost certain that without the Gouzenko documents, the whole communist spy system would never have been exposed.

NOTE ON ROOSEVELT AND STALIN

1. As his first order of business in foreign affairs, in 1933, FDR recognized the Stalin regime even as some 7 million human carcasses stunk on the plains on the Ukraine.
2. Joseph E. Davies was made Ambassador to Stalin in 1936, with FDR's only order, to "win Stalin's friendship at all costs."
3. Pearl Harbor and Bataan in the Philippines were sacrificed with the Pacific Fleet, to permit FDR a place in the war.
4. Early in 1942 FDR gave the Soviets top priority on all supplies, even over our own troops fighting in the Pacific.
5. In 1943 Roosevelt told his personal friend and trusted emissary W. C. Bullitt, "I give (Stalin) everything I possible can and ask nothing . . . ."
6. At Casablanca, January, 1943, Roosevelt thought of "unconditional surrender," son Elliot tells us, while sucking on a tooth, "just the thing . . . for Uncle Joe."
7. At Quebec, August, 1943, Hopkins revealed a "very high level U.S. military strategic estimate," headed "Russia's position." The Soviets "will dominate Europe . . . every effort must be made to obtain her friendship." Sherwood wrote, it "guided the making of decisions at Teheran and Yalta."
8. In the fall of 1939, FDR rejected Adolph Berle's notes from his interview with Whittaker Chamber which Berle (in charge of State Dept. intelligence) had designated as "espionage". FDR refused any information on the Katyn

Massacre. Hopkins had a hand in the Atom Bomb Project, and provided Stalin with anything that he could get away from General Groves[98]:   1,465 lbs. of uranium salts, cadmium, cobalt, heavy water, aluminum tubes, 7 million pounds of graphite. Harry Hopkins was a master spy, as revealed by the Russians recently. He was in the atomic bomb program from the beginning. The FBI learned of it from undercover informants in Communist circles on the West Coast. Communists with contacts among socialists at the University of California, were found by the FBI to be leaking; the FBI was promptly ordered to discontinue its investigation.

9. At Quebec II, FDR promised Churchill $6.5 billion for signing a plan for "pastoralization" of Germany. It is believed to have been given by Stalin to Jacob Golos, a high Soviet official, who gave it to Harry Dexter White who is known to have given it to Henry Morgenthau, Secretary of Treasury. Secretary of War Stimson wrote of reading it back to FDR, who then pretended to be "frankly staggered . . . said he had no idea how he could have initialed this; he had evidently done it without much thought." But the plan was never rescinded until nearly the Berlin Blockade. Some Cold War!

10. At Yalta (but initiated by Harriman in late 1944), FDR promised Stalin full equipment for a 1.5 million man army for Siberia: 860,410 tons of dry cargo and 206,000 tons of liquid cargo, including 3,000 tanks, 75,000 trucks and 5,000 airplanes, some of which apparently could not be delivered until after the war's end. This was given to Stalin plus Japanese Sakhalin, the Kurile Islands, the Chinese naval base at Port Arthur and the international port of Dairen. The

---

[98]"We saw every evidence of pressure". . . to give to Russia everything that could be given (and/was not limited to atomic matters) . . . how delighted we were to get something away from the Russian . . . were very anxious in connection with the gaseous diffusion plant to get certain equipment. If not obtained . . . would have delayed completion. The Russian had a plant on the way . . . it was boxed on the dock when we got it." (Hearings Regarding Shipment of Atomic Materials to Soviets House of Representatives, Committee on Un-American Activities (December 7, 1949) p. 941-957 Jordan testimony p. 932)

Manchurian railroad was to be put under a Soviet-Chinese Company, all of this was to pay for Stalin's entering the Pacific war, which he had professed every intention of doing, on at least three occasions. In any case, Japan was already defeated. MacArthur and Nimitz had told Roosevelt at Pearl Harbor in July, 1944 that Japan would surrender "without an invasion." Yet, FDR and Marshall created a huge invasion force, massive beyond imagination. After returning from England, I was almost snared into it. It was a fraud, unneeded. The "invasion" was an excuse to make concessions to Stalin. Even more concessions would have been made had the Soviets been in the war longer than the two days before Hiroshima.

11.   Communist spies and influence existed most everywhere through the war, even in the White House, with Harry Hopkins and Lauchlin Currie (who skiddadled to South America just ahead of the spy hunts). There were only two exceptions: within the Manhattan District itself, and with the Pacific forces. Eisenhower and Marshall kept Western forces out of Berlin, and denied us even an entrance corridor, and also out of Prague. The Soviets were given, by FDR, rights in Japan little different from in Berlin, but MacArthur froze them out.

12.   Roosevelt made America an accomplice with Stalin in: (1) slave labor, (2) devastating the defeated far more greedily than after WW I, (3) the forced repatriation of some two million people to a quick death, or a slow death in the gulag, (4) and the holocausting of some 12 million people, largely women and children from homes held "as long as London was English," onto the open road with what they could carry, where pillaging Soviet troops plundered, raped and murdered.

THE SPLIT

Writers have commented on the fact that of recent years treacherous conspiracies have become so open -- "open conspiracy," an oxymoron. It began with FDR's WW II. Marshall, Hull and a number of others certainly were aware of FDR's treason; it can, however, be argued as Schlesinger and Truman did that Roosevelt was "forced to do it, for our own good." In fact if Roosevelt had proceeded to act in the support of America's interests in seeking to preserve Western civilization, upholding even the rather vacant propaganda of the Four Freedoms, and freeing the enslaved peoples, his "trickery", as Schlesinger called it, could have been overlooked. But I have already listed for you a dozen <u>major</u> acts by FDR, that benefitted only Stalin, mostly to the exclusion of even the Soviet people.

FDR provided the example, and the evil party recognized that new vistas were now open to them. Conspiratorial treason could be taken as a right, like quotas, sodomy, abortions and hate America were to become. The evil party now held the media; with a little care it could act at will.

People never realized in 1939, they seem not to even today, that socialism with a communist core had taken hegemonic control of the "establishment" in America, and in much of the West. Walter Lippmann declared "no one else is taken seriously"; Diana Trilling wrote "everywhere in our culture's life the Soviet Union exercised control"; Eugene Lyons wrote his *Red Decade* documenting communists in the media in schools, government, entertainment everywhere especially where opinions could be stated and opinion changed. By 1952, Whittaker Chamber found ". . . when I took up my little sling and aimed at Communism . . . What I hit was the forces of socialism . . . which in the name of liberalism, spasmodically, incompletely, somewhat formlessly, but always in the same direction, has been inching its ice cap over the nation for decades."

By 1950 I had been for years a strong rather left-wing Democrat; I had favored FDR and Truman, and abhorred McCarthy and Nixon for accusing Democrats of being communists. But I knew as did all of America that McCarthy was after communists. So it was that the words of Secretary of State, Dean Acheson, "I will not turn my back on Alger Hiss," marked a new level of arrogant power for the evil party. Acheson was a liberal. Nobody at the time except the inner core of the evil party, and a few as Lippmann put it, " . . . who were not taken seriously . . . swimming hopelessly against the tide," realized the enormity of the FDR treason, or realized that what Hiss and Hopkins did was exactly what Roosevelt wanted. Acheson knew.

George Marshall turned down both a U.S. State Department request and one from the British, for a secure transit into post-war Berlin, certainly at FDR's order. Marshall, in 1932 at the generals level in the Army, had been declared "unfit to command troops," and had wandered into the Guards and then to CCC camps. It was there that Eleanor and Hopkins recognized in his modest ability, "their man," who would do as told. Within some three years he was on his way to becoming the real military head of all U.S. armed forces. After Yalta he had to talk with the head of the Polish fighting forces, General Anders, whose men had served in so many critical battles for so long, and would now never be able to go home. Release of the abominable communiqué was only hours away. Irritated and weary Marshall would only say, "We continue to march with the Soviets . . . afterwards, God alone knows." Nothing can better describe the abyss into which the evil party of Acheson, Schlesinger, the *New York Times,* Edward R. Murrow, and all the rest had either pushed so much American blood and treasure or at least stood by saying "I will not turn my back . . ." on those who did.

Who were the American people to turn to? At that time the media had not yet subverted their common sense; they knew that communism was the evil empire. The people recognized in Joe McCarthy, Nixon, Whittaker Chambers, blighted souls though they perhaps were, that there alone with but few additions, stood all who dared match the conviction of the communists: through mud and hatred, Herblock's digs and sneers, children put on TV to tell of their contempt for Nixon. All others when forced a bit crumpled.

The Split gradually became visible for all who would see. There was a "Roosevelt Climate" showing a marked splitting away from America, which continued and grew on his example. That the deliberate and organized evil of FDR's men and policies were continued, following the German collapse, must be noted.

The Soviets have admitted -- hardly necessary -- that it was the NKVD that carried out the Katyn Massacre of Polish officers and men. Yet at Nuremburg, the Third Reich was indicted, at Stalin's insistence for that massacre, although Roosevelt had been advised, and then given documentary proof of the Soviet crime.

Admiral Erich Raeder was given a life sentence as a war criminal for planning the invasion of Norway. Unmentioned was Churchill's 1940 admission that the Germans had been but a day ahead of him.

Herman Goering was not charged with the blitzing of 60,000 Britishers, or for bombing Rotterdam or Warsaw, because Churchill himself had instituted terror bombing; Goering held off for four months. The culmination of the British "Lindermann Plan," for bombing working class housing, where the houses were close together, was the bombing of Dresden. Stalin insisted on it; some 135,000 souls, many refugee women and children, were burned to death.[99]

One of John Kennedy's *Profiles* was of Robert Taft, GOP presidential hopeful at the time. "The Nuremberg Trials," Taft declared, "will forever remain a blot on . . . American jurisprudence." JFK insisted that Taft wrote, "not in defense of Nazis . . . but in defense of . . . traditional American law and justice."

It was our Supreme Court Justice Robert Jackson who established the policy that the protection of the Hague and Geneva Conventions ceased the moment the Germans surrendered (5, 15, 1945). Both Freda Ultey and the Swiss editors of *Weltwocke* perceived that the prosecutors aimed at proving, (1) that the pre-Nazi, traditional structures of Germany, based on free enterprise and European traditions -- "Capitalists" -- were the main support of Nazism, and (2) in

------

[99]If there be any question about the tenderness of Hitler's thugs, read Paul Johnson's *Modern Times*.

obscuring the close relationship and alliance between the "nationalist" and the "collectivist" socialisms, that is, between the Third Reich and Sovietism.

Justice Robert Jackson maintained that the Control Council Law No. 10, drawn up by the Four-Powers for War Crimes Against Peace and Humanity, was based on International Law. It was actually based on Marxist collective guilt and on power. The "war of aggression" had been carried on for two years by the allied Soviet and German forces and the crimes against humanity chargeable to the Soviets were second to none in extent and in barbarism. Yet the U.S. sat with these thugs in judgment of their initial partner by order of FDR and his followers.

Collective guilt meant that anyone in any capacity who aided the German war effort was guilty of the crime of waging aggressive war: a peasant who produced food, an industrialist who provided employment, a soldier who obeyed orders, were all guilty. It was the entire German nation, as a preliminary to pastoralization. When the four-powers refused to sentence more than the top Nazi party members, the evil party of FDR's moved on to Dachau. Hence the most evil trials were totally FDR's, being initiated as a result of his directives. International law at best only provides protection during belligerency; when the fighting stops and there is neither treaty nor agreement, there is no law. Such were the rules for the Dachau trials, and the animals that were collected by the evil party at Dachau were more abominable than many of the prisoners.

Lieutenant Colonel W.N. Everett, the American lawyer who was appointed as defense counsel for 74 Germans accused in the Malmedy case, petitioned the U.S. Supreme Court charging that the Germans had not received a fair trial. The Court refused to intervene but Army Secretary Royall was forced to appoint a commission to investigate the charges. The commission sent to Germany in 1948 consisted of Judge E. L. Van Roden, of Delaware County, Pennsylvania, and Justice G. Simpson of the Texas Supreme Court. Their report was never made public. However, Judge Van Roden gave a series of talks around the country in which he revealed much of the U.S. evil at Dachau. Men were convicted and hanged on the basis of information obtained by beatings, kickings, breaking jaws or knocking out teeth. Agents used many ruses such as pretending to be priests. Judge van Roden speaking at Chester Pike Rotary Club (12-14-1948) said, "all but two of the Germans in the 139 cases we investigated had been kicked in the testicles beyond repair. That was standard procedure with American investigators."[100]

No evidence was produced to prove the existence of Ilse Koch's "human lampshade," so minutely detailed in many U.S. publications. General Clay was forced to take a hand. When he commuted her sentence, he described her as a prostitute, a pervert, but not a war criminal. These were the Dachau trials, totally laid to Americans, perpetrated by the evil party.

---

[100]Freda Utley, *High Cost of Vengeance,* 1949, Chapter 7.

PART II

TRUTH IN HISTORY

The establishment that has gained control over much of America, particularly in the media, universities and foundations, and in education and entertainment, openly declares its purpose to destroy morality and our culture, and thereby truth and human society. Those who may claim that they have not so declared, have never criticized or even questioned those who do. It trumpets one holocaust, for the effect of obscuring not only a greater holocausting, but of obscuring the very acceptance of holocausting as a necessary part of a Statist's "new vision."

Surely it is but common sense to recognize this evil party as such, as the same evil party that has single-mindedly planned and executed (1) the destruction of the necessary education for the maintenance of human society, (2) the destruction of Rule of Law, and (3) the uprooting of the culture without which a human society becomes irrational, as clearly ours is approaching.

This evil had a beginning, a foundation, and a history. Three rather extended assaults that have been much dissembled and "revised," will be examined briefly. The first concerns the undermining of our Social Contract, as contained in the conception of our Constitution; thus it is about freedom, in the widest sense. In time it stretches from the colonies, through the beginning of states-rights demands and Abolitionism in the North, Reconstruction and the 14 Amendment, on to the attack of the Constitution in post-WW I, up to WW II. The second assault was made by Franklin Roosevelt in his WW II and the subsequent so-called Cold War. The third is the Vietnam-Watergate syndrome.

A note relates some misunderstandings concerning black people. Any and all statements of facts or opinions are made only in the interest of truth; where misstatements or error occur, they are subject to correction, on the basis of substantiated truth but not in ideological claims. The actions of many people, particularly adherents to the evil party, which certainly include FDR, John Kennedy and Martin Luther King, Jr., have been tremendously destructive of our culture and of our human society. Culture and society are far more sacred than the memory or reputation of any individual; wrong done by individuals cannot be allowed to reflect shamefully upon nation, culture, or human society. It is one of the important purposes of this section to see to it that the evil opinion that has been placed upon America or our human society for certain events is put where it belongs on the responsible individuals. If that dishonors their memory, it is because their imposed "memory" was fraudulent.

WITCH HUNTING

Witch hunting, like magic, was an invention of intellectuals, whose purpose was "social control"[101] through

---

[101]Following the German revolt of 1848-9, socialist-communist elements began to effect the manipulation of cultural influences and social structures through a new science, *Culture geschicts* (cultural history). This was carried to the U.S. by immigrating German socialists, and was taken up by the then sprouting university network of socialist cells, by Lester Ward, A.W. Small, E. A. Ross and Frank Giddings. These were the founders of American "cultural anthropology," as socialist indoctrination along with other "social sciences." Ross's *Social Control*

terror.   From tribal times, through the god-king empires, Greece, Rome, Holy Roman Empire, and through Hegel, religion was an integral part of the State.   Christ, in "Render unto Caesar . . ." seems to have been the very first to demand a separation, which was continued only with Protestantism, and to some degree particularly with the Puritans.   Through the Middle Ages, and before and after, some very evil men, brutes, held high church titles, because of the principle, "everything in the state."   Remember this when people talk about the evils of religion or Christianity.   Cardinal Richelieu was a good example as was the Borgia family in Italy, Henry VIII and many of his type who long headed the Church of England, and rulers and aristocrats of Germany who headed the Holy Roman Empire.   But these people were hardly Christians.

So it was that witch hunting had long been a favorite way of achieving control and of striking at various policy impediments.   People were also tortured and burned in roughly equal numbers for violating guild regulations.   W.P.D. Bliss, founder of American Fabianism (socialist), eulogized the medieval "socialistic" feudalism; he labeled the burning of two men for guild violations as "just cruelty," much like Auden's "necessary murders" by Communists during the Spanish Civil War in the late 1930s.   Confessions for witchcraft or guild violations bore a marked resemblance to Soviet purge trials.

Far greater numbers of people were accused and executed, usually by burning, in Europe than in America; here none were burned.   By the late 17th Century, witchcraft was well recognized as a delusion; there were no witches.   Cotten Mather in fact wrote a book on how to handle alleged witchcraft so as to prevent a spread of accusations. Unfortunately, he also described how the "possessed" were

---

(1901) declared a new law," the greater the ascendancy of the few (elite), the more possible it is for social control."

"supposed" to behave. Therein was his great error.[102]

A group of young girls, it was suggested from the less orderly end of Salem, used his book to accuse an elderly Indian-Negro servant, as a prank. Flogged, she accused others. The offending children felt caught, and required to keep up their pose, so others were accused. Fourteen women and five men were hanged, four died in jail; fifty-five saved themselves by accusing others. Only one man, Giles Corey, refused to play the game; to plead guilty was to hang, to plead not-guilty was to give legitimacy to a mad evil known to be such. He was pressed, crushed, until he died.

When madness prospers, like today, none dare call it madness. But they did dare, when the mad accusations touched the wives of the mighty. What had begun as a spring prank, by early fall was all swept away; the entire court was disbanded, and 150 were released. In a few years, the convictions were annulled and relatives indemnified. It has been haters of America and racial renegades who have used this brief summer incident, this obvious aberration, to vilify the roots of our human society, and to force the perception that Puritans, whose efforts to create a human self-government as the roots of America, were mean, evil, and narrow minded. In a 1940 thesaurus, under "bigot" will be listed Pharisee, iconoclast; a 1985 thesaurus will no longer list Pharisee, it is replaced by Puritan.

It was not witchcraft, as fear of a superstition; it was an "imposed perception," often more powerful than the truth, behind which is always the "force." It may be a mob of men with clubs who tar-and-feather or hang. Or it may be clerks, the weasel-minded with pens who bring suffering, even deaths to millions. The power of public opinion is the power to exclude, and to be seen to exclude; to accuse and condemn and to be seen to crush; to lie and dissemble while publicly lauded. "When treason prospers, none dare call it treason," in Washington, New York, and Hollywood.

---

[102]See S. E. Morison, *Oxford History of the American People* (1965) p. 124.

The historian S.E. Morison gave the above account in his *Oxford History of the American People.* His is an excellent history, up until about 1920, when socialism began, (as Trotsky said of the slug humanitarianism) "leaving its slimy trail, obscuring intelligence everywhere." Numerous times Morison drags McCarthyism into all manner of topics so, of course, he couldn't resist witch hunting.

Socialism-communism (Lenin's one-time friend, Max Eastman, called communism super-fascism) was and is the greatest evil ever created by the imagination and hand of man. Not only has it murdered some 100 million souls, often with torture in peace time, it is destroying the very concepts of human society, truth, morality, decency, honor and freedom. Yet the whole liberal evil party, the "overhead planners" establishment that Lippmann described, that laid sole "claim to being enlightened, humane . . . and taken seriously," not only never criticize it, but anyone who does criticize collectivism is pounced upon with vehemence and hatred.

Now the effect of their attacks exhibit the power "to exclude and to be seen to exclude"; it is a "pariahizing," just as a charge of witchcraft. From such a charge there is no defense. This is not just a turning around of the liberal's charge of witch hunting; that charge was nonsensical. It forced the perception that since there were no witches, there must be no communists. Well there were communists; Eldridge Cleaver came to claim "under every bed." Even such leftists as Victor Navasky, editor of the *Nation,* declared, "they were all communists." The charge of witch hunting was but an arrogant assault, an usurpation of the power to declare the accepted and the contemptuous, within the human society it aimed to destroy.

By no rational means can witch hunting be in any way related to the aborted attempt to rid our society's most sensitive positions from occupation by its avowed enemies, the Communists. All the while this struggle continued, from roughly 1946 when the so-called Cold War began with some limited attempts by Truman to resist Communist encroachments, until the Supreme Court set up protective measures for communists, everyone knew that they could exist and operate only by a strategy of deception -- "nothin here but us chickens boss." Perpetuating the fraudulent idea that the hunting of communists -- deceitful destroyers of everything we held dear -- was witch hunting, marks that user as a renegade and a member of the evil party.

The charge of witchcraft or witch hunting must be recognized as a panic-driven mob passion. People did <u>not</u> believe in witches; Giles Corey did not, nor did the leaders who shortly stopped it when it began to impinge on them. The evil was not a fear of witches, it was a fear of being charged, knowing that the very charge was a condemnation. But it is a condemnation only for those who have not the power or position to respond, as the leaders did. Communists were not "witches"; it was they who held the power to strike down.

There are two important and rather separate parts or aspects to this charge of witch hunting. The more virulent, evil feature is of recent invention. The witch hunting episode of Salem was a very brief and singular aberration of one summer; it was not witch hunting but an arousal of mob fears. Yet the evil party, particularly liberals since the 1960s, have "forced the perception" that it constitutes the total truth and characterization of the Puritans. All the good works and virtues of the Puritans, founders of our Nation became as in an instant nothing, less than nothing, evil. It would be like mentioning blacks only in connection with cannibalism, or Jews only as the murdering of their neighbors, who had accepted Judaism, submitted to circumcision, and "on the third day when they were sore" the Jews rose up and killed the men and enslaved the women. Salem no more represents Puritan history than that represents the Jews. The same evil Marxian "one-enemy" trick was worked in Vietnam. From the beginning, the Communist Cong's only weapon was terror, terror to force the peasants to snipe or booby-trap the Americans. Burning and torture were their only tools. Then in the wake of the chaos of Tet, hearing that renegades were chanting at home for the Cong to kill them, being sniped and booby-trapped from all around, at My Lai a small group of maddened Americans struck back. Once! and My Lai was a legitimate target. The result was that the evil party in New York made it the symbol of the entire war.

The second or more conventional perception of witch hunting is that of stigmatizing almost any demand for truth. But today the evil party more commonly charges "racism", as formerly they did witch hunting. Those who control the "power" can strike down any opponent with the thunderball of racism, and anyone caught is burned. But simple observation will show that by far the most egregious racism today is by blacks and Jews. With the power of the media they are able to follow Trotsky's tactic of demanding victimhood, even as they attack Aryans, or white males, and force upon them a second class status.

ABOLITION AND THE FECULENT 14TH

Abolitionism had two major aspects, the one most commonly noted having to do with care for the Negro slave as a human being; it is said to have been predominately a feminist movement, concerned principally for the women. The other side is seldom noted: it was a movement of taught hatred for the South. Yankee historian James T. Adams tells us that the Abolitionists "placed their cause above all others, irrespective of a sane sense of values." Slavery was a great evil which was being abandoned by most of the West, but the Abolitionists insisted upon it being ended immediately, and without compensation, and were willing to demand their way even at the expense of the Union or untold human suffering.

There was a far more intense dislike for the Negro in the North than in the South. The violence used against Prudence Crandall's school for Negro girls in Connecticut should be compared with the "house" Negroes being taught in the South. This dislike of the Negro was extended to a hatred for the fanatical Abolitionists, who aroused passion in such a way as to make slavery a burning issue, without providing a solution.   Lincoln declared that he could not blame the South for not settling an issue for which he himself could provide no solution.   There was a time when Virginia missed by only a narrow margin in outlawing slavery. If the North had been sympathetic and helpful to this effort in a real way, it might well have succeeded.   It would have required some compensation, and a distinct plan for dealing with the freedmen, but the North had only fiery denunciations and a desire to secede from the South.   Moderates such as Hawthorne and Lowell, along with most of the fanatics demanded secession: "They take one way, we take t'other." How little they really cared about the Negro.

Historian Adams notes the terrible results of joining the moral fanatics[103] of Abolition with the political fanatics of Reconstruction.   These latter burned with the knowledge that the freedmen, becoming citizens, would increase Southern population, giving it greatly increased power in the House of Representatives and especially in the Electoral College.

Briefly, what the Reconstruction fanatics (the Radicals) succeeded in doing in 1867 was to destroy completely, for a brief period (that was ended only by the death of their chief), our three branches of government.   Two years after war's end, they had locked out of the Congress Senators and Representatives from Lincoln-reconstructed Southern states, even though the adopting votes of their state legislatures were used, and needed, to pass the 13th Amendment ending slavery. But when the South refused to accept the proposed 14th Amendment, which was of an indefinite meaning and born of hate, the Radicals moved. They totally incapacitated President Johnson with the Tenure of Office Act and with the moil of impeachment, frightened the Court into denying jurisdiction in "political" problems, grabbed the Army from its Commander-in-Chief and, two years after war's end, forced a total military occupation of the South.

------

[103]The source for some of the taught hatred of Abolitionism lay in the socialist movement that began in the 1820s.

Puppet state governments set up by carpetbaggers from the North were ordered to revoke the previous vote on rejection of the 14th; even as they rejected recisions from Northern states.   Lacking the Constitutionally required presidential signature and voted under clearly illegal circumstances, the Secretary of State hesitated to declare the 14th's enactment.   Hence Congress ordered it promulgated.

The 14th is an evil cancer injected illegally into our Social Contract, the Constitution.   It has been claimed, and it is being used, as a repeal of all the essentials of the Constitution that constitutes our Social Contract.   It was not the result of deliberations but of force, deceit and incitement to panic, with threats that the South was on the verge of renewed rebellion.   The people certainly did not believe that they were repealing the Bill of Rights, and the 14th, for nearly a century, was never used to aid the Negro.

In 1886, one of the renegades who hatched it, stood before a corrupt Court and reckoned that they'd had in mind that corporations were people.   It was thus that states were denied the powers -- by the 14th -- that they had been using to reduce the economic and political excesses of industry.   The evils of laissez-faire entrepreneurs were not evils inherent in the market or in some abstraction called capitalism; they were evils of corrupt men in government.   Within some 20 years, the power of the states and of the people to protect their human society, at that time largely from the corruption of money, had been reduced, according to liberal historian Beard, to "a mere shadow."

By the end of WW I the second rape of our Constitutional Social Contract was perpetrated.   Some law cases that clearly were wartime national security cases were tried in federal courts as free speech or press cases from which they were Constitutionally barred.   These cases could be accepted legitimately by a federal court only as national security cases; if they were judged to be cases of free speech or press, they had necessarily to be returned to the state court.   But the federal courts saw that it being wartime, and national security being sacrosanct, as was free speech and press -- either way they couldn't go wrong, so they grabbed a new "precedent", for "protecting" the Bill of Rights. It was an evil lie; they were "incorporating" the Bill as a giant reptile incorporates a bird.

There is endless debate today about "original intent," natural rights, activist judges, "incorporation" and other deceptions. Most people seem to apprehend it all as a matter of getting or not getting a piece of candy. Few relate these arguments to the foundation of their security in a human society.

The Bill of Rights is the real and only significant "wall of separation" in our Constitution. It was intended as, and stood for nearly two centuries as, a wall between the great powers of the national state and the naked individual. Social affairs were reserved to the local governments; they alone were empowered to deal with "all that concerned the lives, liberties and properties of the people." "Congress shall not" pass such laws, and only laws that Congress has passed are legal fodder for federal courts, along with Constitutional issues.

A woman was shot through the head by BATF fascists as she held her baby while standing in front of the plywood shack in Idaho backcountry where she lived. If she had been Black or Jew, there would be national "sorrow", with documentaries and all the correct rituals. Her family had been harassed for nearly two years by federal "agents", with trained shooters and high-tech weapons. No matter how much people generally dislike cults, cults there will always be. The cult in Waco came and went freely; if there had been legitimate charges against them, they should have been served. But again the hi-tech "agents" knew there were no charges that would stand up in court. Besides they had all the nice equipment: tanks with demolition arms, gas, high-powered guns to spray walls behind which they knew there were women, and children.

It was sometimes blacks, sometimes Indians; now it is the hated whites that can be shot down or burned out, without even so much as a public ripple. That is the power of the State, the power of fascism to holocaust.

Every citizen should understand, and every father and mother, and every school must teach their children that they are safe from fascism only when they have a Bill of Rights that stands like a wall[104] around communities keeping out the "agents" of the national state. Statism is impossible with Rule of Law. When activist judges are allowed to invoke imagined penumbras and emanations, nobody is safe. Only when people of a society keep the State subservient will they be safe. Your only protection is in a human society.

Of course some people are evil and all of us are evil some of the time, but all normal people in a human society have consciences. A State has no conscience, nor do Statist bureaucrats, "agents."

What needs to be recognized is that the Constitution was our Social Contract for limited government; it denied the national State power to interfere in our schools, our families, or ordinances against pornography and loitering and crime. The national State was barred from interfering with religion or local laws against indecency or libel, from interfering with rules concerning elections: "from all that concerned the lives, liberties and properties of the people."

The people have never agreed to any changes in that Contract. Even the feculent 14th Amendment, born of corruption and illegality was never recognized by the people as repealing the Bill of Rights. Its "equal protection" and "due process" were clearly procedural, taking no power from the people. Any and all powers that the national state has usurped can and must be taken back.

Remember, if you allow the national State to become your protector, soon only its forbearance will keep it from being your jailer.

---

[104]A well known "conservative" legal scholar some years back expressed surprise that the Bill of Rights had been "so little used until the past 25 years." How do you use a wall? Why obviously you tear it down, "Incorporate" it, like a reptile does a bird.

NOTE ON NEGROES AND SLAVERY

America's two greatest humanitarian democrats, Jefferson and Lincoln voiced the near universal belief, held until recently,[105] that whites and blacks could never live together with acceptance. While recent times are claimed to disproved that belief, common sense and the facts undermine such a claim.   If Booker T. Washington's work had been continued and expanded by others, it might have worked out.   But the Negro leadership: of the Black Caucus, NAACP, and from Chavis and Sharpton to Martin Luther King to say nothing of the likes of the Black Panthers, SNIC and Nation of Islam, have very largely set themselves, though usually in a somewhat clouded-over manner, as hateful enemies of America, or at least the allies of such people and groups.

1.   Black leaders refuse to accept as one of the uncontested terms in the equation that blacks were enslaved by blacks themselves or in cooperation with their Arab-Islamic allies. Slave markets existed in Africa long before Columbus and continued almost to the present. What black leader has ever told his people that Livingston, of Livingston-Stanley fame, was in Africa working to close down African-Arab slave markets?

2.   Lincoln warned Negro leaders during the Civil War that they would not be accepted; he urged them to leave and he would help them.   Middle class blacks, such as those he talked to, who had found America good enough stay in, should help their weaker brothers to find a home of their own.

3.   Many black leaders have demanded reparations.   They ignore the fact that America's most horribly destructive war was fought to free their ancestors who had been sold into slavery by their own people. They ignore the fact that our Constitution and freedoms have been undermined to a large extent in an attempt to bring some equity to black people who refuse to take responsibility for themselves -- as per Booker T. Washington -- and now enjoy telling of their desire to kill us, to destroy our culture. Recently a decision

---

[105]James McPherson, *Perspectives in American History*, Vol. III (1969), p. 470.

was being made to convert a school in one of the few predominantly white neighborhoods left in Detroit to an Afro-centered Malcolm X school, something that would reduce not increase young black people's ability to make a living on their own. As for paying reparations, far more white people of today are descendants of non-slave holders who fought to free blacks or had no relations here during slavery, than of people who owned slaves.

4.   There is a further factor that is most dangerous, in itself, and even more so because daring to raise it may well be used as a reason for killing the messenger. Studies have suggested that the great core of the big-city Third-world underclass are people of IQs so low that they can never be expected to care for themselves, let alone carry some of the load of society. Sometimes these "families" run 10 to 20 children. What is bound to happen when some establishment of the future decides that carrying this load is not a part of their "vision"?

5.   The irrationality of the liberal establishment's policies concerning blacks, or "racism" generally, are equally as mad as its policies on education, welfarism, violence, and other social policies. Louis Farrakhan, to their dismay, punches holes in their nonsense, but he adds lies and his own racism; clearly he is not the liberals' boy. M.L. King was, on the other hand, an integral part of the liberal-to-communism continuum. It is not the intent here to defame Mr. King, but rather to demand that white liberals who insist that King be raised to national "icon" status, look at the record: (1) King, on Labor Day 1967, orated in Chicago while bongo drums outside led the chant "Kill Whitey . . . Kill Whitey . . ." He called for revolution "all over the globe". (2) The same year at New York's Riverside Church, King compared the U.S. to Hitler's Germany, calling us "The greatest purveyor of violence in the world", and claiming we had killed a million Vietnam civilians, "mostly children". (3) A 1965 Saturday Review article revealed King's tactics of getting "demonstrators" into the streets to provoke a response. (4) In 1981, David Garrow of Duke University presented partially revealed FBI information in his anti-FBI book, *FBI and M.L. King.* Bobby Kennedy ordered the wire taps, not Hoover, nor Johnson. It reveals years of Communist direction and money, from high C.P. officials:

Stanley Levison, Bayard Rustin (youth arm), Hunter Pitts O'Dell, with King announcing, "I am a Marxist" and denouncing "anti-Communism". There was a banker's report of an account of over a million dollars.

FDR

In 1933, as his first major foreign policy initiative, FDR recognized the brutal regime of Josef Stalin, even as some seven million human carcasses stunk on the plains of the Ukraine.

"Corrupt and gullible" Joseph Davies was sent by FDR to Moscow "to win Stalin's friendship at all costs." As Ambassador from 1936 until the war, Davies reported to FDR on Stalin's "brown eyes, exceedingly wise and gentle," even as he was destroying the embassy's "well-staffed . . . highly professional division of Eastern European affairs."[106] Soviet Minister Litvinov declared its records were better than the Soviet's own. Davies had the library dispersed and the files destroyed; George Kennan, in the embassy at the time, "smelled Soviet influence in the higher reaches" of the U.S. government.

Ten months before Pearl Harbor, FDR fired Admiral Richardson, head of the Pacific Fleet at Pearl Harbor. He was told, "You hurt the President's feelings", by telling him that both the fleet and Pearl Harbor's defenses were totally inadequate.

The Japanese had a secret "Purple" code in whose unbreakability they so firmly believed that they entrusted their highest secrets to it. By sometime in 1940, it was effectively broken and a system called "Magic" was developed for doing so. Very few people knew of its existence. Only FDR, Hopkins, Marshall, Hull, Stimson, a few others, and the actual decoders ever saw the messages. They were not entrusted to a professional intelligence group for analysis.

---

[106]Paul Johnson *Modern Times*.

Churchill was given a Magic machine but Pearl Harbor was not. From the so-called "Magic intercepts", the timing and location of the Japanese attack were known, roughly days in advance, precisely by 9 a.m., December 7th, four hours before sunrise over Oahu.

Roosevelt made some top-secret commitments to British Foreign Secretary Eden late in 1938. In 1939, more were made; the so-called Kent Documents consist of some two thousand "secret and illegally exchanged messages" beginning at the time of the Hitler-Stalin joint attack on Poland in September, 1939, Kent was a code clerk in London and apparently sought to warn America that FDR and Churchill were seeking war. He was imprisoned and the messages may have been destroyed. They must have contained information concerning FDR's urging "Poland to resist the reasonable German demands in 1938-39."[107] More to the point, we know that while people of the West, particularly in America, saw Stalin as a far greater and more evil force than Hitler, in 1941 both Churchill and FDR had men in Moscow offering immediate aid almost as soon as Molotov had returned empty handed from Hitler and following Hitler's attack.

From 1939 until 1941, while Stalin and Hitler were allies, there was powerful resistance within the media and in all of the liberal left establishment, including the communist dominated unions, against the "imperialistic" war. These were the only "isolationists" of any power. The real "isolationists" were not the American Firsters, but the liberal-socialists, the communist oriented.

After Stalin was attacked, FDR scurried to get into the war. He asked the Navy to determine what the Japs would do if their oil was cut off. When told they would go to war, he immediately cut off their oil, imposed a virtual embargo on all trade, froze Japanese assets, and closed the Panama Canal to them. He arranged the Atlantic Charter Conference in the lower St. Lawrence to declare war, effectively to save Stalin.

Secretary of State Hull sent the Japanese an

---

[107]Paul Johnson, *Modern Times*.

"ultimatum" on November 26, 1941; Churchill had a hand in tightening it up to total unacceptability. The FBI was reporting on unhindered Japanese spies on Oahu; they were detailing frequent and precise ship locations in the harbor. The "winds" message and "burn the codes" messages were received, then the "pilot" message -- the first 13 parts of the "final" message. (Remember, these were intercepted Japanese "Purple Code" messages to their Ambassador). FDR received it about 9:30 p.m., December 6, and it was testified that he declared, "This means war!" The 14th part was delivered about 9 a.m., December 7, and the Navy Chief Admiral Stark declared, "I must warn Kimmel!" No one did.

The Pearl Commanders were played for suckers, as were the American people; all information concerning the Magic intercepts had been assiduously kept from them. So too for the FBI spy reports taken along side of them; they knew nothing about Hull's ultimatum. It was known that if they had even suspected something and had made any defensive move, however slight, the Japs would have turned away. They <u>were</u> sent a <u>War</u> <u>Warning</u>, but it merely called for a sabotage alert. Washington was informed immediately of their bunching of airplanes, etc., and there were days to send a correction. None came. A Colonel tried to force a warning through to Hawaii but was stopped. A Navy Captain also tried and was stopped by two Admirals.

Harry Elmer Barnes, noted historian, declared that there were three possible reasons why the Washington war chiefs, Marshall and Stark, did not warn Pearl Harbor: they were idiots, traitors, or under FDR's orders not to.

There is no question but that FDR did knowingly sacrifice the Pacific Fleet, some 2,500 lives or more at Pearl Harbor and many more thousands in the Bataan Death March. Every TV station utilizing a publicly owned frequency, ought to be required to excerpt an hour program, for the afternoon of the first Sunday in December, from Manny Lawton's, book on the Death March, *Some Survived.*

Arthur Schlesinger admitted that FDR had "tricked" Americans into the war, for their own good.   Robert

Sherwood wrote, "I burn inwardly," when he recalled his part in the "trickery." But for what purpose had America been tricked? Had it been to save Western civilization,[108] the people could have forgiven FDR.

The true significance of Yalta lies not in its pretensions as a peace treaty or settlement; but as a great offering to Stalin. FDR's Secretary of State Stettinius, who accompanied him to Yalta (Hull had resigned), when criticized for its provisions, demanded, "What did Stalin get that he didn't already have except the Kuriles?" The fatuousity of that reply is revealed by asking, "Why then send a dying man halfway around the world in wartime, to confirm that?" Why was so much blood and treasure poured into such a rat hole?

Insistence on completing some long-struggled for purpose: that alone can justify such tenacity in a dying man. And certainly that purpose was the same one that impelled Roosevelt to "trick"[109] the American people, and sacrifice the lives of thousands on Hawaii and in the Philippines in order to gain entrance into the war. On March 7, 1942, FDR sent letters to American war agencies ordering a "preferential position" in matters of munitions be given to Soviet requests over all allies and even over U.S. Armed Forces. "Unconditional surrender" was "just the thing for . . . Uncle Joe"; son Elliott tells us FDR thought it up while "sucking a

---

[108]Anyone still believing that will believe anything. The war ended in "peace" with horrors as great as the war; mass deportation of millions of civilians, partitions, spoliation, destruction of all things human on a mass scale. Never was the integrity of Western civilization or human values mentioned. The Atlantic Charter was a monstrous lie to achieve war. See F.J.P. Veale, *Advances in Barbarism,* and Freda Utley, *The High Cost of Vengeance.*

[109]Schlesinger's description. That FDR did, knowingly and intentionally, so sacrifice them in order for him to get into the war is spelled out in detail in official government hearings, and is outlined in books by Morgenstern, Beard, Crocker and others. Captain Oliver Lyttleton, British Production Minister under Churchill asserted 6-20-1944 to the Am. Chamber of Commerce in London, "It is a travesty on history ever to say that America was forced into war" (Morgenstern p. 116).

tooth."   In early 1943, "I give him (Stalin) everything I possibly can, and ask nothing in return."   Roosevelt had angrily rebuffed the Chambers-Berle Report on Espionage, in 1939; he had likewise been infuriated over being presented with documentary evidence of Soviet savagery at Katyn Forest; he initiated the evil Morgenthau Plan for pastoralization of Germany.   FDR and Churchill resisted all efforts to bring an early end to the war, and thereby of the holocaust, by an overthrow of the Nazi government.   As the "Strategic Assessment" circulated by Hopkins announced at Quebec (1943), the U.S. must give "every assistance and every effort must be made" to buy Stalin's friendship.   Lend-lease which legally was restricted to war munitions came to include whole shiploads of not only food and clothing but great tonnages of metals, chemicals[110], polymers, whole plants, and nuclear materials of nearly all kinds, including some 1,500 lbs. of uranium compounds in 1943.   General Groves was to testify[111] concerning the struggles between the Manhattan Project and Hopkins' Soviet project for strategic materials and equipment.   As the war was ending, FDR gave to Stalin 860,410 tons of dry cargo and 206,000 tons of liquid cargo for equipping a 1.5 million man Far Eastern army.

The purpose of Yalta was to document these gifts to Stalin, plus: the Kurile Islands, Sakhalin, "pre-eminent interests" in the Chinese naval base of Port Arthur, and the great shipping port of Darien, and the Manchurians railway. Finally the American people were to be made accomplices in slave labor and the holocausting of 12 million Germans from their homes, on to the open road with a sack on their back, where only freezing rain and snow protected them from the plundering, raping and murdering of marauding Soviet troops.

---

[110]43 million gallons of ethylene glycol (Prestone)

[111]See Major G. R. Jordan's _Diaries_

McCARTHY

All the truth about Joe McCarthy, Martin Luther King, Jr., FDR, JFK, Nixon, and others need not be made into a great issue, but the <u>untruth</u> about them, particularly as their actions and intentions damaged or helped America, must be publicly examined.   The future of free society depends critically upon our past; many unpleasant truths of the past can be ignored, but untruths, pleasant or unpleasant are as poisons or cancer in our society.   They must be rooted out and objectors to the rooting out must be seen as part of the poisons.

McCarthy's career was short and inconsequential.   In spite of what you may have been urged to believe, he fired no one, blacklisted no one and, according to liberal even leftist sources, all or nearly all he accused "were communists." If the awful stain of McCarthyism and fascism and Red-baiting had been accompanied with demands for truth, and the condemning of smear by vague liberal media charges and claims of witch hunting, then America would have gained. The fact is they were used for the very opposite: to conceal the inhuman evil of communism.

People must bear in mind that communism was a great evil; it starved to death some six million peasants for Stalin's convenience; untold millions died in the Gulag, in torture, and in the Purge; it crushed the humanness out of all of its people; and it created environmental catastrophes all over its lands.

People who attacked McCarthy were almost all enemies of America in that they supported our worst enemies, expressed direct hatred for America, or sought to brand as evil policies which were widely supported as in America's interests.   Few spent any time defending, improving, or supporting America.

A fascist became anyone who attacked communism. The Communist Party's media, the *Daily Worker,* charged that attacks on Alger Hiss were in fact a "dagger into Roosevelt (and an) indictment of the New Deal as Communist." This is a double sided charge. Being a rather left-wing Democrat in domestic affairs at the time, I did harshly oppose McCarthy for his attacks seemed of little harm to the Reds, but were crippling to the Democrats, as the Daily Worker said. And certainly this was the connotation they intended. What I have come to see is that the New Deal, and much of the Democratic Party for half a century, had strenuously pushed Statism, and destruction of our free society.

Ellen Schrecker, New Left Professor[112] blundered into the truth, "What made McCarthy a McCarthyite was not his bluster (false charges, etc.), but his anti-communism." I.F. Stone complained about "informers and Communist renegades;" he couldn't comprehend that which was closest to himself: an American renegade. Henry Steele Commager, a consistent running-dog of Communism perceived, like Schlesinger, that Communism was in the same spectrum with "liberalism." These liberals agreed with McCarthy that the fate of Communism involved the fate of liberalism.

Nowhere can the paradigm of McCarthyism be found better exemplified than in Hollywood's *Guilty by Suspicion*. It is, of course, about the Hollywood Ten who were "blacklisted by McCarthy." It is "a restrained, intelligent account of a successful director whose career is ruined when he refuses to 'name names'"; "never a party member, he has been wrongfully implicated." "He's very successful," seen in the "easy self-confidence he wears . . . is his tweed jacket." From "Golden Boy on Top . . . the next day he's unemployable . . . as the result of an accusation forced from someone trying to save his job. The studio bowed to pressure from Washington . . . this fall from grace" is intensely emotional.

This is so filled with lies and dissemblings there is hardly sufficient tissue to discuss. As has been known since Lyons's *Red Decade* (the 30s), Hollywood had long been controlled by the Communists and their evil party. They did the blacklisting; they hired principally Communists.   Of

---

[112]*No Ivory Tower*, a "long whine on McCarthyism".

course, they hired and worked with others, but the "others" always knew who pulled the strings. For the communists to cry "blacklisting" is as hypocritical as Marxists crying anti-Semitism.

But even over and above all that, there simply was no blacklisting in the sense of secret black-balling. And there was no pressure from Washington. You see the Communists wanted, needed to work in secret -- hidden. Like a bunch of cockroaches when exposed to the light, they hated it. It was only pressure from the public that urged, not forced, the studios. And usually they were not fired; rather they took assumed names; they took long vacations until it blew over, and then they were back. And when they came back, boy it was tough on the frogs. You see, the Communists were tightly organized, disciplined; against the unorganized non-Communists, they were like a few hunters after a herd of deer.

"Naming names" tells it all, as one commentator wrote, they wanted to be communists, to despoil human society, and they demanded the right to do it in secret. The whole "Guilty by Suspicion" is a damned lie through and through. "They were all communists" wrote leftist editor Victor Navasky of *The Nation*. "Every one . . . had been deeply involved in Communist affairs . . . They were hostile because they were zealots for communism . . . (and they) ran their own blacklists." One editor waged a long and successful campaign to keep Orwell's *Animal Farm* out of the U.S., and the liberals sneer at the keeping out of *Lady Chatterley's Lovers*.

Finally, of course, the "naming names" had nothing to do with McCarthy. The names were in fact named by the FBI even before the HUAC hearings of 1947, three years before McCarthy. The seething hatred and vengeance of the evil party is demonstrated in their removal of Robert Taylor's name from a Hollywood landmark, replaced by "Cukor" forty years later, by people claiming to be animated by opposition to blacklisting. Victor Navasky's *Naming Names* described Robert Taylor as, "didn't really know any names." Ceplair and Englund's *Inquisition* counts Taylor, Reagan, Gary Cooper as "friendly" witnesses whose "function was not to provide the committee with information, but with luster. They didn't name names; they merely lent their names." One of Hollywood's Ten, Director Edward Dmytryk, called the removal of Taylor's name after nearly 40 years "a small, mean-spirited, picayune thing."

Communists have always presented themselves as martyrs for democracy, helpless scapegoats of American fascism. Yet it was they who forced silence about the brutalities of Communism wherever it took root. They lied about being Communists. As *Partisan Review* founder Phillips noted, as members of a fifth-column they demanded that others "defend their right to lie about it."

One of the Ten, Ring Lardner, pointed precisely at the Communist core in the evil party. "We did play a part in everything that was going on . . . Motion picture committee to aid Spanish democracy, Hollywood anti-Nazi League, League of American Writers, would not have functioned without active communists in their forefront."

"Isn't there a difference between 'naming names' and expressing your disapproval of the Party by working against them?" That is corrupt dissembling. When has naming Nazis been questioned on any basis? Communists repeatedly denigrated "informers"[113], borrowing such slurs as "stooly" from crime or unions. Most noted was Lillian Hellman's *Scoundrel Time.* Underneath this was the forcing of the perception that in a period of national tension with Rosenbergs, Klaus Fuchs, Harry Dexter White, Hiss, Silvermaster, Judith Coplon, Lattimore, John Stewart Service, and many more, it was wrong to root out traitors; the American people had no right to inquire into communist (by its very nature treacherous) influence in movies, unions, schools and government. Any child can recognize a difference

---

[113]I.F. Stone, eulogized a couple years ago by the likes of Peter Jennings, whined of "informer spies, and communist renegades." Did you ever hear of a Nazi renegade, or an American renegade? In the Soviet, informing was a <u>duty</u> that was monitored.

between "tattling" about cookies or, on the other hand, little Johnny lighting matches in the storeroom.

The hard pinch comes with the complaint voiced by both Arthur Schlesinger and the Communist *Daily Worker*, and many in between, including Sidney Hook, that Whittaker Chambers "somehow linked FDR and the New Deal with communism." My, my! See the section here on FDR.

John Roche, and generally Sidney Hook, defended the rights of Communists to jabber about overthrowing the government. That has never been the problem; it was their further demand for a right to hold government positions, university professorships or positions in unions, foundations, and teaching. Our world has been upended as today the evil party denies those positions to upholders of human society.

It must be understood that whatever the force was that underlay socialism-communism (bureaucratic Statism) and drove the fierce attacks on, and fired hatred for the basic beliefs of freedom and decency in Western civilization, that force and motivation for hatred still burns, still corrupts, and still destroys everything protective of human society.

NOTE ON McCARTHY

William Rusher tells a story about McCarthy that deserves to be known[114]. I recall it first-hand.

It was claimed that of 30 "suspected subversives" employed as scientists at the very sensitive Fort Monmouth laboratory "all were ultimately vindicated."[115] The truth seems to be that Joe

---

[114]William Rusher, *The American Spectator* (3,1984).

[115]That is not true. Nor was Judith Coplan "vindicated"; she was caught red handed. The problem was that she was exposed by decoded KGB messages, which the FBI refused to reveal. It has likewise been claimed that Lattimore and John Stewart Service were vindicated or exonerated. Neither was; to make a long story short, in both cases, it was the courts freeing them on technicalities. William Rusher *The American Spectator* (3, 1984).

McCarthy got himself ensnared in the Army hearings and in the meantime the 1954 elections went to the Democrats and so went his committee and investigation.

In the Army hearings, the Army lawyer Joseph Welch pulled out a big white handkerchief and cried into it so realistically that he caught a whole afternoon of housewives. Welch looked like Uriah Heep and could play the part perfectly. He was after Roy Cohn: did he <u>truly</u> know of any security risks at Fort Monmouth? Did he, in fact, know any security risks <u>anywhere</u>? If so, "I implore you, sir -- I <u>implore</u> you -- to reveal their names before the sun goes down!"

Old Joe's patience snapped; he intervened to suggest that if Welch was really so all fired eager to locate security risks, he might start looking at Mr. Fisher on his own staff.

It is believed that Welch anticipated generally such a question, because his aide, Mr. Fisher, had been for some time with the National Lawyers Guild which was on the Attorney General's official list of subversive organizations. So, bringing it up was hardly a smear, nor obviously was it prepared. The *New York Times* had examined the case quite extensively weeks earlier. If Welch baited McCarthy into dragging Fred Fisher's record into national TV in order to weep over the cruelty of his doing so, his performance takes the all time hypocrisy prize. It was suggested by others that Welch had in fact "prepared and memorized his part":

"Until this moment, Senator, I think I never really gauged your cruelty or recklessness . . . Little did I dream you would be so reckless and cruel as to do an injury to that lad . . . Let us not assassinate this lad further, Senator. Have you no sense of decency, sir, at long last? Have you left no sense of decency?" With a large white handkerchief this Uriah Heep wiped a few crocodile tears from his rheumy eyes. Perhaps all politicians are cynical, but Joe had met a master from the evil party and he was dead.

The evil party had found its solid footing in TV; with control there, it could control the world, "leaving its slimy trail, obscuring intelligence." If people could be made to sympathize with communists over anti-communists, then anything was possible.

CUBA

The evil party cut its teeth in the media with

McCarthy. It could now come out far more boldly than it ever previously had dared. The touchstone of the evil party's core, through this period and ever since to a fading degree, has been an attitude toward the Spanish Civil War (see Note). The evil party of a media-bureaucracy alliance struck first in Cuba in the late 1950s, then in Vietnam in the mid-1960s, and in Washington in the early 1970s; in 1990, it took over the government.

Herbert Matthews, of the *New York Times* editorial board, was a fixed supporter of Communists in the Spanish Civil War and, in May, 1956 reported that he smelled revolution in Cuba; it was "inspired" by the Castro attacks on Moncado Barracks in Santiago, on July 26, 1953, and a second attack on the Matanzas garrison in May, 1956, both ending in senseless killings. Ruby Hart Phillips, the *New York Times* correspondent in Havana, was used by Matthews as an intermediary. Late in 1956, she passed on information to Matthews that Castro wanted to see him.

Matthews, surely under *Times* orders, arrived in Havana on February 9, 1957, as a tourist with his wife and set out on a mountain vacation. Thus it was that he interviewed Castro and his "26th of July movement" in the "impenetrable vastness of the Sierra Maestra." He wrote of "thousands of men and women" who "are heart and soul with Fidel Castro." His "revolt . . . Batista cannot hope to suppress . . . His men adore him." There was much more in these articles to the *Times* in February, 1957. Then a CBS special on "Cuba's Jungle Fighters" and a spread in *Life* in May "proved to be a tremendous boost for Castro."

Eisenhower's second inaugural of January, 1957 was routinely accompanied by the resignations of all ambassadors. Arthur Gardner, working very competently in Cuba, wanted to stay on, but rather mysteriously his resignation was accepted shortly after Matthews' articles appeared in the *Times*. Gardner was pro-Batista, and his replacement, Earl Smith, was a Wall Street broker. Smith was told by a friend, who knew his way around the State Department, that "The decision has been made that Batista must go. Be very careful." (The decision was from down in the lower levels.) Smith made a good try to keep from being snared by Roy Rubottom, Assistant Secretary of State, and W. A. Wieland, Office of Caribbean Affairs. Both had been present at the "Bogotazo" (1948), Peron sponsored riots in Bogota, at which 3,000 died; Castro had been a leader, announcing over the radio, this is a "Communist revolution."

By the end of 1957 Castro still had less than 300 men; the media was quoting up to 2,000. Batista agreed to hold elections with UN observers, provide amnesty and establish constitutional guarantees. But Rubottom succeeded in suspending arms shipments to the government over Smith's protests. Matthews and Ruby Phillips provided every possible media distortion, such as "(Castro) exerts supreme authority over large areas." The plan was to force the perception in Washington that Cuba wanted Castro, and in Havana that Washington would support only Castro. Meanwhile Rubottom and Wieland were cutting off all supplies to the government while keeping them flowing to Castro.

Castro arrived in Havana on January 8, and on January 17, in *Times Week in Review*, Matthews wrote "Dr. Fidel Castro is the greatest hero that their history has known." And the mob cried, "Paredon -- to the wall!"[116]

In August, 1960, former Ambassador Smith of Eisenhower's Administration, testified at a Senate hearing: "The United States government agencies and the United States press played a major role in bringing Castro to power." Mario Llerena who had been Castro's major liaison with the *Times* soon broke with Castro, and reaffirmed Smith's statement. Then Major Diaz, who had flown weapons to Castro, defected. Harold Hunt of the CIA wrote that the media's subservience to Castro was so great that the State Department might have deported Diaz if the Senate Committee hadn't subpoenaed him.

In September, 1960, two months before the election, Castro came to Washington. He noted that Admiral Burke

---

[116]Russ Braley, *Bad News* (1984).

had expressed doubts that Khrushchev would fire missiles if Cuba were attacked. Castro said, "Suppose Mr. Burke is mistaken?" In the UN Assembly, Khrushchev took off his shoe and pounded the desk, leading the applause.

NOTE ON SPAIN

Spain had been ruled through the 1920s by Socialists, who were much like British Fabians. But it was civil war within the Socialist Party that generated the Spanish Civil War. Socialist moderation and reforms had done much to effect a peaceful transition from monarchy to a republic. Schools were built and a modest agrarian reform begun. Then came the penetration of the ultra left. Spain's most capable general Francisco Franco warned, in 1935, that "The fronts of socialism, and communism . . . attack civilization to replace it with barbarism" -- exactly what was and still is happening around the world. If the army were divided or neutralized, there would be nothing to prevent a Stalinist forced collectivization.

There was a key election in February, 1936; the communist-led Popular Front, which contained the ruling socialist party, failed to receive a majority, but it didn't wait for the required run-off. It grabbed power and began burning churches and killing church people. The middle-class party was led by Gil Robler, who warned, "Half a nation will not resign itself to die. If it cannot defend itself by one path, it will defend itself by another . . ."

The Popular Front failed to control its militants or to form any kind of stable government. By May, 1936, anarchists began to occupy factories, peasants to claim pieces of land. Killings escalated. Arthur Koestler, in *Invisible Writing,* described how communists invented fascist atrocities; the killings seemed about equal on both sides. As thousands were executed by the Communists in Barcelona, often really a part of Stalin's purge, Guernica was bombed. It was not the first town to be bombed by either side; the target was legitimate and its historical significance to the Basques was not recognized by the German and Spanish bombers. Neither Franco nor General Mola knew of the plans in advance. The Communists, always experts at propaganda, had a field day, used especially to cover the far larger killings of their own, especially in Catalonia. *Time* and *Newsweek* pushed opinions to the Communist side; Picasso made his paint-hoax "Guernica". Auden called for "necessary murders". But Orwell's accounts of communist killings in *Homages To Catalonia* were refused publication.

Navy Communists murdered their officers and used the remaining fleet to prevent Franco's Army from crossing over from Africa. But by July, aircraft from Italy and Germany were able to bring over 3,000 in a single day; in August, 1936, Germans and Italians brought aircraft and guns to Franco, while the Soviets supplied the Communists Loyalists with better tanks.

Franco was not a fascist, nor a lovable man; he had a cool head and great reserves of courage and will. He won because of his capacity for detail and his judgment.[117] The Loyalists lost not only because of a lack of control within their own organization, but most especially due to the very disruptive intrusion of Stalinist agents seeking to make sure that no units had victories that were not clearly under the Communist rule. Stalin got away with 500 tons of Spanish gold while giving them some excellent tanks, but clearly he was not going to let them win unless he gained full control.

The lesson to be learned from Spain concerns what happens when ideology displaces the culture of a human society. Franco brought a recovery to Spain, much as Pinochet did later to Chile. A similar lesson, but quite different in result, occurred in Argentina. Argentina was the first Latin American country to achieve "economic take-off," but during its heyday of the early 1940s, it succumbed to the cancer of government promises, regulation of unionism and welfarism under Peron. He combined the worst of Marxismo and Fascism. Argentina forfeited its opportunity to become a truly modern state in a disaster that spread throughout Latin America - - government promises and a huge parasitic state.

VIETNAM

John Kennedy sat at the round table in the cabinet room of the White House discussing the impending coup. A flash message came in: The Ngo brothers were dead.

---

[117]Paul Johnson's account in *Modern Times* is most complete.

General Taylor, next to him wrote that he saw on his face "a look of shock and dismay . . . which I had never seen before"; the President rushed from the room.

Days afterwards a friend tried to cheer him up: they were only tyrants, he said. "No," answered Kennedy, "they were in a difficult position. They did the best they could for their country".

Years later, Roger Hilsman mused, "We were all misinformed about the obstacles the Vietnamese culture represents . . . nobody had the knowledge to permit the kind of social engineering we were undertaking." This shows some mild humility but little sense, for the same bunch are at it today in Washington.

Renegades in the media and in the State Department had succeeded in "Getting Diem", in order <u>to move the war along</u>; even as Ho Chi Minh was making open overtures towards a settlement! Within a month, Johnson tells us that Lodge had reported that the country was going to Hell in a basket, and Ho was making his own settlement. It took almost ten years to recover; by then not only the media but our Congress was controlled by the evil party.

The transcending legacy of Vietnam is constructive and positive. In the early 1960s, every country in Southeast Asia was beset by a powerful Communist movement: Thailand, Malaysia, Indonesia, Philippines, Singapore. The Vietnam struggle and its terrible outcome almost totally decompressed that Communist force. Today, and for some years, the fastest growing region in the world has been Southeast Asia, except for Indochina.

John F. Kennedy declared at his inauguration. "(We) would pay any price, bear any burden . . . support any friend, oppose any foe, . . . (for) liberty". A blank cheque tossed in the wind.

In 1954, both Ho Chi Minh in North Vietnam and Ngo Dinh Diem in the South, faced chaos in the respective portions of their homeland, partitioned according to a Geneva Conference of that same year. Both were racked by powerful gangster bands, tattered economies, nothing running; Diem had the more severe additional problem of communist subversion. With partition, a million refugees had fled south into a country of 16 million and 90,000 went north.

Diem was a nationalist. He was highly-praised and commended by a number of leading liberals. Certainly Ho Chi Minh thought well of him. Marguerite Higgins has given us a deep understanding of him in her *Vietnam Nightmare*[118]; his hold on the vast countryside was through province and village chiefs and their belief in his leadership for the country. In the city, it was merely through the ordinary police, and in emergencies, the Army. Diem had ended the chaos and the South had become the only exporter of rice in southeast Asia. Diem had beaten Ho in the economic war, and thus became the "major obstacle" which had to be destroyed before the Communists could win. In May, 1959, the Central Committee of the Vietnam Communist Party met and declared war on South Vietnam. So much for the lie of the "Civil War."

Late in November of Kennedy's first year in office, that old Harvard jungle fighter, John Kenneth Galbraith, stopped over for a two day, first visit, to Vietnam. His resulting advice to Kennedy was: "Diem is exceedingly bad . . . only solution is to drop Diem . . . will be neither difficult nor dangerous". It seems that the evil party in Washington had come to recognize that Diem was the core of anti-Communist resistance, and if anti-Communism was bad in Washington and New York, it must also be bad in Saigon. Galbraith's advice flew in the face of liberal Justice W.O. Douglas' evaluation of Diem: "a hero . . . revered . . . honest and independent and stood firm". The historian Joseph Buttinger had just finished a history of Vietnam, *The Smaller Dragon,* (1958) in which he acclaims Diem's rebuilding as the "miracle of Vietnam", after it had been given only six months to live.

In 1961, Kennedy sent General Maxwell Taylor to Vietnam for a military appraisal; this produced the beginning

---

[118]Marguerite Higgins, in *Our Vietnam Nightmare* (1965), has provided an invaluable account of the essential part of the war. Ellen Hammer's *Death In November* (Diem's) (1987) is also valuable.

of a flow of men and equipment. As a result, by July of 1963, the rate of communist infiltration and attacks was way down and many Cong were entering Diem's amnesty program. Also by July, Ho Chi Minh began efforts, carried out openly, to reach a settlement with the South.

But forces were beginning to concentrate on Diem. Much against Diem's advice, Averill Harriman had (1961-1962) succeeded in negotiating a neutrality treaty for Laos; Eisenhower had urged strengthening Laos as a peg to hold back the Communists. Diem foresaw correctly that Ho would pay no attention to the neutrality while he, Diem, would be required to honor it. Without this almost renegade mistake there would have been no Ho Chi Minh Trail (or Harriman Highway), and no need for bombing Cambodian sanctuaries.

By May of 1963, Tri Quang and David Halberstam were beginning to produce events in South Vietnam. It was known that Tri Quang's brother was one of Ho's men in charge of subversion in the South, and that Tri Quang had been associated with a communist school in Hanoi that trained agents to act as Buddhist monks. The first act of Tri Quang was to create the Hué Buddhist riot of May 8, in which eight Buddhists and one Catholic were killed. There had been a mix up in orders concerning flags, but this had been straightened out with Tri Quang. Nevertheless he continued even more violently to incite the crowd. Troops were called. As they arrived, the Province Chief testified later there were "two loud explosions . . . on the veranda . . . then broken glass, gun shots, and exploding grenades. All evidence pointed to plastic explosives (characteristic of Cong work) on the veranda. Bodies had their heads blown off -- no metal splinters, no wounds below the chest. The troops fired in the air and shot U.S., MK III concussion grenades into the crowd (not on the veranda). MK III concussion grenades were used by the government for crowd control; their maximum effect is a non-fatal concussion. It was later admitted that the officer, Major Dang Sy, was sacrificed, tried and executed to satisfy Tri Quang.

Tri Quang moved on to Saigon where he entered into

a loose relationship with David Halberstam, the *New York Times* journalist who had arrived there a few months earlier.

Halberstam had quickly set himself against anyone who had a good word to say about Diem: the CIA station chief John Richardson, Kennedy's new Ambassador Fredrick Nolting, all the military heads, and especially Marguerite Higgins. Halberstam, Neil Sheehan and Pham Xuan An (who was also a Ho spy, a Communist colonel, who worked for *Time*) "had created a small but first-class intelligence network", so wrote Halberstam; they worked in coordination with the puppet Buddhist Tri Quang and his gang of radicals.

The "Buddhist crisis" which had started with the Hue bombing on May 8, turned to self-immolation, burning with gasoline. These were always announced to the American media so that they could have their cameras ready for the event. Street demonstrations and violence by Tri Quang's thugs were all recorded by the media.

On August 19th, word went around that the pagoda which Tri Quang and his gang had taken over, Xa Loi, was to be raided by the government. Tri Quang told Dennis Warner that he hoped "they would kill one or two of us".

None were even "seriously injured", said CIA's Richardson. The goal of the raid had been the arrest of Tri Quang, but he escaped and was soon given sanctuary at the American embassy where a new ambassador, Henry Cabot Lodge, was taking over. Halberstam had reported "impossible to know how many were killed . . the true toll was never known". Actually little damage of any kind was done and the CIA reported none hurt seriously.

There is solid testimony that senior generals requested Diem to order the raid, because Tri Quang's demonstrations, at times three or four thousand strong and with "the Viet Cong right amongst them", were getting out of hand. But whether the generals or Diem's brother, Nhu, directed the pagoda raids (of August 21), was immaterial. Tri Quang was a renegade, openly and admittedly seeking the overthrow of the government during war time; putting him out of business was proper, if ordered by the dog catcher. But he escaped, and was soon given "asylum" in the American embassy -- a man of whom Marguerite Higgins had already written that "he wanted Diem's head wrapped in an American flag." The horror of Vietnam grew from the fact that the American evil party provided Diem's head.

Such stark irrationality can only arise from cross-purposes. There was a clique developing among second level State Department types to "Get Diem", in order to "speed up the war". And, in the media, it was said that after Matthews in Cuba, journalists knew exactly what was wanted in Vietnam -- "Get Diem". And since the generals were the only visible replacements, they must be kept pure, "untainted" by Diem. Ted Szulc of the *Times* had reported, from State Department sources, that a group of the generals had, on August 18th, requested Diem to order the raids, that the radical Buddhists of Xa Loi pagoda opposed any conciliation and resolute action was called for. But Halberstam was coming through with reports that "Nhu did it"; Jimmy Reston who knew nothing about it, declared "only propaganda" from State. And Roger Hilsman used the Voice of America to tell Saigon (who knew otherwise) that Nhu did it, so that that would be the VOA report coming back to New York. Then on August 24th a cable went out to Saigon, ordering a coup and also declaring " . . . whether (the) military proposed martial law or . . . Nhu tricked them . . . We recognize the necessity of removing the taint on the military for pagoda raids . . .".[119] Hilsman again, "after the closing of the pagoda on August 21st, facts become irrelevant". E. R. Morrow wrote, "feelings ran so high . . . that the process of reason could not function." Harriman became so overwrought at Nolting that he refused him a ride in "his" limousine back to the State Department, and yanked out an ear plug, refusing to hear what Diem had to say. The *Times* cabled Halberstam

---

[119]In other words, the truth didn't matter. This momentous cable, ordering the destruction of the government, written and sent by the second level State Department renegades, was not given to the top level U.S. government for consideration and was denounced by them. JFK gave it only mechanical approval that was never rescinded.

concerning the great spread between Higgins' stories and his and he went ballistic. Any more questions about, "THAT WOMAN'S COPY AND I RESIGN, REPEAT RESIGN".

When the generals refused to coup, their pay and pay for their troops were threatened by Lodge and finally a pay hold was implemented.[120] All of Diem's supporters, Nolting, Richardson, the military heads except General Harkins, were removed. In September, Kennedy had sent General V.H. Krulak, head of counterinsurgency and Joseph Mendenhall, a State Department expert on Vietnam, to make a tour to determine the effect of the "Buddhist crisis." On returning, they each submitted reports; JFK called them in and asked them whether they had been to the same country. McNamara and General Taylor again investigated and reported back in October: coup "should not be undertaken". General Harkins, Head of the Military Mission warned October 30: " . . . no one (else) with the strength of character of Diem . . . no generals justified to take over in my opinion . . . Leaders of undeveloped countries will take a dim view of our assistance if they . . . believe the same fate (coup) lies in store for them."

Kennedy held a National Security Council meeting October 30th to consider the coup. It must be emphasized that Hilsman had used the knowledge that certain settlement talks were going on between Ho and Diem to hurry the coup -- "they might sign a peace and kick us out". Also the "Get Diem" movement, for which Halberstam and Sheehan and Hilsman and Harriman had worked so hard, had as its purpose "to move the war along". Now with the coup only a couple of days away, the official minutes of the NSC meeting has JFK asking "that we try to find out who the key people are." Bobby found "no sense to support a coup . . . in the hands of a man not now known to us". President Kennedy did not understand why all the province chiefs would be removed; Taylor had to explain that Diem's men would not be trusted by the rebels.

---

[120]General Minh, "The aid cuts erased all doubts."

A Hilsman memo published by the *Chicago Sun Times* urged that all of Diem's family be brought "under the control of the coup . . . warn the group to press any military advantage . . . destroy the palace if necessary . . . Unconditional surrender . . . for the Ngo family . . . should be treated as the General's wish."

Higgins had reported that the war was going well in August; the Pentagon Papers supported her. The war turned quickly against the South after Diem's death. The *New York Times* gave Higgins a large, two column obituary -- she had contracted a jungle parasite of the liver and died in Walter Reed on January 3, 1966. Unstinting in its praise of her WW II and Korean reporting, it never mentioned that the top of her career was *Our Vietnam Nightmare* which gave an account of the war totally opposite from the *New York Times.*

Some four short months after Diem's death, according to the Pentagon Papers, McNamara went back to Vietnam and reported to Johnson, "the control structure from Saigon down into the hamlets (has) disappeared." Diem's government that had accomplished so much was held together not by secret police, but by his integrity, leadership and wisdom; now his province chiefs were gone. After Diem was killed, with others of his family, most anti-Communist leaders were run into hiding or killed. Tri Quang's demonstrations and immolations increased. Diem left some 300 political prisoners in jail; soon they were to run to the thousands. The only government left was repression. With the country in chaos, it took three years of Americanization to destroy the Communist threat at Tet. That victory was given away by the media. More years of re-Vietnamization were required to put the South into holding their own; that was given away under cover of Watergate when the evil party in the media took over Congress.

Wilfred Burchett, the Australian, Communist-journalist told Keyes Beech, "Diem was a national leader (as Higgins had reported), you will never replace him, never." The NFL (Viet Cong) head, when finally convinced that the Diem's assassination was not a hoax, declared, "The Americans have done what we couldn't do for nine years". Ho Chi Minh, who always admired Diem, was shocked at the assassination. He declared he "couldn't believe that the Americans could be so stupid."

But clearly it was not stupidity, but renegadism, treachery. If the evil party could grasp control of the media and produce that irrational nonsense, use second and third stringers in the State Department to destroy the government of a small ally fighting for its life, it could certainly have put a couple of sharpshooters on grassy knolls in Dallas[121] and convince a court that was renegade to begin with, that "nothing of the kind ever happened". Read of the sheer dissembling of the Court's Justice Robert's "investigation" of Pearl Harbor, in Morgenstern or Beard.

Had there been any truth to the claim that it was necessary to remove Diem in order to move the war along, then there would have had to be plans and initiatives that he was holding up and which could have been activated immediately on his elimination. There was nothing of the kind. Rather, there was the certainty -- the repeated warning -- that Diem's elimination would bring chaos. So what did the "Get Diem to move the war along" bastards do after Diem was gone? Why they took a widow's break and then came out with "the war is unwinnable", then "the war is criminal", and then "America is criminal". They were the criminals.

On the Communist Tet offensive of 1968, and the war generally, it has been said: "The offensive proved catastrophic . . . (but) propaganda (largely U.S.) transmuted this military debacle into a brilliant victory . . .", as wrote Truong Nhu Tang, Viet Cong minister, in the International Herald Tribune (10, 9, 1982). Uwe Siemon-Netto, a West German (five years in Vietnam) correspondent wrote, "I am haunted by the role we journalists played . . . What prompted us to make our

---

[121]Certainly the evil party did destroy the Vietnam government, and thereby any rational basis for the war. If they were so intent on this deed certainly they would have recognized the importance of also getting rid of JFK, who might have been more effective in rallying the U.S. to win the war after Diem than was Johnson.

readers believe that the communists, in power, would behave . . ." We covered atrocities such as My Lai extensively (a single incident in which 109 were killed), but neglected to tell of communist massacres, "infinitely greater war crimes (conducted) as a matter of policy." Some 4,800 were slaughtered during Tet-1968 in Hué alone, 2,500 were bulldozed into one massive grave.

"Never has distortion by the press reached such limits . . . the Western press emerged as the most effective weapon in Hanoi's arsenal". Ian Ward, *London Daily Telegraph,* (1972).

Peter Jennings, on August 30, 1989, touted a book by an Army historian, W.M. Hammond, declaring "the Army has concluded that the media were not to blame". (If treason prospers, none dare call it treason). Ask the *New York Times'* Reston, who insisted in 1975 " . . . historians will agree that the reporters and cameras were decisive in the end. They forced the withdrawal of American power from Vietnam". A *Times* news story (4, 13, 1975) predicted an "Indochina without Americans life will be better for most".

A few months before JFK went to Dallas, Bobby orated, "We are going to stay in Vietnam until we win. The American people want to help a nation that gives of its blood, sweat and tears for freedom". A few short years later, during most of which he served in the highest position of justice in the country, he cried out to chanting mobs, "What we are doing in Vietnam is like what Hitler did to the Jews".

With Harriman's irrational neutralization of Laos, the Communist North transported men and supplies south along the Harriman-Ho Highway -- which followed along the long South Vietnamese border -- in the neutralized Laos. Though the Communists had no right to be there, the media not only called these areas "sanctuaries", but insisted that they be treated as such. Thus, Ho was able to move men and supplies south with, in a sense, U.S. protection. Extending these "sanctuaries" into Cambodia allowed a build up of troop concentrations within some 30 or 50 miles from Saigon and other important centers. Then, at moments of opportunity, they would spring across the border, burning and rocketing.

CAMBODIA

Near the end of Johnson's term in 1968, his Ambassador to India, Chester Bowles, was informed by Cambodia's Sihanouk that he was "not opposed to U.S. hot pursuit in uninhabited (by Cambodians) areas"; in fact it "would be liberating us". <u>But</u> keep it secret what you are doing; we have to live next door to Big Brother. A Viet Cong rocket attack on Saigon on March 15, 1969, pushed Nixon to order a B-52 strike on the Cambodian sanctuaries. There was no complaint, no reaction from Phnom Penh, Hanoi, or Peking. Further strikes were ordered without protest. The real fact was that the communists were <u>not</u> supposed to be there. It was believed that these strikes contributed to the North Vietnam decision to have the NFL (the Cong) offer a peace plan at Paris. The *New York Times* noted this as progress, especially since the offer did not claim to be the only one possible. But, on the front page of the issue containing that editorial, Wm. Beecher of the *Times* Washington bureau reported a story "leaked" to him of the sanctuary raids. This is the kind of damaging leak that forced the need for the "plumbers" -- the leak fixers.

During WW II no journalist, nor anyone else would make public secret information that came into their hands by any means, for clearly it could only help the Nazis. But to let the Communists know, has been held to be a totally different thing by the evil party and all of their jackals. There should never have been any need for "plumbers". Their existence points to a pernicious moral deficiency not just in the evil party that was openly promoting the communist cause, but in all of those, particularly the young and the churchy, who were deceived or wanted to be deceived by the good purpose of peace stretched threadbare over the easily recognized greatest of evils.

Our strikes into the "sanctuaries", despite the leak,

greatly reduced the war in the South, as had the devastation of the Viet Cong by Tet - 1968. Sihanouk broke relations with the U.S. when Diem's government was assassinated in 1963, kicking out all Americans lest they pull one on him. But in July, 1969, relations were restored, following the initial raids on the Communist invaders. In January, 1970, Sihanouk left Cambodia for a two month vacation, leaving Premier Lon Nol and a cousin, both anti-Communists, in charge.

Lon Nol, presumably, organized an uprising of 20,000 Cambodians who sacked the embassies of North Vietnam and of the Viet Cong in Phnom Penh, on March 11, 1970. More demonstrations followed; Nol ordered all Communist forces out of Cambodia.   Sihanouk, then in Moscow, learned that he had been deposed. The large North Vietnamese forces in the border sanctuaries launched an attack toward Lon Nol's forces near Phnom Penh. This provided a unique opportunity for the South and for U.S. forces to hit them in their rear along the border. The Parrot's Beak was a large protrusion of Cambodia into South Vietnam, like an arrow, that came to 33 miles from Saigon; Fishook was another protruding sanctuary coming to 50 miles from the capital. Nixon ordered a strike, and went on TV to announce that it was but a temporary incursion, not an invasion; it was designed to draw Ho's armies away from Phnom Penh, and provided an opportune time to hit these staging areas which were used for assaults on Saigon.

That was the kind of movement that forced the Communists to the peace table, but that was exactly the kind of peace that the evil party did not want. The media succeeded in forcing the perception that the "secret" bombings -- which soon were no secret to anybody -- were Nixonian evil because they were "secret"; and Cambodia was a peaceful little nation which had been madly attacked by the U.S. out of frustration.

When on April 29th, South Vietnamese hit the Parrot's Beak, the *New York Times* headlined, OPPOSITION IN SENATE, "rising peril seen" in subhead, "Senators Angry". As though the South were not allowed to strike back at assault areas hitting its capital. On April 30th, the U.S. strike into Fishook produced a volcanic response. "Military Hallucination" stormed the *Times*. "Time and bitter experience has exhausted the credulity of the American people and Congress . . . clear breach of Cambodian neutrality," Tom Wicker, "The invasion of Cambodia . . . ".

On May 1, at a Joint Chiefs briefing, Nixon ordered " . . . take out all the sanctuaries, knock them all out . . . so that they can't be used again". The media stormed into Congress, which reacted properly. May 2, the *Times* editorialized "Cambodian Quagmire", "can they (we) get back out?" Anthony Lewis, " . . . massive armed attacks in a foreign country . . . " Congress, particularly Senators Cooper and Church, threatened to cut Army funding; Nixon cancelled the order.

At Kent State in Ohio, there was violent student action: trash set afire, bottles smashed against police cars, Viet Cong flags, blacks standing in black military grab, a whole street was set afire. Molotov cocktails, machetes, ice-picks, chunks of wood with nails protruding appeared from nowhere. Some 1,000 rioted on May 1; Saturday, May 2, some 2,000 euphemistically called "students" tried to burn the ROTC building; firemen and equipment were attacked, police and firemen injured by rocks. They moved to burn the president's house but found it ringed by highway patrol. Ammunition in the ROTC building began going off, and about 10:00 p.m., the National Guard arrived.

Policemen and guardsmen were injured by rocks and thrown glass. Six airplanes were damaged by a truck and the airport office was burned. Guardsmen were told "We'll get you tonight you bastards". Ten Blacks walked past the Guardsmen, spitting on them. Bags of human feces were thrown at them. It went on from there; a full gallon can of gasoline was retrieved from the administration building. Tear gas was used at different times, as when some 3,000 converged on the president's house. A grand jury later noted "a level of obscenity and vulgarity never before witnessed".

Monday, May 4, a large crowd of "students" began an attack on the Guards. It gradually increased in savagery, with bricks and golf balls studded with nails. Tear gas was used but the canisters were thrown back among the troops, who were now wearing gas masks. The troops left a sports field and parking lot area and retreated up a grade toward Taylor Hall. Suddenly troops wheeled and fired without taking off their masks; 28 guardsmen fired 55 M-1 rifle rounds and five pistol shots in 13 seconds. Most of the shots went, not into the crowd near to them, but down into the parking lot area.

Several thousand people gathered for an attack on the troops, but faculty members deterred them. On May 5, the school closed.

NOTE ON KENT STATE

The Kent State Riot of the first week of May, 1970, was created by the SDS. It had become a major force at Kent State in 1968, operating by 1970, six or seven communes from which renegades seeking to destroy America operated, making trips to Cuba, Budapest, or around the country to instigate violence. "Regional travelers" moved from place to place tying together militants, and forcing action. Mark Rudd, who led the riot at Columbia, was a "visitor" at Kent.

In April, 1968, Mark Rudd spoke to a crowd of 1,000. Arsonists burned down West Hall. A black renegade newspaper called for "killing of all racists", killing of policemen.

In 1969, SDS conducted a "Spring Offensive" which led to a confrontation over demands. Their campus charter was revoked and 58 arrests were made. The Weatherman faction of SDS operated five communes in Ohio. These were described by the writer James Michener in his book *Kent State,* as "teaching severe discipline . . . to produce revolutionaries programmed to obey orders . . . You surrender all personal money and will power . . . with total dedication." A threat was made in 1969 to burn down the whole campus.

In the weeks preceding the Kent Riot, Bernadine Dohrn visited Kent frequently. She was the one, speaking of the Tate murders by Manson's commune, who said "they killed the pigs, ate their dinner . . then shoved a fork into a victim's stomach." Was it not the one pregnant?

Also in the weeks just before the Riot, Terry Rubin, urged a crowd of some 2,000 to "kill your parents". A professor and five students were arrested for assaulting a police officer.

The following month at a nearby campus, Jesse Jackson was reported to have urged students "to emulate Fidel Castro, and Mao Tse Tung and . . . topple the system". Bernadine Dohen issued a "declaration of war", burnings, rioting, and dynamitings occurred across the country, as at the University of Wisconsin. A Kent State, senior professor, Dr. Sidney Johnson, faculty advisor to the rioters, was eulogized on his death in 1979. *The Daily Worker*, the official Communist newspaper, noted that he had been a member of the Communist Party since 1936.

Much of what is noted here came from an article by D. D. Murphy, who depended on James Michener's book, *Kent State*.[122] In particular Michener looked at the cause of the Riot.

In 1959, ten Democratic Congressmen and 46 "intellectuals" organized the Liberal Project, "to cleanse the haze from the word 'liberalism'". Their book, *Liberal Papers*, effectively demanded surrender to communism. They urged: dismantle NATO, abandon nuclear deterrence, withdraw from Berlin and turn Europe over to the direction of the Soviets, while allowing them to plug in to our early-warning system.

Richard Barnet, of JFK's Arms Control Agency and Marc Raskin, a McGeorge Bundy aide on the top secret National Security Council, met at a Kennedy Conference in 1961. By 1963, they had created the Institute for Policy Studies (IPS) with money from the Stern Family and from Sam Rubin's Foundation. In 1958, Stern's uncle, Al, was indicted on three counts of spying for the Soviets, and he fled to Czechoslovakia. Stern money came from the Sears, Roebuck magnate, Julius Rosenwald. Rubin money came from allegedly stealing the name of Faberge for a trademark from the family that had to flee from Lenin's Chekas. Victor Rabinowitz also gave money to IPS; he headed a law firm that defended Soviet spies -- Coplin and Hiss -- and was "the chief legal bulwark of the Communist Party".

Cora Rubin Weiss, the daughter of IPS financial backer Sam Rubin, was an organizer of the 1967 "March on the Pentagon" and

---

[122]Dwight D. Murphy, *Conservative Review*, March/April, 1993.

helped plan the big scuffle in Chicago prior to and during the 1968 Democratic Convention (that was when I started abandoning my party).

In January, 1970, Cora Weiss held a "news conference" in the Canon House Office Building where she criticized the government's alleging of atrocities committed in Vietnam. (Atrocities were well known to have been the very thrust of Viet Cong activities in the South from the beginning.) For communists to claim "they didn't happen" was typical. Navy Lt. R. Frishman and Seaman D. Hegdahl had testified before the House Committee on Internal Security about the Communist's inhuman, brutal, treatment of prisoners. Weiss jeered, "Since he was captured as a war criminal he was lucky to have an arm at all".

The Students for a Democratic Society (SDS) was a Communist-terrorist group formed in the summer of 1962 at Port Huron, Michigan by Tom Hayden, and others, Bernadine Dohrn, Mark Rudd, Jerry Rubin. Read *Destructive Generation* by Peter Collier and David Horowitz for the details. You will find that the designations "communist" and terrorists" are almost understatements. The SDS was one of the militant groups that the Institute for Policy Studies sought to coordinate. S. Steven Powell, in *Covert Cadre*, presents the most thorough study of IPS (the core of the evil party and in essence a KGB outpost, where they commonly lectured). He wrote that IPS was a "hub" or core that brought together renegades such as Tom Hayden and Jerry Rubin, representatives from SNCC, the Mississippi Freedom Democrats, CORE and SDS.

There are two reasons for presenting this background on the IPS here in connection with the Kent State riot. First, as James Michener explained, in his *Kent State*, at that time students throughout much of the world were being agitated by Communists. In France, they frightened Dr. Gaulle; Japan's young radicals were the most fierce, yet there was no draft, no war; in Venezuela students had none of the Japanese causes, nor of the French nor American, yet their protests were most violent. In all of these, Michener wrote, there was one "fundamental reason causing this worldwide result", "It is Marxist-based -- Mao Tse-Tung, Ho Chi Minh, Che Guevara . . ."

The second reason for bringing in the IPS, goes beyond their being the puppeteer at Kent State. Note that SDS, which provided the site-leadership at Kent, was organized in 1962 before there was a Vietnam War or any of the other pretended reasons for "revolt". The second reason points to the broad spectrum of festerings pricked by IPS; over-indulged young people around the world was but one of the sores given IPS attention. Communists had a purpose and a core to dramatize that purpose and no one would call their arrogant bluff. As the British Marxist Terry Eagleton declared a few years ago, "There's an enormous prize and we're the only players in the arena."

The real Vietnam War was hardly between Hanoi and Saigon. There was a little war between the communist agent Tri Quang and his Buddhist gang against Diem, [123]another between the Defense Department and the State Department plus media, and one between the Vietnam generals and Diem. But the pay-off was war between evil party renegades who sought a Communist victory over America and our boys whom a treacherous Congress had ordered into war and then abandoned. The media, universities, and entertainers lauded renegade rioters as "peace demonstrators", though they marched and bombed, and chanted for a Communist victory.

Eisenhower had, presumably with some aid, decided that it was essential to stop aggression in Vietnam and the way to do it was through support of Laos, across some 50 miles of South Vietnam. This would have effectively stopped infiltration into the South by holding a 100 mile strip. He didn't have the guts to either initiate it or to cut loose from Vietnam so conclusively as to make re-engagement awkward. Henry Fairlie claimed it was the precise mind of R.C. McNamara and the prim intellect of McGeorge Bundy who took "us" into Vietnam, really took Kennedy, and then they deserted, leaving America holding the dirty bag.

Lincoln noted that even in quiet times men have differed harshly, but in times of great tension and confusion, all sorts of evil things arise from the ground and crawl about. But never, even in his time when the country was rent with a most savage civil war, was there the loathsome slimy renegadism so praised by the media and intellectuals that crawled about during the Vietnam War and even after.

Even a President called the Vietnam struggle a "racist war" and a "criminal venture", following the Communists in the evil party. If so, then WW II must have been quite the same; in both cases we sought to prevent totalitarian enslavement. We sought to

---

[123]They were not legitimate Buddhists at all, but thugs paid by Hanoi who violated every Buddhist principle.

prevent from happening what did happen when the evil party's influence in Congress led to cutting off supplies to the South Vietnamese, who were then defending themselves.

SLOUCHING TOWARD WATERGATE

The media, meaning in particular the bell-wether *New York Times*, knew why the Cambodian strikes were to be kept secret. They knew that the incursion into the "Fishhook" and "Parrot's Beak" were limited actions, designed to force the Communists to the peace table; the *Times* had admitted as much after the sanctuary bombing of the previous year, and they served to protect American servicemen from surprise raids from these hideouts. The *Times* knew that Tet-1968 was a near total defeat for the Communists and that My Lai, where 109 died was an aberration, hit during the confusion just after Tet, and that it was in fact a legitimate target. They knew, on the other hand, that the Cong's principal weapon was the sudden attack with the burning of villages a matter of policy. Finally, the *Times* knew or very soon learned, that there was nothing in the Pentagon Papers embarrassing to Nixon; they concerned only the Kennedy and Johnson administrations, and ended before the termination of Johnson's administration. Can you imagine the *Times* publishing top-secret documents during WW II?

Every person who has risen in a position of strength to do harm to the evil party has been attacked most savagely, with hatred: Whittaker Chambers, Joe McCarthy, FBI's Hoover, Johnson, even Harry Truman, Hubert Humphrey and especially Nixon, now Reagan. When Nixon won the 1972 election by a record landslide,[124] the hate in the evil party

---

[124]When people write or say that America turned against the Vietnam War, or against Nixon after Cambodia, note the 1972 vote. Nixon was never a popular person; he had an uneasy way of doing things. He was not well liked, but when it came to a choice between what they conceived of as America or the evil party, the people chose America in a landslide over the "anti-war" renegades.

overflowed into a vow of vengeance, voiced by more than one media baron.

Reneta Adler served on the "impeachment inquiry staff", whose function it was to articulate the precise charges against the President. Here are some of the things she wrote in her article "Searching" (At. Mo. 12, 1976): " . . . most of the work, almost all the time by almost all the staff was a charade . . . a machine was seen to churn . . . but the machine . . . produced in the end, no case." She wrote, "There never was any doubt among Doar (Special Counsel) and his group that <u>unless</u> there was overwhelming evidence of Nixon's <u>innocence</u> (not guilt!) that the President must be impeached". (e.a.).

Then along a different vein, Doar knew that an inquiry, a report, on the conduct of past administrations "would be among the soundest defenses . . . against impeachment . . . (but) the White House lawyers never undertook anything of the kind . . . an error . . . so profound that it still seems hardly credible".

"It was not a story of inexorable processes of justice . . . forces of darkness vanquished. Nixon's chosen successor has . . . retained (Nixon's unindicted accomplices, and appointed some of the closest to (high positions) . . . unthinkable for men so utterly compromised . . . no revelation . . . has any sense of finality . . . unless Nixon did something beyond what is known . . . his departure seems random, arbitrary and even incomplete."

Perhaps it was an intuition which led her to add, "It has always been an anomaly that whatever we know . . . about the offenses . . . is based in one way or another, on what was known to John Dean". New evidence about Mr. Dean has in fact been uncovered. *Accuracy in the Media* asked Robert Sherrill of *The Nation,* a writer of "impeccable anti-Nixon credentials . . . to comment on the new evidence (in *Silent Coup,* by Colodny and Getlin, to have been interviewed on "60 Minutes"):

" . . . the great lesson of this reportage, (is) that certain crucial events are carved in the public's historical memory . . . almost solely by the *Washington Post* and the *New York Times* and the networks. I think the public should be reminded over and over of this dangerous situation". " . . . any effort by outsiders . . . along more accurate lines is almost surely doomed to fail. The *Post, Times* and networks suppress contrary versions simply by ignoring them . . . I don't suggest that . . . poobahs . . . sit around tables thinking of ways to dupe the public as a matter of routine . . . (but) when their version is seriously challenged, they fall into a nasty collusion of defense . . . CYA means 'We'll cover your ass if you'll help us cover ours' . . . the ass that needed covering here, (with) something the size of a Ringling Brothers tent, was the *Washington Post's* . . . the *Times'* and CBS . . ."

The story that people were forced to testify to, with the threat of extreme sentences, was that John Mitchell wanted some information out of Democratic headquarters in the Watergate Complex. He sent some "plumbers" after it and they got caught. John Dean became central to the cover-up. (Hence Adler's perception that "whatever we know . . . is based on John Dean").

What seems to be clear now is that old John Mitchell, and Nixon, knew nothing about the break-in; there never was, in fact, any information that they wanted. Actually John Dean planned the whole break-in for his own interests. There was an address book in there; it contained the names of a call girl ring used for visiting Demo-big wigs. John Dean's girlfriend -- to be his wife -- was in it and he wanted that date book. The burglars were caught with the key, not to Larry O'Brien's desk, but to the desk that contained that book, which then came into the hands of the government, and which Dean still tried unsuccessfully to obtain. What was Dean to do? Why confess to the break-in; but he was breaking in for Nixon. No one ever asked why the burglars were carrying that key. Mitchell and Nixon never knew what hit them; they tried to cover for their people but didn't know for what.

Silent Coup was on the *New York Times* Best Seller list

for several months. As the Watergate anniversary neared, the *Times* ran a full page and a half of Watergate; it devoted eleven lines to *Silent Coup,* concerning only the fact that Dean was suing the authors. Mike Wallace spent much time and money and was "very excited" about a documentary on *Silent Coup* concerning the "black book". Then click! No show.

What is important for you to recognize is that all this is only marginally related to Vietnam, to Watergate, to the Pentagon Papers, to all this crap. These were but skirmishes; the central thrust of the evil party was to defeat, to derogate, to humble, to weaken in any way the human society that they sought to replace. Nixon had Vietnamized the war, withdrawn the troops under an agreement with South Vietnam and ratified in the peace treaty that we would continue to supply the South, which was then holding its own. Removing Nixon was essential to the dishonoring of that promise. It was a mean, dirty, gutless thing to do. The war had been won! It was thrown away by Congress because that is what the evil party demanded. When treason prospers none dare call it treason!

Why was it that the "White House lawyers never undertook a report on the conduct of past administrations," as Adler noted?   Can you find a single person who has any rational, concrete idea of what Nixon did do, beyond some vague "cover up"? If some act was illegal, why need a charge of cover-up. For both what Nixon did and especially what was past conduct of recent Presidents see Victor Lasky's, *It Didn't Start With Watergate.* Check the Otepka case, Ervin's clearing of Nixon, and the planned outcome of the investigation.

SOURCES

There are very few general history books that present an honest account of WW I onwards. S. E. Morison's *Oxford History of the American People* is excellent up to the beginnings of socialism, which begins to take effect following 1900. For WW I, the New Deal and anything subsequent it is incomplete and unreliable. I know of nothing that can compare with Paul Johnson's *Modern Times 1920-1980*. Although it is British, and from their viewpoint, it has an excellent coverage of social and cultural movements as well as wars. John Truslow Adams' *March of Democracy* (2 vols.) is generally and especially very good for the Abolitionist movement.

I know of no satisfactory single account of the New Deal, but Felix Morley, a one-time New Dealer, wrote *Freedom and Federalism* which contains a number of important insights into the New Deal. See also *The Roosevelt Myth*, J. T. Flynn (1956); *Suicide of the West*, J. Burnham (1960); *Memoirs*, A. Krock (1968).

For a good, generally complete, but brief account of WW II and politics, read G. N. Crocker's *Roosevelt's Road to Russia*. For Pearl Harbor read C. A. Beard's, *President Roosevelt* or G. Morgenstern's *Pearl Harbor.*

Vietnam cannot properly be understood at all without Marguerite Higgins', *Our Vietnam Nightmare.* Ellen Hammer's *Death In November* is excellent; Russ Braley's *Bad News* has excellent accounts of a number of Cold War engagements -- of Cuba as well as Vietnam, Cambodia, the Pentagon papers and other important matters.

The treasonous subversions of the past half-century are very important and it is imperative that they be well understood. Read John Stormer's small (1964), *None Dare Call It Treason* (some two and a half million copies the first year). Allen Weinstein set out to vindicate Alger Hiss and Radosh and Milton the Rosenbergs; the resulting *Perjury* and *The Rosenberg File* are detailed texts on the writhing of the entire liberal establishment, seeking to obscure the evil.

8. LANGUAGE AND WORDS

INTRODUCTION

> Cicero: The aim of writing is to make it impossible to be misunderstood. Derridians, please note.

> "When the Tao had no name, that was the beginning of heaven and earth; when it had a name, that was the Mother of all Creation", (the beginning of humanness): *Taō Te Ching.*

Language as communicability is older than words. Communication through ritual is older than fish. Gestures and expressions, or more generally body-language, are common in most mammals. Words apparently began with imperatives, interjections and epithets, growls and purrs; verbs grew naturally out of these.

Much revealing information about culture can be found in philology. Owen Barfield compared the word *cereal,* from Roman Ceres, goddess of corn and flowers, with *panic* from the Greek Pan, the protector of flocks and herds. *Cereal* from the Romans is the name of an object, seeable and touchable; it tells us something of Rome but very little about corn or the Romans. *Panic* is from the spiritually minded Greeks; it relates to man's feelings and inner world of consciousness, ungraspable, unseeable. The "word" *panic* is more closely related to the thing, than in the case for "cereal". "In that intangible inner world, words are themselves all we have."

But they tell of simple men at the dawn of consciousness, gripped by an invisible "force" that could set their minds reeling and their flocks flying in panic. What could it be but some invisible force?

It is often said that the mind thinks in words. But more primitively, we seem to think in images and patterns; later words become symbols for images. The totem was the symbol, the image for the clan, and hence became the word, in a sense the first written word. Words as syntactic speech likely evolved most connectedly with feelings, for there are no images for such as homesickness. The mind began to think in words only after having developed along reliably accustomed paths -- even though these paths run to the edge of understanding.

Man needs an overall view (Schweitzer's world-view) of his universe, his society, and his relation to them, and to the ultimate mystery upon which he and all else is grounded. Comprehending this and his feelings of guidance in this mystery is the essence of religion. Thus new knowledge can be fitted into, and made conformable with a framework of connections, or patterns, in a world-view which gives structure to a culture and makes usable all history and tradition.

It is by the perception of such patterns in the new and unknown, similar to old ones we comprehend, that we come to grasp new ideas and concepts. We might believe that in the far distant past, it occurred suddenly to someone that the pattern of grasping, as for a distant branch, could be likened to the struggle to grasp an idea. The discovery of patterns of unseen, previously unconscious connections between feelings and behavior seems to have urged men to consider unseen connections between things in the physical world, science.

People, even children and animals, have an ability to store a number of bits of information, unconsciously and from short term memory and then presumably somewhat continuously and unconsciously to scan these bits for connections. As some connection rises to the surface of consciousness, we say we have an intuitive feelings about the matter. Physicians discover pathological "syndromes" in this manner; it requires some interest and concern for details of life, and some periods for reflection to allow these intuitions to surface and be recognized. Much of all learning, not memorizing, but gaining new outlooks or perceptions, especially among children, is of this type.

NOTES ON PERCEPTION

Our sensory and nervous mechanisms, optical or auditory, convey to us messages that are the product of highly complex, totally unconscious computations. These mechanisms have sought to abstract from the chaos of accidental sensory data those data which are constantly inherent in that trans-subjective reality which we believe lies behind our sense data (Lorenz p. 14). If one looks first at our cognitive apparatus, then at the things sensed, and if, on both occasions, one obtains results which throw light on each other, then we can believe that all sense knowledge derives from an interaction between the perceiving subject and the object of perception, both of which are equally real. The knowledge derived from these interactions, by way of unconscious computations, leads to our perception and a recognition of objects independent of size, form or color. This recognition and probably every recognition of real things hinges on Popper's "pattern matching."

Imagine in your mind a white rectangular box; there are almost an infinity of orientations of the box and of wavelengths of incident light that will cause the one unchanged box to take on an infinity of different outlines, shapes and colors. Yet we possess a computing mechanism which tells us the shape and color the box should express in various orientations. Thus end-on it may appear as a square, and in blue light appear blue.

The ability to separate essentials from noise derives from sensory or nervous processes which are beyond our observation or control, but which are very similar to insight, making calculations and drawing conclusions. These unconscious processes are called ratiomorphous computing mechanisms. They have nothing to do with conscious reasoning, but possess a similarity to rational processes.

The ability to perceive a constant identification irrespective of variations -- transposability is the most important criterion of a

Gestalt -- is known as the Ehrenfels criteria. Thus a melody can be recognized, regardless of pitch or instrument. The ability to pass over what is contingent (noise) and to <u>abstract</u> the essential (thus to transpose) is characteristic of all perception mechanisms and forms the basis of objectivation.

The abstracted properties are invariably inherent in the object. Elementary functions of perception provide constancy phenomena, a concept determined exclusively by function, for the physiological mechanisms for color constancy and form constancy. Similarly we have the perception of a size constancy, regardless of distance, and a form constancy of a 3-D moving object.

Lorenz tells us that a computer designed to do compound interest was found capable of handling differential and integral calculus. So too the constancy mechanisms of perception for identification of particular objects are also able to work at a higher order and isolate the characteristics of a whole class of objects, and identify the basic, constant Gestalt. This supreme function is independent of rational abstraction and is possessed by animals and small children. Thus not just dogs, but even all mammals, have something in common, a generic quality, and thus may all be called "bow-wows." This higher integrating system, Gestalt perception, possesses new system characteristics, and is linked to learning and memory; it even seems to possess its own system for information storage. The process by which a Gestalt, as a form, crystallizes as a perception, emerging against a background of "noise," may extend over long periods, even years. Ethologists and doctors commonly find recurrent patterns, such as a syndrome of pathological symptoms.

Humans possess a cognition function capable of absorbing unimaginable numbers of individual observations, of storing them for long periods of time while evaluating them statistically for the <u>related</u> individual recurrences -- which then might constitute a syndrome. Such a system must be unimaginably complex. This phenomena has many similarities to rational action, but all these sensory and nervous processes take place in total unconsciousness, the name ratiomorphous being chosen to indicate an analogy with rational behavior.

Intuition's task is to discover relationships among sensory data and between units of higher perception. Perception is an activity of human cogitation, the synthesizing of two systemic units. We say "it dawned upon me", or "the thought flashed," when we bring two formerly independent thoughts into a relationship.

Gestalt perception is at the forefront of human cogitation. At the same time, it is the warden of already known facts whose substance is many times larger than our memory. For example, it is here that our capacity for sensitivity for harmonics, whose complications are so immense that they exceed anything comprehendible through the intellect. Rational thinking could never accomplish the same result, and do it almost instantly.

Gestalt perception is capable of perceiving highly complicated polyphonic interactions as harmonies and of reacting to minimal disturbances with a sensitivity similar to a highly trained conductor discerning false notes among a vast orchestra. But this must be learned. Sufficient data must be fed in until the Gestalt is able to sort out the order from the chaotic background. Thus a Westerner can only, in a long time, come to appreciate the "message" in Oriental music. So too we learn to perceive beauty, and some aspects of truth, justice and charity. A most magnificent accomplishment of Gestalt is the ability to distinguish the sick, the abnormal, from the healthy and human.

The function of abstracting that Gestalt perception performs may not be a prerequisite (ontogenetically and phylogenetically) for the development of abstract thought, but it remains an indispensable part of it. An author criticized sharply the claims that "words are an integral part of thought" and that grammar is the "elementary part of logic." Perhaps words and grammar are but the surface effects of a perception that is far deeper than reason; nevertheless that must not be allowed as an excuse for deprecating words and grammar, as our only real contact with these perceptions.

For the so-called lower senses, such as a tactile cell or scent cell, the stimulus travels from receptor to mind without evaluation.

Emasculation of language leads to spiritual impotence, loss of the vividness of life, and is the death of humanness. This is so because language was constructed by our ancestors as a means for comprehending their spiritual feelings of belonging and of brotherhood and conscience. Words have power to touch the souls of people, if there is comprehension of a sacredness, a preciousness that adheres to you and your people.

All great human scholars from Confucius to Orwell

warned that one thing alone keeps men sane, rational: the sense of unified, agreed meanings. "The easiest way to destroy a people is to corrupt its language." "Organized lying . . . is not a temporary expedient" of modern Statists who seek to destroy human society; it arises from their need for a "continuous alteration of the past." "The present chaos is connected with the decay in language." Orwell went on to warn that sloppy language results in sloppy thinking, and allows lies to sound truthful and murder respectable. The respectable poet, Auden, asserted during the Spanish Civil War (on the Stalinist side), a need for "necessary murders."

When language is corrupted, people lose faith in what they hear, become confused, angry, ripe for believing the slickest demagogue. Human society is voluntary; its coherence and humanness depends on people's admiration for a guiding and cohering purpose. When this is corrupted by lies, garbled by misused words, society becomes irrational, and Statists grab control. Reason and truth become unobtainable when language is flawed.

Right action is determined by an ideal of existence, anchoring all purpose in the reality of human nature. The old American realism of Puritanism informed our nation's creation. Emerson urged "Self Reliance"; it is good, even necessary, but wrong, even idiotic or renegade to assume that it can replace human society. So it is well said that the decay of language was not due to carelessness nor ignorance. The freest nation the world has known was created and nurtured by Puritanism; it had to be destroyed by the likes of misusers of self-reliance before our Modern Language Association could be possible. And it is no accident that it, the MLA, is the "vanguard" of an evil party seeking the destruction of Western culture. It is the "mother lode" of political correctness, or thought control; it is the subverter of truth, morality and reason. A former MLA director called Carol Iannone a "pro-Nazi, anti-Semite . . . a racist," for questioning three book awards for the lackluster *Color Purple* of Alice Walker. An MLA Symposium on Language presented the "outstanding research" of a bright young type: "Writing is a series of marks that convey a message. Animals mark their territory with feces and urination (pause). Would you all ponder: Is the dropping of feces writing? (Silence)."[125] The tragedy of modernity, the great pacifist Bertrand Russell once wrote, concerned "rationality . . . despised as the vain dream of men who lack the virility to kill" in such circumstances.

> "Extremism in defense of liberty is no vice", as Cicero claimed.

> Primacy of will over intellect is not an assumption, but the supremacy of purpose over reason.

> "Slovenliness of language makes it easier to have foolish thoughts".

> "Error is never so difficult to destroy as when rooted in language", Bentham.

> "Superstition - the habit of respecting what we are told to respect:, Lowell.

> Pragmatism goes from what works universally, to what seems to work now, to mere drift.

> "Gay, the most agreeable of words . . . appropriated by a morose(?) group is an act of piracy" which must be undone.

NOTE ON BLOOM

Allen Bloom's *Closing* has in many sections the integrity of Orwell; but in places he suffers the weakness of mental self-cannibalism so common among modern writers. He saw the dangers and the need for saving Western culture, but could not refrain at times from brown-nosing the renegades who control our

---

[125]Here is the paradigm of the liberal university, not in a nutshell but on a piece of bark.

society with digs at their enemies: "I respect Sidney Hook (for) fighting threats to academic integrity . . . that is not me, I admire the theoretical life, not some moralism." You see then how irrationality results from the crossing of purposes. Bloom's predominant concern (purpose) was for his beloved university, without at times seeming to be aware that its slipping away was the result of savage uprootings of Western culture. Transcultural truths were "American imperialism," but when a contract went out on Solomon Rushdie, suddenly what a brauhahah. The Ayatollah was never more evil; how could he deny transculturality?

Bloom has so many good things in his book it is painful to criticize it, but because I urge you to study (not just read) it, I would that you anticipated his errors.

Bloom has a big hole in his comprehension of culture: "condemning ethnocentrism (culture) may be progress". Here perhaps is the core to that which I see as his error. The "canon" is "demagogically intended"; canon he says, is what is established by authority, by the power, not by rational criteria. The debate shifts from content to motives for use of the canon, which is by definition "an instrument of domination." He doesn't say that he really believes this, but does demand to be seen in the center, between the stupid Right and radical Left. He's for a transcultural humanity not a canon and quotes W.E.B. DuBois.

Bloom clearly sets a moral equivalence between "reactionaries" and radicals. Can he be blind to the fact that his "reactionaries" are the thinning ranks of the upholders of Western freedom and culture, who gave Bloom and DuBois the open education they so loved, and their right to criticize it? How could he not recognize that the radical Left is growing while shrinking all freedom, shrinking all thought, as Statists always do until there is no humanness left.

It seems to me that there can be no such position as between reactionaries and radicals, for the reason that these categories are wrongly perceived. The only categories of universal significance are human society and Statism, between which lies the Abyss. The common "reactionaries" or "Right" approximates the upholders of human society: limited government, personal responsibility, voluntary championing a great guiding purpose, always some form of rising up, primacy of families with children, a culture aimed at guidance through innate feelings, or spiritual values. Of course this is transcultural in most respects. But remember man is of a dual nature, naturally good but with the monkey of reason on his back, so there are some poisons in culture, some lies in truth.

The canon of the West includes the greatest efforts from throughout the world to sift the evil, the poisons, the lies from culture and truth. They are the greatest guides known for rationality and freedom in a cohering society. If it be "demogogically" urged at times, surely the demagogue is acting in a good cause. Certainly the canon is established by authority, the greatest authorities that have risen, always with effort to remove the spoiled. In a sense, it may be taken as "an instrument of domination", as a parent, as a university instructor, as laws, as morality, as human society are instruments of domination -- seeking to construct a framework of a nurturing human society within which individuals have greater freedom to "do their own thing," within the limits of social responsibility set by J. S. Mill. Is an American child "dominated" when he speaks his first word in English and not in some language unknown to his parents? Is a child dominated when he is taught that responsibility for himself is the greatest incentive to a productive life? Are young robins dominated by being taught to fly with the flock?

Of course culture is imposed, as one's native language, one's family, one's community and its laws are imposed. All knowledge and customs both innate and cultural <u>must</u> be taught --imposed.

Bloom is equivocal about culture, it is "extremely difficult to discern." He says other foolish things about culture, and the reason is clear. I can find no indication that he has any place in his world-view for society, especially for human society, and culture without society created the impotence, the barrenness of liberalism. I believe it is true that culture can do nothing, is little more than peeled paint, unless fixed on a foundation of human society. Culture is a creature of a society and when the society is destroyed, the culture floats away on the wind.

"Nihilism . . . means the bourgeois has won, . . . overcoming . . . the superstitions of Christianity . . . was perhaps the key to liberating men . . . ; failure of culture is now culture . . ., he corrupts morality, the essence of which is to exist for its own sake . . . What a man has from nature is nothing compared to what he has acquired from culture; Nietzsche concluded that modern rationalism is unable to rule in culture or soul, (thus) cannot defend itself and its human consequences are intolerable. This constitutes a crisis of the West, for . . . all regimens are founded on reason. The very idea of culture was a way of preserving something like religion without talking about it . . . we do not love a thing because it is good, it is good because we love it."

On and on Bloom goes, but then "Nietzsche . . . starts from the observation that a shared sense of the <u>sacred</u> is the surest way to recognize a culture". Then we are on solid ground; man's first philosophy-religion (in the true sense) was "Righteousness is what is loved", loved as most precious meaning sacred, meaning from innate spiritual feelings -- true religion. And it is these feelings which produce the coherence to hold a society together, motivate morality and charity, truth, decency and responsibility for survival and rising up -- for guidance of the cohering group, a human society.

NOTE ON GRAMMAR -- (The word once meant magic)

"Grammar is the most elementary part of logic," the beginning of the thinking process. Its rules and principles are the tools for turning thought into speech. Language is both the medium in which thought is generated and the transfer medium by which ideas move from one mind to another.

Words link images together to form an idea, an expression; they are the building blocks of reason. But it is through grammar that images are organized into a rational statement. An excellent Chinese student once told me that in ordinary things she could think in English, but for the very difficult, she had to think in Chinese.

Much of thinking, the condensation of information into knowledge, is accomplished by "pattern matching." Most people are unaware of the pervasiveness of patterns, everywhere. Myths are patterns, as are all stories and fables; even world-views and purposes have the essence of patterns. A metaphor is a pattern in thinking; in the beginning the concept of lying, in a certain circumstance, was referred to as "plowing in crooked lines," the word for which was *praevericari.*

If language were merely the dress of thoughts we should be able to separate them, but we cannot. Words, arrangements, language and style form the structure of thought and are no more separable than skeleton from body without destruction. But it must be remembered that words and language are used for two different purposes. Factual information can be stored or communicated as a code; thus it is that we discuss science or the physical world. But if this were all, and the evil party in education and elsewhere does seek to force the perception that that <u>is</u> all, then Sir Walter Raleigh, as an acute observer of the world, would never have asserted that morality colors all language. Code communications, as in works of science, are readily translated to nearly exact equivalents in other languages. But in the world of spiritual feelings, in true speech where "we gratuitously disclose ourselves and share our perceptions," most particularly and especially as we seek to do in poetry, here there can be but a suggestion of a translation. Such personal utterances are of spiritual feelings and can only be apprehended, believed or doubted. True understanding is unattainable without respect and detachment. We are told, and most know, that we cannot understand home until we have been separated from home, nor can we comprehend the present values until we comprehend the past, health until we know sickness. Also we must recognize that we cannot begin to understand another culture until we understand our own, and conversely we cannot understand fully our own language until we become reasonably competent in another.

Try now to comprehend the barbaric horror of today, where everything said above is not disproved in any way, just brushed aside. It is asserted with the confidence of Moses or a madman that there is "no scientific basis for standards. Prescriptive grammar is simply the ideology to which standards are imposed,"[126] or it is but "an instrument of racism and class oppression." This can be shown to be wrong by the general way that has been designed for finding the truth: you put one foot ahead of the other; likewise we can examine the footprints of our ancestors. For the past twenty thousand years or more, we can see and observe the efforts of men to seek truth, seek progress, to rise up. Why should people now believe, from a renegade elite that seeks to enslave them, that these efforts and standards for them are not essential?

A more detailed explanation of why grammatical standards are essential for the survival of a society, a people, cannot be given in a TV bite, the way a sneer at "mandarins" can. As said above, true speech requires respect and in a deeper sense it requires need - - need is the true basis of all sacredness, of love, of all belief. If you were with a space crew, abandoned in space, and your only

---

[126]He doesn't even know what an ideology is, but throws in the word is a mere vituperative.

chance for rescue was to follow precisely a message, how that message would be gone over in the struggle to extract from it every bit, and the correct interpretation of each. Awareness of standards would be the golden key to survival.

One renegade professor perceives a futility in appealing to students for standards in grammar whose only basis lies in some musty and rejected "Victorian" idea of culture (why not Platonic or Aristotelian?). He goes on to point out, not as a consequence of this rejection, but as a justification for students' concerns, that literature and the reading of language are no longer socially important or even significant. I tell you that that can never be true while the white man and his Western culture survive. While there is a hope for their revival, language and the great Western canon must be held as of supreme importance for therein lies our culture and our guidance.

We end this section with a quotation from C. S. Lewis. Lewis acted on his interest in words through much of his life by collecting vagrancies of word meanings; these he published as *Studies In Words.* It is worth some of your time. Lewis also authored, among many other books, *The Abolition of Man,* and *An Experience In Criticism.* In the latter, he wrote:

> "Those of us who have been true readers all of our lives seldom fully realize the enormous extension of our being which we owe to authors . . . My own eyes are not enough for me; I will see through those of others . . . in reading great literature I become a thousand men . . . I see with a myriad eyes . . . in worship, in love, in moral action, and in knowing, I transcend myself . . . "

WORDS

Art

We think of art as a mysterious quality to be found in certain things, and proper to be "collected" and celebrated. Human art reached quite a high peak some 15,000 years ago, found in caves of Western Europe, heights it took some 12,000 years or more to re-attain. And it was in no manner an aesthetic experience, nor was Greek or Renaissance Art. Aesthetics as a major factor for intellectuals arose only in modernity. Plato would have none if it; however, Kant and his followers, having given up on religion and purpose were important formulators of "aesthetic values" apart from social purpose, morality and humanness. The "contextualist" view of human society perceives an organic unity, bound by spiritual feelings of belonging. This is the pattern to which a human society conforms, by its own nature and that of men.

Opposed to this is the Kantian or "humanist" conception; it is based on a perceived primacy of "aesthetic" qualities, observed especially when separate from their original context and evaluated according to specified formal standards. The humanist's view is based on evaluations of contrived harmonies, idioms and patterns which are perceived to be independent of historical cultural context. Thus it is said to "transcend merely Western", and to address the timeless and universally human.

It seems clear that this is a micro or bugs-eye view. Nothing transcends purpose. Purpose is Creation, God, Nature, and human religion seeks to comprehend it. Morality depends upon purpose; truth and rationality are co-operators with purpose. To speak of art as merely Western, inferior to the timeless or universal, is like perceiving Western morality in fact culture itself as merely Western. Western is not great because it is Western; it is great because it has been the foremost culture universally for the past millennia, as it was in the Greek era.

Michael Lind, whose article (Public Interest, Fall 1992) has provided some of the basis for this brief note, began by declaring that the art museum like the public school, public library, and we should add public market and church are what Marxists demean as "bourgeois institutions". And you need comprehend that this really means that they are institutions of a purposeful human society whose supreme intent (not at all implying constant tension, only guidance when a significant choice is to be made) is to rise up to that proper to man.

Art museums, as institutions of society, may be said to have made their modern appearance in the West with the opening to the public of the Louvre in 1793 and the British Museum (1753) and the public's National Gallery in 1832. Now it is obvious that Greek art and Renaissance art came into existence not for the expression of aesthetic taste but "for the moral education" of the people. So too with the above museums.

Lind declared that a present "equation of the Western and

the universal would . . . (be) something to be proven." That is what Max Weber professed to prove in his *Protestant Ethic*; he claimed a unique universality of the Western arose from the fact that only it was completely based on a rationality, a guiding purpose. That was that greatest of gifts which we inherited from the Greeks; it is what in fact raises art above the playthings of god-kings and critics; and creates a vast culture of guidance and belonging.

Lind's "classical humanist ideal of a morally and aesthetically normative general nature transcending cultural relativism" and <u>his</u> "ancient regime" are typical modernist obfuscations that would have raised Coomaraswamy's high contempt. Only a human society with a profound purpose, a religion, and a culture to celebrate, guide and advance the society, and to make it human, can have any claim to humanist, normative or natural.

People must come to comprehend that there is no such thing as capitalism, or liberalism, or democracy, except as obscuring concepts. There is only humanness which must be supported and revered, and which <u>must</u> <u>be</u> <u>taught</u>, or intellectuals will create the enslavement of Statism. One has only to recognize the strident vehemence -- douse him with "gasoline and set his putrid ass on fire" -- the abusive arrogance and the inhuman evil of supporters of NEA "art". A more audacious assault, seeking to enslave human minds with obscenities, to befoul the greatest of human efforts and to intimidate with the Nazi-like virulence of their attacks on all who objected to their filthy inhumanness, have not been seen since the Stalin-Vyshinsky purge trials. The hypocrisy of the well-to-do, to rich, crowd of intellectuals and establishment crying Nazi censorship as they perniciously seek to ensnare the common people in a sub-human dependency to their elite can best even Stalin or Hitler.

Censorship? Let someone make a Piss King, or a Piss Hasidic or a Piss Homo, and see how quickly censorship is forgotten for a whine of hate art.

Clinton demanded that the Haitian leadership be banished, for their brutal but far less extensive social destruction than achieved by our evil party. Hence banishment would be fitting for these enemies of humanness.

<u>Blasphemy</u>   Much discussed during the Rushdie and the flag-burning incidents; it also relates to *The Last Temptation of Christ*,

Hail Mary and all the other anti-Christian programs. It is true, as claimed by the renegades, blasphemy should <u>not</u> <u>be</u> <u>illegal</u>. It is a moral problem and therefore is the responsibility of society to correct. Such renegades need only be seen as unrespectable, unworthy of any social acceptance in home, job or in the public square, and they will disappear.

<u>Bourgeois</u> It is not just an epithet of hatred; it is a sneer word for human society. Anger over a wife's infidelity is a "bourgeois feeling." Actually the reported fact of male jealousy being the leading cause of wife beating (and the same is true of husband beating) is explained not on the basis of culture, but on the basis of genes and repugnance against laboring for foreign genes. "Bourgeois" began to be used in the modern sense by Rousseau, and it marks the opening to "modern" intellectual life.

<u>Categories</u> They are equivalent to a golden mean (as courage is between foolhardiness and cowardice) between "stereotyping" and indiscrimination; there is a proper, in fact a socially essential mean, without which right and wrong soon become confounded. In a free country, as the U.S. used to be, the government was held to be, and to a large degree was, subservient to the people. To claim that is still true today, as through elections, is as deceptive as the Soviet's claim for democracy through its elections. Today, the people have only the most impotent influence on government, on schools, on churches, or on most anything. "The concept of definition by the use of separable categories is being rejected as part of the war on culture and society." Society clearly has three domains: society itself, and its two arms: economics and politics.

<u>Change</u> "The savage must not remain a savage, nor the nun remain a nun, and China must not keep its wall."

Everybody wants change; the arrogance of the claim that only certain "perceived to be enlightened" do is but grit for the war. You want change; I want change. Even the bare fact that the "enlightened claimers" want change down, and I want change up is not the central point.

The central point is Hegel's dialectic, which made change the cardinal principle of all who sought to destroy human society. Nothing was to be permanent, only the "strife of opposites."

Permanent revolution it is called, the deadly enemy of human society.

Christianity sought change by teaching each to amend his own life. Socialism, all Statism, seek a Procrustean change: everyone's legs trimmed to produce an "equality." The mad irrationality of modernism is no where more naked than with change. Nobody wants equality they want an edge: his change, his luck, his agenda, his "vision." Every common person knows that there are many, many wrong answers, and generally only one right. We have learned that of the many genetic mutants that occur naturally only a minute fraction are improvements. For a stalled car, only very particular change will effect recovery. Thus we can observe that most all change is destructive, and to no avail.

Yet look at the vast changes that have occurred in the history of our forbearers, always, always, rising, rising! Condensation into a cooperative society, with non-aggression and altruism, parental tenderness; conceptual thought and language; recognition of a spiritual vail unfolding society endowed by Nature's God, guidance for brotherhood.

If nature didn't have a purpose, it certainly acted as though it did, and it produced man with reason. Is reason to be allowed to destroy reason, to end progress, and end man? Change, like morals and truth, must be guided by a rational purpose, to rise up.

<u>Character</u> is a set of habits, an ingrained way of life, seen most clearly not in greetings but in meeting crises, with little time to think. But character must be deep in order to provide support for habit, the habit of facing reality, responsibility and consequences. Personality is the selfhood that meets the community. Virtue is to be seen when choices are made.

Character is that aspect of the soul which wills and chooses. It expresses itself in action, and will is that part of character that chooses the action. Thus character is under duress. Our character is partially formed by our preceding actions, our habits. Habits are formed from teachings and from innateness.

<u>Creative</u> once referred to the work of high excellence, attained by great artists who produced order from chaos, and a personality was one who accomplished this in his own being. But these words, like many others, have been vulgarized by modernity; even children are

creative and have personalities. These words have displaced the formerly more precise attributes of virtue, character, rationality, with a resulting covering over of purpose.

The chance tatterings of children, paint splatterers, and the beasteries of "modern art" are "created" much as a farmer's dunghill. The human soul needs to create, and to see created the magnificence, the splendor which is conducive to noble feelings and reverence. This is the essence of admiration, the vision of rising up. It is a great shame of today's America that magnificence, splendor, nobility, and reverence are unknown, unused words, recognized only here and there amongst antiquities.

Democracy

No word in the English language has been more corrupted than democracy. Confucius and others have warned of destruction of a people through corruption of their language, and a principal means of this corruption is through the distortion of word meanings so that social communication, so essential to human society, becomes poisoned. Orwell's State forced the destruction of words, thus inhibiting communications, but far worse is corruption of meanings, which leads to confusion, quarrels and eventual internal chaos.

Democracy not only has nothing to do with human society or the human imperative to rise up, it is in many ways contradictory to and destructive of human society -- assuming democracy to mean proximately "the people rule". It is contrary to and subversive of human society in that society is innately, implacably hierarchal, non-egalitarian and demands leadership and excellence; it began almost as an army. It is painful for me to admit it, after striving to be a Jeffersonian democrat much of my life, but it is true that it is not so much Christianity that was made for slaves as it is <u>democracy</u>. Democracy, as the people rule, assumes or even demands equality, and it must be understood that the only equality is in slavery. Everything else in the universe is hierarchal. People-rule tends innately to be mob-rule: Red Guards, Cheka, SS, KKK. The whole irrational concept of democracy and equality is a major evil-offspring of the Enlightenment.

Tocqueville was a very able product of the Enlightenment, of France where it occurred monstrously irrational (see Rousseau, or Diderot's *Rameau's Nephew*). And he came to recognize its terrible mistakes well before J. S. Mill's essay on *Coleridge*. Tocqueville gave an emphatic warning to America of the enormous cultural, actually social, price that democracy should in time extract.

Before looking at the price, we need consider a distinction. When a society of men of little humanness and culture face decisions, they are commonly made quickly and with finality. Fifth century Clovis assembled his army in the then open field, the Champ de Mars. Lifting high his great sword and bringing it down in a powerful stroke, he cleaved in retribution the head of a henchman to the clavicle, with the fierce words, "It was thus thou clavest the vase (St. Rimi's and mine) at Soissons". We have noted the great pacifist Russell to declare, "Rationality . . . is of supreme importance . . . not only in ages when it easily prevails, but even more so, in those less fortunate times when it is despised and rejected, as the dream of men who lack the virility to kill where they cannot agree". Note, however, that this statement is tricky and misleading. Rationality is needed most when men lack the virility to kill when attacked by true evil; these are the very men who do not necessarily despise rationality, rather they, like the person caught up in a web of lies and deceit, cannot afford it. The tragedy of modernity is that now when men lack the virility to declare the good and to defend it, they have renounced rationality, even truth.

Now to Tocqueville's price for democracy. With more humanness, by which we mean more rationality and truth, there is less need for violence and killing. More culture as guiding knowledge is needed, and this means more literature, art, manners, and excellence and leadership in all things, with honor, bravery, true valor and a reverence for the spiritually human. It was just these things Tocqueville warned would be what democracy would replace with envy and leveling, alienation and me-toism. And so we have seen.

The most pernicious me-ism is feminism in its radical form, far more destructive than the me-ism of race, as females are the most important component of a society in its efforts for survival. No member of a society of any interdependence has ever possessed anything approaching "control of their bodies", as trumping the essential needs of that society. Millions of Americans have been asked to put their lives on the line, and will be asked again; if you failed to do so you might have been shot, and some were, others disgraced and dishonored. Hence acts or even claims for some "right" that may weaken the society and thus lead to a renewed call for lives cannot be permitted or tolerated. Quite the opposite; only people who actively support society are to be held in respect. It was not for nothing that the evil party lauded Rawl's idea of outlawing contempt.

There must be a whole sea-change in basic education and social attitudes, in line with Jefferson's democracy. Government must be returned as subservient to the people, an arm of society for upholding appointed, coarse discipline. It must uphold at least the essentials of natural law, and it is the right and duty of the people to intervene and to set things aright (with the least disruption of forms) when it fails to do so. We must begin by wiping away a State that audaciously pretends to stand as protectors of criminals, aliens, perverts, louts and renegades -- in opposition to the human society that support the State. No State should be allowed to meter morality; <u>society</u> should take the responsibility for controlling abortions, drugs, abuse, pornography and the like, through the awarding of respects, jobs, and association. It should write most local ordinances through community "civic corporations".

John Chancellor intimated, that the people cannot be depended upon to make policy in most areas; certainly not in the areas of finance and trade, or in science which touches the critical areas of defense, education and communications, or in many other fields even into morality and law. But they certainly can recognize bad policy, and particularly the moral and social aspects of all problems, and must do this with confidence and noise.

It is not so much that something is wrong with the basic machinery of our government, as it is that people have failed to act against it when it became renegade, as for example when the Court's Chief Justice Warren openly began basing judgments on socialistic propaganda tracts rather than law, or when Justice Blackmun expressed his contempt for the people who dared to question his penumbraic abortion decision. On top of everything else, our media, education and entertainment have twisted every happening, every law and every policy, so as to promote destruction of our culture and society, even as they praised and urged our acceptance, ever coerced acceptance, of Statism. And they have dissembled, obscured and lied about all things so as to force socialism as the great vision to be perceived by all who were not capitalists or Nazis. And those who sought to thwart them were demonized. Only the organization of wards can bypass this evil party, for its eventual elimination.

Some idea of how complete the renovation must be is

suggested by the recent report of a *Wall Street Journal* Staff Reporter: " . . . (T)he leadership of the next Congress will be dominated by men . . . (of) the 1960s . . . defined by a lack of any collective experience, like WW II or the Depression . . . Instead they lived in a period of erosion of unions, corporate loyalty and public faith in governments. For Democrats (it will be) harder to reach out to the working class; for Republicans it fosters a libertarian streak that encourages decentralization of government." Is it really possible that these people are nerds and air-heads as to be without education or tradition, without principles or beliefs, without a purpose and a vision for the future? Certainly this Iron Environmentalist's picture is wrong.

People accept this irrational feculence, rather than believe it. These deceptions and lies cover all communications today; they have been taught in school and repeated endlessly in the media, claiming "Puritans are a drag on our culture," (TNR, 5,11,92); and "original intent" in our Constitution is authoritarian, fascist.

But people want something entirely different from this; they want a purpose, to belong to something admirable, to feel a protectedness. Democracy can mean anything from Jeffersonian agrarianism to Communist East Germany's Democratic Republic. Hence, it has no meaning, like liberalism and progressivism; Statists can add their domestic "reforms" until human society is gone. We have seen it.

Equality

Freedom for the individual was the admirable and essential objective of the American republic. "Created equal" is not a condition, but transitive to a doing, an opportunity to pursue in freedom one's life and own destiny.

Equality can only be felt, proclaimed like truth or love; when forced it becomes drab uniformity with loss of the individuality that people love in their community. To equalize the things people enjoy requires severing the connections between qualities, conduct and responsibility on the one hand from the rewards and respect on the other. Social equality and a true sense of brotherhood are at times contradictory. Equality is in many ways incompatible with liberty except as a symbolic ideal -- legal or religious. Equality can only be imposed, by a tyranny, because all people, men and women, are by nature so unequal.

Have you ever known a person who sought equality rather than an edge? Equality is only to be perceived in the mind, like respect; it is of the spiritual dignity of a person. It comes from natural law, as Lincoln defined it: the right to eat the bread that comes from the work of one's own hands, without leave of anybody. This concept of equality has as little in common with today's envy and radical irrationality as the limited government of our Founders has with that tyrannical Statist corruption in today's Washington.

Men desire not to be equal, "but to excel . . . (which) next to self-preservation, will forever be the great spring of human action (purpose)," wrote John Adams. Equality is the death of progress, as exemplified in Statism. Progress of every sort: scientific, economic or cultural, has been produced by people of a will to be unequal. Equality benefits no one; it frustrates and embitters the talented, and reduces the poor to deeper poverty, denying them even hope. The central and innate failure of socialism, or welfarism, is the suppression of abilities not only at the top, but all along the line. It is the innate urge to rise up that produces progress and causes people to rise above bare subsistence. People truly "live" only in a struggle for something to which they can dedicate their lives.

People differ widely in physique, dexterity and coordination, but the enormous differences in mental abilities and motivation are far more enabling. Many people are confused and misled about IQs; these are a measure of the ability of a mind to encompass and construct an image of an idea quickly. But people with high IQs may lack motivation; it may be a huge engine, but if it won't start, it is of little value. Or the high IQ person may have little ability to get along. However, these are somewhat the exceptions; researchers have shown repeatedly that people of generally high IQ, have above average physiques, personalities, and are generally all-around superior individuals. It has been my privilege to have known some.

Equality is urged by renegade Statists to induce resentment, even hate; equality of result is enslavement for all but the lowest. Statism always levels downward, and uses promises of equality and free-sex as come-ons, as bait. Human society, with its purpose to rise up, has the common person aiding the craftsmen, always leveling up. The drive for equality is at best materialistic, goodies now rather than respect and joy of accomplishing. Next to the greed of the intellectual for power it is the great menace to human society, where equality is as impossible as in a home and family.

Forced equalization among demonstrably unequals demands ever finer distinctions, always more regulations and bureaucracy. If a democracy of equality were forced by law, there would cease to be opportunity or freedom for anybody. Equality except before God, the law, and in the minds of our neighbors, can only be imposed by Statist terror.

The German philosopher Kant wrote many wise and profound things, but certainly he was mistranslated or was himself misled when he declared men equal in human dignity because of their capacity for moral choices. But "capacity" for choice is nothing and, in any case, basic morals are not chosen, they are innate standards essential for the stable functioning of a human society. You can no more choose the standards of morality for your society, than you can choose the standards of operation for your car.[127] Both are set by the Maker.

> "He goes on Sunday to the church and sits among his boys. He hears the parson pray and preach, and he hears his daughter's voice singing in the village choir. It makes his heart rejoice, for it sounds to him like her mother's voice, singing in Paradise. He needs must think of her once more for in the grave she lies, and with a hard, rough hand he wipes a tear out of his eye. Toiling, rejoicing, sorrowing, onward through life he goes. Each morning sees his task begin; each evening sees its close. Something attempted, and something done has earned his night's repose. Thanks, thanks to thee thy worthy friend for the lesson thou has taught, and in the flaming forge of life <u>thy</u> fortune must be wrought. And on the burning anvil shape, each burning deed and thought."

Euphemism, Oxymoron, and Other Deceits

Cultural revolution - holocaust
Due Process - a "contextual goal" of a bureaucracy, associated with freedom of information, government regulations, and various

---

[127]A person can, of course, have additional, cultural standards, but these must be conformable with the innate roots.

emotions and agendas arising from a dead constitution.
Public entrepreneurship - socialism

Elitist -- has two nearly opposed meanings, depending upon whether you support human society -- then it is a sneer at a Statist leader; if you are a Statist, it is a sneer at a person who seeks excellence for a human society, as used in the Carnegie Report on education to condemn the idea that "there are certain canon works (our culture) that should be familiar."

Ethicist - hired public snoop for the State

The Git-to -- a whine from black radicals. It consists of large areas in our once great cities where black violence pushed whites from their neighborhoods, often with little or no compensation. After the dust settled, large middle-class communities had become Beiruts, git-tos.

Goodness -- "No amount of peripheral enrichment of life, or education, can atone for a lack of center", for lack of a social purpose administered by a core. Mandeville asserted that the humanitarian Shaftsbury, "seemed to expect goodness in men as we do a sweet taste in grapes." "Political correctness" is a party line. Sensitive -- corrupted from a description to a passion.

Unqualified teacher -- educated person without a clap-trap "ed" course.
Burnouts - goof offs
Government support - taxpayer
Peace studies - appeasement, better red than dead
Pluralism - rule of special-interest group, an oligarchy of the
        radicals
Pragmatism - expediency
Recreational sex or drugs
Anti-anti communist - renegade. A communist is a moderate compared to a die-hard anti-communist.
Skinner's behaviorism - man is but a brute
"Values" - replace good and evil
Self-appointed guardians - watch over language and culture
Ecologists, ethicists, humanists - watch over snail darters, owls
and rats.
Non-judgmental - anti-human society, a New Republic writer noted the persistence of old fashioned moralities among "the less educated."
Gentile - Why are we heathens in our own society?
Peace -- defined as "better Red than dead" and is an irrational renegadism backed by communists. A bloated humanitarianism that

G. B. Shaw called "the stage army of the Good." "On every side the slug humanitarianism leaves its slimy trail, obscuring intelligence and atrophying emotion," was Trotsky's keen observation. It is never a matter of just "peace" nor of simply war; it is always peace or war against somebody, or for somebody.

Hate

      Hate is instinctive, natural, part of our innate self-defense system. Parental tenderness, in conjunction with the equally powerful indignant anger or hate, are the two horns of instinctive familial or clan protection. We recognize non-aggression and altruism as innate standards for social stability, on top of which acquired social standards make up the composite of morality and charity. Likewise we have the innate feeling of hate, and on this may be similarly imposed a cultural component of contempt or cultural loathing. This latter can be fanned into a hate by teaching.

      All of these have long existed, but not until the coming of socialism -- modern Statism -- has hate been purposely taught as an ideological tool, involving great masses of people, often in preparation for a holocaust. This modern teaching of hate began in a sense naturally. The early socialists -- St. Simon, Fourier, Marx -- preached anti-Semitic hatred because they saw early capitalism as a Jewish manifestation. They were unanimous in condemning the mobility and disorganized competition that was upsetting all traditional order with, "naked self-interest the only nexus between man and man." On this basis, there could be claimed a natural right to hate.

      The mass teaching of hate began with the socialists, but hate on a local scale has always existed for many reasons. There seems little doubt that modernity's destruction of religion and thereby of guiding purpose has made possible such rank growth of hate. Lytton Strachey is a glowing example; brought up with all advantages, there apparently was nothing for him to grasp as an admirable purpose to which he could dedicate his life and work. So in some manner he came to hate, with a growing intensity and craftiness, everything about him. Only later did he find Communism, and learned to use it as a wick upon which could be produced a steady and enduring flame from the oil of his hate.

      Henry Adams is another writer whose hate is carefully exalted by each modern generation. In a lifetime overflowing with opportunities to comprehend the purposes of society and the duties of the able, he never really raised a hand. His "antipathy to society" led him to reject out of hand "the judgment of the world," to shirk every responsibility, and to "regard every question open" permanently -- permanent revolution.

Seldom in the history of the world has a small group as the Puritans in America made such a mark in creating models for self-government, models for free public education, for government by openness and minimum coercion. Hannah Arendt has noted in detail the influence of Puritan models on the Founders of America which was widely declared throughout the world to be "man's last great hope," until the 20th Century Socialists renegades began their corrupting. Today the forced perception is that Puritan is next door to Nazi.

Henry Adams expressed his own "pleasure of hating" but imputed it to his home and ancestors as "known New England qualities." Renegade Socialists who began taking over universities in the early 1930s, especially humanities departments, corrupted generation after generation of students with this hate, and it became embedded in all cultural perceptions. A 1940 thesaurus lists as a synonym of bigot a pharisee; by 1980 it was puritan or redneck. Can you imagine "Jew" being listed as a synonym for miser or shystic, or jungle bunny for Negro? Certainly they rank less in abuse than bigot, which has been raised from "an intolerant devotion to party" to the epithetical vituperation of Nazi, "racist," or "American Firster," or more recently of "fundamentalist."

"One of the things intellectuals have done repeatedly . . . is to get people to hate one another, fight . . . tear the social fabric that makes human life possible." So wrote Tom Sowell.

The 1968 Kerner Report blamed "white racism," and hundreds of court orders and billions of tax dollars poured forth. As "block busting" rolled across vast areas people sold their homes for little or nothing to escape with their sanity if not their lives. Square miles of once tree-lined middle class neighborhoods were git-toed. Old people, mostly old church women were left behind; and here and there in Detroit and Chicago a shameful story would appear. First her flowers would be pulled out, her screen door broken, windows knocked in, and then a TV stolen. Police would come and laugh at her for imagining. Finally their broken bodies, desecrated and head bashed would be carted off to nameless boxes in the morgue. A nation that treats its old women that way doesn't deserve to survive. It won't.

In a bull-bear fight the two animals are forced into an enclosure too small for them; they commonly battle to death, usually of both. The eastern establishment arranged one of these in Boston with Judge Garrity presiding. Again the able escaped; only the poorest of the poor blacks and Irish were left to fight to the death -- frightened and naked of human leadership there was nothing else to do. The elite was seeking a "new vision for society," as Anthony Lewis described the most brutal of holocausts in Cambodia.

Why are blacks always "enraged"? Why such intense hatred? "Homosexual artists outraged at society for inadequate concern." *(TNR)*. Why have words such as "puritan," "capitalism," "bigotry," "hypocrisy" become such harsh curses? Epithets not of mere abuse but of hate? Are Jews and blacks so much better than puritans who gave them laws and government that allow them to vent their spleens? Is capitalism more evil than the socialist evil empire, and bigotry and hypocrisy so much worse than communism and the liberals who have supported it?

A few years back I unintentionally became involved in doing a good deed for a black family in Detroit -- the woman apparently had a fairly nice job. Ending up briefly in their closed-in porch, a little kid about two feet tall rushed into the room; seeing me his eyes saucered and, zip, he was gone. Maybe bashful before strangers. A moment later as I was about to leave he was back. Walked into the center of the room with his chest out, "We'eeze black folks! Weee don lik white foks!" His dad guffawed; his mother's face hardened as I left.

How come there is no Jew or black Archie Bunker?

Lawrence Carter, columnist for the Detroit News in 1981 wrote that Naipaul's description of two young Iranians reminded him "of a fellow who sells me sausages and cold cuts . . . with the same surly, self-assurance, the same belief that Allah chose him for a special destiny, to swindle and overcharge black customers, oozes out of his very Islamic pores."

One of the attackers of Goetz, Ramseur by name, apparently grew up like the Washington, D.C. man, who, in his late twenties, coerced his mother into two jobs, to support his "life-style." He tried to squeeze more blood out of the turnip; his mother was found dead with an iron rod forced up her rectum. So too with Ramseur, as described by a lawyer at the trial; he was shocked, appalled at the savage hatred which would not stop flowing, once he was pricked, even when it was so clearly necessary for him to show restraint. The people who burn crosses, paint swastikas or clip their heads generally do it for little more reason than other people spray graffiti. Painting "pissing-on-crosses" or far more indecent abominations, or rapping hate for white people are far different crimes, for they are backed by most of the renegade establishment. Their intent is the genocide of Western society. If Piss Christ is acceptable then clearly a Piss M. L. King must be; as a minister of God, surely King would have insisted upon such a substitution. Sinead O'Connor charged in <u>Rolling Stone</u>, from the history of the Popes, "We've got to realize those f _ _ _ _ _ _ s are running the world, they're running every government . . . the World Bank." Suppose someone said "No it's the Jews"?

At Disney World, in Orlando, the French Pavilion has flowers with French culture; so too the Norwegian Pavilion shows the Culture of Norway. But the American Pavilion was an unrelieved hall of "brutal cruelties": blacks, Indians, Mexicans, Asian, Eskimos and women. No trace of historical figures like Washington, Jefferson, Lincoln; no Bill of Rights, no sacrifice to make the world safe for democracy. Only hate!

Jay Loverstone, head of CP, U.S. 1927, visited Moscow (a few years after Lincoln Steffens, a few before FDR recognized the brutal regime); he called Stalin "a murderer," to his face! Kicked out of the Party, he joined a struggle for worker's freedom around the world -- with Garment Worker's Dubinsky and George Meeny. More responsible for the success of the Marshall Plan that Marshall, he provided <u>unwavering</u> support for Poland's solidarity. Lovestone must have watched in joy as in country after country, Communist tyranny was flushed down the drain.

But in the cultural West, intellectuals had marked Jay Lovestone as an "enemy," like Joe McCarthy, Whittaker Chambers, Richard Nixon, Ronald Reagan.

Some punk singer was to "rip up" the picture of a baby on a TV "comedy" show. Some particle of something informed her that that might not be decent so, on the live show, she ripped to shreds a photo of Pope John Paul and vengefully called for a "war" against "the real enemy." She then launched into a hate, war song.

Hate is a feeling and thereby arises from roots in instinct -- in Nature. So too with sloth, gluttony or greed, and many other anti-social forces. These innate feelings at one time had positive purposes -- to urge rest or eat when possible. Hate is an overwrought indignation. It is a gross misunderstanding to imagine that Nature could have supplied us with the great social forces of parental tenderness, love and reverence for home and family, and yet provided no recourse to brutal attacks upon them. Love and reverence for home are based to a very great degree upon need; without need there can be no real love or feelings for home; it is this need that demands an indignant response to assault.

Thus it is terribly wrong to urge people to believe that hate or racism or contempt of any kind can be outlawed even with a total destruction of human society. Try outlawing hunger. The solution is not to teach non-hate; that too, but not as much as teaching away the contemptible. History of the world is full of examples of respect even honor and, in very special cases, reverence, for quite "different," or "unacceptable" people, when they had something to respect.

There must also be mentioned the case of a normal leeway in a free society. Pat Buchanan was hounded with a full load of venom from the evil party, and from both left and right for objecting to a perceived avidity for America's involvement in war, from the Jewish "amen corner", of which ADL's Abe Foxman had howled for some time. *New York Times's* Rosenthal raged: "anti-Semitism" and "blood libel". About the same time we learn, from the grapevine, not the TV networks, that the Israeli Mossad (CIA) knew of, and deliberately did not warn us of the Mercedes truck bomb which killed over 200 Marines in Beirut. Jewish Arthur Koestler's advise: "write ruthlessly what one believes to be the truth, or shut up". He should of added, "and don't whine when the same returns." That seems overdone for a prudent normality, as does Russell's "kill". Buchanan's remarks were of a gentler give-and-take than Richard Goldstein's (6,1973, *Mademoiselle*) "I never encounter a white Southerner without feeling a murderousness pass between us . . . ", and "There is something utterly sinister about the image of Richard Nixon inviting Merle Haggard to sing at the White House". But then even Florence King went off the deep end and warned that the sad and harmless "Red Necks, White Socks and Blue Ribbon Beer" might become a "Horst Wessel".

Oliver Stone has admitted a burning hatred for America. When a documentary is made, or a fictionalized account of history is written, it commonly has a theme, in fact a truth, that it seeks to demonstrate: the evil of war, propaganda carried by the media, or some other socially justifiable purpose. The purpose for Oliver Stone's *Born On The Fourth of July* is to assert the evil of and to teach hate for America. If Stone had made a movie to assert the evil of Jews or blacks and to teach hatred for them, it would be like pissing on the corner of his brother's bed. On the other hand, making up lies to "demonstrate" the evil of America and teaching hatred for our country and people is like crapping in the middle of the dinner table. Stone should have been tarred and feathered.

Stone lies about Kovic's wrestling coach, "I want you to kill!" Kovic thinks he may have killed a fellow marine. His Major investigates and concludes it is unlikely; then promotes Kovic to a new team leader. He does not "take his head off." Kovic's mother was jeered in the film as a religious fanatic and "robotic" anti-communist. Bar patrons know Kovic was not hassled about losing the Vietnam war. At the Syracuse University strike, there were no police anywhere, no force. Nor was Kovic there and apparently neither was Abbie Hoffman. Kovic was cited for seeking to save a buddy and was wounded in the leg, not the spine. He doesn't go to Venus, Georgia, because there isn't any. Nor did he go anywhere else in Georgia or any other place seeking the family of the man the Major told him he probably did not kill. There was no such family known.

Kovic tried to cause a rumpus at the Republican Convention, after promising not to when allowed in. He was politely wheeled out and supposedly had dinner with Jane Fonda, and Daniel Ellsberg. No dumping on the ground or ripping off medals. Every item was calculated to prove evil and to teach hatred for America.

Lies are to hate as fertilizer to plants. For a peek at the colossal pervasity of lies in the entire communist-to-liberal continuum, refer to Lyons' *Red Decade*, *Chronicles* of Muggeridge, Johnson's *Modern Times*, Hook's *Out of Step*. The whole evil party began its life with conspiracy and subversion, Trotsky advised: always appear to be on the defensive, the scapegoat, even as you attack.

By forced perception, racism in America is perceived as Aryan or Christian with Blacks and Jews exempt. Black racism against Jews or Jewish racism against Blacks both become American racism. A Japanese woman married to a Jew produced a diatribe from her against "overbearing in-laws", and Passover a "ritual of gluttony and hypocrisy", a symbol of the vast gulf-between Japan and American racism.

A few years ago, the San Francisco District Attorney declared officers of the Jewish Anti-Defamation league could face felony charges. Some 10,000 seized illegal dossiers on individuals revealed an immense Gestapo network. Mysteriously the case was closed and the files actually returned.

H. L. Mencken, like many Americans, including Jews, rather accepted the dual and seemingly contradictory stereotypes for Jews as Communist-inclined and given to sharp business practices. Our establishment now rejects these as possible versions of the truth and damns them as harshly anti-Semitic. Yet far harsher and vastly more extensive attacks on Christianity, "poor whites", and America generally were, well "versions of the truth".

Beverly Hill's money-and-influence Congressman, Henry Waxman: "We don't want to see a Hispanic split vote so that an Anglo (Aryan) would win" (*TNR* 7,7,86,p. 18). A couple years later ADL's Foxman complained to *The Wall Street Journal* that those who "counter attack anti-Semitism, anti-Zionism, racism, and gay-bashing found little support".

My, My! M. Rosenthal bashes the Boy Scouts of Baden-Powell as "cynically manipulated". I. Howe claims Jews "view American populism as a nativism" close to Nazism, and the present task of socialism is to defend the "welfare state".

This kind of Dershowitzian chutzpistic wrangling is grossly irrational, dangerous, and deprecated by the great majority. Fortunately most Americans of all categories are beginning to recognize that if the old dog that has been beaten so long dies, so will go the fleas. And that dog is Western culture, Rule of Law and our rightful Constitutionally limited government, all of which has Christianity providing structural unity, and at this stage there is no alternative but fascism.

Hypocrisy and Prejudice

The greatest hypocrisy this world has ever suffered is that of liberalism. It has been the liberals who have made world socialism possible. It is not just the people like Andy Rooney, who, a few years back on "60 Minutes," proclaimed something like the "greater vision of communism." Nobelist Samuelson declared it "a vulgar mistake" to perceive the enslaved of communism as "miserable." The "Christics", the most savage assaulters of those who worked to counter communism in Central America, were given strong support by Bill Moyer, Senator Kerry (Mass. D), two *Frontline* shows and heavy media coverage. Cornell Professor, M. Scammell declared "communism miraculously retained a moral edge over capitalism."

President Reagan was pounced upon when he declared the

Soviets an "evil empire," as was Derek Freeman when he straightened out the lies of Margaret Mead.

Strobe Talbott, in whose hands much of America's future lies relative to Russia, a few years back dismissed the very idea that there was a Soviet threat.

Socialist H.G. Wells and G.B. Shaw (*Anticipations*) admitted "that the ideal of equality naturally meant mass killing," since the "inferior and unfit must go." Shaw's preface to *On The Rocks* (1933) was headed "Extermination" which he said must be put on a scientific basis.

Like Red Guards or Brown shirts, some 200 "students" led by "professors," were reported by *WSJ*, 4-10,91, as "roaring into a quiet lecture hall (some with canes and sticks) and posting themselves menacingly in the aisles and exits." They disrupted the talk, jeered the speaker, an elderly professor who barely escaped a beating. The lecture was to have been on the fall of Communism and the Berlin Wall.

It has been the liberals, who have provided the cover, the support and defense for the enemies of human society, the evil party. Some 110 million souls have been holocausted, mostly in peace time, commonly by their own people (under natural law more heinous than attacking foreigners), often with torture. Has this ever been taught in school, made into a movie, or ever referred to in the media? It would seem that "The Holocaust" has been quite effectively used to screen out the far larger and more general crime. This is renegadism, for the holocausting is by no means over; it is an accepted practice in all of Statism.

The point is that liberals are destroying human society, and have been for a century, in preparation for a socialist take-over. And that take-over generally will not be collectivist, it will be nationalist, meaning fascism.

This evil party, with the greatest of hypocrisy has followed Gordon W. Allport, a Harvard *Who's Who* professor with a record of supporting Communist causes wrote, and has been followed by many like him, that a "tolerant person is likely to be a liberal in his views. Prejudiced individuals are more often conservatives." This is a typical example of this forced perception that anti-Semitism is an American or "conservative" disease. Can you believe that Mr. Allport was not aware of the Marxian and socialist origin of modern anti-Semitism and taught hate?

Christianity has existed for nearly two thousands years. It has made mistakes; some professing to be Christians and even holding high office demonstrably were not Christians. All of us are human beings and subject to the imagining of evil. But nowhere in the history of the world has there been a greater force for good, for decency and humanness. The greatest evils charged to it, such as the Thirty Year War and the crusade against the Cathars of southern France, had little to do with Christianity or even religion generally. Christianity provided the purposeful structure upon which Western culture and civilization was advanced from that high level of the Greeks.

On the other hand there never has been a more evil movement, evil by total intention, then socialism. At the beginning it was merely reactionary, but by 1850 it dropped its idealistic pose, except to some degree used as propaganda. It went forward as a movement of deception and taught hate. Voltaire and the German philosopher Fichte who contributed to socialism's "theoretical" foundation, along with essentially all of the founders of socialism: St. Simon and Comte, Fourier, Marx and Lassalle, Blanqui, the French socialists who instigated the Dreyfus Affair, all of these were generally violently anti-Semitic.

It certainly cannot have been missed by many people that during the 1980s the liberals, the media, and the Congress supported Communism in Central America, and to a lesser degree around the world. The same evil party produced the catastrophe of Vietnam. This liberal love for socialism, communist or fascist, has a long history. In 1940 Eugene Lyons, in finishing his *Red Decade* on the 1930s, wrote: Intellectual red terror spread through New York, Hollywood and Washington, important universities, and large cities . . . The terror was real, though underground, underhanded, and not readily subject to proof . . . its fullest force was (against) "renegades," people . . . who had shaken off the authority . . . of the Communist Party . . . vilification would not be limited to name-calling, but would spread into fantastic smears . . . . The uninitiated cannot be induced to believe how effective the terror was (page 324, read the whole section).

But who was accused of the "smears," of the "black listing", of anti-Semitism, of causing Hitler and "the Holocaust"? Why Christianity, America, "conservatives."

Arthur Hertzberg called the mildly conservative, student *Dartmouth Review's* editor "a pro-fascist thug." The Institute for Policy Studies, which for years cooperated with the KGB, has always had ready access to the *NY Times* and to high government officials. IPS fellow Karl Hess expressing their general philosophy, urged "no alternative but to use violence to destroy the U.S." and was he not declared an icon by John Podhoretz?

Prejudice has the underlying meaning of an opinion held without sufficient grounds and, to that extent, may be charged with being colored or irrational. Of course there are very few opinions held by anybody that are based on sufficient grounds; in fact the very existence of any absolute truth is generally denied. There is hardly a single opinion of any importance in politics, economics, law, social and cultural affairs generally and, of course, in religion that is "held with sufficient grounds." We <u>believe</u>! so it is widely declared for religion, but in politics it is suddenly quite different; it's, "I'm a liberal, and I <u>care</u>."

With corruption of language "prejudice" ceases in a large sense to have a meaning and becomes a vituperative epithet. "If moral duties and the foundations of society rested upon having their reasons, made clear", civilization would never have come into being. That there are ranges of uncertainly, that there is a truth in most things that can be verifiably approached, that everybody lives by uncertainties, that beliefs can be held quite legitimately, and especially that the differences between beliefs do not necessarily have a first cause in evil: all of these become lost in the chaos of vituperation and reason itself is abandoned.

It is often said, as does Bloom (p. 246) that "democracy liberates from tradition . . . prejudices are leveled." Clearly that asserts that experience, as that best teacher, and beliefs that have been found essential for rational progress but perhaps may be not fully justified, that all of these are rejected. What then is left, why, ideology of course: Marxism!

Hence it is that differences of opinion about social goals that ought to be contested get obscured under sneers and contemptuous cries of bigotry. For example, just one of the pernicious results is that the quality of the goal gets confused with the practice. Everything that has always been seen as America's exceptionalism, "mankind's last great chance," gets submerged in an oily froth of "the condition of Negroes in Mississippi." All the evil of 100 million tortured souls, of gulags and purges, informers even as children on their parents, of stark scarcity, along with bulging new bombs, all of this was not the slightest cloud on the "greater vision of communism." Never was bigotry more obstinate and intolerable than in modern liberalism.

<u>Instinct</u> is defined as a natural impulse and aptitude of an organism to respond to external stimuli, below the conscious level; it is hereditary, not involving reason. Thus our instinct for home, community, love, conscience, all that comes from "below the conscious level", as heredity, unlearned and unreasoned is pre-cultural. These may be enlarged upon by culture much as natural looks may be enhanced by care.

Beyond the simple instincts of love, hunger, fear and fight, which are clearly related to biological survival of a pre-social individual, there are other feelings which seem to be "related to biological survival only intuitively," yet surely are hereditary. In some obscure way some seem related to conscience: the urge to admire, to admire beauty and truth. We can suggest that conscience, and thus all of these others, comes only with society. Certainly those deeper instinctual feelings of brotherhood, belonging, and a feeling of protectedness are related to a society.

<u>Justice</u> Justice was to Plato not fairness but a sign of a well ordered soul, doing one's own work, and minding one's own business. Aristotle saw justice as a part of character, not something imposed. It was an activity of the soul. Justice, conscience, morality and purpose exist only in a human society.

Justice concerns only natural rights; injustice is a violation of those rights. "Nobody of men can pretend that justice requires the enactment of any law." Justice like morality is above the law and below the law; it is natural, from the heart, not a part of reason. Like mercy, "It droppeth as the gentle rain from heaven."

Justice, being of the heart like morality, charity and all of human decency, is only of or within a human society; where that society ends or is destroyed so too do they end. Reason can reveal to men that others beyond their own society have similar purposes and that we should seek to include them in our concern for justice and charity. But that is another matter.

To discriminate is natural; it is everywhere, universal throughout nature. All life will find ways to aid family, friends, even those that we recognize as like us. We all seek to be with those whom we have things in common; we prefer the pleasing over the dull, the clean over the dirty, the trustworthy over the unknown.

Discrimination is in truth less against than it is for: in favor of the true, the excellent, the admirable, the known. This is the very Rule of Life, to seek to rise. In a healthy human society people have always, through admiration for the better, sought to choose the better, to aid the better to rise.

Discrimination in favor of true merit must remain an important standard. Those who seek to denigrate it, to insist on an equality that does not exist, intend to destroy human society. This can only lead to the equality of slavery and loss of all things precious.

Dealing with "others" is a great problem of life. It can be solved by reason, but only through an expansion of human society. In the horrible "integration war" in Boston, of Judge Garrity and others, and in other such evil confrontations, there was the very opposite. To get these brutal encounters started many things were said, such as this: the black children live in a community of violence, of non-hope, non-decency; let them mix with the white children and they will come to understand hope through orderly accomplishment; they can learn non-violence from the white children and become more like them. This could have led to acceptance on both sides.

It was never publicized but this "enraged" the black leaders; the very thought that a white could teach a black anything was anathema. If the intent had been consent and acceptance, only a limited number of somewhat chosen blacks should have started a pattern of cooperation. The intent was the very opposite, the crushing fist. Judge Garrity and lackeys consciously arranged savagery: a bear and a bull were to be put into a small corral where they could only tear at each other until one or both were dead. If they had done it with animals, it would have been an act of savagery, prosecuted by law. With children the very "law" performed the act of holocaust, on the most defenseless sections of society. The silk stocking liberals were able to get away when blood started to run. Such was the gutless inhumanness of much of the "civil rights" wars; through them the shame and horror of our Third World cities were created.

Loyalty

There is something hideous about being devoid of loyalty, wrote Simone Weil, a "Jewish Joan of Arc." People have an innate need to belong, not to be a pariah. It was Sartre who said, as must all communists, "My party, right or wrong," which put a dunghill at the center of his life.

Those who prattle Dr. Johnson's patriotism as the "last refuge of scoundrels" are ignorant of Boswell's immediate explanation, "he did not mean a real and generous love, but that pretended patriotism which (so often) cloaks self-interest."

Loyalty is an innate feeling. Society too is innate; it is man's only real protection, the source of all most precious, sacred. Loyalty is but Nature's command to defend.

In a world in which the connections between causes and effects are becoming increasingly obscured, beware of losing patterns of behavior long proven useful and safe. It is incomprehensible that intellectuals who had lamented and opposed a certain moral guidance from Christianity, would abandon all human dignity and stoop to the yoke of the evil party. Millions of Americans followed Lillian Hellman's renegades into a camaraderie with Hitler's tutor, accomplice and superior in evil, Joe Stalin.

Who has not heard the old canard about "having the guts to betray your country," rather than a friend,[128] without some queasiness? A far older sentiment commands, "This above all, to thine own self be true." Your country means your family. All the people and things you have ever cared for. Are you the kind of person who would betray them, and for their enemy?

Loyalty is the hard currency of love. There is no such thing as dis-love, so neither is there dis-loyalty. One ceases to love, to care; if the uncaring is obscured, unannounced, it is betrayal. Then there is the jeer. "My country right or wrong," which G. K. Chesteron set straight. No normal person would say such a thing, except in a truly desperate case. It is like saying, "My mother, drunk or sober." If a decent man's mother did suffer so he would share her troubles to the last, but to talk as though it were of gay indifferences is not the language of a human being. What were the louts doing when their country was embarking on such a mistake?

The great majority of people love their country; it is normal; and they feel a loyalty to it. They are willing, even anxious, to hear and understand constructive criticism of it.

For many years Johnson would snipe at the Scots. After his visit to the Western Isles he acknowledged that a Scotchman must

---

[128]"If friendship is to rob me of my eyes, darken my day . . . set to be right which I know to be wrong . . . I will have none of it." Thoreau.

be a very sturdy moralist not to love Scotland more than truth. Prior to his visit through the Highlands, Scotland had been very cruelly treated by England, and thousands were forced to flee, as for their lives.[129] There was much talk of emigration to America, many had already gone. The landlord of MacQueen's Inn greatly impressed Johnson; "I asked him whether they would stay at home if they were well treated. He answered with indignation that no man ever willingly left his native country."

Johnson believed in patriotism, including local patriotism. To uproot and go to a new country might bring comfort, but man will not live for mere comfort. "That man is to be little envied whose patriotism would not gain force upon the plain of Marathon, or whose piety would not grow warm among the ruins of Ionia."

A person with a strong attachment to his country, to one similarly inclined, would seem loyal; to a globalist he would be seen as nationalistic; to a renegade he would be a jingoist. How often today do we hear of American Firsters vilified. Remember, when you hear such charges of jingoism, or worse, you may well be listening to a person having a loathing or hatred for our country and people.

Contrary to the imposed perception, it is usually not difficult to sift truth from untruth, justice from injustice, or patriotism from renegadism. In fact most people make such distinctions every day. Loyalty is not determined by whether a person "meant well." The most dangerous traitor may be a largely selfless visionary. Loyalty grows out of family and local associations. We must learn to love the little platoons which Burke eulogized in a society.

<u>Majority</u>   "Nothing more obvious; it consists of a few powerful leaders, some accommodating scoundrels and weaklings, and a mass of men who trudge after them not knowing their own minds." Suppression of the best by the worst.

<u>Morality</u>

Shaftesbury took goodness to be "natural to men as sweetness is to grapes," so wrote the 18th Century satirist

---

[129]Some of my ancestors probably came about that time.

Mandeville.

To be human, or good, is no necessary property of man. It requires foremost a grasp on responsibility, in fact on honor. Cicero claimed that it is the spiritual feeling of honor that demands responsibility or duty; only then are "moral principles permanent, invariable, and in harmony with Nature".

Societies exist among insects, birds and mammals. There are very fixed ways, customs, standards given by Nature, by which a hive, a flock, a pack or clan is enabled to cohere and survive. We have seen that these fall into three general categories: (1) pre-society parental tenderness, (2) non-aggression within the society, and (3) altruism within the society.

Before reason, all the "practices, relationships, and organizations" of our forbearers were innate standards. With reason our forbearers become consciously aware of these as feelings: conscience, brotherhood, altruism, a feeling for home and "us," and so on. These are all deeply phylogenetic and usually associated with our deepest feelings and rituals. The society of our forbearers is believed to have been nominally monogamous for three million years or more, hence customs, or standards of society related to the protection and nurturing of families are properly a part of these innate standards.

When our forbearers began to come out of the fog of the unconscious world and to move into the light of objective consciousness they became aware not only that there were rather fixed ways to do things, but furthermore if they didn't follow those ways, they felt an anxiety, or a deep sense of guilt; their conscience gave them no rest; animals even feel anxiety.

Thus our ancestors began to develop, to acquire rituals, often as mere gestures or expressions, to communicate a message of friendship, benevolence or altruism within the clan or tribe. Always these acquired practices, if they were to be implemented or lasting, were necessarily built upon and comformable with an innate custom, practice, or standard as a base. These innate standards, when covered over as by a veneer of culture, became known as morality and charity.

Note that these standards, for the innate base and the cultural composite, are generally not of equal strength. For example the innate drive to reproduce to spread one's own genes, that people actually rarely are even conscious of in their daily life, is perhaps the most powerful. It is rather common for non-monogamous male primates to kill off babies, so that the females will come sooner to heat. So it is not at all surprising that men will be, if not abusive, at least more apt to be less considerate of other's children, including step-children, than for his own. As for so-called racism, all peoples are programmed, both innately and culturally, to at least distrust other people if for no other reason than mere lack of familiarity, of uncertainty.

That brings up the matter of education, particularly by example, and especially the care, prestige or reverence for the example. People can be taught to minimize their concerns for differences, not by declaring them evil but by emphasizing a need, as a part of a social purpose, that overrides the differences. All customs both innate and cultural need to be taught. When societies decay, the things that cease to be well taught, particularly by social examples, are the very things that culture needs most. Reason informs us that human society, guided by a culture of information and assurances, is essential for human survival; further that families are essential for society and culture for human society; both are most implacably essential. It can be observed, as well as reasoned that fornication, adultery, sodomy and homosexuality generally are disruptive, subversive, baneful to marriage, to families, and the nurturing of a competent and stable new generation. But since these are related generally to the erotic force, they are often the first pathologies to appear as society decays. And as society and purpose decay together, it becomes increasingly difficult or impossible to teach, to urge, or even to coerce certain responsibilities on to people, especially the young, for they see no purpose, no real reason why.

Reviewers of J. Q. Wilson's *Moral Sense,* and others, have demanded to know, "if morality is innate, why is it so variable?" Once racism was ok, fornication not; why not vice versa? Wilson answered with the obscurantism, "disposition." The simple answer is that for all societies -- bees, geese, rats and wolves, a cohering, cooperative society is possible only with standards of behavior demanding non-aggression and altruism, within the society. Nothing innate demands these for those beyond the society; any counter to innate urges can only come from culture. And culture must be an organic whole, based on a moral society of purpose, upheld voluntarily through reverence and admiration of the people. There is nothing in non-aggression or altruism, <u>within</u> the clan, that proscribes "racism" (whatever that is), almost the exact opposite is true.

On the other hand, fornication was never acceptable in a

healthy society, though certainly not unknown because of strong erotic urges. Wherever a bonded-pair is the designated producer of children -- in the society of our ancestors into the past million years, and noticeable in many species of birds, and even for the wolf breeding pair -- fornication is most pernicious. It is destructive of the bond that produces and nurtures children, a task coequal in importance, in some ways or cases even exceeding that, of survival itself.

Cannibalism of another society (or tribe) is in no way prohibited by innate forces, perhaps not even cannibalism within the tribe, when of the dead, and in order to survive. However, any detectable interference or endangering of children or mothers is harshly to be proscribed as endangering survival. This rather clearly should include the toleration of cultural factors which effectively force mothers to forsake their children day after day for work.

People today have been led into the rather general assumption that morality, and I refer principally to the innate root, has to do with inter-personal behavior. That is important, but of most particular importance is that behavior which affects children, mothers and families, and the community that consists of and must nurture families. It is in this respect that pornography, fornication and perversions of all kinds are condemned. Additionally, examples of behavior promoting ideals in children conducive to assumption of social responsibility, and positive attitudes towards eventual marriage and families, are to be given noted respect. These cannot be degraded to mere attitudes; they are moral necessities.

To summarize requires only a repetition of the statement that the major task of society is the production of a new generation, capable of survival and rising up. The increasing (1) dumbing-down of our children's understanding or even awareness of our culture; (2) the increasing reproduction of more predominately those of lower intelligence and more unsocialized character, and (3) the uprooting of all training for, or even concept of, a high respect for customs, institutions, and laws that promote normal children, families, and a stable society: all of these are obviously totally counter to an imperative social need.

Even to suggest that the evil perversion of all moral decency in our society today can be blamed on "modern philosophy" or "science" or any other such abstraction is to succumb to a childish irresponsibility that must be rejected. Innate society and, more particularly civilization, demands expressed indignation and contempt for such moral lubricity.

The "great variability of morality", so often noted, needs to be explained, taught and understood. In primitive societies where a subsistence level of living is common, the exact needs, the demands, for survival are visible and understood by all, hence social discipline is quite universally much easier to maintain than in a vastly interdependent modern society, where social needs are often obscure and falsifiable. Such interdependence clearly must be reasoned, but since reason is so variable, behavioral variations must be watched considerably more closely than when all people can readily see and comprehend the obvious needs.

Furthermore with a reasoning society, survival is not threatened by visible and direct assault. Social stability and survival becomes determined by the strength of social coherence. Hence not physical defense but moral defense becomes the major concern.

Morality concerns not only the way people need to act; it must include the way people feel, as a dominant determinant of future actions. Renegades are keen to claim that "Morality cannot be legislated." No, but immorality surely can, up and down; positive morality must be voluntary, rewarded by social respect, and recognized not as "tolerance" but a necessary environment for a cooperative existence.

Only a madman could maintain that the distinction between the honorable and the dishonorable, between virtue and vice, is a mere matter of opinion. Morality rests not on rational acceptance; it demands an emotional attachment established early in life.

It has been claimed that the old narrow group loyalty and rigid family organizations may not enable a person to function well in "a changing world." This is but renegade dissembling. A survival group, high in a wilderness area needs behavioral standards certainly fully as much when moving as when in camp. Furthermore one needs to ask what is changing, and in which way and by whom? Is the change a positive good and who controls it?

Aristotle declared animals to be "incapable of moral actions" and Sam Johnson pronounced men to be no more naturally good than a wolf. No less either; both are social animals, and both were good according to nature before man gained reason. The only unnatural evil that ever came into the world came through man's imagination. Evil has always predominated within the higher or intellectual circles of human society. If inhumaness or violence and corruption ran in sections of the common people, it was due to intellectuals who had been responsible for cutting them off from a human society. J.H. Breasted noted that morals began as folk customs, and had nothing to do with religion (I believe he meant the religion of the court or as we see it too often today.) It has always been the duty of the leader class in a voluntary human society to identify "morals" and to elevate "moral behavior" as something to be esteemed.

The ethical nihilism in, "Nothing good or bad, but thinking makes it so," is a trap used by renegades seeking destruction of human society. It may be used as an amoral perception that the good doesn't really amount to much and the bad nothing to worry about.

The idea that education should, above all, help students to make up their minds on moral issues is completely misdirected. Modernity seeks to force the perception of morality that ethics has to do with decisions: "What would you do if . . ." Morality is about the customs and standards of a purposeful people. Education's principal task is to provide young people with knowledge about its purpose and how that purpose may be furthered. Without purpose, reason is helpless. Honesty with ourselves is the first postulate of reasoned morality. What are we doing? To what degree do people make themselves aware of what they are doing, such as living without a purpose, or ignoring conscience?

Aristotle agreed with Plato and the Biblical prophets and, with perhaps the first philosophers to write it down, that a good man is one who recognizes and does good. Adeimantus defined morality as "actions that benefit society." Aristotle insisted that prudence or wisdom rather than rationality is the central instrument of moral judgment. Anatole France believed morality to be the sum of prejudices of a community. But the most unfeeling of men, Bertrand Russell, accepted the view that "all ethical judgments are (not) wholly subjective . . . we are willing to fight and die" for opinions that certain things are evil.

Hegel taught that the history of the world is not the theater of happiness, but that religion is reason's highest and most rational work, and is the sphere in which the nation defines truth (in essence, defines purpose because truth depends upon purpose.)

Don't get the idea that all "morality" is innate or that all that is innate is "moral." Essentially every appearance of consciously recognized behavioral impulses have been mossed over by a supposed strengthening or improvement from cultural additions. Cultural "morality" would never have come into existence without the pre-existence of the innate roots and is a product of reason. Rousseau declared that Socrates and like minds might acquire virtue by reason, but that the human race would have disappeared long ago had its preservation depended upon human reason. This is deceptive. Had this preservation been in the hands of the common people, their reason would have deferred to their innateness and preservation would have been, if not assured, at least made subject to a desperate struggle. It is from the reason of intellectuals that preservation must be protected.

A leading journal of opinion, a few years back, editorially asserted that after due "reasoning," "if a person or two or three and a billy goat find a way to be happy that strikes most people as revolting, that's hardly reason for the government to thwart them." (In the following, a number of other practices of questionable morality, from abortion to sodomy, might have been considered, in place of the "example" of the billy goat.) Note that in the case of a Statist government, any "thwarting" is not subject to public reason; it is a concern only of the elite. On the other hand, if the government were truly by, of, and for the people, as ours used to be, it would in fact be the people themselves who were doing the thwarting. If the billy goat group were to carry out whatever it was that they had in mind in some old deserted barn, or even in their own living room and, thus in total privacy, obviously no one <u>could</u> object.

It seems rather certain that that was not what the worthy liberal editor had in mind; he clearly desired not privacy but the "sending of a message", "making a statement". We should all agree with the editor, but only on the basis of reciprocity; that another group, or society generally, be allowed to be "happy" too in sending their message, for example that which the "women of Marblehaid" sent to Arn Arnson.[130]

It has been said that every good act of men is but an acting of a part -- taken by many as hypocrisy. Accordingly many conclude that true virtue or morality comes naturally; if it is done for reward, even for community recognition, it is not virtue but scheming. Actually the whole idea that man can be civilized, higher than a brute, is the great "hypocrisy" under which our forbearers have struggled upwards for a million years. If a rich

---

[130]Arn Arnson an' 'is 'ord 'art, tarred and fithered and carried in a cort by the woman of Marblehaid.

man wants to give a million dollars for a new school, take it and thank him, giving respect as perceived to be proper. But judge not lest you be likewise judged.

Marcus Aurelius expressed a thanks to his grandparents, parents, family, kinfolks, tutors and friends. It took all of these to constitute the kind of hierarchy under which standards such as morality and truth can exist. Roman *pietas* was a rendering of homage, reverence, respect, and allegiance to nation, family and hallowed place, with a human tradition that life is a part of some greater whole. Beings become human, not through science or the comforts of naturalism but by becoming a part of a society with an admirable purpose to rise up, and cohering in this purpose as a community with traditions, rituals, and human decency. Language will certainly be diminished without Shakespeare and the great poets and wise men of the past. And language is integral with thinking and comprehending. As it thins so too will human consciousness.

The German philosopher Kant emphasized that the common man in his longings for nobility places himself in thought in an entirely different order of things from his sensual desires. As the possessor of an intrinsic personal worth, he becomes conscious of belonging to a higher world. Kant is translated over and over as declaring the higher world to be "the world of pure intellect or reason." Surely man's "higher world" is his world of will and purpose, of feelings: the innate from whence arises all that is of reverence or spiritualness.

NOTE ON MORALITY

A woman who was just finishing her teens when the 65's feculence hit the fan, tells her brief story in a current "newsmagazine." She answers her presumably coming-teenage daughter's question," . . . Honey I got stoned and missed the war . . . lived my life in a slow stupor, wore sandals and see-through shirts, talked at great length, with utter conviction, about things of which I knew absolutely nothing -- it was then necessary to explain why getting stoned, walking around half-naked, and passing judgments on things you knew nothing about is a bad idea."

She goes on, "I have so much waste in my past that it almost washes away my future, making it difficult for me to go forward . . . There is a permanent record. It lives on in the memories of all the people you have known . . . in your own perception of yourself, coloring and flavoring who you become, what you expect to be able to accomplish . . . your future is in your past . . . your past drives your future."

Anyone who can read this confession and still continue to believe that morality and truth are relative deserve what they get. It is a terrible shame that children are not started out understanding in the first place.

The use of Koestler's quote, that Whittaker Chambers "committed moral suicide to atone" for others is an embarrassment to be left behind the bushes somewhere. To atone is to be reconciled <u>with</u> (a morality), and obviously that cannot be a suicide and certainly not a moral suicide. The very concept of a "moral suicide" is a degradation. Certainly what Chambers did only the communists could have found objectionable. He committed publicly a personal, moral cleansing, and he did that only when forced to by Hiss' libel prosecution. Chambers did not persecute Hiss, he belatedly defended himself before the onslaught of Hiss's prosecution. Again Chambers testified to past history only when forced to, to protect himself.

<u>Poetry</u> Prose is of the mind and reason; it deals with analyses and synthesis. Poetry is of the heart, the soul, a spiritual world of feelings in wholeness and completeness. We are told and retold many things; very little has been added to the Greeks, but for each retelling we need strive for some newness, "Every age is out of joint and the past must rally people to the permanent things," to thoughts and ideas, "the fair and immortal children of the mind." Homer is said to have "looked with high scorn on the brutal and unjust Age of Heroes." Yet they were heroes and he made them so or they would not be remembered.

Poetry is "The records of the best and happiest moments," its great end, "that it should be a friend to sooth the cares and lift the thoughts of men." "Brief is the growing time . . . and brief the flower's bloom . . . things of a day! What are we . . . a shadow's dream."

We are told that the great sweep of song and the strong measured beat of Pindar is unknown in English poetry, but suggested in Kipling: "That night we stormed Valhalla a million years ago". But we are not a particularly musical people, and Kipling is "a good bad poet."

Wendell Berry remarked in criticism that "teachers and students read the great songs and stories to learn <u>about</u> them, not to learn from them." They have been called great, been accepted as great, because of their beauty and the "weight of truth they carry." Such long reaffirmed beliefs become standards, far superior to an individual's "standards" which are, in fact, but his private prejudices at a certain period in his life, and very apt to change with maturity and wisdom.

The new critics reject the idea of truth as a personal goal, and the idea that a text may be worthy of comprehending in its own terms. If those texts that have been thought over and corrected for found error are not worthy of analysis and belief on their own terms, then certainly less so are those of the new critics.

What is lacking in the new critic is any sense of urgent purpose. The sheer idiocy of their position actually corresponds to that of a group of backpackers high on a mountain pass as a severe storm is approaching, who insist that all their maps are but patriarchal arrogance. And they will "imagine a different future," out of the vacuity of their minds. If there is no truth, no responsibility, no need dictated by a harsh world, one can imagine the greatest delights in the very fact of annihilation.

<u>Puritan</u>   A standard thesaurus of the 1940s listed "Pharisee" as a synonym for bigot; by the 1980s bigot had become "Puritan," or "red neck." Prejudice which had been more predilection or prejudging, had become largely racist, to hatred. A Wall Street Journal editorial told of a British columnist on PC: "Pursued by Puritan Furies." Certainly even a rudimentary knowledge of PC has it distinctly Marxian, not Puritan. Calling it Puritan, is like blaming the English for slavery, or the Jews for Marxist hatred. Leonard Tancock, an intellectual of London, wrote in his note on Dennis Diderot, preceding his Penguin translation of *Rameau's Nephew,* a damning of Rousseau for "the intolerance of the bigoted puritanical type."

Does such arrogant bigotry as his own justify the hateful "stereotyping" of other groups, thus: The "stupidity of the idiotic English type" or "the cupidity of the bigoted Jewish type" or "the savagery of the racist Negro type." It is doubtful that any group has been more bigoted in modern times than the liberals, devoted "obstinately and intolerantly to its own party, beliefs and opinions."

Clearly Serrano and Mapplethorpe (of *Piss Christ* and *X*

Portfolio fame) were "ideally suited to inflame the religious and sexual sensibilities of the right . . . those inflammable Puritan sensibilities were ignited again," by more: David Wojnarowicz's catalog (temporarily NEA overruled) with "[dousing] Helms with gasoline and [setting] his putrid ass on fire . . ." Then there was the art critic at the "Cincinnati trial" who judged as "almost classic" Mapplethorpe's bullwhip up his ass and who admired the "opposing diagonals" in a photo of a Negro pissing in a white man's face. So reported *TNR* art editor Robert Brustein. And, again, TNR's David Segal declared "puritans . . . a drag on our culture". Hannah Arendt, in her *Revolution* and Max Weber in his *Protestant Ethic* held totally opposite views. Hence this current vilification must be condemned and terminated.

<u>Reason</u>

"Rationality as an appeal to a universal and impersonal standard of truth, is of supreme importance . . ., not only in ages in which it easily prevails, but even more, in those less fortunate times in which it is despised and rejected as the vain dream of men who lack the virility to kill when they cannot agree." Pacifist, Bertrand Russell.

It seems certain that imagination and reason are one, or that imagination is a manifestation of reason. Clearly, before reason there was no imagination.

How then explain Pascal's teaching that unaided reason cannot win over imagination, and Cicero's claim that man is swayed by two forces: appetite (accepted commonly as nearly equivalent to imagination) and reason. The answer can be deduced from Kant who seems to say the same thing: pure reason was knowledge <u>not</u> from sense experience. General truths must be true <u>à priori</u>, before experience, as in mathematics, that is pure reason; we cannot imagine a refutation from any experience. Now imagination being in reality reason, we see Pascal's imagination (reason), countered by something that he calls "unaided reason" (let us designate it as "R"). Likewise, Cicero's "appetite" is surely the imagination of reason, and he too has something countering it; again to avoid confusion let us designate his "reason" as "RR". The common concept has been that true reason concerns nothing but that from the senses, but Kant for the third instance claims reason of the senses is also countered by something that he calls "pure reason", and hence may be taken as equivalent to the countering "R" and "RR".

Certainly this countering force: Pascal's "R" and Cicero's "RR," and Kant's pure reason, that transcends the sense's reasoned experience, come from a source of knowledge separate from the senses; we know it to be of the genome. Sense messages enter the conscious mind through reason, but so too do phylogenetic messages, "emanations" from the processing of genomic knowledge. It is essential to retain the word "reason" for that facility in the mind which constructs all mental images or concepts and turns them about, and in-side-out, for examination and analysis. It is necessary to distinguish information from the senses as distinct from information from the genome -- feelings, and since many people are not even aware, may even deny, the differences, it is important to specify clearly in each case the <u>source</u> of reason's information: from senses or from genome. Science is largely reasoning concerning information from the senses and religion's (in its humanly spiritual aspects) reasoning is largely based on phylogenetic information or feelings. Thus to contrast, to antithesize, the reasoned with the spiritual confutes logic by confounding categories.

Reason is often placed in opposition, or even in contradiction, to tradition. Nothing could be more fatuous, or dissembling. To begin with, remember that things we call truth or culture or religion are not apt to be totally free of error; they should be free, to the limit of our ability. So too with tradition. It is a common liberal renegadism to claim that "because an idea is ancient and . . . widely received is no argument in its favor . . . in fact that "should immediately suggest the need for testing" -- thus for doubting or even rejection (James Harvey Robinson).

Tradition is made up of these "ancient ideas": Proverbs, Ecclesiastes, Aesop's Fables -- ancient to Aristotle. Tradition must be seen as like science, truths that have been tested over and over; Newton's Theory of Gravitation was taken as absolute for centuries, but was found to be but a mere approximation. If a demand had been raised to have all science put on hold until retested, as Robinson demanded for tradition, it would have been ignored as absurd. Modernity belies its claim to uphold reason by rejecting tradition. "What can we reason, but from what we know?" and have repeatedly tested? Better the liberals should be testing their own claims.

The French philosopher Montaigne declared reason to be a

limited and untrustworthy instrument. Why trust reason when instinct, used by animals, is a safer guide? And Orwell gave up his beloved utopianism because of the "fundamental irrationality of human behavior". Well, we all have moments of weakness. Reason is but a tool; can there be an untrustworthy hammer or knife, or even nuclear energy? We assume the tool to be in reasonable working order; if not, it is not a tool, but a defective tool. And human rationality almost by definition depends upon human purpose; purpose may be defective but to claim human rationality defective is likewise to claim an untrustworthy tool. Human rationality is like a good computer; if you put junk in you will get junk back out. To blame human rationality for our problems is like blaming the hammer for the bent nail. This is no way meant to deny the possibility of faulty reason.

Walter Lippmann in later life declared the "central principle of Western philosophy: that man's reason is the ruler of his appetite." Would it were so. These are not simple errors, nor excusable as a manner of speaking. They are deeply deceptive; the fact that it was not intentional means nothing to the learner. Human error and evil arise most commonly out of a flawed, untrained purpose, producing the bent nail or the soiled reputation. Yet reason is man's most powerful tool, and it is essential in the rebuilding of our society that it be utilized to show the irrationalities of modernity; both science and "religion" must be used in guiding society toward that proper to man.

Religion
<u>Religion</u>

It is of first importance to comprehend what religion is -- of supreme importance, not only for what it is but for its misuse and what it is not. Nothing that is not humanly spiritual in its essence should be given the name of religion. Spiritual means <u>of innate feelings</u>, with all of the sacredness -- meaning extreme preciousness -- of home felt so devastatingly in homesickness, of belonging as felt in love, in the aridity of alienation, and in the at-homeness of community. But beyond these are the most powerful "forces" (as Durkheim called them even though they are so deep as to be nearly unconscious) of a collectiveness of protection, and an urge to rise up. All of these are nearly continuously being scrutinized by conscience.

These feelings are real; they are innate -- phylogenetic.

Their breaking into the consciousness of some remote ancestors marks the beginning of humanness. And it is an implacable want and fact that when these innate feelings are ignored, repudiated, abandoned as social guidance, people cease to be human. Scientists have affirmed what Darwin suspected, that much of basic, human social behavior is determined, guided, by innate feelings. But that guidance must be taught, as young robins and wolf cubs are taught. If instead children are not taught, or are taught that which thwarts or rejects the innate guidance, they cannot, will not, grow to human beings, but rather will become not even animals (innately guided). They will tend to be, depending on the strength of the corruption, beasts with the vast powers of imagination.

It was a tremendous awakening for man when these forces began to grip his mind. Almost certainly it was the event which fired the organizing efforts that produced syntactical language, which in turn marks the gap between animal and human. Furthermore we find a constant affinity between religion and language or the "word", and also between religion and law. Justice was judged by natural law, that "proper to man", irrespective of any man-made judgment. And that "proper to man" was fixed by innate feelings which are the true roots of all religion. Contempt for the law was as evil for the Greeks -- hubris -- as for the Hebrews. Atheism is a rejection of rationality, by rejection of guidance according to that "proper to man"; it leads to the perception of a desolate aloneness in a vast dead universe. It never occurred to the human mind until the modernity of the Age of Reason and Enlightenment -- surely an Age of Irrationality. Bertrand Russell saw man as solitary on a vast and barren plain under a darkened sky trudging beetle-like towards a black horizon.

Comprehension of religion requires consideration of the concepts of science and culture. These constitute the accumulation of efforts of men "to know", and were until the beginning of the rational modernity of the Greeks, pursued in common. Science is of the physical world, "through the senses", concrete and translatable into any language. True religion is of the feelings, spiritual, evanescent, powerful: homesickness, anger, love, belonging, rising up, joy; these are the themes of great poetry and song. Culture is the combination of both the physical knowledge and our comprehension of feelings as guidance, in the service of survival and rising up. And people must be taught to see that the physical is but the house, or the body; the spiritual is purpose of the house of body -- the why and wherefore, the whence and whither.

Common religion is perceived in three aspects: (1) the urgings or source of the urgings for guidance, and (2) the erring human efforts by people gathered in churches or "religions" to comprehend, to celebrate and to teach that guidance, and (3) add a recognition of powerfully imposed false perceptions of religion and/or humanness. Note that we find exactly this same trifurcation for culture and for science: the reality and truth, human fumblings to find it, and vicious calumniators seeking to deprive humanity of the truth. The intent to distort and to stultify is much stronger in culture than in that part we call science, because all culture is purpose, and its essence is guidance -- and for reasoning beings that must be predominately spiritual guidance. It is this guidance that tyrants and renegades seek to grasp into their own control for the clear and obvious purpose of enslavement of the people to an elite. Human culture and religion, like science being the works of erring men seeking an ideal -- the ideal of truth, contain unknown but also arguable errors. Only by teaching all three (science, religion, culture) at home, in K-12, and throughout life, and by example in daily life and in literature, and by holding fast to a purpose and a tradition, which is repeatedly checked, can the error be reduced.

The source of the feelings, "forces", or urgings for social guidance toward that "proper to man" has been the principal point and focus of criticisms and of attempts to denigrate and reject their guidance. It is essential to comprehend that in a rational sense it makes little difference whether our innate feelings, or those revelations claimed by prophets, arise from God or from a Creative Nature that has ingrained guidance in all DNA. Not only do we know that guidance does exist, people always have known it to exist, and have created their most magnificent symbols and works in recognition. The very existence of humanness and civilization and culture are products of that recognition.

Only a stultifying defensiveness and unthinking irresolution can account for the inflexibility with which so many modern Christians hold to some ancient claimed-meaning of religious texts. Christ quoted the prophets but did not go around insisting upon an unflinching rigidity. If the sabbath was made for man, not man for the sabbath, then surely the words of the prophets too were made for the men who were to hear them. Augustine, Abelard, Maimonides, Hooker and others have urged a rational interpretation of sacred works, and a recognition that they were to be understood by unlettered peoples; even Paul followed a mild prudence. The Scholastic philosophers understood and warned of the need to keep religious teachings within the realms of God-given reason. Maybe Moses did talk with God and Christ arose, or maybe these were but means of emphasizing supreme messages: the law and the hope.

The supreme message of all religious has always been, must always be: "Righteousness is what is loved". That is Christ's message. We know, reason and science knows, that we receive messages of guidance that make what is right and proper seem good -- loved. All life does. The explication of that guidance, its teaching and advancement, is the Way, the only way to rising up as human beings. The "truth shall make you free", but we know that all truths in our vale of uncertainty are but approximate; let there be room for discussion by all. This guidance came from somewhere; naming that as The Creator is but placing a fixedness.

Furthermore, people love to love, love to admire, love ritual, and to express and maintain their humanness through all of these. Let there be a Sistine Chapel and a Church in the Wildwood and a Hallelujah Chorus. Let there be a Roscelin and a Loyola, a Shakespeare and a Babbitt. Demand that our churches teach human guidance in their own way. Demand that our schools and universities, our foundations and government teach truth and excellence <u>above</u> <u>all</u>, in a search for that proper to man -- that which is loved. Demand that our media and entertainment exhibit such truth and excellence in ways proper to the rising up of Western civilization.

In the words of Buddha, "Have you heard, Ananda, that the Vajjians foregather together often, and frequent public meetings of their clans? . . . So long, Ananda, as the Vajjians foregather thus often, so long may they be expected not to decline, but to prosper".

People must reform society, through wards and community, if they are to remain human and free. They must learn about and seek to discuss the issues "proper to man", and culture, and plans for rising up. "Observe that of man's whole terrestrial possessions, unspeakably the noblest are his Symbols, divine and divine seeming . . . The Church: what a word was there; richer than Golconda . . . In the heart of the remotest mountains rises the little Kirk . . . Strong was he that had a Church, what we can call a Church: he stood thereby, though 'in the center of Immensities, in the conflux of Eternities,' yet manlike toward God and man; the vague shoreless Universe had become for him a firm city, and a dwelling which he knew . . . worth living for and dying for."

Tradition

Tradition is experienced and verified truth." Ask the ball club manager, the farmer, the broker, anyone who must produce.

History is philosophy teaching by example. It teaches how much the present is a creature of the past, that there is a sternly logical sequence in world affairs, little open to chance or change, only to implacable purpose: Bolingbroke.

Most people have seen in a park some scraggly animal, like a mother deer, wasted by diarrhea, tattering along begging candy from thoughtless people, while a sickly fawn straggled behind. Neither will survive the first fall flurry. That is the fate of those who have lost their tradition. Survival is accomplished by adapting to an adequately nurturing ecological niche. The knowledge as to what constitutes a sustaining diet was stored as innate knowledge in the deer. It was not greed nor sloth, nor a modernity, that has led the deer from her tradition. It was a temptation, against which no defense had ever evolved.

The helping, guiding, protecting hand of a parent is not intended to deprive, or to stunt or frustrate the normal, healthy progress of a growing child. No more does tradition seek to limit people or a society. "(T)he cutting edge of reform and renewal, as opposed to the blunt edge of a tradition and stagnation," is a phrase in a recent scholarly journal on religion. Note the demagoguery, "cutting-edge," "reform" as opposed to "blunt" and "stagnation." But take an example. The Bill of Rights poses a "blunt edge" to force "stagnation" of efforts to destroy our freedoms, while activist judges provide a cutting edge to destroy liberty in the name of "reform." The tradition of the "three Rs" has received the "cutting edge" of NEA "reform," to our great loss and shame.

Those renegadisms were planned and pushed to execution by an evil party. Loyalty to a people's tradition and culture is not the product of untutored minds. Folly can be avoided only by understanding and a guiding purpose. Loyalty grows out of family and local associations, but tradition can evolve only from a long-held purpose. The great value of tradition is that it provides the helping hand, across barren and trackless stretches when the path to purpose is unclear. You do what you have learned to depend upon. "Stagnation" and irrationality arise from failure of reason and decay of purpose, not from the tested wisdom of experienced tradition.

That point needs emphasis, readily achieved by considering

custom. It is often said that tradition is knowledge of how things should be done, or is that part of a culture that concerns customs. While tradition and custom certainly overlap, custom is but a habitual way of doing things, in order to take advantage of learned motor skills, as an aid in avoiding mistakes, and other such secondary purposes. Tradition is a far broader concept; it is our sole aid across barren ground where landmarks are absent.

Tradition is in fact closely allied with "uncontested terms". To begin with, the meaning of most all words must be uncontested or it is impossible to communicate. As agreement decreases, the possibility of accommodation, and thereby of avoiding conflict, decreases. But uncontested terms go far beyond words. American and all of Western tradition has back into prehistory, held that "motherhood" was sacred, rule of law was sacred, that there was a power above man that spoke to him through the voice of conscience and other spiritual feelings. Only a few years ago, these were still uncontested traditional beliefs -- not beliefs but axioms -- and people were no longer taught <u>why</u>? Then when the question arose, no one or few could answer. Contrary to Max Weber, tradition and its authority are only "perceived" to be sacred because of age, but this is misunderstanding. The wisdom of tradition and thereby its authority arise not from age, rather it is old because of validity under long testing. But being a human construct -- like all culture, religion, and accepted truth -- it contains errors which it is our duty to define and to remove.

So renegades in the hegemonic media rejected the use of the word "motherhood," "as a ploy of the pro-lifers." Rule of law was jeered as denying to the people "what they wanted." And fascism, as the glorious promises of "change" and "choice," became the "cutting edge" to destroy human society, Western culture, and rational humanness.

Modernists who denigrate tradition forget, or ignore, or are ignorant of the fact that the great freedom and creativeness of Greek philosophy was fixed and protected by tradition. There was a tradition that still exists today in science and engineering, that allowed and encouraged critical discussions between various schools and within a school. Certainly this did not begin with Thales, as Popper suggests; it was at least as old as the tradition of the tribal elders settling problems. It seems that the shamans, the intellectuals, have never accepted it, but rather have always sought to gain power by ruse, by dissembling, by fear. In the beginning all knowledge was one, but when science became separated out from other knowledge, it apparently became exempt from the suppression of criticism by intellectuals.

Neither democracy nor liberalism require abandonment of tradition; they, in fact, need it for guidance because reason is not enough. Tradition is, by its nature, truth as nearly as is discernable. Thus arises the extreme importance of real history. History to the scientist is the literature, with all its subsequent corrections; to the farmer, it is his record book and his memory. That too is tradition because it has been shown to work, not just as expediency for the moment, but as dependable over generations.

Tradition has been charged with "setting limits to the possibilities of human action." This is nonsense. It is purpose, what you want most, that sets limits, but even there one is really concerned with the objectives and how to overcome natural limits that interfere with the attainment. It is traditional that athletes exercise, get proper rest, don't smoke, eat proper foods. Those are limits?

Teaching children and youths the joys of unrestrained sex, to say nothing of masturbation and anal and oral sex, can have as devastating an effect on their lives and the life of their society as candy for the deer. Teachers, university professors and intellectuals generally denigrate and seek to destroy tradition without comprehension or even consideration of the consequences. But, some do understand yet persist in uprooting civilization, intentionally.

We are fast becoming a people without social roots in tradition, principles, or history. Our free and open society is given the name of an abstraction, a straw man: capitalism, and it is blamed for all the sins man ever committed, all the cruelties and vices ever imagined. Yet when the state rules and determines all, as fascism, it is given the glowing name of social democracy and is endowed with all the virtues ever imagined in earthly utopias or heavenly paradise.

Modernity scourges tradition as a great evil when, in fact, it is what has stood the test of time, of crises and change and been found sound and valuable. Even outworn traditions or habit seldom becomes detrimental. Commonly they merely slide into irrelevancy, as in the example of a British study of artillery crews during WW II under a need to speed up operations. Movies of gun operations were found to show a very puzzling act. At a certain point in a gun crew of five, just before firing, two of the men simply stood at attention for three full seconds before resuming activity. No one could explain why; it was just part of a learned motor pattern. Officers and men at the gunnery school all knew that three seconds were "necessary", but for what was unknown. Someone recalled an old retired artillery colonel who long ago had come up through the ranks, and he was called in to observe the movie film. He was puzzled too, but asked that the film be rerun. The officer watched the old man's arms and feet jerking faintly as he imagined going through the operations of the firing sequences. When the mysterious three seconds were past, there came a quick "Ah ha! Of course. They are holding the horses." Horses hadn't been used for many years.

Note the non-adverse nature of the anachronism. This is characteristic of tradition for a very concrete reason. If there be in a tradition something that skirts unknown danger, sooner or later the inevitable variations will find it. Hence some procedure that has been followed for a long time is bound to be safe. Change, except for clear and certain reasons, is generally not worth the risk.

"Change" of any kind was used by the New Deal to stretch the Depression into a decade, and "change" was used as an excuse to put the iron straps of the federal bureaucracy on the giant health care industry.

<u>Truth</u>

The most incessant occupation of man is the ascertainment of truth." J.S. Mill

"If that is true, what else must be true?"

"Our age is so impregnated with lies that even a voluntary blood sacrifice cannot give us back the truth." - Simone Weil.

Self-deception is common among liars. A British pro-Communist publisher of books in the 1930s commissioned an editor for a book, *Christianity*, which was to contain a number of contributions. He informed the to-be editor, "I am anxious to publish nothing with which I am not in agreement. Its starting point must be that. Christianity is not solely a religion of salvation, but must concern itself with politics and go 'all out' for immediate socialism." Yet, he complained, when the bias was too blatant, "too much a left wing exposition . . . was to be avoided." "All sorts of devices will occur to you" as long as "the   reader inevitably draws the right conclusion."

Truth wears a different face for everybody. She is said to be at the bottom of a well; whoever looks down in search of her sees his own reflection at the bottom and is persuaded not only that he has seen the goddess, but that she is much better looking than he imagined. So wrote poet Lowell. But that is capricious; truth is far more peremptory. Sir Walter paid with his life for slipping on his own warning: it is dangerous to follow truth too near the heels.

Truth is central to all human endeavor. It shares with purpose and rationality an often, yet unrecognized, oneness that guides all humanity. It is impossible to have any one without having all three -- a fact deserving attention.

A scholarly conservative, a few years back, wrote of an "irredeemable duality": Right and Left represent such ordinaries as "Roundhead and Cavalier, Whig and Tory, down to Wet and Dry," and on to juxtaposing communism and capitalism. The writer seemed totally unaware that the final pair represent unconnected levels of inhumanness and humanness far beyond the realm of politics.   It is sheer perniciousness to fail to realize that "communism vs. anti-communism" pairs totally unlike categories, non-comparable.   The writer also tells of a Chinese student in London, having fled there from Tiananmen Square, saying, "Now I know what fascism's really about." "Fascism?" cries the writer, as though he had never heard of Lenin's one time friend Max Eastman who declared communism to be "superfascism." When communism fell, the Hard Left overnight became the Hard Right. Of course that was but liberal dissembling; what it was before and remained, was an evil inhumanness.

There is truth and right and when a person denies it, try to help him, but if he will not see, Paul advised, "have no company with him that he might feel ashamed." Schopenhauer had a different idea. He explained that when we argue against a man with reason and explanation, taking all pains to convince only to discover that he _will_ not understand; it has to do with his _will_. Logic is useless, you must appeal to his self-interest, his desire, as Machiavelli advised. The intellect may seem to lead the will (purpose), but only as a guide leads his master, as the lame man who is carried on the shoulders of the strong blind man. Men are driven by what they feel, instincts that are much of the time unconscious. Character lies in the will and is continuity of purpose. So-called intellectuals say, with Spinoza, that good and bad, truth and falsity, are relative terms, mere prejudices, yet every person soon must face actual human needs. Schopenhauer demanded that people face the "raw reality of evil." Real people must seek to rise up. Help them to see the brilliance of hope, the enabling worship of heros, the wisdom to be found in history, but only with truth.

Any common person <u>knows</u> that there is truth: a turn left takes you to Chicago, right to New York. Purpose defines truth, and you must know whither you are bound, or it doesn't make any difference. First there is the simple truth of conformability, as rationality, or is it definition: one-half of two-thirds equals two-sixths. Hence the original <u>pattern</u>. We cut two-thirds of an apple into two parts; each will be one-third. It is all rational, it fits, it is conformable. One can go on to the real and imaginary solutions of a particular differential equation and observe the two principal characters of light waves.

Next there are truths in the physical world. The sun will rise tomorrow. No, No! the sun never moves (in that sense); the earth turns. Once the earth was wrongly believed to be a sphere, because in olden times a sphere represented a higher perfection; nor are planetary orbits circles. Newton's gravitational mechanics, once taken as the very acme of the power of reason, is now known to be a mere approximation. And as we go away from something like definitions, two plus two, we find that truth is always a way-station in throwing off error.

Finally we arrive at the social-spiritual world: "and the greatest of these is charity," or modesty is the soul of feminine grace. If you seek to live in freedom in a voluntary society, it is necessary to comprehend that which people have always known: that it is desirable and admirable and that there be charity and feminine grace. If you would rather submit to a sub-human tutelage to the State, you don't need them, nor decency nor morality; you need only obey.

Truth, in this social-spiritual world, can often be sensed from feelings, as can morality, brotherhood, purpose and conscience. Otherwise it must be sought. We find truth by experience. That's why tradition and history are so important for a human society, and mean little or nothing to Statists. (That is in fact a way of identifying them.) We put one foot ahead of the other, squirm for footing and then another step, sometimes having to try a different step. That is the way to truth for the mountain climber or the scientist; that is the method of the Creator's evolution. Some steps lead into dead ends and must be retaken. Genius is but the mountain climber who can look to the past, look ahead, and see farther where good steps should be possible.

Lowell warned over a century ago that the belief was spreading that truth should be settled by a show of hands. This has become the raging monster of liberalism, consuming all rationality. J.S. Mill and jurist O.W. Holmes urged that truth be exposed to the market place, trial-by-combat. Let them try their wives' virtue there; as well leave beauty, honor, all decency, as leave truth. As well use a bright sword for moving dirt and stones. Men go to the market to win, not to reflect upon purpose in the world. Truth is little better than a fair, farm boy for the con men at the market.

Truth requires connections. Anyone who has assembled a do-it-yourself kit knows that when things fail to fit, error exists. It is the great beauty of Nature that all things are connected and fit; the parts required to assemble an atom, a gene, or a galaxy. Thus, in science, the great restraint is that it cannot be truth unless it fits together. Accordingly, Einstein declared beforehand that three connections had to be proved, otherwise his theory would have to be discarded. Even with fantastic luck it took nearly two decades to prove them.

In 1923, the third, the red-shift, was confirmed and Karl Popper pointed out how diametrically opposite to this truly scientific attitude was the attitude of Marx and Freud. Over and over again, these pseudo-scientists, charlatans, had stretched their theories or ignored the facts, yet they were glorified for it. Their errors and deceptions are today beyond doubt, but they continue to whirl upon the stage of the modern university, almost unnoticed in the surrounding irrationality.

Toward the end of the Red-thirties social engineer, Karl Mannheim complained, "The most disastrous effect of events in recent years is not that certain groups have abandoned themselves to irrationality. Far worse, other groups from whom we have expected some resistance to irrationality, have overnight lost their belief in the power of reason."[131]

George Orwell declared in 1940 that "one ought to

---

[131]*Man and Society In an Age of Reconstruction* p. 40, Karl Mannheim (Harcourt, Brace).

recognize that the present political chaos is connected with the decay in language." A few years later he wrote that "the idea that history could be truthfully written" was being abandoned. He blamed totalitarianism for destroying the "common basis of agreement," and questioned whether the "liberal tradition" could be kept alive if all the world were ruled by fascism.

Hayek (p. 155) declared that "totalitarian propaganda . . . (was) destructive of all morals because it undermines the foundation of all morals: the sense of and respect for truth." He went on to add "the complete perversion of language" is its major characteristic.

Hayek was certainly a little shortsighted. Totalitarianism surely destroys truth, but it is but a part and a rather small part of the Western modernity where truth is also destroyed. Today, everywhere in the schools and churches, in the government and in entertainment, lies and the teaching of hate are pervasive. It was Hegel who proclaimed there to be no other criterion of truth except that which serves the State. How completely this principle has been incorporated into all government in Washington. The great liberal, J.S. Mill, believed that society cannot presume to decide between truth and falsity, or to lend support to truth once decided. This is to reject rationality, education, and the very ideas of purpose, progress and justice.

Until 1964, rumor played a minor role in the respectable media because truth was allowed as the basic defense against libel. Therefore, "sources" had to be evaluated. Then the Supreme Court intervened with *NY Times v Sullivan,* and decided to change the law; "public figures" could not win a libel suit on the basis of untruth.[132] If the media, academia or government were interested in truth, they would have devised a satisfactory way for people to distinguish deceits, lies and evils: in education, socialism, in racism and welfarism, and in human society. *Sullivan* declared it unwanted.

Russell Kirk has reminded us of the lesson, the myth, of

---

[132]In California, a police sergeant lost his protection from gross libel by the mere fact that the evil party in the media raised him, on their own assertion, to a "public figure." On the other hand, Lillian Hellman, who had spent a lifetime making herself a public figure, sued for libel and through her money and evil party influence demoralized an enemy for telling the truth. The savage grip was released only with Hellman going to her "just deserts".

Perseus who sought out the terror and struck it down with all his might.   King and company demanded to see what they were supposed to ignore. When they grew menacing, Perseus held forth the awful dead face of the Medusa; the blood curdling stare and grin. The dripping snaky locks turned King and courtiers to stone. We know not the original lesson, but we do know that some centuries later the fixed stare and snaky locks had become a frigid beauty, the mask of a woman beyond good or evil. Two centuries more and the evil beauty shows life, a faint sensual smile starts along the lips, but a note of haunting terror now lurks behind the eyes.   The monster haunting man's dreams had descended to concupiscence.[133]

The desire for the truth has been dying with God and human society, of which He was the Spirit, yet people of half the world have been struggling to stamp out of their midst the organized lies and terror of Statism. So it is beyond rationality why the liberals, the intellectuals, the great humanitarians of the West have struggled for years to lie about and to hide the horror of Statism, while forcing in every way the destruction of human society and its replacement by the State. The leer of the Medusa has become a smile, an invitation. Even a Jew has insisted that that most horrible holocaust of all, in Cambodia, was a legitimate attempt at a new vision for society.

The very purpose and essence of a large fraction perhaps most speech is to "impose." When people urge or even coerce you to believe or at least outwardly accept and conform to the perception that to "impose" is evil and that all culture is imposed, and therefore is evil, they too are imposing. Teaching that culture is relative is imposing a belief, as is the urging of any perception. Propaganda and indoctrination are imposed.

At one time our forbearers had no conception, no awareness of truth because they lived according to instinctive, phylogenetic

---

[133]Families must be protected from the obscene, but the core persons of a society must know the worst. Long after writing of terror lurking behind the eyes I came upon a quote from a modern Medusa (The Am. Spect., 12,94, p.92; from Anna Quindlen, recently of the *New York Times*). " . . . the smallest boy -- in on a first offence -- into the shower room, while the guards pretend not to look and leave him to find his own way out, blood trickling palely, crimson mixed with milky white, down the backs of his hairless thighs, the shadows at the backs of his eyes changed forever." Your society!

guidance. In time, they became aware of untruth and of reason's vagaries. The truth was always local, immediate -- is it prey or predator over the hill -- always visible for survival. But, with affluence, problems became longer range; answers required more knowledge, were more abstract. All of this was sharply impressed on the minds of the Greeks, much of 3,000 years ago. They knew that they valued freedom and, in time, they perceived that the only way to protect themselves from falling under the terror of a bureaucracy, which they observed in the neighboring god-king empires, was to struggle hard for that inside themselves which they could conceive of as "proper for man." Only by consciously struggling upwards could they escape the abyss of Statism. It was that purpose, to struggle upwards, that determined truth. Nothing is relative, except as being more or less up. To imagine that it didn't make any difference, of no more concern than right or left, was irrational nonsense that they couldn't imagine.

> "I do believe that there are gods, and in a higher sense . . . the noblest way is not to be disabling others, but to be improving yourselves:" (*Apology*).[134]

What you must see is that the mind's central concern for a billion years (remember the thinking protozoa) has been survival and rising. For the phylogenetic there is nothing else; so too even for reasoning man, but beyond are such artifacts as ignorance or chance, and ideology: some theory that will promise rewards unearned by struggle upwards. By propaganda and indoctrination, such fantasies can be imposed even as truth's struggle upwards for culture is jeered as "imposed." Human society is not an ideology, nor does it ever depend upon an ideology. It seeks to relate the truth to experience and to tradition, and to the spiritual inner voice.

Hence we can see that a purpose "to rise," or morality, truth and human decency are as truly "imposed" as a young robin's learning is imposed. But indoctrination, propaganda and all things contrary to man's spiritual needs are imposed as the sentence of the condemned is imposed.

---

[134]Plato's Socrates.

9. FAMILY

INTRODUCTION

"The family does not symbolize human continuity, it _is_ that continuity."

"In light of what we know now . . . it is not permissible for us to go on destroying family life when we know that we are destroying it." Society has always, for reasons of self-interest if for no other reason, educated its children so that they grew up law abiding, with socialized aims and purposes.

"The old tribal system", for all its faults and for all its superstitions, "was a moral system. Our people today produce criminals and prostitutes and drunkards not because it is their nature to do so but because their simple system of order and traditions and convention has been destroyed . . . by the impact of our civilization". We have "an inescapable duty" to rebuild a system of order and tradition.

That was the essence of what was written by a Western intellectual about the destruction of black society in South Africa, and it was acclaimed as a great humanitarian statement.[135] But equal destruction has been visited upon the common people of America without one word of a similar objection. Is it not shameful that our intellectuals, our professors, and government bureaucrats could discern this truth in a far away land, but ignore it in their own society?

---

[135]Alan Paton, <u>Cry</u>, *The Beloved Country* (1948), p. 143.

Look at our great problems:

1. Crime, violence, abuse on the streets and in the homes.
2. Education: we teach children of sex, sodomy, and hatred for their society, but nothing of the social and cultural reasons for attitudes of discipline, personal responsibility, and a joy in learning.
3. Culture and government: both nearly cease to exist as supports for humanness, and decency, for a human society.

There is not a knowledgeable person in the field of crime and abuse who does not recognize that the root of our disaster here lies in the deliberate destruction of family order. Look at the major reports on education; every report, if it is at all comprehensive, points to the central importance of homes, in pre-school particularly. It is claimed by competent authorities that by the age of 6 months, a child has fairly fixed its central attitude toward life nearly permanently. Certainly we know that by the age of five or six years if a child has not developed a positive _attitude_ toward discipline, personal responsibility, and a joy in learning, he is not likely ever to do so, and if a child has not learned to read and with some enjoyment, by the time he is 9 or 10, he likely never will.

If a nation is to survive and to progress, it must make its number one priority the nurturing of a new generation. Through the ages, as our ancestors developed Western civilization, the raising of families was held up as the prime function of public institutions, of religion which long performed many of the responsibilities of today's government, and of government itself. This requires a culture with institutions and laws wherein that purpose is recognized as predominant. Such a purpose rejects all relativism.

Make no mistake! When the renegades in Washington and New York paint their glowing pictures of nationalized health care, and nationalized education in "Goals 2000," and in a nationalized information highway, and nationalized criminal justice, they are talking about Statism. And they certainly are not talking about collectivization, so what they are talking about is national socialism or fascism. They have prepared you for it, through destruction of morality, and truth, destruction of rule of law with the resulting destruction of families and a human society.

All of these problems demand the rebuilding of families. And the rebuilding of families obviously requires that we <u>intend</u> to do so. Oh, it is said, the women don't want families, and the men don't want to support them. That is simply not true, not of the great majority. And if true of a small minority, it is only because that is what our tax dollars teach them in school, and that is the lesson our advertising dollar provides on TV. We have the power and the <u>duty</u> to turn off those dollars.

It is all very simple. You can see it in the past. Many children will not learn to read, and many more will not learn to read for enjoyment (history, philosophy, literature) if what they are given is "look-say": "See Spot run, run, run . . ." reading instruction. Nor are the problems of crime and abuse going to be solved with police, and gun control, and an army of arrogant bureaucrats with their regulations and lawsuits. Nor are men and women going to raise families in the cultural rot of today. Families and education, discipline, decency, culture, and humanness are the products of voluntary human society, and regaining one is the only real and permanent solution. People must be given a real sense of participating in an admirable purpose; then they will want to know, want to do their best, want to have and to belong to families, and have culture because these are all innate needs of human beings.

The obvious fact is that the evil party has struggled for a century to destroy these very things. Two centuries ago, even before socialism, Rousseau noted the decay of families in the liberal societies of Enlightenment's individualism. He sought to persuade women to claim a positive family contract and to shun the soul-less embrace of the state. Twenty thousand years ago, the Council of Elders in Aryan tribes conducted so-called male "initiations" for young lads reaching puberty. The Elders "waged a systematic assault lasting over months on the bodies of the youngsters." They were taught obedience and responsibility and, through religious activity their aggression was sublimated into a mature sense of power which does not need violent exhibitions.

Lorenz has described the relatively monogamous and lifetime commitments of greylag geese pairs. The female, as is almost universally the case in nature, does the choosing; the male will be kept for some extended period exhibiting his abilities to perform the functions necessary in the raising of a brood. In the end, the female makes sure that he has all the stability and perseverance necessary. Only then is he accepted.

Nature knows that the female cannot, except in the most unusual cases, raise her young by herself. We know too that a woman cannot, except in rare cases, raise a boy, certainly not so that he has much prospect of becoming an adult male capable of raising a family of his own. In fact, she cannot so raise very certainly even such a female. To raise children to the age of five or six with attitudes of discipline, responsibility, and positive outlooks on learning and cooperating is not a part-time job. For even two devoted parents to succeed demands an entire environment of other families in a human society.

We spend billions of dollars on aliens, tens of billions seeking to remedy the curse of look-say reading and hundreds of billions on wastrels and druggies. It's time this was ended and that raising a family was made the most respected and supported of endeavors.

We have job quotas now; so it would be nothing new to give the top quota to undivorced heads of families with multiple children. Furthermore, a girl could marry at 18, have available high quality video or TV courses in history, English, foreign language, science and beginning law or medicine. She could raise four or five children and by the time she is about 30 take two or three years of professional training and then share a top quota with her husband as a lawyer, doctor, or in business. The problems of crime, education, importation of aliens, drugs and culture could be made to disappear in a few years. It is in fact the intent of the renegades who control the media, universities, and entertainment that this not happen. Their plan is State enforcement in every phase of life -- fascism.

Families must be the platoons, the building blocks, for a society of people seeking to survive, and culture is all the knowledge, customs, and ritualized communions essential for its cohesion and guidance. A civilization is the whole: of people, culture, institutions and homeland, organized for survival and rising up.

And what, asked Rousseau, that prince of liberal renegades, "is the surest mark of their (a society's) preservation and prosperity? Their numbers and population. Seek nowhere else this mark . . . of a good government . . . The government under which a people wanes and diminishes is the worst . . . No, whatever they may say, when, despite its renown, a country is depopulated, it is not true all is well."

"(T)he family of the last few decades has grown even more unstable, until it has reached the point of actual disintegration," wrote Harvard Professor Sorokin in 1941.

Especially in the wilderness of our cities, Redfield[136] wrote in 1946, there is little to reinforce family ties, and much to break them down and to weaken all that could sustain them: the church, the schools, entertainment and public figures, commercialized distractions, and the proclaimed respectability of the divorce court.

Increasingly the family was presented, not as an organic structure to be handed from generation to generation, but rather as the individual creation of a generation, unconcerned with the past, with the future, not even concerned with people's real needs. It is always much easier and satisfying to fill the need for amusement, or appetite -- a beer, sex, or a ball game -- than the need to fill the far

---

[136]Margaret Park Redfield (*Am. J. of Sociology*, Nov., 1946)

greater joy in a great purpose. Young people are taught that they have a "right" to condoms and lifestyles, with no regard as to who is going to support them, provide the executive style jobs, the pleasantly ordered society, or a meaning to life itself.

I recall vividly watching PBS's Robin MacNeil, sitting on his fat ass, a quirky smile on his face, responding to the problem of a man who had committed suicide, over his son and the Vietnam war: "Isn't it a shame that his government couldn't have given him something to live for."

Before 1940 he would have been laughed out of town, even by a bunch of farmers. The whole idea of the Enlightenment, of Liberalism, was that there was <u>not to be</u> some power to give people "something to live for." The Church, Christianity that provided the basis for our freedom, our government, our morality and responsibility for our fellow men, had been denied and driven from the public square for seeking, much more flexibly than the State ever could, the privilege or duty of doing just that, on a far higher level of humanness than even imaginable by a bunch of bureaucrats. What a person will "live for" or die for must be taught in the home, reinforced in parent and society-directed schools, and exemplified throughout a culture. To conceive of that as something the State ought or even can do is to reveal a soul of rot and a mind of renegadism. Millions of young men did not volunteer or assent to go and kill millions of Germans, but to destroy the idea that the State could dictate that for which one was to live. You see that idea still lives and is the very purpose of the liberal-supported evil party.

AGGRESSION

Nature has provided a non-negotiable "reality principle": that there exists certain inevitable facts and limitations in survival. Man was not designed for civilization because he was not designed for reason; he has yet a long way to go in learning to live with it in safety. The "reality principle" must begin at the beginning, with survival.

All authority, order, indignation, and law itself, spring from aggression, the very essence of the implacable commitment to survival. In nature, it is controlled by other instincts, but in reasoning man, it must be controlled by reason. In early tribal society that was the task of the Council of Elders, particularly as mentioned through the influence of initiation rituals.

The principal means by which society has come to control male aggression has been through marriage and family. Monogamous pairing is not uncommon among animals, particularly (non-herd) social animals, and its purpose in nature is exactly that of traditional human society. The male must show not his hardware but his spiritual character; the female looks for stability, responsibility and aggressiveness only to a degree necessary to protect her nest. He is chosen for his fathering qualities because the female is unable to raise her young alone, and this is no less true of modern women. It is gross dissembling of the evil party to force the perception that restraint is unnatural and a tyranny devised by Puritans.

We do have natural instincts but they need instruction and directing, just as with animals and, furthermore, certain natural controls are largely missing in civilization. We teach children not to be greedy, gluttonous, slothful and lazy because the natural need for these in a harshly competitive environment is no longer present. So too sexual restraint must be taught -- <u>imposed</u> -- so that the role of the human female approaches that of her counterpart in Nature. It must be done to obtain the nurturing of two-parent families.

Male aggression is a central problem for human society. Much of culture is directed toward checking violence, as through ritual, and channeling it into constructive activity. In the *Iliad,* at the beginning of Western culture, the ultimate concern was how order was to be restored after the most powerful warrior loses control. In primitive societies, the Council of Elders very early became aware of the disrupting tendencies of young males when not kept busy. It was the beginning of ethical education, as the bodies of youths were systematically assaulted over months of severe testing to teach obedience, responsibility, and the sacredness of the tribe. Aggression was channelled into a concern for social order through religious activity.

As culture weakens, the will to maintain order fails and there is increasing danger that young male gangs will riot. The principle tactic for taming male aggression is by limiting their access to females through marriage, while requiring support of the family.

But repression can be carried too far, by mother or family, by wife, or by modern psychological repression. The result may be a wimpish indifference which may even include a repressed violence. When aggression is blocked, the erotic instinct is inhibited, resulting in a sissy or a homosexual, or the weakened male may be attracted to a dominating woman and become henpecked.

Obviously the taming must aim for a balance that results in the aggression being converted into a calm sense of power which does not need violence or arrogance to prove itself. Cultural failure on one ends leaves violent and incorrigible brutes, while the other extreme may produce ineffectual males, afraid of women and with an aversion to children.

Nuclear patriarchal families have been an integral part of the survival and progress of our forbearers for some millions of years. Footprints believed to be of father, mother and child have been found as fossils. Aryan languages: Sanskrit, Latin, Germanic, Celtic, Slavic and others, have names for father, mother, brother, sister and daughter that are so related as to assure a common origin and thereby that families predated Sanskrit. There the root "Pa" meant protector and supporter.

Mother's roles are well defined in nature; Ma in Sanskrit stood for the maker; in biological terms, females of all mammals are similar. The quoted observations on footprints sets father at least three million years old, which biologically is not very old, yet far pre-dating culture. The father's role, both innate and cultural, has been as harnessed to the raising of offspring, not unlike that which Lorenz cites for the monogamous greylag geese. The male aggression that had, previously no doubt, gone to effect a more widespread placing of genes was harnessed by an evolutionary adaptation to the raising of specific offspring from a mate. The male role, more so than the deep innateness of motherhood, requires teaching, learning by example and emulation of a respected and revered figure, ancestors and tradition.

There are definite indications that a strong patriarchal role of protection and guidance by males is characteristic of natural tribal societies, both pre-human and human. But when social stability sufficiently negates any necessity for protection, the males become increasingly unneeded for physical survival. It would seem that when this condition was reached in a number of cases, the male role deteriorated to something like a "warrior class", or became piratically parasitic. It was then that the feminine remainder of a corrupted society became matriarchal until destroyed by male tribesmen.

Predominately in animals, it is the male who exhibits the sartorial finery while the female is quite plain. That is because the male must be dressed-up in order to be chosen. The females doing the choosing have no need for attractive dress. This was distinct for man through the age of chivalry and remained largely true through the Enlightenment, but was beginning to change. By the 19th Century's Victorianism, the change of the fancy headdress from male to female was nearly complete. As society and family broke down, the man more-and-more did the choosing and the woman was thereby forced to attract. By the end of the 20th Century, many women had abandoned all modesty in their attempt to attract, becoming more and more courtesans or whores. And the men tend to a wimpish, weakly potent, "black widow's" mate. But the real black widow's mate adapted to his ways over ages; man has been to some degree thrust into this role (Sonny-to-Cher) <u>not</u> by culture, but by pernicious opinions and forced perceptions, anti-culture.

Of course, children will and are being most devastatingly malformed in this corruption. Mothers say, Oh I don't think so, they are growing out of it. Fine spirit, but misjudged, for the obvious and simple reason that there is nothing to grow into, no purpose, no rationality.

The sub-human horror Tocqueville warned of 150 years ago is here; the young fail to mature -- children remain children. Scientists have claimed that domestication of animals has interfered with normal physiological processes in particular ways; some signals which activate changes to adulthood are no longer received. They don't grow up! A master to a dog remains as his mother for all his life; he continues to play. Not so with a wolf. At a certain age he becomes an adult, and his master (mother) ceases to be his guide; he may obey if he wishes to. The responsibility for adulthood is not being taught to our children.

"Like all students, they're looking for moral wisdom and intellectual guidance . . . they want to grow up; instead they're exposed to talk . . . misguided political advice about the beauty of political protest as a prominent way of life; advertisements featuring beach parties and fancy cars . . . implicitly encouraging them to remain children. This is the deepest sense in which they are ill-served," (C. Lasch, *First Things*; 3, 94, p. 62). Compare this recent comment with the thoughts of W.H. Whyte in *The Organization Man*, written as the 60's revolution was germinating (in the following section on "Youth"). It concerns Whyte's presumptions about students' reactions to *The Caine Mutiny*, and students' actual reactions; as here they wanted to know what was <u>supposed</u> to be right.

"The world we inhabit is becoming less and less adult . . . so little work to do . . . so little suffering . . . answerable for so little . . . they cannot recognize when they move from being led to moving on their own free will . . . required to take charge and protect instead of demanding care. The loss in public responsibility comes from abandonment of morality . . . compromise follows compromise. Activity is discouraged, in politics, in scholarship; no decision has consequences because people have no power. Pleasure, promiscuity, drunkenness breaks all families and all humanness." (Lee Lescaze, review of Ivan Klima's, *Judge On Trial, WSJ*).

Homes even of caring parents, unselfishly devoting the best years of their lives to their children have nothing lasting to give them (recall the attitude of the canon who deposited the document in the Gotha church, p. 10): no sensible vision, no high models of action, no real sense of connections with past or future, or even with peers. The family -- the womb of society -- requires recognition of feelings, instincts, conventions, and of an unfolding spiritual veil within which each soul is accountable. Though bodily reproduction and training in living are its actions, the result must be civilized human beings, with a vision of belonging to an admirable purpose and understanding the essentials for survival. (See Bloom's, p. 57)

YOUTH

To be a child means to go barefoot after the rain, with soft water and grass below and birds and rainbow above. It means to feel the snowflakes fall, hear water chuckling down the draw from melting snow. It means to fish in the river, to lift the heavy bundles of golden wheat into shocks, and watch the horses plunge their noses deep into the water barrel. It means to believe and to trust in all things.

Man was not designed for civilization, but he has shown that it in fact can lead toward something proper for humanness. The real problem is the city; it was never designed for families, and is in fact the death of them. The city has no real use for children and they have ceased to be a public good. They are made into Murphy Brown playthings, yet we know that children raised so unnaturally are not likely to become human beings and raise families of their own. It is very clear to anyone who will look that far that in two or three decades more and more children will fail to become adults.

A column was written by Suzanne Fields after Mike Dukakis had been asked the Rape Question -- if his wife were attacked, what would he do. She wrote that the Duke had been fed a fat, fastball right over the plate, begging to be sent screaming over the fence. But the Duke popped up weakly behind the plate. No passion, no heart or instinct, no "take-it-or-leave-it masculinity", the kind of virility a woman instinctively knows she can count on "when in the wee hours there is heard the sound of breaking glass." She pointed out that while the Duke was studying for the debate, his stand-in at a fund raiser was Alan Alda.

Alan Alda, like the Fonz, Woody Allen, Dustin Hoffman, the Beach Boys, and all the rest of our "liberal culture," and The Duke and Bill Clinton, never grew up. Fields wrote that the point of *High Noon* and *Shane* was that Gary Cooper and Alan Ladd responded with the full measure of manhood on behalf of exploited women and children, and even an undeserving community.

The retarding of adulthood had become visible with James Dean, in *Rebel Without A Cause* (1955). His was a protest against the <u>failure</u> of masculine virtue and adult authority.[137] That is exactly what Dewey's education for socialism or even for his "socializing," was intended to eliminate. Western culture, as the books written before 1900 which he declared should not be read, is about "the masculine virtue and adult authority" that Jimmy Dean missed; his father was the gelded male in an apron. The teaching of that leadership is exactly the purpose of the Western "canon," and that purpose is exactly what the whole renegade liberal world forces people to perceive as being so offensive. Children, all

---

[137]*Rebel's* author was not the discoverer of this failure. Of the many who had noted it, the words of sometime Stalinist Dwight MacDonald in 1950 were: "Americans have been made into permanent adolescents by advertising, mass culture." Actually young people had become increasingly susceptible to mass culture and advertising because of the removal, from education and from our culture, of all the lessons and examples of human, responsible adulthood -- responsibility for human society -- by Dewey, Boas and the entire evil party.

people, must be taught how to live, even as do the robins and the wolves; and, as reasoning beings, with susceptibility to the mischief of imagination, they need taught-guidance far more seriously. In approaching this problem of what to do about young people, listen to a young man (age 20 in 1991) and an older woman from the 60s generation. The young one, a senior at a University of California branch, wonders what it would be like to grow up when you could "count on" things, like a career, a house, a family. He accused the boomers (his parents) of being the first middle class who failed to tell their children, "Someday this will be yours." Instead you taught us to be "young and stupid". "After legitimizing youthful rebellion you never let us have our own innocence (sic?) -- perhaps because Vietnam and Watergate shattered yours. That's why we're mature enough to worry about racism, the environment, abortion, the homeless, nuclear policy." We were fed on the video culture of bimbos, beer commercials and racy TV, "you created to idealize your irresponsible youth." "You thought you were 'giving America' a major re-evaluation of its identity."[138]

You gave us "freedom" of the latchkey, with missed parents and broken homes. And what about the "negroes in Mississippi" you cared so much about? "I'm (not) angry at you for selling out the system. It's that there won't be any system for <u>me</u> to sell out . . . the money isn't there any more." But "I can't blame you . . . (it's the) cutthroat capitalism . . ." Being angry at racism and the war in Vietnam, "that's not the same as allowing the system to unravel out of greed." Cable TV, BMWs, cellular phones, the whole mall culture reduced 12 year olds to wanting "everything <u>now</u>." At least (your parents) gave you a chance . . . "our kids will be even dumber, poorer, more violent . . . you missed your chance to change the world and robbed us

---

[138]Remember the famous journalist, quoted earlier, who declared that from 1933 to 1967, America had dropped its identification with every thing it had ever stood for. And the boomers found it in further need of change?

of the skills and money to do it . . . we could really use (help) . . . it's your last chance . . . (and) our only one."[139]

How terribly sad; how totally misunderstanding. A woman who was 20 in 1961 recently wrote her story as one of those (from above) who were "reevaluating America's identity" in the 60s. As a female, there was no tradition that she was responsible for external social order, but actually the rot began in homes where the female was supreme. "When asked 'Mommy, what did you do in the war?' . . . I honestly replied, 'Oh, Honey, I got stoned and missed the war.' Then I had to explain to her horrified expression that I didn't mean people threw rocks at me until I passed out, but that I lived my life in a slow stupor, wore sandals and see through shirts; and talked at great length, with utter conviction, about things of which I knew absolutely nothing. (Now it was) necessary to explain why getting stoned, walking around half-naked and passing judgment on things you don't know anything about (remember Roger Hilsman admitted the same thing after pushing the extermination of the leadership of a small country fighting against communism[140]) is a bad idea." She admits having "to choose my words carefully . . . cautious not to reveal embarrassing . . . ex-husbands." "I didn't want my daughter to think getting married and divorced is no big deal." Before, "I thought time flowed over things and covered them . . . I thought I had no permanent record . . . I didn't care what other people thought about me . . . Life wasn't precious, it was a commodity, a vehicle . . .

"It wasn't worth it. I have so much waste in my past it almost washes away my future . . . sometimes I hold my breath when I have to put down a name on a reference list . . . what may they know . . . think . . . There is a permanent record . .. your life history. You may be able to redeem it .

---

[139]*Newsweek* (7-1-91) "The Terrible Twenties". I was 20 in 1941, and the stories of the lad of 1991, and of the women (next) of 1961, are both as foreign as anything written in the previous 2,000 years.

[140]Hilsman was also of her generation; so much for "Vietnam shattering your innocence."

. . You can't shake it."[141]

The fifty year old is mistaken in largely blaming herself. The pressure for her to run wild was too great; today Suzanne Fields writes, "the pressures on women to work because it's (PC) are enormous." Both pressures have come from the evil party. Talk about things being <u>imposed</u>!

The twenty year old is a far more difficult case, he believes he has been done wrong, as certainly the 50 year old did, when 20. They were in fact both done wrong, denied a decent education, proper examples and guidance in understanding the responsibility and the rewards of a human society.

His down side is what sticks. "Vietnam and Watergate shattered your (innocence)"? My God! They created them; one of them said, "If Vietnam hadn't existed, we'd have had to create it." SDS began creating "Kent State" shortly after 1962. As for "racism, environment, abortion, homeless, nuclear policy", where is there or where has there been one Marxian socialist country, among the dozens that have or do exist that gave one second thought or one cent to the whole lot?[142]

Children can stand terrible hardships: famine, work, discipline, as long as they feel a part of a family, of a purpose. Children and wives need support, reassurance, and direction. Providing them has been the duty of the male for millions of years, and is the reason the family loves him, for love in daily life is 99.9 percent need, with only an occasional spiritual glow. Consider now two cases: first a pre-60s case in which that need was corrupted, and second a post-revolution case in which it failed.

The movie, *The Caine Mutiny* of the early 50s, presented a situation of the young, perhaps impetuous,

---

[141]*Newsweek* (12,13,'93 p. 8) "Not All Brides Can Be Burned."

[142]That fact, that socialist governments paid no attention to racism, environmentalism, abortion, and homeless, suggests that these might be "straw man" issues -- totally dissembled.

grabbing control from the established and staid, perhaps stagnant order. The chief mutineer is presented as sincerely believing that the ship was about to be destroyed if he did not act immediately, but there were bases for equivocation. In the end, after brilliantly defending the mutineers, their lawyer harshly denounced their uncalled for usurpation. Hence the problem: conscience versus the order, or the individual versus the system.

Whyte had students of a superior group each write an extensive paper upholding one side or the other: conscience or the establishment. Grading would depend upon the supporting reasoning, not the choice. Whyte "expected" the youthful students would uphold youth and individualism; intellectuals were already largely anti-system. He was shocked when they all favored the system except for one, who worried through much equivocation before finally insisting on a "moral duty to act as he thinks best." " . . . (T)o act as he thinks best!" exclaimed Whyte, "Has this become an anachronistic concept?" "Anachronistic?" you might reply; the apotheosis of the young wasn't even due here for another decade. Whyte was forcing perceptions that denied centuries of experience, of experience since well verified. The important fact is that the students understood that they weren't supposed to know -- so much for "value clarification". They spent far more time trying to find out "What was supposed to be right," according to author Wouk, or elsewhere, than with imagining things of which they had no experience. "To have his path made clear is the aspiration of every person . . . "

Consider now a quite different situation, a post-revolution case of the son of two California State University professionals who were apparently very PC, "espoused racial tolerance" and lived in a racially mixed area in Long Beach. The boy had a reputation as a "soft-spoken, intelligent, one-time choir boy," Boy Scout, and honor student. That was the only side of Chris that a 21 year old Vietnamese student saw of his "best friend."

But there was a problem. A transformation began in

Chris who had always upheld racial tolerance; in the chaotic halls of Long Beach Polytechnic High, he "came to view himself as a victim of discrimination." Polytechnic's 3,700 students were over three-fourths Black, Mexican, Asian, Filipino and Pacific Islanders, and there were special days, rooms, and organizations for each, from Black Pride to Cinco de Mayo, but none for whites. Chris felt a real need for someone to stick up for white people. This became a controversy with his parents and the school, and he griped to his friends.

In the fall of 1992, he entered City College of Long Beach; racism was worse, so he and some friends organized a club: White Youth Alliance. Members testified that the club functioned as a support group, as a replacement for family support or official college concern. They confided personal problems and sought to avoid alcohol, drugs and violence. Chris "was their role model". A member testified, "We felt like we were being pulled apart. I was the only white person in my science class. All the time we heard about black things and black shows and after Rodney King, it was like they had hate for every white kid."[143]

Apparently in April of the second year, a Reverend Joe Allen enters to support Chris's group; he "equipped a warehouse hideaway" with gym equipment, "racist literature, guns, discussion of white supremacy and White Aryan Resistance," and a video camera. But Joe was a government entrapment "agent", a Gestapo, a Fagin for four months' time. Then Joe reported to his NKVD that an "attack was imminent," presumably on a black church. Chris is alleged to have "bombed" the home of a Chinese "Spur Posse" member, an organization that boasts of "sexual conquest of young

---

[143]Remember in the racist King affair, a felonious parole breaker and wife beater, endangered lives, attacked police repeatedly, and was finally brought in with "minor lacerations", largely self-inflicted. He was presented by the renegade media as a "motorist," and was given millions of tax dollars, while police who endangered their lives bringing him in are given federal prison sentences. Chris's story is also from L.A., the *Times,* Aug., 1993.

girls"; he faces up to 45 years in a federal prison. Sobbing throughout the hearing, he was "led away in shackles". Where the boys' (ages 17 to 20) activities ended and Gestapo entrapment began will probably never be known. But it is the duty of parents, of colleges, of all government employees to foresee and to avert such actions, not to entrap youths into lifetime prison. Where were the parents, the college officials, the ACLU and all the other civil liberties groups?

The system has unraveled, but not out of greed, corrupting as that is. It was unraveled, intentionally by unravelers: John Dewey and the NEA, Morris and Felix Cohen, Earl Warren, Brennan and Blackmun, Roger Baldwin and the ACLU, Franz Boas, Mead and Benedict, and by Franklin Roosevelt, Hopkins and Eleanor, the liberals who fought Joe McCarthy without once attacking the far greater evil of communist infestation, particularly in our schools, universities, and media and entertainment. These people did far more damage to our human society than did Alger Hiss, the Rosenbergs and a dozen more spies put together.

A remarkable type of young man is being bred. He rarely leaves his mother's pap before his thirties. For a "van" or such he will sacrifice family life and children and, when not working to pay for it, or keep it running, his attention is held by TV, random sex or malls. The state increasingly directs his future as advertising con-men form his thoughts. He may protest mildly on occasion but his real dislike is for "fundamentalists" and conservatives who would deprive him of his "rights," and yak about freedom. He looks to the "gov'ment" to straighten things out, as medieval serfs looked to the *seigneur*. He soon will exist in a world that resembles a gray anthill or one of those vast chicken farms in Arkansas.

Meanwhile women wonder where the "responsible men are," writes Suzanne Fields. "They share an anger at the men who passed through their lives . . . It's easy to feel sympathy for women who have come of age when . . . men refuse to accept paternal responsibilities." They become bitter over the paunched and hairless Hefners who become fathers in their fifties. But women can't wait; they want children. "Now we have to be happy if men bathe;" forget any idea of marriage and all that crap.

Perhaps the sexual revolution is responsible; some blame feminism; others blame men who choose not to be tamed. What kind of a civilization is this in which children have children because they are afraid to be alone.

"The old taboos are dying . . . a new permissive society is taking shape . . . nudity, obscene language, candid lyrics, erotic art and TV . . . People are breaking the bonds of puritan society and helping America to grow up." Asinine when *Newsweek* published it in 1967. "This revolution has been made by young people and nothing will thwart it . . . the truth will out . . . strip away the sham and cant of their elders . . .," by David Susskind. Tell that to the above "20 year old". You can't have everything.

Today the number dead or dying of AIDS is well over 100,000. In 1990, it was reported that every year produced 10 million cases of sexually transmitted disease (STD) -- two million new cases of gonorrhea, with 70 percent undetected, and 100 times more powerful penicillin is barely effective. Herpes -- painful, incurable, life threatening to infants -- infects a growing fraction of the young people. Syphilis, parasites, bastards and teen suicide rampant in broken families. Free at last! to squander hundreds of billions on global warming, acid rain, ozone, radon, asbestos, alar, racism, lawyers and bureaucracy.

"We have become accustomed to saying one thing and thinking another (lying). We have learned not to believe in anything, not to care about one another . . . love, friendship, compassion, humility and forgiveness have lost their depth . . . a stray relic from the past, rather comical . . . I mean all of us . . . None of us is merely a victim (of communism or anything else), all of us helped to create it . . . the sad legacy of the past forty years (is not) something alien . . . On the contrary, we must accept this legacy as something which we have brought upon ourselves . . . and (we must now) act on our own initiative, freely, sensibly and quickly . . ." to remove it. So spoke President Vaclav Havel in January of 1990 to his new nation.

Has America not been similarly humiliated, and by exactly the same or related evil party?

Those people who promised "a new permissive society," an "America growing up, strip away the sham and cant of the elders" were of the same lying, evil party of socialism of John Dewey destroying education, Morris Cohen destroying our Bill of Rights, and Franz Boas our culture. They were subversive liars as was FDR, Earl Warren, JFK, Brennan and Blackmun, and a host of others. They all moved toward the destruction of our human society.

Huxley warned that "man's worst difficulties begin when he is able to do as he likes." Of what use then is freedom?

This of course is shallow misunderstanding, true only of a "lad," who has yet no purpose in life. It is said of the modern that he has ceased to believe in his society, but will believe in anything else. The modernist too is an adolescent, suffering the tragedy of never having grown up.

This is best exemplified in the life of the "mythical" Henry Adams, the lad who never really grew up. He admitted rejecting totally "the judgment of the world . . . (came to) regard every question as open . . . (shirked responsibility), had an "antipathy to society . . . looked on the world with instinct of resistance . . ." Why could he not have learned, as both Aristotle and Aquinas taught, that manliness was man's achievement of fullest humanity, as womanliness is the human female's?

Addiction by the young to "entertainment" -- junk food, TV, rock and drugs -- displaces the joy of creative purpose, that society failed to teach them. Even prehistoric man recognized that youth in a reasoning society must be taught to reason -- even imposed as initiation. In order for a culture to be transmitted, the receiving generation must be able to identify with and have reverence for their elders and their culture.

The British scholar Michael Oakeshott follows Nietzsche in accepting the claim that "education as socialization", as taught to John Dewey and the current educationalists, portends the "abolition of man." Education begins, he urges, when a human inheritance of feelings, beliefs, understandings and activities supervenes on momentary desires and imaginings.

LEADERSHIP

A human society is absolutely unique. The only other form for organizing the activities of people ever discovered is Statism. Society is voluntary and probably long before it became human, it was guided in large decisions, especially when the path was unclear, by a Council of Elders. The Elders were always guided by a purpose: the welfare of their grandchildren and therefore of the continued rising up of the tribe toward something better. Statism is enforced submission of the masses to a "higher elite." It is guided by a theory, an ideology, which has as its core the principle that an "elite" is essential for guidance. Thus survival of the elite is its guiding purpose.

A prime example of a human society was the covenanted structure of our Puritan fathers, whose pattern was used by the Founders of our nation and whose subsequent disciples were praised for their abilities in self-government by Tocqueville. Being voluntary and very open, it is necessary that it cultivates a vigorous core to ward off anarchy on one side and Big Brotherism on the other. The leadership that evolved millions of years ago to do this was the Council of Elders. Their authority probably seldom conflicted either with the young warrior's hunts or raids, or with the social customs; it was used largely in urging compromise and adherence to tribal wisdom and customs. This may be taken to be authoritarian, but it was never so intended, and probably seldom was; the intent was in effect to provide a framework or house for the tribe to live in and for the raising of replacement generations. What people did with their time and efforts otherwise was largely up to choice. Their concern was tribe survival and rising up.

A good example of the work of their leadership is the covenanting of the "Mayflower Compact." Another, much older and quite different incident of leadership (whose origin I have forgotten but is supposedly legitimate), concerns a baboon pack. Lions ahead had been scented; the pack halted and the warrior bulls ringed the pack. Slowly two very old bulls moved forward in the direction of the scent of the lions, and disappeared into the brush. Sometime later, after determining just where the lions were, the old bulls reappeared far to the left, heading for tall trees, and the pack followed.

Thus human society is innately tribal. Leadership is more closely related to social structure, to society, than it is to culture, which is principally knowledge for survival and rising up. Of course anyone can, like Humpty Dumpty, define words the way they wish. But for people who are concerned about the greatest, and now most pressing issues to man, uncorrupted names are essential, especially for such prime concepts as his natural organization for protection, and his knowledge for guidance.

We commonly read or hear such as: don't try to impose your religious beliefs on me (concerning almost any and every social problem), or, these reactionaries are trying to impose patriarchy, or Western culture, or your morality on me. Let us have it straight; culture is imposed: education, morality, religion (as purpose), all of these, including a language and street signs are imposed. No less is socialism and hate-America imposed today. You must understand <u>that</u> to be your major "choice", and urging recognition of it is a main purpose of this *Guide*.

How many times, if ever have you seen, heard or read in the major media, or in the universities, of someone objecting to the imposition of Marxism, of communism, imposition of obscenities, or anti-Americanism, or the imposition of Statism by Washington. Look how horribly America has been devastated since 1960; this hasn't been by chance or accident. It has been imposed.

If culture should not be imposed, if children and young people should be allowed to make up their own minds, then it follows that babies shouldn't be taught to speak, or be toilet trained. Wait until they are old enough to decide for themselves. Oh, you say that is silly . . . Well it is not silly; it is that the whole problem is misstated. There is one great law, survival, and it imposes all things.

In the wild where all things live close to the edge of survival, it is as when man saw the "glowing eyes of the great cats." Nature is not free and without restraints; there, too, much is imposed by survival -- read the stories of Mowgli, which were written to teach children the need for order, rules and responsibility. Survival is imposed only as a simple desire to live. But, with reason man have built bulwarks and institutions that have separated people further and further from the edge of survival. Not only must the nature and importance of man's innateness and spiritual guidance be taught, the great importance of the 'bulwarks and institutions,' as culture, must also be <u>taught</u>, <u>exemplified</u>, and advanced. The institutions are human society, culture, marriage and families. The bulwarks are standards of morality and truth, and truth in language, without which the institutions are unstable and purpose fails. Society brings protection -- all people's only sure protection -- but it requires responsibility for its maintenance. Reason brings all evil, but also it is on reason that we must depend for understanding that all of these institutions and bulwarks are not for enslaving people, as is Statism; they are merely to provide the minimum order for stability and safety, beyond which people are then able to seek in freedom their own vision of life.

Finally then, and most importantly, it must be understood that families are the ultimate building blocks of all these institutions, and that it is only through families and their nurturing human society that it is possible to achieve ultimate survival. Our forbearers for eons have killed, eaten, or enslaved "others"; but treason and renegadism, as the very intention to destroy your own culture, and as certainly therefore as night follows day to destroy your own people, was a thing almost unknown, and when it did occur was a matter of ignorance or madness, not reason. All rituals and songs, all great literature and music have been created to celebrate, in exuberance, in reflection and reverence, one's human society and families. <u>That</u> is culture!

Lack of purpose is the malaise of modern man. He seeks "happiness" even knowing that happiness like virtue is not found, it is made: the result of whatever best effort toward a good end that one can achieve. Material things have become so important that women must abandon their children even motherhood to go to work, making families and survival endangered, even terminal.

Purpose must be organized and enforced for it to produce progress, and we have seen that the male authority for not only that enforcement, but even for the protection of human society, has been undermined, degraded and in certain aspects abandoned. Your human society and culture, all that is most precious in life, will not and is not being protected by the State; in fact, it is increasingly subversive to all decency, truth, morality, culture, all humanness.

The media and "entertainment," going way back to Lyons's *Red Decade* of the 1930s, has been the leader in this genocide. R. Hobby has used movies as markers of the destruction of male authority and protection.[144]

1. *The Birds*, 1963, showed three generations of women receiving male guidance and protection.
2. *Jaws*, 1975, had the mature male sacrifice himself so that the boy and a middling one can be saved.
3. *Aliens*, 1986, presented a woman and a robot as saviors of ineffectual men. In the meanwhile, I lost count of how many times blacks were shown giving white people lessons on how to live. Imagine the reaction to an oppositely

---

[144]*Chronicles*, 7, 88, p. 42.

directed story.

4.   In *Fatal Attraction*, the man is unable to protect his family or even himself from a knife wielding 'crazy' that he has aroused. A woman must save him.

Such presentations reinforce a perception that duties, standards and responsibilities no longer exist. This is a major subversion that must be exposed and obliterated, and the renegades that coax these pernicious conceptions must be banished from human society.

But even as that is being done, our youth and young men must be given an education that will accomplish the ends of prehistoric initiation rites. Families and societies are not to be parasitized by young men who have never been taught to do otherwise.

WOMEN

Of all God's gifts to man, Eve is far above all else; surely some women would say the same about men. There was Helen the beauty, Cleopatra the charmer, Sappho the soft, and Boadicea the warrior. Genevieve rallied the people of Paris when Attila stood at the gates; for centuries her peasant bones were carried through the streets of Paris in a box to ward off threatened danger. And there was Joan the Maid and Elizabeth the Virgin.

The world is full of Annas: little charm, less talent, no wealth nor wit. Ordinary Anna with thick lips and spreading nostrils. What devotion, what slavery, even unspeakable for a man of the nobility. She apprehended more than understood his genius, his needs, his fever of creation. She softened the torment of his soul with care and devotion, made him a home, bore his children; she, a girl, lifted him up, saved him from debtors prison and grasping relatives, took dictation, sold his book to obtain just payment. This wild and evil man was to her "the purest being"; without her, there would have been no Dostoevsky. The handmaiden to Mother Russia was robbed by the Revolution, and died in privation in Lenin's early year of 1920.

Isaiah saw women as loving fine raiment and ornament. "The daughters of Zion are haughty, and walk with stretched forth necks and wanton eyes . . . mincing as they go, and making a tinkling with their feet."

"Women's cosmic dominance" through motherhood and control of sex is one of the prime facts of life in a human society. Hence women have the prime moral responsibility to prevent rape; men the prime legal responsibility. Nature and women demand that the male be the aggressor; hence the female must not only <u>not</u> invite sex, but must early on do the "choosing" to dis-invite. When society fails and Statism takes over, women become little more than slaves, except of course, those "kept", as by the elite.

An excellent review article on women and families appeared in the *Salisbury Review* (9,89, p. 51). Briefly, some of the findings discussed concern the growing feminization of the workplace, which has long been male turf, as the home was female. Some half of U.S. women with children less than a year old work   partially because of intense liberal-socialist pressure, says Suzanne Fields, and partially because of the evil party which the liberal-socialists support. Most of the ages-old social and governmental foundations under families have been destroyed: the concept of a family wage, the legitimacy of the marriage contract, tax support for families, and generally the social, cultural, and legal supports for families have been uprooted.

On top of this renegade savaging of the families, which are so desperately needed, there is taking place an even more pernicious abomination. Every one of those (above) policies, which increasingly are being denied to families with the increasing destruction of them in the face of growing dis-education and crime and violence-based rot, is the increasing demand and obtaining of those very benefits by sodomists and pederasts.

Another set of findings demonstrate the importance of

mothering, as by close physical contact, for up to 2-1/2 years of age for children; only then can play group-activity be beneficial. Infant monkeys separated from their mothers shortly after birth soon became maladjusted, both frightened and aggressive, and incapable of eventually raising their own children. Maternal deprivation is as serious a malady as diphtheria and typhoid. Children with a first year of life spent in a day-care kindergarten of top grade quality were found to kick, push, threaten, swear, and argue and to be apathetic and unresponsive. "Lousy day-care centers won't let researchers in."

"The correct development of a child requires the commitment of mature parents who understand that children do not grow like Topsy . . . Mothering is probably the <u>most important</u> <u>function</u> <u>on</u> <u>earth</u>. It is a full time demanding task."[145] Abandoning their biological purpose, the bearing and raising of children has long been known to have a deep psychological effect on women, making them domineering and aggressive prunes. Dr. Voth, of the above reference, notes that such types dominate the "women's movement." Sensory deprivation of babies is claimed to produce damage to the neuronal system that controls affection and aggression. A correlation has been shown between people who exhibit little physical affection and high levels of violence.

It is modernism that destroys families. Feminists, as modern historians, use non-existent and ambiguous evidence to damn human society, marriage and two-parent families. Children watching animals know better. Worldwide, where families are strong, usually through religion and tradition (ethnics) as among peasants, children are prized and nurtured. Cicero declared, "nature implants in men above all a strong and tender love for his children." The only real security for women and children, for the common man and his family, for the weak and needy is in a human society. The state will sacrifice all or any of these, all decency and the environment both physical and cultural, for its evil purposes.

---

[145]H. M. Voth, *Families* (1984).

We have <u>seen</u> it.

The "Lying and the Obscening of America" is like a vast thundering herd, moving towards the horizon on all sides. Christina Hoff Summers, in *Who Stole Feminism* charges that renegades propagate myths that vilify men, demean women, and derogate Western civilization. *Time* and the *Chicago Tribune* (1993) reported a lie that battery of pregnant women was the leading cause of birth defects. Actually Professor Graham of Johns Hopkins estimates that 60 percent of the U.S. infant-mortality rate results from the effects of promiscuity and drug abuse. Naomi Wolf, Gloria Steinem, Ann Landers, and various college textbooks publicize the lie that anorexia kills 150,000 U.S. women yearly; the true number is around 100. The American Association of University Women reported that girls claiming "happy with the way I am" dropped from 60 percent in elementary school to 29 percent in high school. AAUW fibbed; actually when added, the "always true," "sort of," and "sometimes" "happy with the way I am" came to 92 percent. Not mentioned by AAUW was the finding that girls are more likely to be proud of their work than boys, and that no correlation was found between "self-esteem" and academic success. HHS's Donna Shalala produced the whopper: 25 to 30 percent of women's emergency room visits are caused by domestic violence -- probably having their knuckles treated.[146]

The renegadism is that once these lies get told, they never really get untold. As for censorship, little gets into textbooks (K-12-U) that the evil party does not want. Removal of the "Sex Respect" curriculum, which argues against promiscuity, homoeroticism, and suction abortions in the home, is demanded by ACLU and Planned Parenthood types because it advocates "two-parent heterosexual couples" as "the sole model of a healthy family." They insist it is "censorship" merely to use the text.

Neither men nor women, unmarried, had a "right" to sex within the lifetime of many; fornication and adultery

---

[146]Collected by the New Jersey writer, Cathy Young.

might have been dealt with harshly. There is no more "right" to one bodily excretion over any other. "As long as nobody gets hurt, what's wrong with sex between unmarried adults? . . . Just about every time the bus brought us back to the hotel", Magic Johnson explained, "there would be 40 or 50 women waiting in the lobby . . . some were secretaries, some lawyers . . . actresses and models . . . teachers, editors, accountants . . . college professionals . . . every day hundreds of perfumed letters . . . pretty explicit." Certainly none were mothers. They were whores, lacking any connection between sex and motherhood.

POPULATION

Ludwig von Mises, in *Socialism* (1920s), warned of an assault on families waged in the name of feminism, as part of the renegadism of socialism. Paul Samuelson's *Economics* contains no index entry for "family." It is typical of the ignorance or renegadism -- take your pick -- of Marx and Engels to declare "bourgeois claptrap about the family will disappear with private property"; hence the war on property.

Society tends to decay and requires more concern for its survival as people move into cities, move from farms to factories, as income goes up, as education increases. And as society decays, family structure decays and reproduction declines.

Added to this birth reduction was the war that the U.S. government declared in 1965 against white babies,[147] the same year that the immigration gates were opened to a massive Third World invasion. A memo on population-control put out in 1969 listed ways for discouraging Americans from reproducing white Americans:[148]

---

[147] J. Kasun, *War On Population* (1988).

[148] Julian Simon, *The Ultimate Resource*.

"Economic deterrents" and "social controls"
Revision of tax policies to reduce exemptions. (now to
be reversed for homosexual "marriages")
Discourage private homes
Restructure family
Encourage homosexuality
Denigrate manhood

Renegades and the misinformed talk about population
the way Clinton talks about "change." The question is what
population, what change. The boom in babies peaked in
1957, and went into a "strong cycle of fertility decline." Eight
years into the decline some renegade bureaucrat declared the
U.S. overpopulated and declared the war on births.
What that must be balanced against is the
catastrophically exponential increase in Third World
population; the tabulated increases in world population are
occurring near totally in non-Western countries.

1850 1 billion	2000 6 billion
1930 2 billion	2100 10 billion
1975 4 billion	

Ben Wattenberg's, 1987 *The Birth Dearth* looked at the
problem of "what population." It is accepted that a birth rate
of 2.1 is a zero growth rate. Today among much of the
world's white population the rate is in the range of 1.7; in
Germany it is 1.35.; In the Third World it runs generally from
4 to over 6. Wattenburg wrote "The Birth Dearth in America
will yield an even smaller proportion of white European
'stock' (to use a census term) and this will cause more ethnic
and racial tension and turmoil than would otherwise occur."
This was pounced on by liberals with the backing of
the entire evil party; it was declared to be the cry of
"racism," the "yellow peril" all over again. Note that when
East Germany implemented programs for raising the birth rate
there were no such cries of racism.
It is madness for the media and even the government

to promote Afro culture, Hispanic culture, Jewish culture, Islamic culture and Asian culture, while Western culture, <u>which is the only institution that can prevent our country from tearing itself apart</u>, other than the brutality of fascism, is not merely denigrated but rejected and destroyed. And, as culture goes so goes population. Rousseau has warned that when a country's population wanes, something is not well.

It has become common for one relatively small African country to forcibly expel, hundreds of thousands of people dissimilar from themselves largely in name only. It has been reported that Japanese families that went or were sent by the government, in past times, to Korea are not permitted full citizenship on returning generations later. Perhaps no country is stricter than Switzerland on keeping out "others," and for good reason; immigration would soon destroy their federal system of self-government, as it has been instrumental in destroying ours.

There are two fronts on which reform must be effected immediately. First, the naturalization process must be completely ended, until a degree of social stability is regained, and gradually and on a humanitarian basis, all who came here illegally must be returned. Second, for nearly fifty years or more imposed government or social forces have inhibited the development and growth of white generations while those of non-whites have been uninhibited or promoted, even with massive taxes on white families. These inequalities must be reversed, again until social stability has been rebuilt.

10.   THE INDICTMENT

No greater crime can be found in the history of man, barring nothing, than occurred in the Twentieth Century. It was not the savage often torturous killing of some 100 million souls, evil as that was. The real inhuman crime was the ruthless effort, continued decade after decade by liberal intellectuals, to destroy human society and to replace it with the global slavery of world collectivism. People can be replaced, but the rational human society based on the greatest ideals that man has ever perceived, in Western culture and Christianity, probably cannot anymore than can an ecological niche.

The reality of this barbaric devastation is almost beyond conception. To comprehend it requires a complete education, perhaps by showing videos of schools, their financing, and the product of 70 years ago compared to today. Do the same with families and with music showing the singing groups with the songs of quartets and choirs; and also how few laws, locks and police then, compared to today. Some of these comparisons have been made here, but groups as wards must be formed to examine and to prepare to end the barbarism.

In recent years, the attack has been carried out in the name of fighting capitalism, or McCarthyism, or the Vietnam War or poverty, or racism, but the central intent was always to devastate human society. It began with the socialist cells organized in our best universities at the end of last century.

The first stage of the struggle consisted of the corruption of the foundations. The aborting of education by John Dewey's "reforms" was warned of early as illiteracy and emotional problems arose. But the evil party's "reforms" held. Rule of Law was to be replaced by judicial dictates; it was proudly announced in 1935 that "no part of the Constitution or law . . . could not be demolished . . . in the name of the Constitution." And the success of the Nazis was presented by Felix Cohen as proof. Culture was attacked directly under the cloak of "cultural anthropology" by Franz Boas, Mead, Benedict, Myrdal and many others. These assaults were always kept from the public view, "while making the most solemn promises that nothing of the kind was intended."

During the second stage, mid-1930s to mid-1960s, the cells of the first stage metastasized and a totally new establishment took control, as described by Lippmann and Lyons. If you were not a collectivist, you were not taken seriously, you were a nobody, a mossback. During these years "the United States merits the dubious distinction of having discarded its past and its meaning in a briefest span . . .," wrote the most knowledgeable and ethical journalist of the time, Arthur Krock. Even as FDR was declaring, to gain the 1940 election, ". . . again and again and agaaaain, your boys are not going to be sent to a foreign war," he was preparing the bait of Pearl Harbor that would provide access to a war to save Communism.

Before his brother went to Dallas, Bobby Kennedy promised, "We are going to stay in Vietnam until we win. The American people want to help a nation fighting for freedom . . . ". After a few short years, during most of which he was the highest official of Justice in the government waging that war, he rose to cry to a chanting mob, "What we are doing in Vietnam is like what Hitler did to the Jews." He ignored being the head of Justice in that "we", that massacred the government of our little ally, thus tying America irrevocably to a horror. In the third stage (1965-82), the evil party's establishment would step forward from concealment openly and damn America. This was a period of diabolical madness, unequalled in history; well-to-do and educated individuals would bomb, demonstrate in the streets and chant for the defeat and death of their own brothers, sons, friends.

A president would be driven from office by jackals of communism; Renata Adler, a leftist, who served on the "crimes committee" declared the attack on the presidency to be a farce. She wrote, "the Church Committee Report, and the other documents . . . support a claim that Richard Nixon was hounded from office . . . and that the impeachment inquiry was just another phase of the cover-up." Cover-up? ". . . Whatever we know . . . about the offenses (of Nixon) is based one way or another, on what we know about John Dean." John Dean's doings were known to Democrats who were aware of his plans. The only key the "burglars" had was to a subordinate's desk, containing a black book with the names of "dates" for visiting Demo-bigwigs, and Dean's later to-be-bride was on that list. But this break-in and Dean's cover-up were merely to distract, and to detract attention from the real goal. Watergate was actually far more about the "bombing in Cambodia" than about John Dean's break-in and cover-up, as indicated by a Senator's expostulation.

Nixon had brought home over 500,000 Americans who had been sent into a foreign war by the Democrats, who then sought to disown the war, after they had connived to have the government destroyed. He had succeeded in having a Vietnamese army trained and supplied, and a peace treaty signed in which the U.S. promised to supply the South Vietnam government. This could not be allowed to stand; not after all the tremendous effort the evil party had put forth to defeat America in the 1960s. "There's got to be a bloodletting. We've got to make sure nobody ever thinks of doing anything like this again," from a powerful editor[149]. The crimes of the courts and of Congress far exceeded those of Nixon. Nixon was destroyed so that his Vietnam victory

---

[149]Read Paul Johnson's, *Modern Times,* p. 649 and the entire section in Vietnam.

could be abandoned. The media and Congress were the real criminals.

Then came a short hiatus in the war. It began about 1982 when people came to recognize in Ronald Reagan something they had not really felt since Harry Truman: that he was a true friend of Americans and a leader to be trusted. It collapsed about 1990 amidst taxes, quotas, and bureaucracy without end.

The fourth and final stage of the attack, not just on America, but on humanness and human society, began about 1990 with the Bush blows to Constitutional government: quotas, disability, environmental mandates.

Today, it is clearly evident that the United States is moving rapidly and irreversibly into fascism; the possibility of collectivization is almost nil. On the other hand, there is no powerful element, such as the Catholic Church once was, that could retain some small sovereignty. Fascism by the nationalization of all authority is already far advanced.

A Gestapo-like BATF, finding no proof of any broken laws other than claimed minor infractions, nevertheless assaulted a compound in Waco with high-tech equipment: tanks, gas and assault rifles firing into plywood walls behind which they knew were women and children. In Idaho, the same evil BATF hassled Randy Weaver's family for over a year, again with special weapons and a dozen sharpshooters. They wounded Randy, killed his son and a Ron Horiuchi shot his wife in the face as she stood on a stoop in front of a miserable plywood shack holding her baby. The evil Gestapo had described this basementless box as a "fortress." Ocie Mills and his son spent nearly two years in prison for "sassing" some Washington bureaucrats over their putting sand in a small ditch on their quarter-acre retirement lot. Three people in Berkeley were threatened with $100,000 fines for each person and each incident for objecting to the reasons for a zoning change. Each day brings more fascist incidents, proving that when you have no human society, you have no protection. It is not, nor was not, the Bill of Rights that protected the American people for nearly 200 years; it was the citizenry of a coherent human society that stood behind it.

Most Americans are not aware and seem not to want to know the extent of the destruction to our human society caused by the evil party over the past 60 years. The encroachment and resulting devastation and corruption have been kept hidden, denied, obscured in every way, keeping people blissfully unaware of their transformation from citizens to Clintonian "consumers", like chickens of an Arkansas poultryman.

You must help to make people aware that the only difference between the Statism to which they are acquiescing and the horrors of fascism is the fractious forbearance of a priestly elite holding all power. This perilous situation has resulted from long planning by the evil party and an unwillingness of the people to awaken to the danger. Many an American, who has been granted high position and great honor, has refused even to speak up, to say nothing of acting in the name of freedom.

I was proud to purchase and to read Dean Acheson's book when it first came out, *A Democrat Looks at His Party*. Let us examine a couple of critical points in Mr. Acheson's career.

Acheson was a mid-level official during WW II, and "a gentleman in politics" that Harry Truman came to know. If Acheson did not know at the time of Pearl Harbor, he certainly knew (being a lawyer) by the end of the Congressional hearings (1946), of the trickery of FDR, Hopkins, Marshall, et al, and certainly before 1950, of the treason-during-wartime of Alger Hiss. And he knew that the evidence was incontrovertible, and that the American public, while near totally unconscious of FDR's guilt, was quite sure of Hiss's.

In spite of all of that, on the day of Hiss's sentencing, Secretary of State Acheson pushed forward with a press conference, at which he volunteered, "I do not intend to turn my back on Alger Hiss." Allen Weinstein[150] discussed this event, noting that Acheson "had to satisfy only one critic, H.S. Truman," and nothing helped him so much as "the Republican's reaction." That, of course, was not the essence of the truth. The real critic should have been recognized as the American people, but it wasn't; the real "Boss" was the evil party -- the media and intellectuals, and Lippmann, Trilling, Lyons and many others have told us where they stood.

But that was not the end of Mr. Acheson, nor of his influence; we can afford one more look. Lyndon Johnson consented to meet with the "wise men," March 25, 1968, two months after North Vietnam had shot its whole wad on the Tet 68. Mainly they were jackals of the evil party, as you can judge: Acheson, Ball, Bundy, Lodge, etc., plus some generals. Acheson talked the most, and someone objected that he was portraying America as seeking "to impose a military solution on the communists." That was said with the assumed understanding of all that the North was known to have declared war on the South in 1959; it was the North that had sought to "impose a military solution," and clearly could escape such by staying at home. But Acheson blew up: "What in the name of God we got 500,000 troops out there for, chasing girls? You know damned well . . . the enemy won't sue for peace -- not in any time the American people will permit." And apparently with all the generals there: Bradley (WW II), Ridgeway (Korea), Taylor (Vietnam), Wheeler (Vietnam), not a one dared to rise to counter Acheson's calumny. The evil party was far more in command than it had been in 1950[151].

---

[150]Allen Weinstein, *Perjury*, p. 505-7.

[151]What a tragedy. "Someone poisoned the wells," Johnson knew, but he believed Acheson's, ". . . the American people will (not) permit." "America had collapsed on the home front," he wrote <u>wrongly</u>; the following week he announced his retirement. Even after four more years, that was the precise question between McGovern and Nixon in 1972, and Nixon, who had nearly ended American participation in the war by then,

We can believe that Acheson knew that in order to save his career (from evil party attack in 1950), he had to stand with Hiss. Perhaps General Taylor felt likewise in 1968, that he would be torn to pieces if he challenged the nonsense of Acheson. But there was a glut of air-head kids running around, who may not have known much about the war, except what they saw on TV, but were smart enough to sense the gutless rot, so they rioted, even went to Moscow and spilled their guts. Today the top level people who run the government and the media, were among them: unprincipled, untrained, unexampled in social responsibility, jackals of the evil party and its ideology.

Suppose that on the way to Johnson's meeting Mr. Acheson had reflected on his part of the treason in WW II; suppose he had asked himself: if we force Johnson out, will the Communists allow us to leave, or will we have a Dunkirk and, in any case, what will happen to all the South Vietnamese who are beginning to get things together? The only answer is that we must give Lyndon another four years to Vietnamize the war and get out. To hell with the evil party; we will tell the nation. That is, of course what Nixon succeeded in doing even with fierce Democratic and evil party opposition and, since he had succeeded, an excuse had to be found to undo it. That was possible only with Watergate.

But Acheson didn't do that, even though reason forces us to believe he must have thought of it. Dewey's treason had made Roosevelt's easier and FDR's made Acheson's easier.

Attacks on America, on Christianity and upon our human society and decency were made possible by the lies and treachery of renegades of the 1960s which were and still are supported by the "liberal" establishment. The "Freak 'em outers" of the 60s were puppets, stooges of evil party renegades who had taught and guided them. A major tactic was indecency, flouting of all standards: old torn clothes, filthy hair and beards, bad grammar, obscene language, open

---

received one of the largest popular landslides in history, and he was not a popular leader.

sex, squatting on the floor or ground. My children came home from school with, "They said we didn't have to use good grammar anymore," "They said we shouldn't talk to our parents about that." Lack of standards destroys human society and rising up.

Central to the renegade bombers and peace demonstrators for a Communist victory in the 60s was SDS -- Students for a Democratic Society. It came into being in 1962, well before any concern over a Vietnam War, and by 1963: it had over 100 chapters. Read of their evil by former leaders in *Destructive Generation* by Collier and Horowitz. It was guided and backed by IPS, the Institute for Policy Studies[152], for years the most important KGB stop outside of Moscow. Kent State, and elsewhere, was being taught the violent riot long before Cambodia. Cambodia was but an excuse. As one of them said, "If the Vietnam War hadn't existed, we'd of had to invent it." So too if John Dean hadn't gone looking for a "black book" of call girls containing the name of his to-be-wife, the evil party and its editors would have had to invent Watergate.

Dr. Ken Masugi, a fellow of Claremont Institute, testified before Congress in 1984 that the intent, "one of the goals of the Sixties (was) to show that America is a racist society, even in WW II America was corrupt, having its own concentration camps." I would remind you that this did not arise from the Vietnam War; SDS and other radical groups coalesced out of the New Left of overt Communists that began to take shape after Khrushchev's attack on Stalinism and on unarmed citizens in Hungary -- 1956 and afterwards. The New Left began by identifying needed action-groups and causes to be pursued: America as racist and corrupt was joined by others such as Japanese "internment" in WW II, "The Holocaust, and radical cut-and-burn hate groups wherever there was an opening.

Dr. Masugi asserted that "Japanese-Americans who

---

[152]IPS was created by dropouts from JFK's top secret National Security and Arms Control agencies, leaving contacts behind.

were activists in the Sixties became the lawyers and organizers" of the demands for "internment reparations." You will note that if America had had an even mildly effective core, even mildly honest editors, even a mildly loyal academia, these dissembling assaults would have been blunted aborning. But it didn't; even the people had become spiritually lethargic from corrupt education and deprivation of responsibility.

Note the way one renegade's lie leads to another. Virginia Postrel, editor of *Reason* no less, wrote in Policy Rev. (Sum. '94), damning Americans for the "imprisonment of innocent Japanese-Americans and the confiscation of their property." Worse yet this was used as one of her major points in support of the fatuous idea that we are further from Hayek's *Road to Serfdom* today; "a long(er) way from serfdom" in fact, than in the 1940s. Reality is obviously the reverse, in those 50 years our Bill of Rights has become mere penumbras and emanations, no more a solid wall against Statism. Government by, of, and for the people has simply disappeared in massive clientism to the State, and culture, scholarship and human decency have all but disappeared under a cloying bureaucracy.

In order to understand the Japanese "internment" claim, it is necessary to be familiar with the hundreds of "Magic intercepts" of Japanese Purple coded messages. FDR <u>knew</u> not only what Tokyo was doing, he knew what the Japanese-Americans were doing, not only from the Magic intercepts but from extensive FBI surveillance, guided by Magic, for confirmation of actions. FDR <u>knew</u> what the Japanese were doing. It was known, and the Japanese-Americans knew, that wherever the Japanese army went, Japanese nationals were organized, by orders of the Emperor, to prepare the way. It seems probable that at least a third of the American-Japanese were so organized; theoretically they all were. And any who failed when the Army came were to be shot. Some 3,000 were imprisoned immediately after Pearl Harbor as known traitors; eventually some 20,000 demanded repartition[153]. Moderate Japanese have protested the "unjustified doubting of their loyalty." Not so; separation of the loyal from traitors was impossible; the huge minority of activists put all under heavy and brutal pressure to conform.

Note an important quirk of the situation that has confused the activists: FDR knew all about the spies, here and on Oahu, hundreds of them active, yet he let them be. You see to have disturbed them too much would have queered the Jap attack, right down to the end. Their fleet was ordered to turn away if there was the slightest sign of loss of surprise. And that was the last thing FDR wanted.

The activists who thought they were so smart, going undetected, didn't know that they were playing on FDR's stage. So people like Abigail Van Buren who whine and cant about "our (e.s.) everlasting shame for putting 100,000 loyal Americans in concentration camps," must be seen as more pernicious than ignorance or credulity can excuse.

The Japanese were not imprisoned nor interned; in Canada they were, and were not completely freed until 1948. Military authorities urged the removal of dangerous aliens from West Coast identified defense districts. Evacuation was not ordered until February 19, 1942, well after the peak danger; the order allowed the Japanese to move on their own, out of the forbidden zones, and some 4,300 families did just that on their own initiative. But movement was too slow and immediate evacuation was ordered, in May, 1942, to "collection points" to await assignment to a relocation center.

An initial 10 relocation centers were reduced to nine when the Tule Lake Center was converted into an internment camp to hold the incorrigible activists who, for example, brutalized other Japanese in order to enforce Japanese authority. The centers were not for internment, the Japanese could leave at any time and many did for jobs, 4,300 left to

---

[153]Some 5,000 renounced U.S. citizenship and roughly an equal number refused the draft, although over 30,000 did serve in some capacity, some highly honorable.

attend universities. The centers were havens with good food, excellent schools and free medical care, libraries, sports facilities, movies and stores. Inmates lived in the kind of buildings, and received the $21 per month pay, of draftees. Havens because living was free; outside certainly many would have been beaten or killed by people who had lost loved ones at Pearl Harbor, Bataan, or the islands. Jobs outside generally depended upon the Army's urging. Congress appropriated $4 million to aid those who wished to go into business. Americans sent them library books, sports equipment, musical instruments, arts and crafts supplies, even graduation robes.

Senator S.I. Hayakawa wrote that the civilian-run War Relocation Administration was "headed by the wise and human Dillon Myer . . . made life as comfortable as possible;" no families were separated and they were housed and cared for as well or better than millions of Americans temporarily housed for war work in places like Willow Run.

Exclusion from defense districts ended November, 1944, and by January, 1945 disassembling the centers started. It is revealing to read Manny Lawton's *Some Survived*, on the Japanese taking of prisoners and the Bataan Death March, and civilians as Jap POWs according to Agnes Newton Keith in *Three Came Home*, or to examine the picture of General Wainwright on release.

Considerable effort went into safeguarding Japanese property; at the beginning items were shipped by the government to owners. Wartime profits from government-leased, Japanese-owned farmland were banked for them. In 1948, Congress passed a Japanese Claims Act, appropriating $38 million (close to one billion dollars today) to cover all losses caused by the relocation, and declared the "award final and conclusive for all purposes . . . and shall be a full discharge . . . with respect to all claims . . ."

In the late 1960s, when denigration of all America was the game of all sorts of renegades, Japanese activists began a drumbeat for "reparations" that continued until the 1980 Congress voted a Commission on Wartime Relocation $1.5

million and loaded it with hate-America types and provided a paid staff, 40 percent of whom had Japanese surnames. Japanese activists held mock hearings and dress rehearsals for those allowed to testify; opponents of redress were harassed and insulted by members of the Commission and by the primarily renegade Japanese audiences. Assistant Secretary for War during the relocation period strongly condemned the Commission's hearings for the Senate: "utterly biased character . . . a disgrace to the good traditions of our procedures." Other high officials repeated this charge. In 1981, Senator Brooke, who should have known better, asked former Col. K.R. Bendetsen, Army director of the evacuation, about the disparity between the commission's "voluminous testimony" and what "you've described." Bendetsen replied that "a great part of (your) testimony was given by people not yet born;" more came from people who were babies[154]. Many people (Japanese) were not given an opportunity to present "opposing testimony", and were "physically intimidated by" renegades who clogged the hearings from beginning to end. The Commission, until some last minute doctoring, refused to admit any wrong doing on the part of any Japanese, so well documented by FBI and Magic intercepts.

Some $1.65 billion were paid to people without regard to background; $20,000 tax free went to thousands of enemy aliens, or their survivors, including those imprisoned for spying, 20,000 who demanded repatriation, to some 4,000 families who were never in a relocation center, and even to non-Japanese spouses and parents who voluntarily accompanied relatives and lived at taxpayers' expense. Efforts are reported now underway to pay Peruvian-Japanese, who were deported via U.S. and, at war's end, were refused by both Peru and Japan.[155]

---

[154]6,000 babies born in the relocation centers received better care, or much better care, than the common people of America.

[155]This account of Japanese-American "reparations" has utilized information from various news and government sources and from the Journal of Social, Political and Economic Studies, Sp., 1993, and Conserv.

FDR's collusion with Stalin was smuggled in with post-Pearl Harbor chaos and "wartime necessity and security." Communist concealment and legitimization was accomplished in the confusion, partisanship and furor over McCarthyism. The recent L.A. riots were sanctioned by the lies, the deceits, and intimidation under the calumny of a "miscarriage of justice," "innocent motorist, beaten into insensitivity," and the forced perception that the last 20 seconds of the video told the whole story.

Those who do not show anger at things that shame them are fools: Aristotle.

To be angry is to care: playwright John Osborne.

To those who let things happen to them, worse will come: Tacitus.

In the world today a bitter struggle rages between two idealogies, and in this struggle no one can be neutral: Khrushchev.

Vietnam was shameful, for the evil party's policy: "Friendly to neutrals, neutral to the enemy, and hostile to friends": Allied diplomat.

At the time of Pearl Harbor at least 80 percent of our people were American Firsters, in spirit, urging preparedness. Before the Stalin-Hitler Alliance, the communists and company were for stopping fascism, but during it, from mid-1939 to mid-1941, communists and many of their liberal allies acted violently against the "imperialist's war," using pressure tactics to tie up defense industries in strikes, as did Communists in Harry Bridges' Longshoremen Union, or at Allis Chalmers. After mid-1941, when their alliance failed, Communists wanted America to go fight their war, and FDR "tricked" us into it.

America was a Christian nation then; it still is in basic law, morality and culture. Much of our real literature, which is primarily pre-20th Century, is structured on Christianity. It was <u>because</u> America was a Christian nation that people volunteered so willingly to the "good war" that they thought

---

Rev., Jan. 1994.

so mistakenly was intended to save Christian-Western civilization and all the enslaved peoples, including many Jews. We did not come too late because we never planned to come until thrown into the war by Roosevelt. And the war was extended in time, permitting the killing of more Jews as a result of FDR's <u>intention</u> to provide for maximum Soviet penetration into Central Europe; it was extended by the evil demand for unconditional surrender -- "Just the thing for Uncle Joe" -- condemned by nearly all authorities, by the inhuman Morgenthau plan for pastoralization, and by a renegade strategy that provided for maximum Soviet occupation. If rail lines were not bombed, it was Roosevelt's order, about which the American people knew nothing. FDR had a number of official and unofficial Jewish advisors.

Yet abomination of abominations, America and Christianity get blamed! We were named as the most evil essence, responsible for "The Holocaust." And a great "finger of shame" is erected on the National Mall of the people of America, memorializing an evil "beyond comparison." Never was there ever a more dastardly insult, never a more shameful acquiescence. This vile libel has been repeated many times, is close to Geo. Will's statement, and is the message of a "Holocaust" video which runs constantly on our National Mall.

Modern anti-Semitism was a construct of socialists, as Jewish E. Silberner documented extensively. Taught hate focused on "one enemy," exactly what Hitler used, was the gift of Marx.

But far more evil than this shameful vilification of America and Christianity is the whole corrupt concept of "The Holocaust." And that is not because of its arrogant belittling of the suffering of ten to twenty times as many people, many as in Cambodia who were far more savagely murdered than by somewhat surreptitious gas ovens -- criticism of which Anthony Lewis declared to be "cultural arrogance." No. The real evil, as declared before, is the obvious fact that is impossible to deny: the intent is to obscure, to hide the Armagedonian destruction of a humanness and human society, and to cover over and keep safe under a welter of distracting propaganda, the priceless jewel of Socialism. All the evil of 70 years of Socialism, around the world, is to be cloaked by a babble of confusion and irrational charges, just as Pearl Harbor was concealed, as the 60's attack on humanness was concealed, as the mad idiocy of Rodney King was covered up, even by a massive riot.

Let us look for a balance in a comparison. The cultural war waged against Germany during the pre-Hitler, Weimar Republic had as an intent the destruction of society in favor of communism (socialism). Jews were a minor part of that assault, but a leading and noticeable part. Not Hitler, nor even fascism, would have been possible without that attack. It was a small radical minority of Jews involved, and their activities caused the majority of Jews to fear the future; many changed their names or moved to the country, seeking to escape. Post 60's America may well be duplicating that horror. Again, Jews have been a small minority, but leaders in the attack upon our society. Elliot Rothenberg a number of years ago (and there have been others since, even recently) noted that the American Jewish Committee, largest and most prestigious, asks for donations to counter the "religious right," the evangelical Christians of radio and TV. They point to "communal obligations" to combat "threats to the very foundations of our democracy," to "Pat Robertson . . . a dangerous trend." They raise alarms over opposition to "some women's and civil rights issues . . . to judicial review, the doctrine of original intent of the Constitution . . . an interpretation sharply at odds with most Jews." Rothenberg answered that these efforts and "a great deal of money" are not to protect Israel or Jewry, but are the social agenda of liberalism: quotas, busing, abortion, unfettered judicial activists. Why should Jews resist criticism of these? Liberal theology has been more detrimental to Jewry than to others. A letter writer of "50 years of Jewish communal affairs" asserted that Jewish organizations "predominately reflect . . . ultra liberal-professionals who dominate these institutions."

What must be made clear is that all of these attacks: from the war on decency, war on the Vietnam War, war on "racism," quotas, demands for reparations from Japs, from blacks, the war on Christianity and the building of an arrogant "finger of shame," all of these were but thrusts in the big war to destroy human society for the apotheosis of a fascist elite. These attacks would not have been possible had not Dewey, Cohen, Boas, FDR and anti-McCarthyism prepared the way.

We know that if people are pushed away from a belief in a power that can bond a human society together, as people even in this century believed in Christianity, they will be forced to support a belief that is inhuman. There is really no middle way. Ideas do have consequences, and the teaching of mass hatred, which for these last thirty years has constituted the core of the liberal idealogy, more so today than ever, must lead to chaos and violence. Schlesinger, Arendt, and Hook, wrote Allen Weinstein (not accidentally all Jews), were harshly critical of Chambers for the sharp unrealistic division . . . (of) participants in a "Manichean morality play", "dividing the world into communists and anti-communists."

This charge of an "unrealistic division" of "Manichean" participants should be recognized as the Big Lie of American Liberals. Schlesinger, Arendt, and Hook, who denounced Chambers, were obviously aware that less than a score of years earlier (1936) Lippmann had declared that the division into humanitarian "planners" and "mossbacks" was recognized by everyone. Could anything be more Manichean? In 1921, Columbia's President Butler had noted the Dewey educationalists socializing of education, "while making the most solemn assurances that nothing of the kind was intended." Morris Cohen's destruction of Rule of Law and subverting of our Constitution was to be accomplished under the dissembling claim of "civil rights". FDR used America in his effort to save Stalin and to push Communism into world supremacy -- so much so that it was ordered that we had to toady to it. In the early 60s, one group of renegades was to leave JFK's top security agencies and set up the most important KGB stop outside Moscow (the IPS), while another stayed on to engineer the destruction of the government of Vietnam -- under the lie "to move the war along". The anticipated and warned chaos that followed provided the opportunity to turn against the war in a few months and to assault America as evil. In the 80s, we had the spectacle of the media and Congress supporting Communism in Central America, while the people and President supported "freedom fighters". So much for denying a Manichean division.

The central evil of "liberalism" resides in its providing and long having provided, a sheltering sanctuary for all who hated America and supported the evil party. I.F. Stone was honored by the evil party's media when he died (6,16,89). Peter Jennings named him Man of the Week with credo, "write the truth . . . defend the weak . . . fight for justice." Izzy Stone was a renegade, a traitor, for over 15 years a paid KGB agent. Oliver Stone's hatred for America, extreme as it was and is, is shared, reinforced and vastly amplified by his audience. His movies: "Scarface," "Salvador," "Platoon," "Wall Street," "Born on the Fourth of July," like PBS documentaries, like The Smithsonian Institution, much of social studies in our schools, and the principal products of the over $20 billion Department of Education are all uniformly intended to make people hate their own people and society, to teach hate and frustrated guilt.

A major purpose of this *Guide* is to show that a "Manichean division" has been fixed by the evil party with intent to destroy the human side. Mankind has known from the earliest times that there was a sensible division; "Righteousness is what is loved," and it is the purpose of education to teach that which is to be loved and that which is to be rejected. "The most incessant occupation . . . (of man) is the ascertainment of truth."

We must demand that a line be drawn between what is tolerable to a human society and what is not. Here is a good example from the recent past:

After four years of Communist post-war bloodbath in

South Vietnam, some of the renegades whose actions had brought it on got squeamish. Joan Baez, somewhat a leader with R.J. Neuhaus, James Finn and other anti-American demonstrators, presented a plea to the "conscience of Vietnam." It criticized the Communists and called for an end to the Vietnam violence; the signers called on the Communists to live up to the ideas of social justice and rights of the oppressed that they had been demanding in their war against the U.S.

The answer came swiftly and with authority; "The government of Vietnam should be hailed for its moderation and extraordinary effort to achieve reconciliation." Baez and her bunch were "stooges," "agents of the CIA." Where from came this answer? From the *New York Times*, paid for by Cora Weiss, and signed by Richard Barnet, William Sloane Coffin and Dave Dellinger: the evil party.

POVERTY

NBC narrated a "White Paper" (1, 28, 1962) on "The Battle of Newburgh (NY)" and its welfare reforms. It was to be an indictment of the "rich mossbacks," just as in the case of housing for Yonkers a few years ago. Poor people were presented as starving, children without clothes, the "whole nine yards." Particularly held up for ridicule were the "cruel" and "inhumane" demands being made on the poverty stricken people as welfare reforms; the "White Paper" condemned them in various images as vicious.

It was one of the original staged TV lies. Prominent people who supported the reforms were edited out; the only supporters shown were in a bar. The whole city was pictured as a slum, and officials were ridiculed by savage film editing. The city manager was shown declaring, "No truly needy person has suffered"; next was a sequence of a man crying, then naked children. Later the man, Thomas H. Weygant, in a tape recorded interview with the City Council, confessed he had received $50 for his crying and undressing his children.

The whole lie was staged.

Note particularly the "reforms" that the city sought to impose, not described by NBC except as "cruel":

1. Able-bodied men on relief had to report for work in city maintenance departments.
2. Refusal of offered employment by "reliefers" would automatically terminate relief.
3. Relief payments to any family could not exceed the take-home pay of the lowest paid city employee with the same number of children.
4. Mothers who continued to bear illegitimate children would be denied relief.

Think! Think if you will, of the human misery, the suffering of children, the awful violence and destruction, the hundreds of billions of dollars that could have been used for constructive purposes, and especially of the awful tearing of the social fabric of humanness that holds us from bestialities that something like these simple, human, true reforms, could have averted.

There you see, in its most ugly and irrational form, the abysmal split between human beings and the evil party. Donna Shalala criticized attempts to limit welfare for unmarried girls having babies, by declaring, "Abandonment of responsibility by government or by citizens, is un-American." Certainly the prime responsibility lies with the girl and especially her family and community (church). The general people of America have little or no responsibility for her, they do have a responsibility for their country, for curbing poverty and indecency. They have gone along with a liberal policy of no-fault bastardy. It hasn't worked; in fact it has caused a deep rot to spread. It is time to try new policies.

Myron Magnet claims, "Without the "cultural revolution . . . there would be no underclass." His cultural revolution is a cop out, a euphemism; fear to say the truth. It was, and was intended to be, a rejection of human society, of human decency and responsibility. The real problem is not material want but spiritual misery. Big-city children are reported eating more meat than middle class children.

To be responsible, to work, be honest and loyal, decent and willing, even to know, requires effort, will, a commitment especially to self and family and community. Dependency is easy, not going to school, not doing work, not being responsible. A person becomes dependent, quite generally, only when he is allowed to be. Even in the Great Depression, there were very few people who allowed themselves to sink into dependency because there really wasn't very much "dole" to sink into.

It was the particular evil of the New Deal's encroachment upon human society that a degree of dependency was "imposed" by the bureaucracy. Even those at a subsistence level of existence were told, and understood, that the "dole" was quicksand -- today they say "the welfare trap." At that time "the moral factor" in poverty was emphasized; containing or eliminating poverty meant eliminating the causes: extramarital sex, and male ruffianism. Bastardy and youth violence are the core of today's shameful rot. It has resulted from corrupt government subsidization; if it were not paid for by the productive, it would not exist.

Renegades forced the perception that bastardy and violent behavior should not be stigmatized. A young male need not work; he can display his "self-esteem," which today means hubris and arrogance, parasitizing on the ignorant, unprotected, unwed girls or mothers.

Such activities were not tolerated until the evil party began to determine policy. Fifty to a hundred and fifty years ago children of unwed mothers were adopted out as orphans. It was not an easy life, but better than in today's Third World cities that we have. Little Orphan Annie was a real orphan, as was Herbert Hoover, some state governors, and many successful people. Pregnancy centers, such as Erring Women's Refuge, were generally charitable, church institutions, receiving little or no money; generally they were capable, honest, efficient, offering little unrealistic "esteem."

Ruffianism was harshly prohibited. A policeman's club would play a tattoo on a vagrant's head all the way back to the quarter to which they were confined. There were no open pornography shops; a man could be fired on the spot for drug or alcohol use. Statutory rape, sex even consenting sex with a girl under 16 or even 18, and breach of promise -- failure to marry after sex -- could bring 10 years, and judges were lauded for severity.

Since the New Deal, the emphasis has shifted to blaming "environmental" factors for poverty. Note the pre-welfarism perceptions. Jacob Riis (d. 1914), a social-worker journalist, was a tireless worker for the poor. He demanded both moral and environmental help. There was a great deal about the poor that needed mending, and it wouldn't be accomplished "by stuffing the one you would help with conceit and gratitude." First of all, he blamed alcoholism. And he did not make it an excuse, or a disease; it was something to be stamped out. He fought for better water, ending tenements, establishing clubs where people could meet "respectably and for companionship not inimical to domestic virtues."

Next was Riis's indignation with "pauperism" -- a moral distemper, the undeserving poor. The poor needed "habits of thrift and ambitious industry," along with "steadiness, sobriety, and cleanliness." The "dole" was worse than poverty; it was what "pauperized" the poor, degraded them, robbing them of all human attributes, from simple responsibility and respect for themselves -- like the earlier-mentioned deer in the park.

There is a discussion of social control by J. Schwartz, in *Public Interest,* No. 103, Sp 1991, p. 21. He says this new anti-social control thesis, of socialists fighting human society, has resulted in mental patients in the streets, rejections of all standards for welfare recipients, abandonment of control of students in colleges and even in high school. He might have added this throwing away of all the controls is the cause of the cancer that has metastasized and is destroying all that men have fought to gain for thousands of years. Western civilization or culture implies control, hence is to be abandoned, so too with all standards; the churches must be rejected from the public square, parental discipline in the homes, and teachers' control in school. Judges are not to be controlled by law or Constitution, nobody by any principle of morality, truth or humanness, on and on.

Schwartz writes that social policies aimed at helping the poor are damned for seeking to control their behavior. He concludes that the critique of social control is in effect a larger rejection of moral norms: the dissolution of the concept of community, indeed of normality. No action can be justified as for the common weal; the concept of a harmony of interests is deceptive. He quotes the historian David Rothman: we neither can nor ought to attempt to restore a moral consensus; our belief in the superiority of morality and humanness, and all that meant to the ability to define and to implement norms . . . has disappeared. Historian Paul Boyer: the quest to moralize the masses was abandoned in 1920, with the realization that the pressing danger was not disorder and degeneracy, but conformity. Schwartz "suggests" that we know better, but that seems to be much less than a commitment, to morality, humanness, and Western Civilization.

Myron Magnet declared that poverty and race were inseparable. Talk about "social policies and arrangements scrutinized," leads to the next stage of the defiant criminal as every man who rejects "workin' some jive job for chump change," and finally to Statism, in which the State is responsible for the fall of every sparrow. Of course, that is only an "interim thing," to be forced into the public's perception until the State has a full grasp on the levers of coercion, then "gulags" and "sending them down" become wholesale answers to unwilling workers or resistant citizens.

Magnet ends his book with the story of a Ghanaian cab driver who was contemptuous of beggars, asserting, "They have freedom and don't know what to do with it." This is true only in a special sense. The fact is all normal people will know what to do when they get hungry enough. It is only necessary that people be brought up to see that work is not for mere survival; work is the very essence of life. People who conceive of receiving nothing more than money from working are going to find it very unrewarding, and the "chump wages" they receive may be more than they are worth. Each job is a step up; it will be for any person who accepts it as such; a step toward a more meaningful life in a broader world of responsibility, of family and contributions to a whole human society.

CRIME

In 1993 prisoners filed 53,000 lawsuits in federal courts against states. Nevada alone spent $700,000 in direct legal costs, but this is overshadowed by the fact that the meddling of federal judges has been making prisons ungovernable. These complaints, which have gotten into federal courts, have covered such as too tight jeans and demands for special peanut butter, and "Man-Boy Association" newsletters. In 1993, 80 percent of state prison systems and one-third of the 500 largest local jails were placed under federal court orders. Federal courts specify publications that must be supplied, the number of law clerks to be made available to prisoners, specific recreational equipment, guitars, playing cards, air-conditioning and TV sets, basketball courts, weight rooms, workshops, single-occupancy cells.

Under a dissembled claim of a Constitutional mandate renegade federal judges have nearly destroyed the right and the ability of local communities to provide police protection. And it only takes one rotten apple to start a new precedent; the status of prisoners has been elevated to that of tax-paying citizens, or even higher. They have removed the concept of prison as punishment. An Illinois convict demanded the right to use his cell for private drug-related activities. Right to cross-dress, to artificially inseminate, number of bread rolls, salads, pornography, have all been the subjects of litigation. Prisoner's rights groups demand that punishment be made illegal.

At age 15 Willie killed two subway riders, "for the

experience," and subsequently tried to kill two prison guards. It was to prevent this from reoccurring that he was routinely chained in his cell for five minutes each day during a danger period. A federal judge has afforded him a jury trial to determine whether the chaining should be continued. He told jurors his only regret was that he failed to kill the guards, and vowed to try again. Prisoners come in denying any wrongdoing, and this namby-pamby convinces them that they are right, thus undermining rehabilitation programs. In fact, federal judges have even prohibited certain rehabilitation programs, such as linking parole to reading proficiency. When a governor prohibited all pornography as a part of a rehab program, a federal judge started contempt charges against the state.

Congress, in its irresponsibility, passed the Religious Freedom Restoration Act enormously empowering vast prisoner demands; "churches" seek the right to distribute hate literature, and are seeking damages under the new law for previous denial of such a "right." The idiocy of this Congressional-Court renegadism is exacerbated by the inability of the Court to define a "religion." Black Gangster Disciples, Satanists, and other hate groups seek "religious" protection. Providing claimed special "diets" for these religions is a new load. California's Attorney General estimated that if only 2 percent of the nation's prisoners demanded special diets, the cost could run to $177 million per year. Even if the state wins the case, the RFRA allows the state to restrict religious practice only in a manner that is "least burdensome" to the prisoner; hence any demand will require hearings, expert witnesses, transportation, state witnesses, legal fees, guards - - to determine "least restrictive." And since RFRA applies retroactively, cases already won or even lost will require re-litigation. Finally since all "religion" will be entitled to equal treatment, these gangster churches can demand anything of legitimate religious programs, and these will necessarily need a cutting to avoid demands for equal funding.

Federal judges everywhere have vied with each other in releasing more and more violent criminals. Loran Cole was released to alleviate overcrowding; he had served 18 months of a 66 year sentence for grand theft; 8 months later Cole murdered an 18 year old college student and kidnapped and raped his sister. Michael Blair served 18 months of a 10 year sentence for an assault charge; when released he raped and murdered a 7 year old girl from an upperclass Dallas community. Kenneth McDuff, sentenced to death for killing three teenagers execution style, was paroled and since has been linked to the murder of four women. On and on. Nationally nearly one-third of all violent crimes are committed by parolees. Federal courts are only concerned with rights of criminals. They were not hired for that; we must have a number of impeachments, with full prejudice. The underlying problem, however, everywhere today is the irrationality, the madness as described above. But the people who control not only the institutions but the making of public perceptions seem unable to see the wild irrationality. Currently a "crime bill" is under congressional consideration. It seems aimed largely at protecting bureaucrats, and at gun control, with a payoff to the big cities. Compared to today, crime seemed non-existent during the Depression when many people were truly needy. Why not try what worked then: respect for religion, morality and responsibility, along with intention to punish criminals? Liberal welfarism has created a steady supply of criminals by paying girls to have children without homes, by destroying entry level jobs with mandates and regulations, and by forcing retention of a corrupt and renegade education monopoly.

The ways to cut crime realistically have nothing to do with the "crime bill". Currently we are told that the <u>average</u> actual punishment for murder is about 2 years, 6 months for rape, 2 months for robbery, just over a week for aggravated assault, a half week for car theft. Make crime costly. Phase out plea-bargaining, along with exclusionary rules and exclusion of evidence. There is seldom reason for hiding prior convictions, or for juries to reach unanimous verdicts, or to disallow frisking of violent suspects.

The human way to reduce crime, which would have a

tremendously beneficial effect on all of our worst problems, is to rebuild families. It is wrong to buy more guns, hire more cops, build more prisons; when federal programs continue producing more criminals.

"The old system was . . . a moral system. Our (people) today produce criminals and prostitutes and drunkards, not because it is their nature, but because their simple system of order and tradition has been destroyed." This was a liberal cry of pain for black Africans. Why can no liberal make the same case for our own people? Today's results are catastrophic: "Sixty percent of rapists, 72 percent of adolescent murderers, and 70 percent of long-term prison inmates grew up in fatherless homes."

There is another type of crime. Dean was described as "an almost excellent student," a "quiet gentlemen," never had a discipline problem. " . . . (L)ike the most normal, well-adjusted kid? Probably not, but not outside the norm. Yet kids just picked on him." One former high school mate who admitted taunting Mellberg said, "Yeah . . . we water ballooned him . . . it wasn't like we hated him, he was just there. Everybody was pretty much cruel to him." Cruelty followed him into the Air Force; rumors were floated that he was a homo, they stole his things, flattened his bike tires. Perhaps central to the Air Force problem were the psychiatrists, where he was likely "ordered" as a result of his complaints of harassment. The "psychiatrists" tried to get him discharged for "psychiatric reasons." His mother spoke of "the horrible horrendous things that Spokane did," she didn't elaborate. He was shipped to another base and was given an honorable discharge, but we are not told whether these were requested or forced. He returned to the base of his harassment with an assault rifle, obviously after the "psychiatrists." We are not told whether he got them, but this former choir boy and chess club member killed four and wounded 25 before being gunned down. Imagine the furor had he been Black or Jew.

ENVIRONMENT

An environmentalist from Ann Arbor a couple years back urged "environmentalism as a commitment to sanity . . . to your grandchildren." Life without commitment, he wrote, is empty, futile; a commitment means a spiritual purpose," a form of religious commitment."

The American people have been asked, and have wanted, to help the needy, the negro, the enslaved of Europe, the people in poverty, and to improve education and laws and housing -- on and on. They have cooperated, given their sweat, their blood and billions. And have reaped one disaster after another.

Edward Krug was an environmentalist who participated in a study of "acid rain," supported by half a billion dollars from the American people; he found no evidence of an environmental crisis. For this information, as Warren Brooks and others sought to make known, Mr. Krug and his scientific credibility were attacked and he was effectively barred from government research.

In the 1970s renegade pseudo-scientists declared that imperceptibly small doses of dioxin could deform unborn babies and alter genes. The U.S. government, meaning you, squandered unreported billions for relocating residents and cleaning up Love Canal and Times Beach; the Veteran's Administration still has a flood of claims. And it was all a giant hoax, like Alar. Dioxin was nearly harmless.

But there is more. Love Canal was one of the first environmental rages, with hate, hate, hate, evil America, evil capitalism spread about, like Nazi ruthlessness. Contaminating chemicals dating back to WW II, produced in the Niagra Falls region, were disposed of under orders and direction from the best scientific advice obtainable. Love Canal, nearby, would be floored with clay, the contamination emplaced and then a very thick clay envelope would enfold the chemicals. The area was declared off-limits and enclosed. But not for long. In a few years the local real estate shysters began eyeing this prime location. Their first move was with their influence on the school board. The very center of the site was exactly where judgment called for a new school. There were rounds in court; the company told the judge of the contamination and of the exclusion of activity. Legal action was threatened until, under a court order, the company turned the property over (they refused to sell it) for $1.00. Soon huge sewer and water lines were laid from one end to the other; schools and subdivisions went up. And then the gunk began to trickle out where the clay sheath had been broken. Then the eco-freaks came, and the lawyers, and all the hate-America.

It was determined that the space shuttle Challenger crashed because the "asbestos scare" caused a California company to cease manufacture of a component.

Most people know that NBC "rigged" the fiery crash of the GM truck by planting a "rocket" in the chassis, but many may not know that CBS's Ed Bradley showed TV viewers that "transmission pressure" could make the accelerator pedal go down on an Audi, with resulting "sudden acceleration" and a crash. Mr. Bradley <u>did</u> <u>not</u> tell them that, for the demonstration, a hole was cut in the transmission and high pressure air injected. Thus was the transmission pressure fraudulently produced and the lie presented to the public.

When editors canardize about our society as "hormonally panicked, wildly litigious," they force the perception that subversive and lying attacks are merely "part of the process," and no longer unacceptable renegadisms, as formerly before 1960. The book *Apocalyptics*, published by Edith Efron in the mid-1980s, gave the proper name to the Statist bureaucrats who set whole freight trains of lies, cannon-balled by the Courts, crashing catastrophically into our economy and society.

In 1978, OSHA, using figures developed by Dr. Irving Selikoff, projected that 58,000 to 75,000 persons per year would die from asbestos related cancer. In 1988, EPA's Marvin Schneiderman obtained a precedent-setting ban on asbestos. In another five years, the actual deaths were corrected to 13-15 per year, and these unprovable. Though the EPA order was denounced immediately here and abroad, in *Science* and *Lancet,* as having been written "for political not scientific reasons,[156] it hammered full speed ahead. A dozen companies went bankrupt with thousands thrown out of work. Some $50 billion was spent on removal, disrupting schools and businesses across the country and 150,000 tort cases clogged courts. At the end of nearly five years of chaos, a U.S. Court of Appeals finally was forced to throw out the EPA ban on asbestos when it failed to make a case for even 13 to 15 asbestos-related deaths a year from cancer among heavily exposed workers.

Note the excuse. Schneiderman's justification was, "We did what scientists often do . . . use estimates without questioning them." That is a lie. Non-governmental scientists nearly universally use peer-review; bureaucrats have "power"; they don't need to. The fact is, they were questioned, before and during the ban, but that didn't stop the destruction of Johns-Manville Company, and others, or the wasting of tens of billions of dollars.

The recent story of a "Buchenwald Touch" concerned the use of "dozens of mentally retarded teenagers as guinea pigs . . . by government scientists in 1946 . . . (who) were fed radioactive food (at Boston's Fernald School)." "In Nashville 800 pregnant women were given radioactive iron," and at Los Alamos, the atom bomb laboratory, "18 people were injected with plutonium to see how much they could tolerate." "Hundreds of radiation experiments were performed in the 40s and 50s, on thousands of Americans without their knowledge."

ABC's Beltina Gregory warned of "a scandal of enormous proportions." Diane Sawyer asserted, "for 40 years the documents were locked away . . . (government) scientists did not make a mistake. They were warned . . . and did it anyway." The implication was that the "Department of

---

[156]Claimed by Sir Richard Doll, of Oxford University, the epidemiologist who proved the relationship between smoking and lung cancer.

Energy," (actually their predecessor the Atomic Energy Commission) "a nuclear lap dog," was responsible for all this as part of the "Cold War."

The topper came from NBC's Tom Brokaw, a "radiation scandal." Elmer Allen was a black Pullman porter. Brokaw's "News" (1, 5, 1994) had Allen's daughter saying, "They injected him with plutonium 239 . . . from what I read tumors began immediately. I also knew that, with the injection of plutonium, it did not give them any choice but to amputate three days later." Even Secretary O'Leary got into it, "Mr. Allen . .. incapable of taking care of himself . . . had been caught up in a giant machine." CBS also spread "the Buchenwald Touch."

All of the above were lies. They must have been known to be lies, for the slightest checking would have revealed the truth. It was a "blatant attack on America" and confidence in government. The Fernald teenagers were treated by an MIT-Harvard program on nutrition, using only minute amounts of tracers, less than given commonly today for millions of cases. Mr. Allen had terminal bone cancer and had been given less than five years to live; so he volunteered for the plutonium injection program.

It was a far, far different world then, than what has evolved since 1960 -- renegades running off to Moscow or Hanoi, "giving aid and comfort to our enemies." People were sacrificing their lives; eighteen terminally ill people, with less than 5 years to live, volunteered through, and with the advice of their own physician, to receive plutonium injections to serve a vital national interest. Mr. Allen was one of three of these "Cold War victims" that lived many years, with absolutely no known effects; he died in 1991, 44 years after the "plutonium poisoning." None of the 18 ever showed any effects of the plutonium; seven lived longer than 10 years.

The TV renegadism is not to be tolerated: Ted Kennedy, shown on his way to Fernald School, was asked by Katie Couric, "Has it surprised you that MIT's president has defended these experiments?" As though callousness rather than comprehension was the reason.

It was much like the renegade, feminist-journalist who asked one of Rodney King's first-trial jurors whether she had not considered the "public reaction" to a not-guilty verdict. Stupid and renegade people have always existed, as peek-throughs; never have they flourished in the "mainstream" as they do today. A free society with constitutional government cannot survive when the presence of such poisoners is not only tolerated but are awarded honors.

The Rodney King Affair shows every sign of being planned. The last twenty seconds of the video were played over and over and over; it contained almost nothing of the essence of the police encounter with King, an obviously PCP-maddened, dangerous felon breaking parole. Yet the public was brainwashed into believing that was all there was. Competent attorneys watched the trial, and we have to believe did tell the media, "Hey, there's not going to be a guilty verdict." Yet the entire media, almost to a man, expressed "astonishment, indignation, anger" at the verdict. It was a TV "victory" over racist America, putting a massive hole in the right of a jury trial, the very essence of democracy.

The same renegadism surfaced again, here, with the Cold War radiation experiments." Keith Schneider of the *New York Times,* wrote how Secretary of Energy Mrs. O'Leary's radical deputy (leader of a massive effort to block nuclear energy development), Dan Reicher, pulled O'Leary out of a meeting with the news that "People were injected with plutonium back in the 1940s." O'Leary ordered, "Get on it," Schneider remarked that, ". . . the (radiation) investigation has been a triumph for O'Leary and has produced political benefits for Clinton." It came out, filling front page and TV morning programs -- just as Troopergate and Clinton's Watergate were surfacing.

People had no more idea that the radiation story was all lies than they knew of the Rodney King lies when Sam Donaldson, his face twisted in hatred, declared that an innocent "motorist" had been "beaten into insensitivity."[157]

Both cases required so little to obtain a check that it simply cannot be accepted that the intention was other than to savage the confidence and integrity of America, and skip out free by the time the truth came around.

In the "global warming" debate climatologist Dr. Patrick Michaels of the University of Virginia asked, "Would you march down the road towards a policy which people have rightfully said requires an economic restructuring of the world, knowing that the world (climate) is behaving opposite to what the basis for the policy said?"[158]

NASA's director of Goddard Space Studies, James Henson, proclaimed on a hot day, (6, 13, 1988), ". . . the greenhouse effect . . . is changing our climate now." Butterfly specialist, Dr. Paul Ehrich, NBC's "environmental expert", warned of "melting polar ice inundating Washington."

The British Equinox program produced a widely-praised documentary on warming, entitled *The Greenhouse Conspiracy*, in 1990. Prestigious London *Financial Times* named it "one of the best bits of television journalism of the year . . . the four pillars upon which the theory of global warming rests . . . not one can be relied on". Evidence that the earth is warming is weak; proof that CO_2 is the primary cause is non existent; there is no ability to predict for future climate changes, and the underlying physics is in doubt.

The producer Hillary Lawson began the project believing in warming; he invited contributions from both sides. British TV magazine, *The Listener*, declared that "the

---

[157]Note how Sam seemed to be saying, "beaten nearly to death," yet he really said nothing at all, "insensitivity" not being a word. Old Sam counted on that.

[158]John Richardson, the CIA station chief in Saigon prior to the assassination of the Diem family, tells a story of "Shining Lie" Neil Sheehan. Richardson had "told him that we had carefully and continually canvassed alternate leadership possibilities and had found none. Did he want us to take a flying leap into the dark in the midst of a guerilla war? His answer was 'Yes'."

main alarmists (were reduced) to bashful inarticulacy . . . almost a witness for the prosecution." Experts from around the world agreed with MIT's Richard Lindzen, "Not only is there little evidence to support a catastrophe, there is ample evidence to the contrary."

Why then, asked Lawson, is it we have been led to take talk of catastrophe seriously? NASA's Roy Spencer answered, "It is easier to get funding . . . (for) a disaster." PBS not only refused to show the excellent British film, it used tax money to produce its own propaganda dog. Vice President Gore, then a senator, defended PBS censorship in a floor speech, and went on to denounce Lawson's documentary as "some ridiculous program from another country." He insulted the outstanding world scientists interviewed calling the documentary a "nut show," that claimed the moon landing was a hoax.

The Bush Clean Air Act tremendously expanded the size and power of the EPA; it will regulate every company that emits any among 181 substances. The people paid half a billion dollars for a 10 years study of acid rain; the result was the determination that the forests, lakes and streams are not dying; "acid rain" is a hoax. The "ozone hole" has always been there, at least well before CFCs were manufactured in any quantity. There is no ozone problem; the billions of dollar turnover to new and very expensive refrigerants is another hoax. Nearly all the chemicals on the foods you eat are not pesticides but natural plant toxins or by-products of cooking. In 1991, the Health and Human Services Department lowered the danger line on blood lead from 25 to 10 micrograms (40 in much of the world). That change raised the number of "children at risk" from 400,000 to 4.5 million, and set in motion a litigatory and regulatory monster that could reach a half trillion dollars. Unmentioned was the fact that, a few weeks previous, the two leading world science journals, *Science* and *Nature* had called into question the basic studies (by Herbert Needleman for "data manipulation") upon which the HHS regulations were based. Congressman Dingell declared "something fundamentally wrong with much of the science . .. on asbestos, dioxin, and PCBs, where risk may have been dramatically overstated at immense costs to the public . . . (the 10 micrograms for lead) is far, far below the level considered dangerous in other countries."

Then there was the radon scare, and the entire radiation hype that has destroyed nuclear power and irradiation of foods for destroying pathogens, and Alar. Lies and deceit seem in everlasting supply. Now we have a multi-billion dollar breast-implant giveaway, and have discovered "no problem."

FASCISM

Not only is our government approaching irreversible Statism, there is nothing solid preventing its moving further. There are, on the other hand, powerful anarchical forces forcing it on, in special interests, minorities and aliens.

When a government succeeds in taking control of the police, of education, enforcing rigid controls on industry, even on the thoughts in people's minds, when it has destroyed Rule of Law and substituted administrative judges who "can give the people what they want," and finally when a centralized and powerful enforcement agency such as Stalin's NKVD or Hitler's Gestapo, exhibits its power with ruthless violence, much as BATF has been doing in Waco, Idaho, and elsewhere, that is fascism. It has been said that power corrupts man; equally true is that men corrupt power. An elite, that has gathered to it such power to command, will soon see itself as above the people, justified in correcting them to some "new vision." Joint Task Force Six has been described as a "military resource (for) civilian law enforcement". The 3rd Battalion, 3rd Special Forces Group trained the BATF group for the Waco assault and observed the operation. Also, it has been reported that enlisted Marines at a California desert station and Navy Seal platoons (reported on Internet and rumored for Delta Force) have been questioned concerning whether they "would fire upon U.S. citizens." Older servicemen were reported negative by over 85 percent, but younger men "agreed" or "strongly agreed." That is how holocausts arise, when only forbearance restrains the organized might of a trained and armed BATF.

Dependence upon the forbearance of powerful rulers, as the only saving protection of people has been rejected and overcome by a long struggle for written laws: as trial by jury (so befouled by the media in the Rodney King case); as freedom of religion or of conscience; freedom from an elite telling you what to think; freedom in your home ("a man's home is his castle") and to assemble together and own property. Fifty years ago or more, the American people did not have to trust the forbearance of a savage bureaucracy for their safety. We had <u>four</u> <u>bulwarks</u> still standing between the naked individual and the awful power of a national state.

1.   Rule of Law and a Constitution. Today an arrogant elite flaunts "penumbras and emanations" instead of law. Our Constitution and Bill of Rights are jeered and ridiculed in the privacy of the Court.

In 1913 Morris Cohen, with the help of John Dewey, unfolded his plan for "judicial legislation." In 1935, his son, Felix, used "the Nazi march to power" as an example of "accepting the forms . . . but substituting a socialist . . . revolutionary party . . ."[159]

2. Federalism was still enforced.

Federalism and its central purpose was long the most highly praised feature of our Constitution. The Constitution was to be our Social Contract; federalism was to be a wall between the national State and people in their local communities. Powers of the national State were specified in the Contract; all other powers were retained by the people. The Cohens, Warrens, Brennans and Blackmuns have turned our Constitution upside down. Now the powers reserved to the people, by "penumbras and emanations" have become the power of bureaucrats to tyrannize.

---

[159]American Socialist Quarterly, Nov. 1935, "Socialism and the Myth of Legality," by Felix Cohen p. 21.

3.   Churches

Our nation was built on churches. Today the media and entertainment and government jeer "fundamentalists" and urge they be driven from public affairs. Many of the older churches, even a fair cut of the Catholic church, have rotted into renegadism. But radical Blacks and the Jews know how and are bent on using their churches as centers of power to attack our free society.

4.   Human Society and Families

The only sure protection that any person or people ever had is a human society, built of families, holding to a purpose, to rise up. Our only hope of regaining freedom, of pulling back out of the horrible abyss that we have been tricked into is for the common people to gather together, into Jefferson's wards, and learn about human society and Rule of Law and the evil party that has nearly destroyed us. A people that has lost its history, lost its comprehension of its ancestors and its culture is like a flock of blind chickens ready for the pot.

We must get our children out of the public schools and have them taught about human society and decency and truth and about the history of our great nation. We must reclaim our Constitution, and thrust back the snout of the bureaucratic government and its regulation and thought control. But an area of most critical concern is crime. Crime not only destroys families and human society, far more critical right now is that it has provided an excuse for the development of heavily armed, hi-tech forces in the hands of a renegade government for the purpose of subjugation.

The visible danger is the BATF, more heavily armed but as ruthless as the NKVD. After harassing the Weaver family for over a year in Idaho, killing the son and wounding Randy Weaver, a sharpshooter drilled his wife in the head as she stood holding her baby on the doorstep of her pitiable plywood home. It was laughed off in Washington as the killing of a "white supremacist." They wouldn't have shot a Jewish supremacist, and black supremacists have been <u>given</u> tax money, from both Washington and Moscow. The Waco

Massacre was an unmitigated genocide, and must be investigated and punished.

The invisible danger is far more treacherous, and it covers many things. The intent and actual movement is to criminalize activities, not just owning of guns, but thoughts and beliefs. Putting clean sand in a small ditch on a quarter-acre retirement lot put Ocie Mills and his son in prison for 22 months. People in the financial markets have been hauled away in chains for no specified offense. In LA a 30-man police and a federal-agents raiding party beat down the door of a rich man's home and shot him dead; the killer claimed some rumor that his wife used drugs -- none were found, but they had an appraisal all ready in case of seizures.

Even more threatening is the change in the whole philosophy of "police." Their job today is far less to protect you than it is to enforce an agenda, or just keep out of trouble. During much of 1987 citizens in Detroit complained to police of a crack house: dealers firing guns in the air for fun, actual street shoot outs while children played, girl prostitutes soliciting old men and adolescents. Finally two men burned it down. The police were there in minutes, jailed the two for two counts of arson and assault with a deadly weapon. But the jury of common people acquitted them. On the other hand liberal media and journalist William Raspberry called for armed soldiers to police the streets of the nation's capital; they were recently joined by the mayor.

What you must realize is that the disaster in crime, as in education, abuse, misery, hate, didn't exist in the 1930s. There were then nearly as few eight year-old school children who couldn't read as who couldn't walk. I believe it was in the fifties when I first read of a place where you dared not walk at night -- a white man in East St. Louis. You could sleep on a park bench at night with no fear -- I have. There was no graffiti, no prostitutes, bums, burned out Beiruts -- not in the open. You will get what you allow, or even pay for. We allow and pay for illiteracy, we allow crime, we allow all manner of violence and indecencies that are destructive of human society, of families.

With such madness, it is obvious that there is no intention of protecting the public. A few years back it was reliably reported that the spouse of a candidate for high government office was involved in producing child-porn, at least indirectly. It was never investigated, and was declared a non-issue. Some old farmer-bus-driver out in Nebraska received an ad for child porn in 1987, through the mail. He foolishly answered the ad; when he returned home on picking up the response, he was met by federal agents. He lost his farm, his bus job, his standing in the community and friends. The Supreme Court exonerated a broken shell.

The most evil crime in the history of man concerns the holocaust, invented by socialists, effected by the anti-Semitism of socialists, especially of Marx who perfected the teaching of mass-hate, by focusing on one enemy: the Jews. Socialist George Bernard Shaw (and others), no Christian, taught that "mass extermination" of undesirables would be necessary. It was first pursued by Lenin and developed on a massive scale by Stalin. Neither Christianity nor America had anything to do with the introduction of holocausts. In 1940, America was near totally against involvement in the Soviet-German War, but was "tricked into it" by FDR. Being a Christian nation, we picked up the burden of saving Western civilization and freeing the enslaved peoples of Europe. If decisions were made not to bomb rail lines or to make demands and policies whose certain effect was to lengthen the war, the people knew nothing of it. Today we have an abomination, a "finger of shame" in the National Mall of the American people, pointed at America and Christianity, and voiced endlessly by a tape.

The obvious effect, and presumably the intent, of this savage symbol of hatred for our country and religion has been to obscure the holocaust as an integral part of the tactics of socialism. That the often tortured lives of 100 million souls could be crushed out by such an evil, and pretend they don't count, and to pretend in fact that the evil fault is with human society not socialism, is a crime more vast than that of Hitler's. All lives are expendable for a cause, both yours and mine. Human society and the very concept of humanness is sacred. It is socialism that would destroy it. If the money spent on the "memorial" had been spent to teach people that simple fact, the effort of the Jews should have received the world's honor. Someone chose to teach hate and to obscure the real evil: the fascism that is enveloping America and the world. Therein lies the Manichean Split.

Jews must be urged to remove that evil fraud and to build somewhere an institute or academy for a rigorous study of socialism or Statism. Edmund Silberner has in fact made a good start in revealing the lies and evils of socialism; but it must be taught.

NOTE ON COMMUNISM AND FASCISM

It is well known that most domesticated animals, and even wild animals after extended captivity, are unable to survive in the wild. In an exactly analogous manner, man loses not only his power of independent social survival when his bonded and purposeful society has been destroyed, with it also goes his humanness, his very comprehension of responsibility, and all that makes life sacred. Since Marx's *Manifesto* of 1848, there has been no reason for people to be unaware that communism had declared families, morality and human society as the enemy to be destroyed.

The early socialists who began subverting our universities a century ago understood this very clearly. One needs to spend at least an hour with *The Red Decade* by Eugene Lyons to realize the power not just of the communist core but of the liberal establishment described by Walter Lippmann, Diane Trilling, Whittaker Chambers, and others -- all quite different kinds of people who had once been a part of this evil party.

Turn now to new material. Read the Introduction by David Horowitz to S.S. Powell's *Covert Cadre*: "My parents were members of the Communist Party, together with all our family friends. The same deceptive exterior that hides the political agenda of IPS hid theirs. Outwardly . . . middle class . . . progressives, espousing views liberal and democratic . . . idealistic and concerned . . . active in unions and civil rights . . . Democratic . . . But inhabited another secret world as soldiers in a revolutionary army was what really mattered . . . were secret agents with code names -- for . . . abandon(ing) the facade of progressive politics . . . to lead the revolutionary struggle . . . a secret conspiracy to war against the (U.S.) fascist state." While making the most solemn assurances that nothing of the kind was intended.

"What those who mistake the left's idealism for innocence fail to understand is . . . (that) their faith <u>can</u> commit acts of enduring evil without causing so much as a ripple." Horowitz recalled a neighbor teacher who accepted the Party's order and became part of the chain that reached from Stalin to the insertion of an ice pick in Leon Trotsky's head in Mexico.

He then tells of the *Khrushchev Report* in 1956, and the subsequent rise of the New Left, denying servility to totalitarian states. Cuba and the Institute for Policy Studies (IPS) would provide the link between revolutionary youth, in SDS and Weathermen and a horde of satellite "spinoffs," and the old

Stalinists. Youth would find its new Stalin in Fidel.

Read the Introduction and "Notes" to the *Rosenberg File* by Radosh and Milton; there is the same universe of relatives and friends all of whom are Communists. Radosh began with intent to clear the Rosenbergs, as Allen Weinstein sought to exonerate Hiss. Radosh tells of the New York Town Hall meeting (1983) to attack his book, filled to standing-room-only with Communist sympathizers. Meetings with several people are described: a lawyer, "Of course they were guilty . . . What's so bad about helping Stalin . . . the responsibility of every good communist . . ."

Then there is the story of the Bernsteins, by son Carl, and Vivian Gornik's story and Ellen Schrenker's admission: it was not McCarthy's methods of bluster, "it was his anti-Communism." But there is a simpler method; merely take an honest look at what has happened.

Students for a Democratic Society, formed in 1962, had over a hundred chapters by 1963. IPS, formed by two dropouts from JFK's National Security and Arms Control agencies (leaving informers behind in these top-secrecy councils), described in *Covert Cadre* as the most powerful KGB stop outside of Moscow, soon began the task of coordinating SDS with other revolutionary organizations. SDS, with IPS guidance and support, turned a generation of students from young people with intelligence and ability to reason in three or four years into a mob whose only argument was F _ _ _ You! The groundwork for Kent State and all the rest, blamed on Vietnam, began before Vietnam.

In 1987, an eminent scientist, who had held nearly every major post in American national science, reported on a study of the Strategic Defense Initiative as presented in a report. The report, he declared, was not worthy of support. It contained errors of "100-fold", "always in one direction,"[160] to make the plan for nuclear defense always seem more difficult than it is. Then there was an Executive Summary which contained errors and inconsistencies, again always in one direction, more negative even than the Report. Finally a prepared public statement for the media, "goes beyond even the Executive Summary . . . abandons all pretense of being scientific . . ." He compares this with what happened to German

---

[160]Whittaker Chambers in *Witness* claimed "a socialist revolution in the name of liberalism . . . formlessly but always in on direction has been inching its cap over the nation."

science under fascism[161].

"Historians" have forced the perception of a moral equivalence between Rightist's assaults in academic freedom in the 1950s to Leftist's assaults in the 1960s. This is but part of the effort of liberals to obscure the evil of Marxism, and to equate Stalinism to American's reasonably free society -- denigrated as "capitalism." The assault in the 50s that involved academia was a rather mild attempt to reveal the dangers of allowing communists in our academic system. It was carried out as much by Democrats as by Republicans. The failure of this effort -- far from equivalence -- has been manifest in the nearly complete take-over of much of our universities by "Marxists," by the evil party. Radosh and Milton, writing on the Rosenbergs, asserted that it was their "worship and devotion" to the Soviets that had led to the "terrible things" with which they had been charged. Ellen Schrecker claimed that the communists were committed to "objectivity and fairness," but Theodore Draper who "knew most of them" advised that any Communist novice knew that classless "objectivity and fairness" were bourgeois deceptions.

Today it is evident that the United States is moving rapidly into fascism; the possibility of collectivization is almost nil and, on the other hand, there is no powerful element such as the Catholic Church that could retain some small sovereignty. Fascism, by the nationalization of all authority, is already far advanced. Rule of law under a Constitution, and even a concept of limited government, organized religion of any power, families and culture, all of these have been corrupted to near impotence, and these have always been the essential supports of a core for a human society.

This year, 1994, there has been a powerful thrust to nationalize not only "100 percent" of the entire health and medical industry, but to pull the entire judicial and police system of the nation under a nationalization, and to nationalize, even more completely, the nation's school system. These are all in addition to massive regulations for environment, racism, poverty, work rules, the financial world and increasingly even into people's families.

Over and over in this century we have seen confirmed Plato's observation on the freezing of forms and solidification of thought under an elite bureaucracy. Even under the most dire need both Stalin and Hitler allowed their ideology to constrain -- with

----

[161]*Academic Questions*, F. Seitz, Spring 1988.

Lysenkoism and against Jewish science -- critical progress. During WW II and on into the 60s, tremendous new technological adventures in nuclear power, jet engine aeronautics, electronics and computers, and then space travel were critically dependent upon new materials. The forced-draft applied to these efforts produced a total revolution in material science. With the 70s, the establishment's appeasement of the Soviets turned to outright "agreements" and the efforts in technology were throttled and the tremendous tools and techniques that had been developed in basic sciences, and the financial support, were transferred to a large degree to studies in biology and medicine. There then occurred a similar, perhaps even greater revolution in these areas. And the advances have created enormous new problems. What people must be warned of is the "freezing into a permanent structure present medical technology" as a result of national socialization of health care.

Housing, racism, and AIDS policies, and discrimination laws, are based on the claim that "dysfunctional individuals," even in excessive numbers and of voluntary disabilities, are of no more consequence than anybody else. Even speech or writing to the contrary will be punished by huge fines and imprisonment. A Berkeley city official chastised residents for implying that addicts with AIDS should be treated any differently than anyone else. It is a federal law that even voicing an objection to such a concept (which is now the law) can bring $50,000 fines for each infraction, for each person of a group, and a year in jail for each. In addition, the cities are held liable, under penalty of still larger fines, for enforcement, to provide the teeth. "Cases are legion in which cities have been held liable for statements by its citizens . . . opposition has been severely chilled," (Wall Street J.,8,8,94, editorial page). In Seattle, a community group's attorney complained that defining drug abuse as a disability makes "every panhandler on the street with a cup a member of a protected class."

The indecent and the contemptible have been made, in violation of the Constitution and common sense, a protected class. Many insane people are indecent, as are many severe alcoholics or druggies, or even very poor people, but it has never been necessary or considered proper to have law to protect them, though they nearly invariably received protection. Most people have compassion for the poor, the perverted, the addict, but the usual case does not command nor even invite respect.

Exposing children to such indecencies is as wicked as

exposing them to violence, lies, abuse; anti-social behavior should not be tolerated. Indecencies drive out decency; tolerance of the contemptible drives out the respectable, and human society deteriorates. Who but fascists would want this?

CONSTITUTION

Cass Sunstein declared, "Everyone agrees the Constitution is law" and as such, "it stands above politics."

This is misunderstanding. The Constitution, as is well known, is predominately a Social Contract and for most of 200 years was understood as such. It contracted power; the states would give to a national state certain "enumerated" powers to be used for the benefit of all the states: defense, control of foreign affairs, interstate commerce, and so on. In return, the national State made specific guarantees to the states and to the people. That was the accepted Constitution. It was the encroachment of Statism, particularly with and following WW I and WW II, that sought to obscure this truth. As Morris Cohen and son Felix recognized, socialism must subvert the Constitution in order to crawl above it. Law is not above politics; law is the very result of politics, however, it should be guided generally by natural law. It is the contract that must be above politics.

Sunstein reveals his purposes when he declares the Constitution "extremely vague."[162] The Constitution proper can hardly be perceived as anything but the very opposite of vague, and so too with the Bill of Rights. An eminent Constitutional scholar a few years back declared, probably less in complaint than in curiosity, that until the recent decades the Bill of Rights had been "little used." But how odd. How do you _use_ a wall? In spite of rabid and vicious propaganda, the "Wall" in the Constitution is _not_ between "Church and

---

[162]C.R. Sunstein, *The New Republic*, 3, 11, 1991, p. 32.

State"; such does not exist by any implication.[163] The "Wall," particularly evident in the Bill of Rights is between the national State and the people in their local governments. As Madison declared, "all that concerns the lives, liberties, and properties of the people," all social affairs, were to be the nearly sole concern of the individual states and of the people.[164] My God, that is what federalism meant! "Congress shall not . . ." assumed that should the time come when that would be corrupted to "No but the Court can . . . ," no one would be interested in freedom anymore anyway.

What is vague about the Constitution exists almost wholly in the feculent 14th Amendment whose very intent, as admitted at the time, was to deceive, to hide, to appear to be something it was not. The 14th most certainly was never by any stretch of the imagination legally passed; it was "declared promulgated" by a savage and revolutionary junta. After the power of this junta had passed, the Court which had fearfully renounced all claims to jurisdiction over "political" questions, took probably the best and only step it could take; it declared that the 14th only referred to the "war issues" and did not repeal the Bill of Rights.

Sunstein and the company which consists of the entire collectivist establishment find the "Constitution vague," because they insist on trying to "read entrails," after having

---

[163]" . . . (T)he most profound and penetrating of the causes that have transformed society is . . . (of) the thirteenth century . . . (Then) the psychology of Conscience was closely studied for the first time; men began to speak of the audible voice of God, that never misleads or fails, and ought to be obeyed always . . . When (this voice of good and evil was) recognized as something divine in human nature, its action was to limit power by causing (it) to be heard above the (accepted) and settled custom . . . (T)he soul became more sacred than the state . . . That is the root from which liberty of Conscience was developed, and all other liberties needed to confine the (State) . . . that it may not challenge the supremacy of that which is highest and best in man." (Lord Acton's Essays, p. 400; see p. 66-77 and 81-83 for "constitution".)

[164]Summarized most succinctly in the Tenth Amendment, and as supported in the Ninth and First Amendments.

disemboweled all of the Contract, all of the Bill, and its foundation even within the Constitution. It is through the needle's eye[165] of a few words in Sect. 1 of the 14th that these Sunsteinian magicians spew forth the entire guts of our most sacred Contract, and then they laboriously sort through the deconstructed offal to piece together their desires.

The audacity of these scholars can be found in its full-blown essence in statements such as, "The Constitution does not say that it should be interpreted in accordance with the original understanding." It seems to follow then that neither should the Ten Commandments be restricted to an "original understanding." If "Congress shall not . . ." can be newly understood by these Shamans as "Congress or Court shall . . ." then surely "Thou shalt not kill," can likewise be drawn through their magic eyelet and come forth as "Thou shalt kill."

Of course, as Sunstein assures us, some interpretations of the entrails "are better than others." Furthermore, these readings of the entrails "remain in a primitive state"; I should think so.

As long as judges may declare "penumbras and emanations", judicial dictates, without the certainty of immediate impeachment with full prejudice, there are no real freedoms, no rights of any kind, except as a forbearance. Our historical "limited government" was buttressed by Bill of Rights' denials, whose "shall nots" required no interpretation. The feculent 14th has been perceived as destroying those restraints, making all freedom subject to judicial acquiescence.

The purpose of law is to inform people of what is prohibited. Some noted scholar recently stated that culture was mainly a matter of "interdictions." That is an unacceptable misunderstanding. There may be some interdictions in Aeschylus or in Shakespeare, but the vast predominance is always with the positive, with the greatness

---

[165]Through this needle's eye comes what is known as the "substantive view"; therein lies the source of all chimerical visions of "due process" and "equal protection."

of the universe and man's purpose in it. Culture guides; law must restrain the vagrant.

So when we think of crime, education, poverty and alienation, we must plan not for controls, "police saturation," more computers and condoms in schools, more abuse centers, day care and the like. We must plan for people wanting to admire, wanting to rise up, being busy with hopeful tasks and purposeful living, not forever squeezed between restrictions. People must see some hope and purpose in their doings.

Society and culture must be admirable or at least aimed so. Law is separate, and it separates out that which is poisonous to society and culture. He well may be classically liberal but even J.S. Mill put on rigid limits. Untruth cannot be called truth, indecencies must not be allowed to challenge decency and humanness, renegadism may to some degree be tolerated, but only at or beyond the fringe of decency. Deceit must be curbed as a cancer. But always keep in mind that these controls are, as a little dirt in a good home, not allowed to interfere excessively with family growth. It is the purposeful doing that must occupy our principal efforts. But the knowledge of that which is loved and that which is hated must always be known and well marked.

RULE OF LAW

> "The Americans combine the notions of Christianity and of liberty so intimately in their minds that it is impossible to make them conceive of one without the other." That America of Tocqueville has nearly been destroyed by liberalism.

Primitive man was bound by elaborate rituals in all of his daily living, by taboos and customs; he could little more conceive of doing things differently than could a bee or a baboon. As people became aware of conduct, the systemization was relaxed and the concepts of morality, responsibility and justice arose, thus circumscribing a sphere within which the individual had freedom to choose. The growth of civilization has been marked by a continued expansion of this sphere of freedom.

Primitive life was intensely demanding, lacking in any choice; behavior was circumscribed from birth for all individuals, hence each was as alike as birds in a flock or animals in a herd. With freedom and choice, differences blossomed and inequality entered. This made morality and altruism even more necessary, and written laws were introduced to provide a coarse screening of behavior.

As inequality and individuality grew, the bonds of society were increasingly distended, leading to social corruption and decay. We do not know how really aware the Greeks were of this, but we do know that they adopted, seemingly for the first time, a general social purpose for guidance, particularly as to maintain freedom.

Feelings, as conscience, were felt as "forces" coming from the outside; innate customs, rooted far back in pre-human times, were comprehended quite similarly. Thus it is that in all primitive tribes or peoples, there is an element in the most fundamental law that is or was accepted as of sacred origin. Sacred should be interpreted as implying innateness, not unlike conscience or brotherhood.

Natural law arose from innate conscience or the feeling for justice -- the right and wrong. All written law should seek to approximate it as an ideal. But much of modern law is "administrative" or Statist's law, the very antithesis of natural law.

Rule of Law (a form of Law of Contracts) binds the government to the use of fixed rules, announced beforehand, that make it possible for people to foresee, with fair certainty, how the government will use the law. Thus unknown people may use the law for uses and circumstances unforseen by the lawmakers, and individuals can make plans with the knowledge of how the State will react. Thus justice was seen as blind. If, on the other hand, the State were to direct individual actions so as to achieve compliance with <u>plans of the State</u>, individuals would no longer be able to plan their lives with any assurance.

Until WW II it was widely accepted that America had Rule of Law as a Christian nation; that did not mean that others were not allowed full freedoms. It was a recognition that the "uncontested terms," the accepted morality, both in government and in social life, were supported by a social core whose outlook and purposes were Christianly human. Government and laws and morality and social institutions were not cardboard signs as for socialist governments.

A free society cannot exist without laws (and Rule of Law), but it also cannot exist with only laws. Our Founders and scholars of the past have insisted and explained that laws simply are not enough to make freedom work; they have commonly insisted that in addition a religion-backed morality was essential to urge people to want to be moral and charitable. What is undeniable is that people and their children must be taught that a guiding purpose is essential for social rationality, and a culture supported by a hierarchal core of scholars and leaders must provide the spiritual and intellectual incentives to the people so that their consent and support is in fact more than merely acquiescence; it is freely offered, by participating supporters.

This bonding, this feeling of participation in a community or brotherhood, the feeling of belonging, and reverence for a life of some preciousness, or sacredness, is what makes a human society. It is the source of social coherence, discipline, and leadership. And all of this has been built up over millions of years and has become an innate need of human beings; without the guidance of these feelings, people cease to be human. They become monsters with reason.

It is this purpose, this morality, and the teaching and guidance that must support it, that for nearly two thousand years was Christian. It was this that undergirded not only law, morality and institutions; it provided the foundation and structure upon which all people of all beliefs could find space and freedom for arranging their lives. It has provided even unconscious guidance for nearly all of us.

If people lose purpose, they obviously become, without purpose, irrational and even mad. If people lose morality, or are taught that morality is relative, or is but an imposition, then everything is permitted. We can see the madness and violence growing like a wild storm that will soon carry everything away. We must regain purpose and a core to teach it and to lead us back to sanity.

SHAME

Shame properly is the pain felt as a result of guilt for an impropriety or shortcoming, disgrace or dishonor. But shame, no less than guilt, is equivocal. Shame may be forced upon the innocent. Guilt is primarily the <u>fact</u> of an offense, but it may be only the "feeling of culpability," and again this may be forced, as an assault.

George Orwell noted that his was the only great country whose intellectuals shamed their own nationality. There was the forced perception that there was something disgraceful in being an Englishman, something that called forth a snigger at every English institution. An Australian recently noted sadly that his country had pursued "multiculturalism . . . as a means of dissolving" their identity in the hope that Asians would thereby look more favorably upon them.

It is shameful that we have allowed our society, our country, and ourselves to become so irrational, slothful, base as to slink from the responsibility for angry indignation and action to end the cultural and social genocide forced upon us. This is doubly shameful in that we have allowed, even approved of, a "memorial" as an accusation of genocide against us to be raised on our national Mall. No other country would allow such a public humiliation. It is triply knavish in that only a Black man and a famous Jewish scholar have raised significant points against it; William Raspberry jeered it by likening it to a "memorial to slavery" except that we had no part in "The Holocaust"; the Princeton scholar, Arno Mayer, questioned the intent of genocide.

Far more shameful, however, is toleration even acceptance by the media and the academics' of a pretense, that we still have a Bill of Rights and Rule of Law, without which there is no barrier to fascism. It is in fact thereby inevitable. Our nationalized and bureaucratized education is a world disgrace, as are our Third World cities, our "entertainment" feculence, and the uprooting of everything decent.

Sir Walter Scott who, in the Waverly novels made of human society "a loving and tender thing" -- (Russell Kirk), was teased by a Whig trimmer, until protesting he was moved to tears. "No, no -- 'tis no laughing matter. Little by little, you will destroy and undermine, until nothing of what makes Scotland Scotland shall remain."

Everyday's news brings more that is contemptible. It took leftist "social engineer," Congressman John Dingle to pronounce BATF, "a jack-booted group of fascists, " and Nat Hentoff of leftist *Village Voice* to damn as "Barbarous . . . pain-compliance techniques used routinely on elderly people." How long has it been since police dared to pain-press a union thug doing violence, or a homosexual or black rioter? A Detroit News photo showed a black policeman, gun in hand, manhandling a 70 year old white man protesting a bigoted anti-Catholic film. Bull Connor in reverse, but not on TV.

Law after law, many written badly enough, but others well written, are used as clubs by fascist judges. Hubert Humphry's Civil Rights Act is the prime example -- used to legalize racial quotas, which it specifically rejected. The Clean Water Act, requiring permits for filling "navigable water," does not mention "wetlands." Yet the federal bureaucracy and courts used it to destroy a 73 year old retiree who purchased a small lot that had been used for a combination fish-bait store and campground with latrines and beer cans. "Agents" spied on him from across the street with telescopic cameras, at the cost of perhaps tens of thousands of dollars, while he cleaned up the mess to the gratitude of the community, and built a house. Then these "agents" hit him. He is under federal court order to move his house and to restore the land to its "pre-adulterated" condition -- sheer nonsense. He is facing contempt charges for failing to beg permission for "added vegetation."

The "Mondale Act" of 1973 ordered states to provide child abuse prevention programs which guaranteed accusers immunity from prosecution, and made it a crime for teachers, doctors, etc., not to report "suspicions." These mandates quickly created a vast bureaucracy of "social workers," psychologists, counselors, etc., often poorly trained, but zealous for notoriety, knowing that reporting "suspicions" brought larger grants. In Stalinist Lillian Hellman's play *The Children's Hour* whispered gossip of children brings devastation and suicide for two young teachers; now government agents and informers are more efficient than gossip. Recently, a 30 year veteran teacher in Minnesota was accused of sexual abuse, later determined to be a dare by an older student, but unfortunately the teacher had already driven in front of an oncoming train.

Jewish Oliver Stone's self-expressed hatred for America has not been satiated with his half-dozen hate America films. Now he presents "a pair of 'white-trash' lovers . . . fetishizes violence . . . the audience recoils from itself . . . festering roadkill . .. grisly chain saw mirrors a deranged imagination . . . repressed sadism . . . Japanese stilted commentary as (white-trash) are plummeted (a la Rodney King) . . . freedom just another word for nothing left to kill." Quoted from the *Detroit News* (8, 26, 1994, D1). This kind of race-hate bigotry must be ended. The Jews themselves, who mildly disapprove of this evil hate-mongering, have a prime responsibility to do so.

Clintonists were widely recommending banishment for the Haitian junta. While their crimes were more violent, they were few relative to the vast devastation that will certainly result from Stone-taught hate. Hence banishment *au chemise* would do for Stone.

It is necessary to say a word about prejudice and bigotry. The traditional meaning of prejudice was that it was a pre-judgment, held with incomplete support. But few beliefs or opinions are held, and few groups adhered to, on the basis of complete knowledge; the very words "beliefs" and opinions admit it. Bigotry by the *Oxford English Dictionary*, and traditionally, refers to "an obstinate and unenlightened belief." Thus a bigot or a prejudiced person is not a witch, madman or criminal; he is anyone -- as you or I -- that holds strongly to an opinion without adequate basis. Who does this fit better for the 20th Century than the entire liberal to communist (fascist) continuum, from the old "Party line" to "PC"?

Race is a word of rather recent centuries; racism is not even listed in *OED*. Race long meant a family, tribe, or people of a common ancestor. Tribes have killed off each other, even as they were from a common racial stock, among all the major people of the earth. In Europe, the Celts killed off predecessors, Teutons killed Celts, Teutonic Danes killed Anglo-Saxon, Franks killed Danes. So, too, in Africa, and Asia, tribes decimated tribes; Bushmen and Hottentot had nearly suffered genocide by Bantus when Aryans arrived and saved them. In America there were, among certainly many others, the Mound Builders, the Mayans, the Zunis who were nearly exterminated by more warlike tribes. Semites have been decimating each other from the beginning of history. The Jewish Testament tells of neighboring people who, in the interests of peace, agreed to accept the Jewish God and be circumcised. After these ceremonies and on the third day when the men were very sore, the Jews rose up and killed the men and enslaved the women.

Jews have historically and presently been less troubled in New York than in Shanghi or Nairobi; otherwise that is where they would be. And they have killed, discriminated against or expressed hatred for the jeered gentile, meaning heathen, when historically opportunity has presented itself, no less proportionally, than the reverse. Furthermore the Jews have always used their organized racial-religious hegemony as a tightly disciplined force, especially in economic and cultural affairs. This has been widely noted in recent years by the

Soviets, by Blacks, and even by Jewish scholars.

The decay of Western civilization is the direct result of the failure of Aryan leaders; let that not be obscured. But they had help; read the admissions of David Horowitz, Ronald Radosh, Carl Burnstein and Vivian Gornick. There you find a vast organized fifth column of Communists far more pernicious than the KKK, because they did not go about in conspicuous white sheets. Rather they made an art of subversion, professing "assaulted virtue," and were far more dangerous than the derided "red neck," nativist or America Firstists, because they are learned and strategically positioned. The good news is that Jews are becoming increasingly aware that the end to Western culture and Christianity could well bring an end to Jewry.

A few years back, the London *Economist*, not an American Firster publication, admitted America to be one of the least racist of countries. Our most terrible war was fought to free the Negroes. Our Constitution and Bill of Rights have been nearly destroyed, except as mere forms, by liberals seeking to satisfy black radicals -- as in the present Haitian "invasion." That wasn't enough so they made white males second-class citizens, in their own country that sent them to war to save the Jews -- among other things -- and got a "finger of shame" for their pains.

The black slaves brought to America were sold into slavery by their own people, many times even by parents -- it is said for a piece of red cloth or an umbrella. Blacks were sold into slavery into Arabic or Muslim lands for over a 1000 years before being brought to America; where are their offspring? You may find the answer in the treatment of black slaves by Moslems, in St-Exupery's *Wind Sand and Stars*, in the 1930s.

America's two great democrats, Jefferson and Lincoln, along with most everyone else at the time, agreed that blacks would never be accepted into white society. They never have; those blacks who appear to have been accepted, now reject it. Perhaps Booker T. Washington could have provided the bridge for them, but he was discredited by white "liberals," socialists. The Reconstructionists manipulated the Negro into a fake freedom; now black radicals have followed a new evil party into more fake unreality. Dennis Prager has worried about what a post-Christian society will be like; let people reflect on the nature of a post-human society.

Simone Weil warned of conflicts between groups of men, where there is "no definable objective." Such conflicts are most bitter. Helen, Weil asserts, was not the issue in the *Iliad*; a "real issue . . . did not exist, and the role which Homer attributed to the Greek gods, we attribute to mysterious economic forces," or to racism. "But there is no need of gods or conspiracies to make men rush headlong into the most absurd disaster."

11. WHAT TO DO

<u>**INTRODUCTION**</u>

Young people, of all ages, need to make a commitment to something admirable to give meaning and motivation to their lives. Most people recognize the disaster of the "welfare trap", but far, far worse is the catastrophic abyss of Statism. Hence the intent here is to provide a rapid expansion in the number of people who can see for themselves and comprehend the danger, while, at the same time, recognizing the positive, the exuberance possible in a life of purpose, in the rebuilding of our human society.

Consider the intensity of the Paleolithic cave drawing: of the wild horse of Montespan, the "twisted perspective" of Lascaux, or the languorous ladies of La Madeleine. These all clearly represent a reaching for something. Some few thousand years ago, it was written, the earliest recognition was thus much earlier, that "Righteousness is what is loved." Durkheim's analysis of studies on primitive peoples, corresponding to our ancestors of maybe some tens of thousands of years ago, led him to the recognition that they had become aware of outside "forces", feelings that urged guidance toward a brotherhood of belonging, in a protectedness. Also they felt a powerful need to understand, to discuss and to ritualize these feelings -- a need to rise up. Plato guessed that somehow the "world pre-existed in the being" of a Spirit; it had been written that " . . . the pathways of his purpose are hard to find. Yet it shines out

. . . in the dark chance of life. Effortless and calm He works His perfect will."

It was these inspiring thoughts that drove the Aryans to build great temples, the Parthenon and the magnificent cathedrals of Europe, also those of the mind, in the Western canon: of Homer and Aeschylus, Dante and Shakespeare.

Scientists know much more today, than did Darwin, about man's natural society and of his innate guidance. We know that the most elemental "particles" of matter carry their codes as to how they are to behave, energetically and statistically, and these carry their influence out into giant galaxies. So too we see that all life behaves as if DNA carried codes that specified the "forces" of guidance, particularly urging a rising up.

Now it is important to learn and to recognize that these "forces" are at the core of social belonging and cohesion, of all that is felt as guidance and most precious. This is simply what is meant by sacred -- like the sacredness of a picture of your mother, only more so. It is toward the comprehending of these "forces" that syntactic language evolved, and that "religion", originally a synthesis of science and philosophy with metaphysics, evolved as social guidance for rising up.

Our current comprehension of humanness and human society is far beyond Rousseau's "natural man"; far beyond Durkheim and Darwin. Science and religion are regaining their original congruence. The astounding promise of working out a true comprehension of "how things really are," through a scientific understanding of what seems to be a Creator's given direction, is at hand.

But beware of intellectuals who scorn humanness. It was they who invented and sought to subvert humanness with magic, and angry gods; "Craft of many words . . . brought terror, to keep men afraid." These intellectuals again bring lies, in the name of many subversions: social justice, environment, and plain envy. They believe they are on the verge of a new Statist god-slave empire.

Liberal intellectuals have worked, with increasing

vehemence and audacity for most of this century to subvert the foundations of our society so they could gain a total control in education, law, culture, and families. Understanding this then demands that, with indignation, a deep line be drawn between our society and those who would destroy it. We should try to be neither enemies nor friends of those across the line; we should encourage all who would rebuild our society to come over. But those who will not, we "will have nothing to do with them." If we are reasonably successful soon only a small core of the evil party will remain to be dealt with.

The core of the evil party has, from the beginning, been in the top universities, but its force for action now resides in the major media and entertainment. It is through a monopoly of nearly all of the channels of opinion formation and distribution that they are able to control nearly all political and social activity, even into the churches. Hence, it is most pressing that that monopoly be bypassed. This can be accomplished by the organization of people into Jefferson's wards, or cells. These would supply truthful news, and serve as forums for discussions and planning. By creating an immediate sense of community and protectedness, of cohesion and belonging, the wards can function directly to renew our human society. They can serve as centers of education and of action, as did communist cells, Jacobin clubs, and early Christian groups.

The first rule must be to avoid violence or even confrontation. All people, but particularly young people, must see that this is their opportunity to work for a great human purpose, and to shape their own futures. Cooperation and help must be sought. There are many groups that can help provide the nucleus for new wards: veterans organizations, churches, youth groups, and social clubs, college newspapers, professional groups and unions. And there are many action groups, from Accuracy in Media, to ethnic, family, and cultural groups that are already active and will help.

Enthusiasm and learning can come from immediately doing something: forming   new   wards,   improving communications or finding and working with allies. Be careful when beginning alone; search for a companion or two or three that can be counted on. Be slow to reveal all your plans; give new people simple tasks. Have them begin communications with other groups, form new wards, or get information on home schooling, or on aliens from Americans from Immigration Control, or on which companies support porno programs on TV from Concerned Women.

Be prepared for attacks. Ridicule and intimidation are standard liberal tactics. But undoing the pervasive obscuring of reality and truth by liberals and their allies to the left, is our initial task. Thus anti-Semitism has been blamed on Christianity and Aryans by liberals, when it is well known to be the product of Marx and socialism. The savage blacklisting was done not by McCarthy, but by liberals and their allies. Morrie Ryskind was one of the highest paid writers in Hollywood, "welcome at every studio" in Hollywood. "After I testified against the Hollywood Ten, I was never again to receive a single offer."

Truth is your most valuable weapon. It is findable by putting one foot ahead of the other, as does science and Nature's evolution. As you have seen, most everything today is shrouded in deceit, irrationalities and lies: history, our culture, the nature of man and his society, law and crime, education, and environment. Especially is there corruption of language and meaning of words; "When words lose their meaning people lose their liberty," wrote Confucius thousands of years ago. Culture, democracy, capitalism, morality, racism and bigotry have become useless except for propaganda. In Orwell's *1984* words are destroyed by the State, thereby destroying the people's concepts for thinking and humanness. So too our liberal renegades have destroyed valor, honor, nobility, modesty, gentleman and lady, even family and motherhood, as well as lout and pervert.

"Mainstream" intellectuals refuse to recognize truth and rationality for if they did their whole evil world of socialism would be forced into the open light and seen for the tyrannical corruption that it is, with its history of taught hate, brutal horrors of holocaust, and its centrality in Chekas, Red Guards and SS, smashing all human decency.

If you feel this to be an exaggeration, note that Washington bureaucracy's yuppie *National Journal* for June 18, 1994 contained the prediction that in some twenty years a million soldiers will patrol the ghettos (already called for in Washington and L.A.), and a million convicts will rot in huge prisons. The wealthy will live in terror, pass through checkpoints, barricades, and secret tunnels to enter their fortress townhouses. Already we are told that Chicago's Mayor Daley has called for a ban on public phones -- as drug dealers' offices.

Human society and Christianity have not been destroyed; though badly battered, they still exist. Most people still recognize the value of the 3-Rs: arithmetic in your head, enjoyment in reading Aesop's Fables and Hamlet, and the ability to construct an "English sentence," as Churchill put it. Goals 2000 will smother all of that in indoctrination. Most people can recognize that children raised in a one parent "family" will <u>not</u> grow up even like the parent; they will be even less human. So too people can recognize that the "diversity" of L.A., Washington, and New York is neither going to last nor stay confined -- the *National Journal* has warned you. We are descending into an abyss of horror with increasing speed, and Lebanization will be but a passing nightmare before fascism. Most Americans recognize that their government, even their public institutions, no longer even pretend to protect them. Government is more openly and increasingly the enemy of white people and Western civilization.

Who has demanded an end to the Gestapo-like BATF, and HUD and EPA government "agents"? Who has denounced and called for impeachment of high government officials who urge the teaching of young sodomists in schools "what to do in the backseat," who attacks Christian leaders, declaring they "have slavemaster mentalities?" Who has demanded an accounting of those who urge a fascist nationalization of police, education and health care? Who has demanded an accounting for the awarding of a felon and wife-beater with millions of dollars of tax dollars, after he endangered many lives while high on drugs and violating parole, repeatedly and savagely assaulted police who tried to arrest him? Officers who endangered their lives bringing him in, with only superficial lacerations largely self-inflicted, were subjected to double jeopardy in order to have blacks have a chance to imprison them, the terms of which are even now being screwed higher. Radical sodomists "featuring" a pedophile contingent and nude men pranced down Fifth Avenue, as the Mayor ordered police to stand by. The President and staff, Congressmen and academics, the Jewish Anti-Defamation League and EEOC have repeatedly attacked Christians. In time, the favor will certainly be returned.

When so-called liberals insist that morality, or culture, even truth, must not be imposed, you can observe their deceit by noticing the way they favor imposing their own "P.C." and ideology, and how they, for much of this century, followed closely to the "party line" of the Communists. It is not a matter of imposing, or not imposing; every nation, tribe, or society must and does impose an order. But understand that what is imposed will determine the shape and quality of our life, just as in imposing toilet training, and manners, and a love for life and knowing on children.

Survival is what imposes all that must to be imposed, plus that required for rising up which is just a bit more. An eagle and a dog, a lion and a snake all know the life that has been imposed upon them. Man, with reason, has had an increasing problem. Eons ago, while our ancestors still lived in a clan of a couple score of individuals, or a tribe some number of times larger, the failure of one person to act prudently could bring immediate pain to someone. That is not so today; each person is so hedged in by circumstances that there often is no recognized connection between a wrong and its cost, which often falls to some innocent or to "society."

We have seen how education was dumbed-down for socialism in the name of "reform", how our Bill of Rights has been bypassed by "penumbras," our culture uprooted by "cultural anthropologists" or just plain renegades, and our government corrupted in the name of "rights." The authors of these evils have been honored and rewarded, and those who have sought to expose the evil have been savagely attacked (See following Note). The power and the bigotry of the liberal establishment in concealing this renegadism has been nearly complete. When some nonentities, presumably unaware of the "sensitivity" of the issue, documented the treason of FDR, Marshall, Hopkins and company on the 50th Anniversary of Pearl Harbor, they were attacked, using the brazen implication that American Firsters were Nazis. And when a scholar revealed dissembling of Margaret Mead, the implications and influence of which is not common knowledge, he was pariahized.

NOTE ON LIBERAL HATE

The increasing savagery with which the liberals attack any and all who they perceive as offering resistance to Statism must be recognized, and a great indelible line visible to all must be fixed between those who support and those who attack human society. Sidney Hook noted that, of those communists whom Whittaker Chambers expected to confess, none came forward. To have done so, Hook explained, "would have exposed them to the concentrated hatred and mass campaign of denunciation" by the entire liberal establishment. Going against the liberal establishment brings the "most intense vilification you can imagine," wrote Tom Wolfe, a couple years ago in the American Arts Quarterly. "We must identify our enemies and drive them into oblivion," wrote our Secretary of Interior, Bruce Babbitt. Al Shanker of the Teachers Union declared Jesse Helms and Jerry Falwell "easy choices . . . must be denounced for the evil of bigotry." But as bigot is defined as one obstinately and intolerantly devoted to an opinion, who has been more bigoted than the entire educationist's bureaucracy?

One of the goals of the 60s was to force the perception "that America is a racist society," so testified Dr. Ken Masugi before Congress a few years back, with its own "concentration camps" (for Japanese) and "Holocaust" (with a Mall "Memorial"). Brown

University uses tax or tax-exempt money to hire race agents; one Don Kao saw his job as forcing the perception that racism was everywhere in America; Kao's "standard . . . if you feel comfortable or normal, you are probably oppressing someone".[166]

"Overhead planners" require that the public be kept constantly agitated as for war, but for peace time Statists have developed agitation propaganda for: "rights", racism, sexism, hatred for America or Christianity and fundamentalists, for homeless, AIDS "victims," on and on. These attacks were started in the 60s by renegade groups; they have since been increasingly sponsored by tax money and, today, have become a major part of our government's attacks upon us. When human society's restraints in morality, family, and community respect are dulled with condoms, violence, perversions, then the Big Stick of the State, exposed at Waco and Idaho will be used. (End of Note)

The media took over leadership of the evil party from the academics after their victory over McCarthy and by the 60s to the 80s had forced the agenda of communism, in Saigon, Washington and Nicaragua, to be supported over the interests of America. The struggle today in Washington to enshackle us with socialized medicine, socialized education, a nationalized police (Gestapo), and nationalized thought control through various -isms, is a continuation of that struggle, as can be perceived in a Wall Street Journal front page, major story (10, 11, 94). Still marching today are, "Those who marched" on "the Vietnam War" (peace demonstrators chanting for a communist victory), nuclear proliferation (unilateral U.S. disarmament in the face of a hectic Soviet buildup), environment (one hoax after another), and the covert war against Nicaragua (media and Congress backed the Communists against the Freedom Fighters)." Note the subtle, propagandized, forced perception that these were all "good" marches, by the good people of liberalism, who are still in control. In truth, they were all marchers against America, and in support of Communism, and their followers today seek our final enshackelment in Statist fascism.

---

[166]C. Sykes, *Nation of Victims.*

Liberal J.S. Mill defined "culture as what each generation gives to its successors in order . . . for at least keeping up and if possible for rising . . . " When authority and reason were to be perceived by all "in the glowing eyes of the great cats", deceit and imagination's evil were minor disturbances. But when progress pushes survival's authority into the background, culture as knowledge for survival became necessary and commanding.

The innately hierarchal society of our forebears had been monogamous for some millions of years -- not unlike the geese Lorenz studied in which the female did the choosing of a mate as a protector and helper for raising her family, where she largely ruled. In the contract, the male received an assured sex mate and recognition as protector of the family and of society, and hence largely ruled external affairs. This contractual arrangement received a significant strengthening with the initiation of a "breaking" of young males, to the responsibilities and rules of society under the supreme tribal authority of the Council of Elders.

In time, this authority became largely transferred to a religion. This was the essence of social authority until the Enlightenment when "intellectuals," ignorantly or treacherously, undercut human society by destroying religion's authority in favor of a proclaimed individualism. Society has been spiralling into irrational chaos ever since; for what was abandoned, besides reason, was a social core, social authority and social purpose.

Note that the prime reason for the organized core, and the social authority and purpose, was for the encouragement and protection of nurturing families. As authority and purpose were abandoned, the significance of society, morality, and all the innate emotions of a spiritual nature, which beget not only art and literature but social cohesion, failed. The material world and irrationality gradually displaced spiritual guidance and human society. Money began to buy more sex and social power than could social honor. Women found it increasingly necessary to attract men and they took over the bright headdress and raiments previously necessary for the male. As women and families were increasingly marginalized, so women began to demand entry into men's worlds.

In the past, social authority made intact families with children the only beneficiaries of social or governmental "affirmative action": job preference for the male parent, tax preference, and legal, voting, and social privileges. Rejected were the louts, the homosexual, the drunkard, aliens and the purveyors of violence, pornography, graffiti, and indecencies of all kinds.

It is not compassion nor rationality that has made these social dregs the prime recipients of Statist's care and feeding, replacing families; it is simply the authority or the evil party. You see our society has been turned up-side-down just as we have seen our Bill of Rights turned up-side-down; that wall and bulwark against Statist oppression has been inverted into authority for manipulation and tyranny.

Along with this topsy-turvy madness, there has been the <u>forced</u> <u>perception</u> of Carterian "malaise", of "a sense of the irrelevance of history and bleakness of the new age . . . we face impossible choices": from a distinguished Harvard historian a few years back. Then last year, self-proclaimed "media elitist", John Chancellor, denounced the very idea of government of, by and for the people; there has to be "a better way of running the country."[167] The perception is forced that personal confidence and responsibility and hope of rising up are ridiculous, just as honor, respect, decency, standards, excellence, nobility, courage and heroism are detested. The gibbering effeminacy or immaturity of "impossible choices" exemplifies the sub-human being that Tocqueville predicted under Statism. Of course, we are not surviving, as Harvard and the entire liberal establishment has long apprehended: "the center cannot hold", "mere anarchy" has been loosed upon the world.

But ability to recover demands that we understand where we are, how we got here, and which way is up. History, tradition, memory and ritual, all that Orwell's *1984*

---

[167]*Human Events* (2-20-93, p.14).

rulers, like our own evil party, sought to obliterate are essential for comprehension of the very meaning, the hope, the joy of rising up.

The problem that we face is quite simple and its essence the West has seen before. The Greeks faced a very similar problem when they recognized the abyss of elitist Statism with its mass enslavement. There is also a similarity in the chaos that the early Christians faced. Clearly, you can see that the Enlightenment in discarding religion effectively discarded <u>purpose</u> and hence, rationality, and culture, and therefore all guidance. Thus we have sunk into the corruption of relativising, even of truth, the idiocy of "imposed" culture, and the renegadism of "rights" over survival. The Greeks' answer was what we call culture and the Christian answer, we call religion. The Enlightenment and its followers have uprooted both.

Our Founders likewise faced great problems and expectations, but they did not whine about "impossibilities", nor did they doubt the ability of rude settlers to govern themselves. They rejected a strong, bureaucratized, centralized state; instead they gave us federalism, which has been judged by scholars to be the central genius of their work. People were to solve their own problems in human communities.[168]

What we must do is to rebuild education, starting with the home and family. It must be recognized that a child brought up without a father and a mother guiding him until at least four or five will not generally grow up to raise a family of his own. Thus we must rebuild culture starting with the home and the Western canon, Aesop's fables.

Religion, in essence, is purpose for guidance, toward that "proper to man." If you do not have a purpose and a

---

[168]In this regard, another example of our up-side-down condition today may be noted in the assertions of a promoter of the 14th Amendment; Senator Trumbull declared in a Chicago speech (1867) that the evil Section 1 was probably a "needless reiteration". Later he declared that "The States were, and are now, the depositories of the rights of the individual against encroachment". How innocent he was.

strong belief in it, you are bound to become the tool of others who do. To the Greeks, religion concerned not "each man seeking his own truth", rather it was an absolute authority to which each person must submit as "proper to man": "There is a life which is higher than the measure of humanity; men will live it not by virtue of their humanity, but of something in them that is divine. We ought not to listen to those who exhort a man to keep man's thoughts, but to live according to the highest thing that is in him, for small though it be, in power and worth, it is far above the rest". So declared Aristotle.

Most Christians of the last four centuries have followed religion in much this manner. Long before that, Saint Augustine declared that it was not necessary to believe in the Creation. Probably God created a nebulous mass, within which lay a coded seminal order. "What we believe by the Word of God is not so certain as that which we perceive by sense" (reason is also a divine gift and revelation).[169] Innate "feelings", or spiritual imperatives are real; they are Nature's or Nature's God's guidance. To reject these is to reject humanness so the Greeks understood. We have seen that our entire liberal establishment rejects, seeks to uproot, all humanness. This justifies naming them the evil party, and drawing a line to mark them off.

Whether the West can again become a community of humanness, with a human society and a purpose to rise up, or whether it is to continue to sink into a "disinherited, disfranchised nonhuman" Statism, as Tocqueville warned, depends upon you individually, and upon me. Are we willing to move people up to the door of seeing a truly human vision of human progress?

---

[169]This is the Four Hundredth Anniversary of Richard Hooker's *Laws*. He also declared "He that goeth about to persuade a multitude that they are not so well off as they ought to be, shall never want attention and favorable hearers."

SUMMARY

"The American . . . has weak loyalties to his family, his community, his country, his religion . . . His concepts of right and wrong are hazy. Opportunism is easy, but he is frightened and insecure. He underestimates his own worth, his own strength, his ability to survive. Largely ignorant of social values, there is little understanding of American history and philosophy, of federal and community organizations, of states rights, of safeguards to freedom, even among university graduates. Exceedingly insular and provincial . . . Indoctrination programs for American prisoners proceed as planned." Written by the Chief of Intelligence of the "Chinese People's Volunteer Army" in North Korea in 1951, concerning some of our best young men taken as prisoners.

Statism, whether as socialism, communism, fascism or modernity's liberalism, can flourish in a free society only through the indifference, sloth and ignorance of the majority. By the 60s, our young people were even more "ignorant of social values". Nothing was learned from the astute Chinese observer. Even this high Communist official recognized that there was "that proper to man": loyalty, society, religion, concepts of right and wrong. Strength of character comes through recognition of and a responsibility for these essentials of humanness.

Long, long ago people became consciously aware of a preciousness, a sacredness in their brotherhood, and of right and wrong. They became aware of a guidance through feelings. These feelings are the basis of all spiritual life, all that is held most dear: home, brotherhood and love, belonging and respect, decency and rising up, morality and charity and conscience that oversees all. This is the essence of all human religions. It was to institute a respect and a responsibility for these in young males that "cave men" instituted education for them. Culture was to become the explication of them, through literature and art. That was the central purpose of the Western canon and of Christianity, from Homer to Hobbs. The teaching of them has normally been predominately done by a church, as containing the core of understanding and purpose.

By the time of the Enlightenment, the West was clearly off the track. It was due in part to the refusal of the Church to acknowledge the need for a more clearly reasoned purpose and to see to it that young men were taught it rather than an outworn ritual that increasingly contained little as a message. Just as important was the success of the intellectuals in teaching individualism and "rights", and that all was to be rejected except "that which came through the senses". But we learn predominately through patterns, and spiritual patterns for guidance don't come through the senses. They are innate, coming from Nature or Nature's God.

Hence from the Enlightenment on, spiritual or innate guidance towards that proper to man, or religion, has been increasingly rejected, and "only that which comes through the senses" is given consideration. This rejection of religion involved the rejection of everything human, and since man's spiritual realm is central to culture, it marked the rejection of culture, and of purpose and rationality. That is the measure of the enormity of our crisis. The rejection of all things human, as can be noted, means the rejection of decency, morality, truth, honor, reverence, even the concept of beauty. As Walter Scott saw this beginning to happen nearly two centuries ago, he was brought to tears by a Whig trimmer: "No, no -- 'tis no laughing matter, little by little, whatever your wishes be, you will destroy and undermine, until nothing of what makes Scotland Scotland shall remain."

The complete calumniation of the truth and humanness is seen every day in the socialization of health, and of education, and police power, presented as "reform"; in the Rodney King affair; in the lives of nearly all "celebrities" in Washington, New York, Hollywood, and points in between. But few examples are more revealing, and go to the very depth of the corruption, than the recent furor over I.Q.

"Know Nothing" stupidity or more commonly bigoted renegadism even dragged in *Forrest Gump.* Surely most people saw the movie, unrealized by some, as teaching the lesson of Jesus: put doing good above fighting. Just as important was the additional lesson that even the least of us can be successful. Of course, there are differences in intelligence, more significant in fact than differences in physique. But just as there can be no humanness under "Marxism": no decency, morality, truth, even culture, so there can be no excellence, and hence I.Q. Only the reflexive monotony of an anthill.

The I.Q. fracas is used to obscure something: the abyss into which we are being led. Pearl Harbor was used to obscure FDR's evil push for the hegemony of Communism (certainly in Europe and Asia). Fake "reform" was used to hide the corruption of education. McCarthyism was used to make Communism acceptable. A fake Buddhist uprising was used to force the destruction of the government of South Vietnam and thus the subsequent calamity. During the 60s, a whole covey of corruptions was marched out with the openly avowed intent to brand America as evil, and to destroy it. Both "Vietnam" and "Watergate" were lies and fakes as has been shown. Concentration camps and confiscation of property of Japanese during WW II were lies. All of these were corruptions of the truth, forced onto the public for one purpose; to supply a facade of respectable indignation to obscure the evil of renegades seeking to destroy us.

There were two more recent evil frauds whose purpose was to denigrate, for the destruction of our existence as a free people. The finger of shame memorial to "The Holocaust" was erected on the falsehoods that America and Christianity were the evil perpetrators. Its purpose, certainly its clear result, is the cloaking of the enormity of the <u>whole</u> Marxian holocaust; even far more significant yet is the obscuring of the Marxian intent to destroy all humanness. The other was the renegade manipulation, deceit and lies which used the pretext of a few scratches on a savage felon violating parole -- who had wildly endangered the public and repeatedly attacked police -- as a basis for excusing and even justifying, a holocausting of L.A. with 55 dead, thousands injured, untold billions lost. Additionally, these scratches were used to justify a pernicious attack on our perhaps most sacred liberty, right of trial by jury, and on America itself -- a justification for further racist attacks.

The I.Q. imbroglio is equally malignant. In the first place, I.Q. is <u>not</u> the one-all that "trumps everything", as Forrest Gump showed. Among most people motivation and character are distinctly more important. I.Q. only provides an edge, and you don't need such an edge for an ax, only for a scalpel; it predominates only on the mountain peaks. Nevertheless, we all know that the edge docs count.

But what maddens the renegade elite is that the existence of an I.Q. difference denies equality. Equality is fake! -- the equality defined by the elite. Hence, the whole basis for the welfare state, for affirmative action, for permanent welfare, for "rights", and the whole corruption of welfarism is undermined. If people are equal and some are not doing well, it must be somebody's fault and, furthermore, they deserve help, not charity but deserved help. But, if people are not equal, the bottom drops out of the whole mess.

There are greater ramifications. Giving the people "welfare", not charity to the deserving, but a "dole", is like tourists in a park feeding a mother deer on candy bars, or it's like drugs, robbing people of the desire even the need to rise up. They are denied the opportunity to be human to be part of a human society. The motivation to rise up comes not from I.Q., but from a human society. There is no way to live and to receive social respect except through responsibility and work. If the so-called "underclass" had had to work and earn the respect of those, including blacks, who are driven out by anti-social behavior, there would have been no separation and there would be jobs. Welfarism made work unnecessary. Thus education and respect and decency became unnecessary.

Vast billions in tax money is squeezed out of people who do work and is poured into these inhuman cesspools. If that flood of cash were stopped,[170] it would cripple or destroy the drug trade; it would nearly end fatherless families, and would end violence for the millions. But think of the vast horde of bureaucrats who would have to be let loose.

Seeking to survive as human beings requires effort, struggle, motivation, and it requires social cooperation in a culture. Welfarism and victimism are the principal paths by which Statists have sought to pander to those "who think they are not so well off as they might be," and thus to corrupt and subvert human society.

You must understand that "giving people jobs," or an "environment," or anything as a policy, will destroy them as human beings, as Tocqueville and many since have warned. Pandering to racism, feminism, welfarism, homosexuals, aliens, louts, and the entire liberal feculence is only intended as short-term policy. As soon as the BATF and other Cheka-Gestapo-Red Guard Units, get firmly in control, all that will fade like drugs in Saigon, when Ho arrived. All that will then remain is that which contributes to the power or jollies of the elite.

Voluntary human society is the only alternative, where only those things are imposed and only those prohibited that are essential for its survival and rising up. Social behavior must be restrained as must economic behavior; but only to the extent necessary for stability, justice, and rising up. Laissez faire began as an attempt to counter anti-social Statist monopolies, but core intellectuals sold out to it and so-called capitalism resulted as merely a corrupted human society. It

---

[170]Even *The New Republic* admitted it would improve the quality of parents.

is that society that renegades seek to destroy, under the deception of "capitalism."

Very clearly what must be done is to rebuild our human society and its culture. Only then will there be the sacredness of brotherhood and belonging, and the protectedness and joy of rising up. Culture is like an organism that can only exist as a unitary whole. It is a human construct like religion (purpose) and thus is subject to human error or even corruption. It is the task of a core, a Council of Elders to keep vigilant guard to counter such decadence.

Organization of wards, Jefferson's "cells," is essential for a reforming of community, for providing truthful news and information free from media lies, for education and preparation in building a new society. Only through such a network, organized by councils, can the social authority be attained to rebuild education, to end all naturalization and immigration until some social stability is regained, to rebuild our Constitutional federal system under the Bill of Rights, and especially to regain these special preferences for families that have always been necessary.

We need no authority to assure us that without truth there can be no purpose and no rationality, and we can see people of our society running madly about like the swine of the Gadarenes. This *Guide* examines only a small fraction of the liberal establishment's lies, and when the truth has been thrust forth liberal renegades have denounced the messenger, almost without exception, as a Nazi, a racist, a fundamentalist, a bigot. Harvard's Soroken warned a half century ago of the "obliteration of the boundary line" between truth and falsehood, reality and fiction. "Human invention has never produced anything so valuable, in stimulation and of description to the inquiring intellect, as the dialectics of the ancients": Aristotle in theory, Plato in practice. "No modern writings come near to . . . the way to investigate truth" both by precept and example. For these and a number of other mentioned reasons, J.S. Mill declared it "important to retain (both Greek and Latin and their literature) . . . as a part of liberal education of all who are obliged . . . to discontinue their studies at an early age."

And surely for the Greeks, as for Christianity and human tribal societies everywhere, freedom was central to all purposes; not freedom for folly but for that search for a proper dignity. The drawing of a boundary line marking off that which poisons it must be done immediately. It is of greatest importance where the value is highest. "He who attacks marriage . . . who undermines by word or action this foundation of all moral society, is my enemy . . . if I cannot defeat him, at least I will have nothing to do with him." So wrote Goethe.

All people must be encouraged to recognize the greatness of human society and the catastrophe of Statism, with welfarism being but the first giving-away into the abyss. We must encourage Europeans to help us and to help themselves, lead the way if they can and will. The West is not apt to survive alone in either America or Europe. Finally the only good and human globalism, for all people, must be based on a rational human society.

NOTE ON ESSENTIALS

If people are taught or allowed to assume the "right" of individualism, to do one's "own thing", to reject responsibility even for self, to claim moral relativism and the right not to be punished or treated with contempt; if people are taught only rock and TV violence and sex, and the right not to have anything "imposed" upon them, then that people are not long for this world. "If a society lets any number of its members grow up mere children, incapable of . . . rational consideration" it has only itself to blame.

A survivalist's society survives by smarts and knowing when to react quickly and whom to fawn before; there isn't much of anything for if there was it would soon be taken. There isn't much education because there isn't time and it proves of little use because everything is so tentative. If you plan, others will not and connive to reap your harvest. Everything is slash and burn.

A high culture requires stability and thus requires standards to guide expectations and tradition to provide certain knowledge;

it must be ready for and capable to progress as people succeed in rising up, and it must be able and intent upon protecting its own, its tradition and its purpose to seek that proper to man. And it must beware of change for the sake of change, for that is permanent revolution.

Everybody knows that there exists a group of people who will live off others if allowed to, who will act irresponsibly and expect others to take care of them, who will goof off, filch or even kill, if allowed to do so. We also know and have seen near universal responsibility for selves and family, only fringe criminality and sloth; when all people are brought up in a society where to do otherwise would draw immediate contempt and even punishment, such things do not prosper.

The evil party succeeded to near hegemonic control of our Establishment, and openly after their success in making anti-Communism evil and Communism acceptable. Its power lies in its control of all channels of public opinion. It thus determines what you are to believe. It is the purpose of this evil party to destroy our human society and our culture -- of families, decency, rule of law and limited government. Through control of opinion it holds the "power to exclude and to be seen to exclude" . . . to pariahize, "swimming hopelessly against the tide".

When Stalin and Hitler were allies Eugene Lyons wrote of 1939-41, "An intellectual red-terror spread through . . . New York, Hollywood, Washington . . . college campuses and large cities . . ." In 1987 Sidney Hook wrote of the power of the evil party, even during the so-called McCarthy era and afterwards: to expose themselves to the concentrated hatred and mass campaigns of denunciation by Communists and their sympathizers . . . has been a potent weapon" against all who would seek to come forward with the truth. Professors have been forced from their classrooms, denied tenure, students and speakers have been harassed and threatened. Duke's Fish sought to have members of the National Association of Scholars -- essentially supporters of Western civilization -- denied admission to important academic policy committees. Fish's rhetoric has in fact been exposed as "a deliberate attempt to supplant reason with rhetoric, truth by persuasion". A criminal indictment (in Canada) was brought against a professor for presenting and explaining some research data on race. The Willie Horton story was brought to light by liberals, who also "exposed his race", yet the evil party was able to make this into a smear of "conservatives" or of America generally.

Finally in the dust-settling after the *New Republic's* frenzied fracas over IQ a Harvard professor, whose name was "withheld" from a "relatively innocuous letter", declared he was upset by the irrationality and desperation expressed . . . (and of) and hominem attacks". His obscurant addition, "Racists never need facts . . . and facts cannot change them" would seem to damn the *Republic's* editors; clearly it was to them that it fit. Another writer commenting (12,26,94), suggested that the professor "feared that if (his) name (was) revealed, the slings and arrows of outrageous retribution might be unbearable".

I have summarized these cases of the rather mainstream liberal mad irrationality that seeks to close off, to censor all discussions counter to the efforts of the evil party to destroy our human society. They have long used "racism" as the meat-grinder for destroying our Bill of Rights and education. Eugenics is another topic that has been labeled Verboten. These are such important topics that they must be moved beyond the censuring media and academia and <u>looked</u> <u>at</u>.

Eugenics was a liberal or reasoned attempt -- when liberal did not obscure a bigoted Marxist -- <u>not</u> to change our genetic inheritance, but to study the factors under social control which may impair or improve that heritage.[171] We need to know what we are doing -- where we are going. In the past a recognized major factor in opposing natural selection has been medicine which, as it became effective, allowed reproduction by weak individuals who under natural conditions -- of God if you will -- would not. However, in our technological society the impairment of our genetic heritage -- and impairment or dysgenics is the real problem for no one seeks to make supermen -- through reproduction by the mentally weak is far more critical than by the physically weak.

It must be recognized as one of the most irrational of invitations to future horrors for our children that billions of dollars are bled from families in need to <u>promote</u> to production of criminals and millions of people whose genetic capabilities do not permit them to become self-supporting, to say nothing of sharing in social support.

---

[171]Margaret Sanger, a major founder of Planned Parenthood, along with many liberals and socialists, such as B.S. Shaw, "evidenced a zeal to bar the brooding of the socially and genetically unfit" (*Nat. Rev.*, 4,12,93,p.5).

Until sometime in the last millennia all genetic changes were eugenic; not only did only the strong survive but especially it was the strong that dominated reproduction -- as in all nature -- and there was a monotonic rising up. This came to diminish in the West almost certainly due to the West's abandonment of reasoned purpose; the church abandoned reason and the intellectuals abandoned purpose. The church claimed to be rejecting heresy and the intellectuals claimed their rejection of superstition, but the real rejected was the reasoned purpose of Christianity which had built such things as universities at Bologna, Paris and Oxford and cathedrals at Chartres, Cologne and Canterbury. With decline in purpose has come a decline especially in all things human, social and cultural. Today to even discuss the very essence of a rational future relative to our genetic inheritance has become a most horrible crime, for both "liberal" and "conservative". This must be changed.

There are a great many people today who do not know these facts, or they insist that times have changed and somehow the guv'ment will see that they are taken care of, without regard to their irresponsibility or even on account of it. But most people can see that such a condition can only be temporary. The very idea of <u>any</u> <u>rights</u> <u>guaranteed</u> <u>by</u> <u>guv'ment</u>: to be free of want, free of contempt, free to "control my own body", free to catch AIDS, become a druggy, a welfare addict on and on, lasts only a short time until too many people drop out. A gulag may be required to regain reality.

We have an excellent example of this today in Social Security, and it is a very mild case -- nothing like the corrosiveness of AIDS, rock, violence and sex. It has, however, been corroding much longer. It will soon collapse as the number of recipients supported approaches the number of supporters. Don't blame me for trying to take away your rights or your check. I don't want to take anything. It is, however, essential for your own welfare and of your society that you face realities. You must keep in mind that it is the guv'ment that has provided you these things, and you know that it has nothing, can have nothing, that it has not grabbed from someone else. And when the number of people demanding begin to exceed the number to be robbed, everybody quits or hides, and there is suddenly nothing. And any rational person can see that coming in a few years in Social Security and in the whole corrupt welfare -- beggar society -- state.

The above essentials must be comprehended, believed and made a reality before there is much need of going on. Most people really know these to be true, but they have been allowed to, and have grown accustomed to, denying them by avoidance. That will work no longer.

What I wanted to say in the first place is an extension really of the above. Children will not learn to read who see that their parents don't and are watching TV instead. They will not learn to appreciate music if they hear largely only rock from the time they are born. They will not be responsible, or non-abusive, or non-criminal, they will never learn to become decent human beings from TV. Young people will not be responsible for anything unless they are firmly taught to be so.

Renegades will try to make out this is "back to the old regime." This is an obscuring falsehood. Human society does not permit the individualism which spurns society's standards; but the very aim of society is to permit maximum private purpose, restrained only by the essential needs of a society to maintain order and decency for the nurturing of families and a guiding culture. The most absolute of possible absoluteness in this world of change is the trustworthiness of tradition, defined as those truths which have been proven by countless generations.

People of shallow understanding or evil intent urge confusion and distrust by rhetorical proofs that it only depend on who is boss, who determines. One of the most fatuous of obscurantisms; life and the future depends upon the _purposes_ of those who are accepted as a core to advise in social guidance. Even a Council of Elders dedicated to the welfare of their grandchildren can rot to oligarchal schemes. Hence, the constant teaching, exemplification and advancement of purpose, through all forms of excellence, and by various competing groups alone can provide the promise of continuity.

The 1994 election turned on the basic urge and need of people to rule themselves in a free human society. The abyss of Statism had become real. We lost our free society, our Bill of Rights, decent education, protection of families and communities through failure of a social core. You must comprehend that the 1994 election will not bring them back. It was but a demand; action must follow. Effective uprooting of the Statist core depends upon accurately locating it, _and_ upon immediate action to recreate a new core of social authority that will rise to the task, not only of the uprooting, but to the inspiring task of creating the new.

Congress does not, <u>has</u> <u>not</u>, been ruling. Rather they have relinquished power to the 15,000 staffers, to thousands of federal judges and their staffers, and to a permanent bureaucracy. Any Executive Branch official who challenges, or is merely distasteful to them risks the Star Chamber of the special prosecutor. This relinquishing of power by the Congress was an inevitable consequence of Statism's dependence upon a vast bureaucracy.

Thus the 1994 replacing of Congress merely replaces a figurehead. It is the core and root that must be destroyed; talk of returning power to the states is fatuous if that is not done. Not only must hordes of bureaucrats be removed, as states regain their proper federal power, but beheading of a few federal judges by impeachment, with full prejudice, is needed for them to regain their attention to their oath to uphold the written Constitution.

Additionally it must be recognized that the essential policy core for the bureaucracy resides in the media-academia-entertainment complex, and the new core must displace it. People have no "right" to freedom; they do have a duty to demand freedom from non-human ends. People possess the ultimate power, but only if they have the understanding and the will to use it. The 1994 election proved the existence of some of both. But it will be but a lone cry ripped off in a cosmic wind, unless there is a wide movement among the common people to create wards and councils as the only effective way to structure a new core that can grow in power in 1996 and 2000. Only in this manner can the inspiring task of building a new human society proceed.

BEGIN NOW

1. Understand, through reading and discussion; form wards to teach others.

2. Bypass media and begin re-establishment of a coherent society through wards and councils. Corrupt and poisonous culture, "entertainment" and education must be pushed from the public square.

3. Halt all naturalization and squeeze off immigration until stability is regained, lest we drowned in Lebanization. All who are here as a result of illegal acts by natural law are illegally here, and must be returned. Clinton's Immigration Service Commissioner,

Doris Meissener, has declared that she "should be more than a vassel for Congress", meaning ultimately the American people, and exults in, "We are transforming ourselves". She and all others who are subversively thwarting American's desire to regain some stability must be sent back with the illegals.

4. Get children out of state schools, and begin the teaching of the 3-Rs, human society, the Western canon, and the joy in learning.

5. Reassert family prerogatives in jobs, taxes, laws and policing, in all society, politics and economics.

6. Impeach with full prejudice, judges who fail to uphold the <u>written</u> law, and who violate their Constitutional oath. Judges who seek to make rather than interpret law must be snouted.

7. Return responsibility to the person, for self, family, community and nation.

8. Rebuild our human society and culture; regain government subservient to the people; re-establish a religion of purpose in the public square, and reawaken the concept of freedom and that "proper to man".

The 1992 election was a signal for even the mainstream currents of the evil party that it was no longer necessary to conceal its "great hatred" for America and Western culture. Hopes raised by the '94 election will end in another "long withdrawing roar", like the brief light of the 80s, unless there is a great movement to bypass, cut-off and strangle the renegade media, academia and entertainment, and create a new order committed to Western freedom, self-government and human society.

ESSENTIAL BOOKS

In the following Bibliography are a number of the books that have been important in the writing of the *Guide*. The nature and significance of a few of them should be noted.

The books that early on got me started in the project were Chambers' *Witness*, whose introductory "Letter To My Children" should be read by all high schoolers, and Paul Johnson's *Modern Times*, a factual account, an unmatched history of the corruptness of modernity. Likewise *Our Vietnam Nightmare*, by Marguerite Higgins is absolutely essential for understanding the real hidden evil of Vietnam, as is Morgenstern's or Beard's account of the treason of Pearl Harbor. Crocker's *Roosevelt* details the subsequent treason of WW II.

Nothing was more influential and time consuming than Lorenz's, *Behind the Mirror;* the elements of this are a necessity in a new high school education, with an introduction even in grade school, to replace the fatuous "dinosaurs," and sex. Bloom's *Closing* is a must. Then there are Barfield's *Words*, Edith Hamilton's irreplaceable *Greeks*, Breasted's *Conscience*, Babbitt's humanism and Trilling's *Arnold*, which are more specifically about culture and, of course, Durant's bookshelf.

The evil and deadly poisons that our society has been subjected to began in education. Blumenfeld's *NEA* gives a quick, vivid presentation, Damerell and Powers are meatier.

Remember, if history was not of a very high importance, renegades would not be so frantic in their lying and obscuring of it. In a reformed education all of the corrupt social studies must be replaced by something like the old *American History* by Muzzey. Morison's history is excellent up to the onset of socialism, roughly Wilson's WW I. Flack is most trustworthy on the 14th Amendment's feculence, and Wedemeyer exposes the rot of FDR and followers. Arendt's *Revolution* is an excellent account of our Founders and gives a presentation of Jefferson's wards.

The evil party is followed in detail in Utley's account of "Our Crimes Against Humanity," communism in *Red Decade* by Lyons, and Weinstein, Radosh, Powell, and Colodny on subversion, with Horowitz on the Sixties, Magnet on the resulting Nineties, and Jared Taylor on "racism."

Finally, and of equal importance with Lorenz, is Durkheim on the origin of man's spiritual needs and religion. The Durant's *Civilization* provided a Golconda of information and enjoyment. In a somewhat different direction man's spiritual needs and experiences were examined by the Greeks, as J.S. Mill assured us, to a degree never matched. For a delightful introduction read Edith Hamilton, and for a deeper guidance read Bloom. Also an excellent brief introduction is presented as the first essay in Weaver's *Rhetoric*. Mill and Hamilton would be saddened with substitutes for the original, but far better this than without them.

BIBLIOGRAPHY

Acton, Lord; Essays in History, (1967).
Adams, James T., March of Democracy, (1937).
Arendt, Hannah, On Revolution, (1967).
Arnold, Matthew, Culture and Anarchy, (1869).

Babbitt, Irving, Democracy and Leadership, (1924).
            Literature in the American College
Barfield, Owen, History of English Words, London (1953).
Beard, Charles, A., Roosevelt and the Coming of the War, (1948).
Berger, P., Social Construction of Reality, (1966).
Bloom, Allen, Closing the American Mind, (1987).
Blumenfeld, S.L., N.E.A. Trojan Horse (1984).
Braley, Russ, Bad News: NY Times, (1984).
Breasted, James Henry, Dawn of Conscience, (1935).
Bury, J.B., The Idea of Progress, (1920).

Carlyle, Thomas, The French Revolution, (1837). (Part I, Book I, Chapter
            2,7,7; B.V, Chapter 1,2; Part III, B.I, C.4; B.V, C.1.2; B.VI, C.2,7;
            B. VII, C. 1,7)
Catton, B., This Hallowed Ground, (1956).
Chambers, Whittaker, Witness, (1979).
Childe, V. Gordon, The Aryans, (1987).
Collier, P., and Horowitz, D., Destructive Generation, 1989.
Colodny, L., and Gettlin, R., Silent Coup, (1991).
Conrad, J., Under Western Eyes, (1911).
Coon, Carleton S., The Story of Man, 1962.
Cooper, James F., American Democrat, (1838).
Crocker, G.N., Roosevelt's Road to Russia, (1959).

Damerell, R.G., Education's Smoking Gun, 1985.
Diderot, Denis, Rameau's Nephew, (pub. after his death in 1784).
Dobbs, Z., The Great Deceit, Veritas Foundation Study (1965).
Donohue, W.A., The New Freedom, (1990).
            Politics of the ACLU, (1985).

BIBLIOGRAPHY 370

Dostoyevsky, Fyodor, The Brothers Karamazov, (1881).
        The Possessed.
Durant, Will and Ariel, The Story of Civilization
Durkheim, Emile, Elementary Forms of Religious Life, (1915).

Flack, H.E., Adoption of the Fourteenth Amendment (1908).
Fowler, H.W., Modern English Usage, 2nd Ed., Oxford, (1965).

Gallagher, M., Enemies of Eros, (1989).
Gasset, Ortega y, Revolt of the Masses, (1957).
Gatto, J.T. Dumbing Us Down, (1992).
Gilder, George, Men and Marriage, (1989).

Hamilton, Edith, The Greek Way, (1942).
        The Echo of Greece, (1957).
Hammer, Ellen J., A Death in November, (1987).
Hawkins, W.R., Importing Revolution (1994).
Hayek, F.A., Road to Serfdom, (1944).
Higgins, Marguerite, Our Vietnam Nightmare, (1965).
Hoffer, Eric, The True Believer, (1951).
Hook, Sidney, Out of Step, (1987).

Johnson, Paul, Modern Times, 1983.
        Intellectuals, 1988.

Keller, Helen, Story of My Life, (1902, when she was 22; died in 1968).
Kelly and Harbison, The American Constitution, 1963.
Kimball, Roger, Tenured Radicals, 1990
Kirk, Russell, The Conservative Mind

Lamphere, R.J., The FBI-KGB War, (1986).
Lippmann, Walter, The Good Society, (1937).
Lorenz, Konrad, Behind the Mirror, (1973).
        King Solomon's Ring, 1952, Man Meets Dog, (1954), On
        Aggression, 1963, The Waning of Humanness, (1987), Eight
        Deadly Sins.
Lowell, James Russell, Essays and Addresses (1904) and
        My Study Window.
Lyons, Eugene, Red Decade, (1941).

McDonald, Forrest, Constitutional History of U.S. (1982).
Magnet, Myron, The Dream and Nightmare
Mill, J.S., The Philosophy of; Edited by M. Cohen.
Milosz, Czeslaw, The Captive Mind, (1981).
Monod, Jacques, Chance and Necessity, (1971).
Morgenstern, Geo., Pearl Harbor, (1947).

Morison, S.E., Oxford History of American People, (1965).
Morley, F., Freedom and Federalism, (1959).
Muggerdige, M., Chronicles of Wasted Time, 1973.

Nisbet, R., History of the Idea of Progress, 1980.

Orwell, Geo., The Orwell Reader.

Popper, K.R., Popper Selections, Ed., D. Miller, 1985.
Powell, S.S., Covert Cadre, 1987.
Powers, R.H., The Dilemma of Education, 1984.

Radosh, R., and Milton, J., The Rosenberg File, 1984.
Reed, John Shelton, Southern Folk.
Ropke, Wilhelm, A Humane Economy, 1960 and
        The Social Crisis of Our Time, 1992.

Schumpeter, J.A., Capitalism, Socialism, Democracy, 1942.
        (predicted that capitalism would be killed by its success, by
        creating a "hostility to its own social order.")
Schweitzer, Albert, The Philosophy of Civilization 1949.
Smith, Huston, The Religions of Man, 1958.
Solzhenitsyn, A., Warning to the West, 1978.
Sorokin, P.A., The Crisis of Our Age, (1941).
Spencer, Herbert, Man Versus the State, (1884).
Stacy, P., and Lutton, W., Immigration Time Bomb, 1985.
Stern, P. VanDorn, Prehistoric Europe, 1969.
Stormer, John, None Dare Call it Treason (1964), and 25 Years Later
        (1990).
Summer, W.G., Folkways, 1940.

Taylor, Jared, Paved with Good Intentions, 1992.
Tiger, H., and Fox, R., The Imperial Animal (1971).
Tocqueville, Alexis de, Democracy in America.
Trilling, Lionel, Matthew Arnold, NY, (1949) Beyond Culture, (1968).

Utley, Freda, The High Cost of Vengeance, 1949.

Weaver, Richard, M., Ideas Have Consequences, (1948) Ethics of Rhetoric,
        (1953).
Weber, Max, The Protestant Ethic, (1930).
Wedemeyer, A.C., Reports, (1958).
Weil, Simone, Reader; Ed. Panichas, G.A. (1977).
Weinstein, Allen, Perjury: The Hiss Case, (1978).
Whyte, W.H., The Organization Men, (1957).
Wolfe, Tom, Radical Chic and Mau-Mauing, (1970).

INDEX